LOGIC AND EXPERIENCE

LOGIC AND EXPERIENCE

The Origin of Modern American Legal Education

William P. LaPiana

New York Oxford
OXFORD UNIVERSITY PRESS
1994

Oxford University Press

Oxford New York Toronto
Dehli Bombay Calcutta Madras Karachi
Kuala Lumpur Singapore Hong Kong Tokyo
Nairobi Dar es Salaam Cape Town
Melbourne Auckland Madrid

and associated companies in
Berlin Ibadan

Published by Oxford University Press, Inc.
200 Madison Avenue, New York, New York 10016

Oxford is a registered trademark of Oxford University Press

Library of Congress Cataloging-in-Publication Data
LaPiana, William P.
Logic and experience : the origin of modern American legal
education / William P. LaPiana.
p. cm.
ISBN 0-19-507935-3
1. Law—Study and teaching—United States—History. 2. Case
method—History. I. Title.
KF272.L27 1994
349.73—dc20 [347.3] 93-21928

2 4 6 8 9 7 5 3 1

Printed in the United States of America
on acid-free paper

For my father and my Aunt Fanny
and to the memory of
my mother and my Jerry

Preface

The genesis of this study of the origins of modern American legal education is to a great degree personal experience. As a trained historian, a lawyer, and a teacher of law, I have been taught by the case method, have used it to teach, and have also been puzzled by the emotions it evokes in both its defenders and detractors. As a law student I was exposed to the typical picture of Christopher Columbus Langdell as the important but basically uninspired creator of this peculiar method of education. I was also taught that Oliver Wendell Holmes, Jr., was the anti-Langdell. Certainly during the time I was a law student, Grant Gilmore's judgment of the relative worth of the two men was widely held: "Langdell's thought was crude and simplistic. Holmes's thought was subtle, sophisticated, and, in the last analysis, highly ambiguous."[1] As a law teacher I am party to many (indeed, too many) discussions of the worth or lack of worth of the case method. Today, it is fair to say, legal education generally accepts that the case method lacks *something* and that Langdell took too narrow a view of legal education. Holmes's tag—that his contemporary was "the greatest living legal theologian" who could not understand that the life of the law is not logic but experience—is forever attached to Langdell's reputation, especially among his academic descendants.

The study of American intellectual history first led me to believe that the narrowness might be on the part of Langdell's critics. Thus this volume is an attempt to place Langdell in context, within the intellectual and to some degree the social world in which he carried forward his reforms of legal education. The conclusion is that Langdell was no fool; indeed, he was an accomplished practitioner whose ideas about law and how to study it not only were well grounded in contemporary jurisprudence but also strongly reflected the experience of practice under the great changes wrought by code pleading.

I also suggest that the appeal of "Langdellianism"—of the case method and the careful creation of a structure of rules of law—was based on its practical effects. To be sure, the skills of case parsing that it taught were truly useful; moreover, the rigorous academic legal education it fostered helped assure the social position of the bar in a rapidly changing world. The construct Langdell and his contemporaries worked to create was a melding of logic and experience: the use of science to better understand and practice.

This volume began as a dissertation written under the direction of Donald Fleming. His patience and encouragement have meant a good deal over the many years it has taken to complete this work. The possibilities in a study of the case method were first suggested to me by the late Stephen Botein, whose teaching introduced me to the pleasures of legal history. Morton Horwitz encouraged me to pursue my interest and provided both emotional and material support for my graduate studies.

During the course of my research I have incurred many debts to the skilled and patient staffs of many libraries. Without the intention of slighting any, I would like to single out the staff of the library of the University of Pittsburgh School of Law and its director during my time on the faculty, Jenni Parrish, and the staff of the library of The New York Law School under the leadership of Joyce Saltalamachia.

The New York University Law School legal history colloquium and its leaders, John P. Reid and William E. Nelson, have been an unfailing source of advice and encouragement. I also thank the readers for the Oxford University Press, especially Laura Kalman, whose suggestions have done much to improve the manuscript. Robert E. Sullivan lent his eagle eye to my prose and has saved me from what seemed innumerable barbarisms. The index was meticulously prepared by Barbara Wilcie Kern. Needless to say, I have full responsibility for both the form and substance of the work.

New York, New York W. P. LaP.
May 1993

Contents

LOGIC AND EXPERIENCE

1

Introduction

The appointment of Christopher Columbus Langdell as Dane Professor at Harvard Law School on January 6, 1870, is widely acknowledged to mark the beginning of the modern American law school.[1] Langdell's discovery of a new world of legal education was only a start. His disciples, especially James Barr Ames and William A. Keener, developed what we recognize today as the case method of legal education.[2] What generally has been overlooked, however, is Alfred Z. Reed's observation "that literally all good things are not first thought of in Cambridge" and "except on the score of practicality, there was nothing startlingly original in [Langdell's] idea."[3] Reed was clearly on the right track. Aspects of Langdell's method of teaching, his beliefs about the scientific nature of law, and the rhetoric with which he justified them resembled those of the past. Yet the first dean of Harvard Law School has acquired the reputation of an innovator of the first order, and a perverse innovator at that. His thought—and by extension the form of legal education he helped create—has been identified as one of the principal sources of the sterile formalism that supposedly marked late nineteenth-century American legal thought.[4]

It is clear that Langdell's view of law emphasized the logical coherence of legal rules. In Langdell's formulation, legal education is the study of a few fundamental principles that are found in the original sources—cases—and, by implication, are derived from those cases by the process of induction. Thus the student thinks for himself rather than merely accepts the secondhand formulation of some treatise writer. This construct justified the study of law as a science.

When it comes to deciding what was new in Langdell's thought, Reed had it partly right. Langdell's ideas do share certain qualities with those of the preceding generation of American legal thinkers. Teasing out the innovative from the continuing opens a new prospect on late nineteenth-century American legal thought; it also sheds new light on the significance of the changes in legal education associated with Langdell's tenure at Harvard. Any such effort must be grounded in an attempt to understand the intellectual world in which Langdell lived his life in the law. For purposes of analysis, that world can be divided into two parts: the realm of law as ideas—as a system of principles that must be rightly understood if society is to be correctly governed; and the realm of law as procedure—as a system of rules for resolving disputes in the courts, knowledge of which gives lawyers an opportunity to make a living.

Langdell's professional world underwent significant change in both aspects during his lifetime. After the Civil War more than one thoughtful American lawyer turned their minds to the idea of law as science and subsequently encountered the writings of John Austin. Some recoiled in horror; some, often those most involved with transforming legal education, found something that struck a chord, that resonated truly. The spread of the new structure of pleading (which was embodied in the code of procedure—the Field Code—written primarily by David Dudley Field and first enacted in New York in 1848) helped change the way lawyers put the law into action, a change Langdell lived as a practitioner in New York.[5] Both developments helped shape Langdell's legal science.

The legal profession does not exist in a vacuum, of course, and the changes that occurred at Harvard during Langdell's deanship parallel changes in society as a whole: changes in ideas of pedagogy; changes in ideas about the sort of training that would equip young men for life in the world; changes in the nature of professionalism and in the structure of the legal profession. Modernization is a term used so often in historical explanation that it sometimes seems to be bereft of meaning. If the modern is equated with ideas and social structures we recognize as more like those of the present day than not, however, it can be said that Langdell and his colleagues lived during, gave impetus to, and even helped shape the modernization of American legal education and legal thought.

The chapters that follow sketch the intellectual and institutional history of these changes. In chapter 2, the often told story of the changes the new dean brought to the law school in Dane Hall is placed in the context of larger changes in both the university and society. To a great degree the narrative becomes the story not of Langdell, but of Charles William Eliot, whose vision informed not only the institutional nature of the law school, but even to some degree its most distinctive educational attribute—the case method. The case method, viewed as a method of instruction, is put into the context of changing ideas of pedagogy in higher education and changing social visions of the way young men are to make their way in the world. In order to emphasize further the degree of change that overtook American legal education and legal thought after the Civil War, chapter 3 describes the alien world of antebellum legal thought and education. Antebellum legal science had two aspects: one shared the general American view of science as the process of inducing from facts general principles which in the end are reflections of the mind of the Creator; the other was based on the supremely useful technical science of common law pleading. Antebellum legal education drew on both sorts of legal science, although antebellum law schools were devoted primarily to inculcating the science of principles, a process that was not particularly rigorous or demanding.

Chapter 4 investigates in detail Langdell's writings on contracts and equity procedure to investigate the case method as an approach to understanding the law rather than as a pedagogical tool. Langdell's legal science is described as a modification of the antebellum science of broad principles in the direction of narrow, technical expertise. This change in focus is traced to the influence of broad social and intellectual change, especially the growth of the positivistic view of law as the command of a sovereign rather than as the reflection of eternal right, and to the highly technical changes in practice and procedure brought about by the adoption of the Field Code in New York, where Langdell practiced for more than a decade before returning to Harvard as dean. The new legal science, then, was the product of changes in both broad and technical aspects of the antebellum legal world.

The relationship between the changing law school and the legal profession is the subject of chapter 5, which necessarily focuses on broader themes of social change. Whatever the novelty or wisdom of Langdell's approach to legal education, the success of the reforms at Harvard seems to require more explanation than the talents or luck of its dean. Just as Langdell's views mixed elements of high abstraction and the influence of the techniques of practice, the success of his school rested on the service it performed, both in meeting the needs of the bar for social position and prestige and in training young men for the realities of practice in a legal world transformed by an early version of the information explosion. The relationship between case method legal education and social standing is illustrated by a discussion of the revolution that swept Columbia's law school when the Langdell method supplanted traditional teaching. The importance of practical training is shown by tracing the growth of law reporting and the concomitant growing importance of research in the decided cases as the principal technique of legal practice.

Langdell's colleagues in the first generation of modern law teachers appear in chapter 6, where their thoughts, as well as those of Nicholas St. John Green and Oliver Wendell Holmes, Jr., are analyzed in terms of positivism, the heart of the new legal science.

While much of modern American legal education and legal thought seems to have appealed to at least the most articulate members of the profession, the new method held its terrors, which chapter 7 describes. The rise of law schools as the setting for legal education, supplanting law offices, led some practitioners to emphasize the need to educate prospective lawyers in the skills of practice. The resulting attack on the diploma privilege actually received the support of Langdell and Eliot, support that emphasizes the degree to which new ideas of legal education differed from the old. Some of the fears and doubts, however, were directly related to the idea of law promoted by teachers working at the reformed Harvard Law School and were not so easily allayed. The case method, in fact, became a prime focus of discontent. For some critics of the new law school, the case method threatened their own cherished view of the nature of law. Their vision lived for a time at Yale Law School, only to be supplanted in the early twentieth century by the Harvard model. Just as the revolution at Columbia illustrated the social power of the case method law school, the evolution at Yale illustrates the changing intellectual underpinnings of legal education.

Opposition finally began to disappear, however, with the new century. Chapter 8 examines some of the factors leading to détente, and places special emphasis on the American Law Institute as the means of reconciliation between school and profession.

What follows, then, is an attempt to place the history of the formative years of modern American legal education in as complete a context as possible. It is an attempt to write a cultural history, a story of both intellectual and social change in one area of American life. The area is a limited one, at least when the number of people directly involved is taken into account. A handful of professors, a small number of articulate practitioners who may have taught a bit, a university administrator here and there, and perhaps a few thousand students, all male, are the actors and the audience. What they set in motion, however, has had broad repercussions. Their creation triumphed as the model for legal education. As the American legal profession grew in numbers and influence, the importance of understanding the roots of modern legal education has also increased—or at least become more interesting. American legal education in the late twentieth century is in the midst of a period of intense introspection and self-criticism. Much of this self-analysis has focused on the history of the enterprise. Most earlier historians have been concerned primarily with the unique contribution of that first generation of teachers, especially Langdell: the case method and the idea of law which was assumed to underlay it. The final conclusion of this work, however, is that the story is more complex, and the forces involved in the creation of the modern law school are more varied than has been realized.

2

Harvard's Transformation

The outlines of the new model law school that Charles William Eliot and Christopher Columbus Langdell created at Harvard are familiar to us today. The ideal institution selects its students through rigorous entrance standards and teaches them using the case method in a graded curriculum that features yearly examinations in each course. Perhaps most important, Langdell's and Eliot's new model school claimed to provide the only true method for training future members of the profession. A system of apprenticeship dominated by active members of the profession gave way to academic training dominated by a new division of the profession—full-time teachers of law.

Langdell is almost universally regarded as the guiding force in this transformation.[1] It was Eliot, however, who hired Langdell in circumstances that help reveal his plans for the school and explain many difficulties the school confronted in fulfilling those plans. Eliot guided the internal transformation of the school in conformity with his view of a properly rigorous academic environment, mediating conflict among the faculty and playing the major role in selecting its members. Eliot even had an important part in establishing Langdell's most remembered contribution—the case method of teaching law. Eliot was a major actor in the reform of Harvard Law School from within.

Appointing a Dean

Eliot hired Langdell as part of his campaign to raise standards in the university and the professions. He outlined his views early. In 1869 the youthful chemist and soon-to-be president of Harvard published a two-part article on "The New Education" in the *Atlantic Monthly*. In a footnote he observed that the paucity of Bachelors of Arts among holders of LL.B.'s and M.D.'s debased the professions—"The term 'learned profession' is getting to have a sarcastic flavor"—and thus foreshadowed the difficult and costly effort he pursued as president of the university to raise the standards of the professional schools. Even more important, however, was his assertion in the same article that "no subject of human inquiry can be out of place in the programme of a real university.'' Vigorous action on that belief ensured that the law school would become a new institution for the training of lawyers separate from, and sometimes antagonistic to, the practicing bar.[2]

Eliot shared in what Burton Bledstein has identified as a general ''mid-Victorian'' propensity to think ''in terms of professional studies versus practical ones, academic studies in any field versus on-the-job technical training, persons who discipline their minds versus persons who do not, qualified practitioners versus quacks.''[3] In Eliot's mind the ideal profession was neither learned nor practical but rather scientific: ''Reforms during Eliot's administration moved the professional faculties away from practical preparation for a craft and toward theory and research.''[4] Yet Eliot never lost sight of the practical aspects of professional education. What his outlook meant for law schools is clearly expressed in a brief address he gave in 1882. The legal profession, Eliot said, ''has infinite need of the condensing, simplifying, reducing, distilling class of minds which are capable of getting at the lowest terms, the gist or essence of an involved and bulky mass.'' These few words express with unusual succinctness what most lawyers and law teachers of Eliot's day meant when they exhorted themselves to greater efforts for legal science. At the same time, Eliot maintained that Harvard Law School wanted ''its work brought to two practical tests'': the test of whether its graduates could immediately be useful as clerks or, if necessary, earn a living on their own, and the test of whether they would eventually reach ''the first ranks of the American bar.''[5]

As a professional educator, Eliot probably saw no great difficulty with the union of scientific and practical aims in law schools. For professors and practicing lawyers, however, the union was frequently in danger of collapsing into civil war. Relationships between practitioners and teachers, among law schools, and among members of the same faculty would all be strained by attempts to achieve the ideal that Eliot helped promulgate.[6]

Those struggles lay in the future. When Eliot became president of Harvard, the law school was anything but the sort of institution he had described in ''The New Education.'' The course of study occupied only eighteen months; students could begin studies whenever they pleased and could likewise end them. There were no examinations, and many students did not bother to stay long enough to obtain the degree. In Professor Joel Parker's words: ''With the exception of the requisition of a certain term of study, the degree is honorary.''[7] This state of affairs had governed for some time. Since the late 1840s the school had been led by the same faculty: Joel Parker, former Chief Justice of New Hampshire; Theophilus Parsons, son of the great Chief Justice of the Massachusetts Supreme Judicial Court of the same name, both of whom had taught Langdell; and a former governor of Massachusetts, Emory Washburn, who joined them in 1855. Although Parker resigned at the end of the 1867–1868 academic year to be succeeded by Nathaniel Holmes, when Eliot was elected to the presidency on May 19, 1869, Harvard Law School was still the school of Parker, Parsons, and Washburn.

After Langdell was appointed, the reign of these three men would be looked on as a period of educational decadence. Whatever disappointments their students may have had with the intellectual stimulation they supplied, however, the quality of instruction became a matter of contention only at the end of the 1860s.[8] At the height of the old regime, controversy was directed at management of the school and of its greatest resource, its library. This tempest in a book stack was fueled primarily by a jurisdictional conflict between two visiting committees of the Board of Overseers.[9] Both the committee charged with visiting the university library and that charged with visiting the law school claimed the right to worry themselves about the state of the library in Dane Hall. The library visiting committee decided in 1861 to make an issue of the number of books discovered missing in recent years and the general lack of supervision of library users. The committee to visit the law school upheld the status quo, and the matter was finally put to rest—with the law school's faculty vindicated—in 1863.[10]

At the beginning of Eliot's presidency, criticism of the school's management was being voiced once again in terms similar to those used earlier in the decade. The library made the news, quite literally, in 1870. On October 17 the report of the committee appointed to visit the law school was published in the *Boston Daily Advertiser*. While the report made some comments on the way moot courts were run and on possible improvements in the methods of instruction, its major criticism of past practices at the school involved the library. Although it "was formed on a comprehensive plan," the library had not been maintained. Purchases had not been systematic, and the condition of the books was "not agreeable to the lover of books, or the lover of learning."[11]

Clearly a library run on such a basis did not belong in the sort of university envisioned by the man who wrote "The New Education." But it was not only the administration of the library that drew criticism. Francis E. Parker authored both the 1869 and 1870 reports, the former urging nothing less than a full-scale assessment of the law school "by a committee so constituted as fully to represent and command the respect of the legal profession as well as to have weight with the Corporation, the Overseers and the public."[12]

The following fall saw a more public criticism of the school in the form of a brief anonymous note in the October issue of the *American Law Review*. The fame of these few sentences rests on the subsequent career of one of the editors of the *Review*, Oliver Wendell Holmes, Jr. Beginning provocatively—"For a long time the condition of the Harvard Law School has been almost a disgrace to the Commonwealth of Massachusetts"—the author went on to emphasize slack standards of admission and the lack of examinations for the law degree, the very matters with which Eliot was most concerned.[13] By the time these criticisms were in print, change was already under way. Parker's 1869 report caused Professor Parsons to resign. At the age of sixty-three "he felt . . . it was too late for him to remodel all his old views and to co-operate in the novel projects of reformation which the new President was already proposing.'' The passing of an era could not have been better symbolized. On January 6, 1870, the very day Parsons's resignation was accepted by the Harvard Corporation, Christopher Columbus Langdell was elected Dane Professor at the insistence of President Eliot.[14]

Whatever inchoate ideas about the case method Langdell may have had, it seems likely that Eliot's views on the need to stiffen both academic and administrative standards, as opposed to changes in the method of teaching, were the most important factor in the choice of Langdell to fill the vacancy left by Parsons's resignation. ''The New Education'' had made clear Eliot's scorn for the academic pretensions of professional schools that did not require a college education for admission. The institution of such a requirement was no doubt one of the changes Eliot had in mind, as were both the rearrangement of the curriculum into a definite progression of discrete courses and the institution of examinations. All this was part of what Eliot's official biographer called the ''Campaign for Professional Standards.''[15] The administrative changes were foreshadowed by the new University Statutes of April 8, 1870, which established the position of dean of the faculty in each of the professional schools. Presumably this new official was not only an administrator—keeping records, preparing agendas, and presiding at meetings were the only functions mentioned in the new legislation—but also a commander in the great campaign.[16]

In that campaign the law school library was clearly an enemy redoubt. Not only was its administration sloppy in a way that a professional educator like Eliot no doubt found abhorrent, but it was also a symbol of a school that did not belong in the university envisioned by ''The New Education.'' Joel Parker defended his and his fellows' decision to let students borrow volumes, especially textbooks, from the library by noting that ''this is no more than the usual privilege accorded to students in offices.'' For the old regime the school was a variation on the traditional method of training lawyers. For the new it was to be a specially adapted department of the university, investigating its branch of knowledge in a scientific way; it was to resemble the other professional schools rather than other methods for training lawyers.[17]

For several reasons Langdell was a sensible choice to lead the transformation of Harvard Law School along the lines Eliot envisioned. Since management of the library was such an important issue, it is significant that, as Eliot recalled, ''to Professor Langdell books had a kind of sacrosanct character.''[18] When the new president began his search for the man to head a remodeled law school, Langdell's devotion to books may have been known in Boston and not just from his brief tenure as student librarian of the school fifteen years before. In February 1870, the new Dane Professor received a letter from R. W. Haynes, an English publisher and exporter of law books. After telling Langdell of his recent meeting with Charles

O'Conor, Langdell's first legal patron, Haynes went on to lament the confused state of the library committee of the New York Law Institute:

> Now that I have (thanks to you my friend) obtained not only the patronage but the approbation of the library authorities at Boston, Philada., Baltimore, & Chicago, it is mortifying to find that one's efforts to do well & right in New York should be frustrated by ignorance & indifference.[19]

This slight hint that Langdell may have had a national reputation in law library circles provides a possible explanation for Eliot's consideration of the New York lawyer as Parsons's successor. The former student librarian must have appeared to Eliot to be capable of salvaging the "grotesque remains of the law library [which] were little more than an open quarry whence any visitor might purloin any volume he chose—provided he could find it."[20]

Whatever specific goals Eliot may have hoped to accomplish by appointing Langdell to the faculty of Harvard Law School, they play no role in the traditional account of Langdell's selection. Eliot promulgated this official version at the dinner meeting of the Harvard Law School Association on November 5, 1886, held to commemorate the 250th anniversary of the founding of Harvard College. Faced with Parsons's resignation, Eliot recalled his undergraduate days when, during visits to a friend in the divinity school, he often "heard a young man who was making notes to Parsons on Contracts talk about law." In 1869 Eliot "recalled the remarkable character of that man's expositions, . . . and induced him to become Dane Professor."[21] Fifty years after the event itself, Eliot amplified his recollections in only the most general way, recalling that the possibility of becoming Dane Professor "attracted [Langdell] strongly," not the least because "clearly he had in mind some reform in legal education."[22]

Having written his version of history, Eliot preferred to let it remain undisturbed. When he was soliciting letters of reminiscence for his history of Harvard Law School, Charles Warren wrote Eliot asking for information on the appointment of Langdell. He received the very next day a rather testy reply from Joseph Warren, assistant secretary of the university: "President Eliot directs me to inform you" that the changes Langdell introduced were not "under contemplation before his appointment," that the idea of appointing Langdell was Eliot's alone, and that Langdell was not promised the deanship at the time of his appointment.[23] Clearly, Dean Langdell was solely President Eliot's idea—and that relationship was not to be disturbed by prying historians.

Fortunately, the Harvard archives contain materials that shed further light on the decision to bring Langdell to Cambridge. Even before Parsons officially resigned on December 1, 1869, Eliot was looking for new blood for the law school.[24] In mid-November, James Bradley Thayer wrote Eliot to propose several names for the president's consideration, most particularly Richard Dana, Jr., the author of *Two Years before the Mast*. A member of one of the oldest families of the commonwealth, Dana had returned from his experience at sea to take up law and by this time was a prominent Boston practitioner. He seems to have attracted Thayer's approval because Thayer judged him "a fine, thoughtful and cultivated creature." It appears, however, that the men proposed by Thayer—all practitioners like Dana—were being suggested as alternatives to Langdell. At the end of his letter Thayer concluded that "after all one comes back to Langdell with great confidence."[25]

Eliot shared that judgment. In December he solicited opinions from those who knew Langdell. George O. Shattuck—Oliver Wendell Holmes's future law partner—wrote the president that "I know of no man who in my judgment would be of such service to the School." He also warned Eliot about the personality of the man he commended:

> It is [illegible] true that Langdell has faults of manner and of temper, and that he is out of relations with the present state of things in New York. He is disgusted with their courts and general mode of doing business. It may be that his appointment would be attended with some peril.[26]

Shattuck closed by suggesting that James C. Carter was better able to give a full character of Langdell.

With his response to Eliot's inquiry, Carter began to play an important role in the life of Harvard Law School. He proved himself to be an active, independent, and influential alumnus. His remarkably frank and open letter of December 20, 1869, apparently played an important part in Langdell's appointment—Eliot sought and received Carter's permission to lay it before the corporation.[27] It is worth setting out at length.

> My acquaintance with him from the time we were in the Law School together until some five or six years since was very intimate, and during that period I had the best opportunity to become acquainted with the powers and characteristics of the man. . . .
>
> In the points of professional learning, clear thinking & speaking, and perhaps I may add the other particular you refer to, fondness for expounding, I think he has no superior within the range of my acquaintance.
>
> His fine natural powers, the high ambition with which he started, and the devoted industry he has always exhibited would surely make, as they have made of him, a scholar of the first order. . . .
>
> The other side of the picture (for I must tell you all), if there be another side, is this. Langdell entered upon the practice of the law in this city with the high purposes natural to such a man. He would scorn to win, or to struggle for, any success which was not the legitimate reward of merit. Very far from being an enthusiast generally, in his profession, he was one; and I think he soon conceived a hearty disgust for the means & methods by which business, place & reputation are here [in New York City] gained. He was not sufficiently content to take the world as he found it, and the result has been a failure on his part to reach that place in the profession to which he would otherwise have easily risen.

> I think he must have felt, and perhaps still feels, much disappointment, and the effect of it may have been in some degree to impair the freshness and elasticity of his character and encourage a sort of dissatisfaction with himself & the world.
>
> He was never distinguished for what is called *self-assertion*, and if he is wanting in any of the qualities, which you are seeking to secure, it will be found to be in aptitude for affairs and the skill and resources to deal with society and men as he finds them. . . .
>
> If you had the whole world to choose from, you could find a better man than Langdell, but your list must be a limited one. If you could replace a portion of his learning and abilities with the popular manners, and personal attractions and the arts of rivalry which have such a powerful influence on building up such an institution as the Law School, it would be well to make the sacrifice; but unless I was sure of these points I should prefer such a man as Langdell. (Don't understand me as undertaking to advise you. I am only seeking to give you my impressions.)[28]

The events of Langdell's deanship would prove Carter a most acute observer of human nature. In fact, Langdell seemed determined to prove Carter's judgment of his "dissatisfaction with himself & the world" and his lack of "the skill and resources to deal with society and men as he finds them" even before he assumed his position.

Securing Langdell's confirmation by the governing boards proved to be difficult. The corporation consented "though with some reluctance . . . probably out of some general purpose to support their young President."[29] The overseers proved to be far less tractable. Langdell would to do nothing to promote his own cause. He refused to supply the Board of Overseers with the names of lawyers who knew him well and even turned down an invitation to dine with some of them. Difficult as they made his appointment, however, such attitudes were not necessarily a handicap for an intended commander in Eliot's war for educational standards. Growing out of Langdell's presumably unhappy experiences at the New York bar, his unwillingness to temporize and the "hearty disgust for the means & methods by which business, place & reputation" could be gained probably made him the more adamant an advocate of reforms in legal education designed to better the profession. His unswerving advocacy of those reforms would be an important factor in the eventual success of his school.

The negative elements in Carter's assessment did not deter Eliot from going ahead with Langdell's appointment. The need to set the library on a proper course and Langdell's love of books, as well as his practical experience in the book trade, may have helped lead Eliot to take a calculated risk.[30] As far as administering the public services aspect of the library went, however, Eliot made a bad bargain. The new dean did try. He installed a rail separating the reading area from the books, abolished the expensive practice of buying enough texts and treatises to supply each student with copies of the required reading, and ended the practice of professors' sending books to the printer in order to have quotations used in their own works set in type directly from the sources. Or, rather, Langdell *tried* to effect these changes. It took Eliot's authority to prevent the faculty from sending books off to the local print shop.[31] Eliot even had to intervene to protect the book stack's newly acquired sanctity. One student, remembered William A. Everett, who was librarian from 1870–1871, kept ignoring the new barrier: "So finding myself of no account with the man, I reported the case to Dean Langdell. He was thoroughly alarmed at the crisis. 'What can I do! What can I do!' was all that he could say."[32] All that he could do was report the matter to Eliot, who wrote the offending student a letter which had the desired effect.

Whatever Langdell's failures as a day-to-day administrator, the institutional changes of Eliot's campaign for reform were gradually implemented. In September 1870 the students found themselves confronted with a new pattern of courses that assumed progression from a first year of required studies to a second of electives. Pursuant to new university regulations, accomplishment in each course was to be measured by written examination. In addition to these opening moves for strengthening institutional standards, that same fall Langdell introduced a new method of teaching law, based not on lectures and the reading of treatises, but on the study and discussion of appellate cases. This new teaching technique would eventually overshadow Langdell's other contributions to shaping the modern law school. It was highly controversial even within Harvard Law School, where Langdell's single-minded pursuit of his own views on the substantive law he taught helped divide the faculty well into the 1880s. Outside the school, discussions of the merits of the case method involved not just questions of pedagogy but also deep disagreements over the nature of law itself. At the same time, many of the institutional changes in the school were quite popular with practicing lawyers who concerned themselves with improving the profession. These institutional changes, however, were controversial, and their implementation risked danger for the school.

Developing a Law School

The ultimate success of Harvard Law School has clouded the memory of the difficulties the school faced for some years after Langdell's appointment. Harvard Law School did not spring full-blown and vigorous from the minds of Christopher Columbus Langdell and Charles William Eliot. For some twenty years after Langdell's appointment the school was still evolving toward its modern form. The dislocations caused by introducing the case method and by stiffening standards were overcome only slowly. The relationship between experience in practice and teaching remained unsettled as Eliot took note of criticisms of the school, and new faculty members did not immediately take up the case method. Most important, the school's position in the legal world was uncertain.

The trials and tribulations of the changing school have been chronicled several times. Charles Warren's two-volume history; the *Centennial History* published in 1918; and the volume by Arthur Sutherland, *The Law at Harvard*—all chart the fluctuations of enrollment and the gradual development of the modern school with entrance requirements, a graded curriculum, and examinations in every course.[33] Not surprisingly, the story tends to have the air of the inevitable about it. The eventual success of the school colors the assessment of events. A close examination of the record, however, shows the intensity of the struggle within the school and Eliot's crucial role as the ultimate arbiter.

One of the most important features of the reformed school was the creation of a full-time teaching corps. The most significant step toward this end is usually assumed to be the appointment of James Barr Ames as assistant professor in 1873. Ames had never practiced law and was a devoted disciple of Langdell. Subsequent appointments to the faculty did not follow the same pattern. Both James Bradley Thayer, appointed in 1873, and John Chipman Gray, appointed in 1875, were practicing lawyers, albeit of a scholarly bent.[34] Neither, at least at first, saw much good in Langdell's teaching methods.[35] Eliot meant their appointments to strengthen the school's reputation with the practicing bar. The school for the first time had four resident instructors after Thayer took up his teaching duties in October 1874—Langdell, Washburn, Thayer, and Assistant Professor Ames.

The increase in faculty allowed the school to dispense with the services of lecturers and to rely wholly on full-time teachers. Eliot's explanation of this change in his annual report for 1873–1874 indicates how thoroughly he, like Langdell, believed in the academic pursuit of professional training. A false analogy between medical education and legal education, Eliot wrote, had led many to believe that practitioners would make the best teachers of law. Medicine can be learned only from the bodies of the sick and wounded; law, on the other hand, "is to be learned exclusively from the books in which its principles and precedents are recorded, digested, and explained."[36] The place to find these principles and precedents, of course, was not the courtroom but the library. Foreshadowing Langdell's 1886 analogy between the law library and the natural scientist's laboratory, Eliot maintained that "the law library, and not the court or the law office, is the real analogue of the hospital." These observations naturally dictated certain conclusions about the qualifications of the teaching force. The medical teacher "must be a practitioner to have cases to teach with." The legal practitioner, however, may not have the temperament or talents necessary to make a good teacher. He is also too busy to be a "thorough student." Given these considerations, the corporation appointed Ames as assistant professor "that they might see if it were practicable to breed Professors of law by the same gradual process by which competent teachers are trained up in other departments of the University." While this experiment has "thus far been perfectly successful," the corporation does not "overlook the advantage of having some men of large experience in actual practice as resident Professors of Law." The appointment of Thayer presumably carried out this dual appointment policy. The basic assumption, however, was that full-time resident teachers were indispensable—another foreshadowing by the president of later comments by the dean.

Eliot's 1873–1874 report and Thayer's appointment illustrate the interaction between the goals of the dean and the president. Both men accepted the proposition that law was a science best investigated and taught through examination of its original sources, the cases found in the books.[37] Eliot then spun from that premise a corollary about teaching law, not publicly articulated by Langdell until 1886 but implicit in his support of Ames's appointment—that law teachers should be full-time teachers and scholars. Practitioner-lecturers played a suitable role while appropriate appointees were being sought, but their role had to end. Whatever this change in the nature of the teaching force meant to Langdell, for Eliot it was a development that brought the law school closer to other departments in the university and more surely under the president's authority. To create full professors by promotion from junior status meant to control their careers; to require teachers to refrain from their practice meant to curtail their financial independence and to focus their professional aspirations on those academic matters over which the president had great influence.[38] It is not surprising that some practicing lawyers transferred their allegiance to the new law school at Boston University where the legal profession appeared to be firmly in control.

Whether or not this competition was the reason, Eliot continued to seek out established practitioners to fill vacancies in the faculty. The selection of Emory Washburn's successor in 1876 clearly showed that something of the past could rise through change and storm. Charles S. Bradley was fifty-seven years old, a prosperous Providence, Rhode Island, lawyer, former chief justice of his state, prominent in its Democratic party, and a sometime lecturer in Harvard Law School. He "lectured in a fashion recalling the old days [and] was absolutely untouched by the case system."[39] He also retained his practice. Gray, of course, continued to practice in Boston, but seems to have been able to devote a full measure of attention to the school and was in every sense a "full-time" teacher and scholar along the new line who "always put the law school first."[40] For Bradley, however, "the School was but one care of many he had in hand."[41] It is reported, in fact, that "the notes for his lectures were frequently jotted down on the backs of envelopes during his train journey from Providence the same morning."[42] Bradley's appointment to full professorial honors while maintaining his practice may have angered his full-time junior in rank and salary, Ames, as well as making the younger man fear for his future. Ames tendered his resignation in March 1877 to take effect September 1, one year before the expiration of his original five-year appointment. The corporation responded by creating a new professorship, and Ames assumed a status equal to Bradley's.[43]

Bradley resigned at the end of the 1878–1879 school year to devote himself to his practice. He seems to have passed through the school without leaving much of a wake. While his departure may have endorsed the policy of staffing the school with full-time teachers, it did not indicate that Langdell's sway was unfettered any more than did Washburn's resignation. In fact, there seem to have been deep divisions between the dean and Ames on one hand and Thayer and Gray on the other. The faculty voted June 28, 1878, to establish two courses of study, one of which led to the degree *cum laude*. To gain the more distinguished status, students had to elect courses dealing with the doctrines of equity; for those in the "ordinary" course, all subjects after the first year were elective.[44]

After the vote, Gray and Thayer seem to have shared second thoughts when confronted by the interpretation of the new rules advanced presumably by Ames and the dean. Gray wrote Thayer that he had thought that equity procedure was simply part of the honors course. It now seemed that the faculty's action meant more than had first appeared:

> To divide the school into two classes one of whom is to be entitled to a higher degree because they have studied equity procedure, though their marks may fall far below those attained by men who have not taken eq.[uity] procedure, this I cannot consent to.[45]

Equity pleading and jurisdiction were among Langdell's primary scholarly interests. He produced a finished casebook on equity pleading (1875) and parts of a casebook on equity jurisdiction (1879, 1883). In 1905 the *Harvard Law Review* published a volume of his essays on equity jurisdiction that had appeared in the *Review*.

As matters worked out, Ames taught courses in jurisdiction and procedure in equity in 1878–1879 using Langdell's book. In 1879–1880 Langdell and Ames taught the two required honors courses in the new third year.[46] This monopolization of the honors curriculum by the dean and his protégé seems not to have set well with Thayer and Gray, especially with the former, who apparently felt his own subject of constitutional law deserved a place among the required courses.[47]

These divisions continued as attempts were made to find a replacement for Bradley. Eventually, Thayer received Eliot's permission—in spite of Langdell's and Ames's pessimism—to seek the funds necessary to endow a chair for the younger Oliver Wendell Holmes. Thayer and the prospective donor, William F. Weld, reached agreement in a short time; on January 19, 1882, Harvard Law School had its new chair—its donor remaining anonymous for the time being—and on February 11, 1882, the overseers confirmed Holmes's appointment.[48]

The appointment of the author of *The Common Law* reveals several facets of life at Harvard Law School in the early 1880s. In the first place, Langdell and Ames doubted the possibility of raising the necessary funds, perhaps because of the prospective appointee. As Ames pointed out several years later in his course of lectures on legal history, acceptance of some of

Holmes's views on the history of uses "would be difficult for anyone who has studied his equity under the guidance of Professor Langdell."[49] Holmes was also an intimate of Gray and well acquainted with Thayer.[50] Perhaps the division in 1878 over the honors course was only one episode in a continuing story. Finally, it was Eliot who approached Holmes.[51] The president's crucial role in guiding the law school was clearly continuing. Eliot's independence in that role is also clear. *The Common Law*, based on Lowell Institute lectures given in November and December 1880 and published in March 1881, was certainly a scholarly work, but Holmes had also been actively engaged in practice for twelve years when his learned efforts finally bore fruit. Twice the precedent of Ames's appointment had been ignored. The new profession of law teaching was off to a slow start.[52]

Holmes, of course, soon left his professorship for the bench. The search for his successor opened up old wounds. On May 14, 1883, the corporation appointed William A. Keener to replace Holmes. Out of law school but four years, Keener was appointed assistant professor as Ames had been before him. In his annual report for 1882–1883 Eliot used Keener's appointment to confirm the experiment begun with Ames. He noted that Keener preferred "the life of a student and teacher," had taken every opportunity to teach, and did it well. It was still an unusual appointment, "but its results have already proved satisfactory."[53] The decision to appoint a man who had been trained at Harvard and had not practiced long was a considered one.

Sometime between Holmes's resignation and Keener's appointment, Ephraim Gurney, dean of the college faculty, wrote Eliot the thoughts of a sleepless night. The dean professed great admiration for Langdell and Ames, but he was sure "that Langdell, running the School at his pleasure, would wreck it. He is as *intransigeant* as a French Socialist, and his ideal is to breed professors of Law, not practitioners." In Gurney's view the appointment of Keener might well mean the triumph of Langdell's view. Committing the school "to the theory of breeding within itself the Corps of instructors" would sever it "from the great current of legal life which flows through the courts and the bar" and would be "the gravest error of policy" possible.[54]

Professor Gurney was not the only person who doubted the wisdom of selecting Keener. The young practitioner accepted an offer conveyed to him by Eliot and Langdell on December 28, 1882, three weeks after Holmes's appointment to the Massachusetts Supreme Judicial Court.[55] During those weeks probably several names were canvassed, and as late as December 27 or 28 the name of Judge William Gardner Choate of New York was being circulated.[56] At least one member of the law faculty was surprised when Keener's appointment was revealed at or shortly before what was almost certainly a faculty meeting held on January 2, 1883. For John Chipman Gray, Keener's selection was the last straw.

On January 3, Gray wrote Eliot "to say what I could not well say last night."[57] He reviewed the ways in which the school had flouted the opinions of the profession at large—by hiring teachers who had not practiced extensively, by instituting admissions examinations, and by extending the course to three years. The result had been a severe reduction in the number of students. Even if the profession were wrong, therefore, the school should not defy professional opinion against inexperienced teachers "on which lawyers are much more unanimous than on the others [examination and the three-year course], and if the thing is to be done it should not be done until we have recovered from the effect of our other changes." Such was simply the counsel of prudence, and said nothing about the soundness of Langdell's vision of the law school as a European-style faculty of jurisprudence. "But now I want to say the profession is right." Gray told Eliot that law was not at all like the natural sciences whose "truths and the best means of applying them are independent of opinion." Law was quite different because "in law the opinions of judges and lawyers as to what the law is *are* the law." The professor has a difficult time in restraining his desire to promulgate his opinions, some do not succeed—"Langdell's intellectual arrogance and contempt is [*sic*] astounding." Should the tendency be strengthened, the school would be doomed:

> The idols of the cave which a school bred lawyer is sure to substitute for the fact, *may be much better material for intellectual gymnastics than the facts themselves and may call forth more enthusiasm in the pupils*, but a school where the majority of the professors shuns and despises the contact with actual facts, has got the seeds of ruin in it and will go to the devil. The very excellence of its methods will send it there all the faster.

Gray's almost desperate desire to forestall the creation of "a majority of the faculty made up of professors whose opinions and training will more and more tend to divorce the school from the facts which the students have to meet in the world" indicates the unsettled condition of Harvard Law School thirteen years after Langdell's accession to the deanship, as well as the continuing influence of those aspects of Langdell's personality that Carter had so acutely observed. Langdell's capacity for leadership was becoming even more problematic as the dean's eyesight began to fail. Enrollment had not recovered from the double blows of the entrance examination and the three-year course of study. The faculty was fundamentally divided over the policy to be followed in appointing future members. In spite of the move to Austin Hall, the school's new home, Eliot was saying a good deal when he wrote in his annual report "the year 1882–1883 was not a prosperous one in the Law School."[58]

The doubts expressed by Gray, Gurney, and perhaps others led to the withdrawal of the offer to Keener. He did not let the circumstances anger him and wrote Eliot: "I hope, and I do not now see why I will not be able to accept the position if offered later in the year."[59] Whatever search was undertaken for an alternative to the young New York lawyer, none was found and the corporation elected Keener to the faculty on May 14, 1883.[60] The Board of Overseers was not ready to concur at once, but rather sent the matter to a committee, which reported back on June 15. The committee found that Keener was indeed a worthy young man of great talent and promise.[61] Far more important was the admission that it was entirely unlikely that any search would ever find a successful practitioner willing to trade the material rewards of practice for the sort of salary the school could afford to pay.[62] The necessity of paying well is clearly illustrated by the report that Judge Choate was then earning $20,000 a year from his practice, whereas the salary of a professor of law was $4,500.[63] Practicality, then, settled the immediate question of finding a successor to Holmes.

The broader question of policy, however, was not settled by Keener's appointment. In 1890 Keener resigned when, because of his relatively short service of two years as a full professor, he was not included in the $500 increase in law professors' salaries. The search for a successor focused on Jeremiah Smith, whose name had been mentioned in spring 1883.[64] After Keener's appointment, Smith continued to practice in Dover, New Hampshire. He had been associate justice of the New Hampshire Supreme Court—at that time the chief trial court as well as the appellate court of the state—and a colleague of the celebrated Charles Doe. In 1874 tuberculosis forced him to resign. After regaining his health, he resumed practice in 1882. Smith was well connected politically, at least well enough to help promote the possibility of Doe's appointment to the United States Supreme Court. He also regained professional prominence. One of his friends from college days, Edwin H. Abbot, receiver of the Wisconsin Central Railroad, called on Smith to argue several important cases. Abbot's reaction to his friend's appointment as Story Professor is perhaps typical of the reaction of other practicing lawyers: "I know this man," he wrote President Eliot; "of the strength he brings both of learning and character. The appreciation of it will grow, & he will be a tower of strength, & add to the school what it somewhat lacks."[65]

Not all of Smith's new colleagues were quite as enthusiastic. Ames seems to have been a strong partisan of Keener and an opponent of Smith. So emphatic was he, and so conciliatory was Langdell, that Eliot ventured to suggest the existence of a "difficulty" between the dean and the Bussey Professor. Ames hastened to assure Eliot that no breach existed, and then went on to tell the president politely that he and Langdell were displeased. While Ames admitted "if consulted I should have made no objection" to Smith's appointment "in view of its probable effect upon the students now in the school," the entire matter "compelled me to recognize that you and I take widely different views as to the function of the Law Faculty." Ames nonetheless insisted he was not "at all disaffected towards the School."[66] In spite of Ames's protestations, his disaffection grew over the next six months. In September he wrote Eliot: "I have decided that, in the interest of the Law School, I ought to sacrifice my personal preference to remain out of the Law Faculty." Again he told Eliot that their views were incompatible and assured him that "your conception of the function of the Law Faculty must work to the detriment of the School."[67] Samuel Williston, who also began his service to the school in 1890, perhaps understated the initial difficulties the judge faced when he wrote in his memoir of Smith: "He was not without discouragements in the early years of his work, and even the contribution which he brought to the School of a new point of view on disputed legal questions did not always work to his advantage."[68]

After twenty years Eliot was still largely shaping Harvard Law School according to his own vision. The appointment of Jeremiah Smith was his decision, although it certainly coincided with views expressed in the Board of Overseers when Keener was appointed seven years before. Tradition, however, makes the crucial decision Eliot's alone. On February 25, 1890, Smith gave a talk on "Law as a Profession" before a group of Harvard undergraduates who occasionally gathered to hear such edifying addresses. Edwin Abbot's son was president of the group and had invited his father's friend to address his fellows. Eliot was present "and was so impressed by the words and the personality of the speaker that he decided that this was the man to fill the Story Professorship."[69]

The talk was never published, but notes—really almost a complete text—survive.[70] Smith devoted most of his time to an examination of major problems of legal ethics posed by practice: Should one take on the advocacy of an unjust cause? What should the lawyer who has been deceived by his client do when the deception becomes apparent after proceedings have begun? Can and how should one defend an accused whom one believes to be guilty of the crime charged? Those questions are still alive today, as are the answers Smith gave in 1890. He advised a thorough investigation of every cause before taking it up, the withdrawal from a falsely presented cause through the discreet suggestion that it would be unprofitable to proceed further, and a defense limited to putting the guilty defendant on the stand and letting him tell his own story. His specific advice was followed by a refutation of the charge that the lawyer battens on the sins of humanity. Most of a lawyer's business was noncontentious: drafting legal documents, advising clients as to future conduct, working to avoid litigation. In fact, moral turpitude was not the basis of legal work: "Law business springs from the intellectual limitations which Providence has seen fit to impose on human nature. The imperfections of human language, and the defects of human memory are the foundation of many differences of opinion."[71]

Smith then turned from the moral to what he called the mental side. The aspiring lawyer needed first the habit of industry, then a knowledge of legal principles, and finally the ability to apply them to the confused facts of daily life. He should not depend on rhetorical ability and mere eloquence to win verdicts but, rather, should pay closest attention to content, especially in making an opening statement to the jury. Finally, there is not much work for the mediocre lawyer. The collection business, checking of titles, and acting as a trustee have passed to specialized corporations. Even the best young lawyers must expect to spend a good deal of time waiting for clients, time best spent in study.

Perhaps Eliot saw in this talk what the experience of practice could bring to the classroom. Smith did talk about problems faced by the working lawyer, and apparently did it well. Eliot was not indifferent to the practical aspects of professional education—he wished to have Harvard Law School graduate men ready to do useful work.[72] For many years he had supported the claims of theory and the spirit of scientific scholarly investigation. The result had been a constant struggle to maintain the material prospects of the school. His attempt to add a different perspective to the school by hiring Bradley had not succeeded. Judge Smith might be the man to redress the balance—at least Ames seems to have been afraid that he would.[73]

Whatever hostility met Jeremiah Smith when he began his duties in autumn 1890 seems to have melted quickly away. He worked hard at conquering the fields he undertook to teach, especially torts. Ames had taught torts and the measure of his acceptance of the new Story Professor is their eventual coeditorship of a torts casebook, which is the direct ancestor of a book still in use. Smith compiled several other casebooks as well and exhibited "unusual sagacity in finding significant cases."[74] He also wrote many scholarly articles.[75] Most important, Judge Smith was a thorough advocate of the case method: "It was his immediate adoption of the case method of teaching which Langdell regarded as the mark of its complete success."[76]

Birth of the Case Method

The symbolic importance of Smith's conversion to the case method of teaching law indicates how thoroughly it was identified with the reformation of Harvard Law School, as well as how it had been transformed from a cause of disagreement among the faculty to the bond that unified academic lawyers. To understand that result requires first an understanding of what the case method was, how it differed from the sort of law teaching that went before, how it corresponded to new ideas of pedagogy, and how it was related to developments in the profession and in society generally.

The case method is most widely recognized as a teaching technique. Samuel Batchelder's description of Langdell's first class is well known:

> The class gathered in the old amphitheatre of Dane Hall—the one lecture room of the School—and opened their strange new pamphlets, reports bereft of their only useful part, the head-notes! The lecturer opened his.
>
> "Mr. Fox, will you state the facts in the case of Payne v. Cave?"
>
> Mr. Fox did his best with the facts of the case.
>
> "Mr. Rawle, will you give the plaintiff's argument?"
>
> Mr. Rawle gave what he could of the plaintiff's argument.
>
> "Mr. Adams, do you agree with that?"
>
> And the case-system of teaching law had begun.[77]

Whether people realized at the time that something new had happened before their very eyes is uncertain. The catalogue issued in 1870 described the method of instruction "in much the same terms as in the Catalogues for the previous forty years,'' mentioning recitations, lectures, moot courts, and written exercises.[78] Fifty years later Franklin G. Fessenden, who entered the law school in that fateful autumn, claimed that ''instruction . . . in recitations . . . was new to the school. It originated with Professor Langdell.''[79] Even if Fessenden's identification of Langdell's method with the recitation is correct, the rest of his statement is not. Although today the ''case method'' is often equated with the Socratic dialogue of the classroom, Langdell was not the first law teacher to question his students.

In fact, Langdell's innovation may have been designed, at least in part, as a *revival* of the recitation and thus as simply one more attempt to meet one of the criticisms voiced in the visiting committee's 1870 report to the overseers. Apparently not satisfied with the faculty's announcement in fall 1869 of some changes in the method of teaching—the most significant of which was the distribution of questions for written answers which were then discussed in class—the committee suggested a course that would make instruction in the law school resemble that in the college. Perhaps they, too, were embarrassed by the school's resemblance to an office. If so, it is ironic that they chose that method of lessening the likeness which would soon be phased out of college instruction.[80]

Eliot took the committee's suggestions to heart. He attempted to persuade Bradley, then a lecturer, to add recitations to his courses. Bradley resisted, citing, first, the difficulties ''of inaugurating a new system which bears hard often upon the self esteem of young men''; second, the unsettled nature of the school with Washburn on leave; and, third, the time it would demand, time Bradley felt belonged to his practice. Eliot made no progress, and Bradley went on lecturing as before.[81]

Even if Langdell's innovation was primarily an attempt to carry out the visitors' suggestion, it was quite controversial.[82] Perhaps seeing only what was old in the new technique the students, according to Fessenden, belittled Langdell's teaching as ''grammar school recitation,''[83] and the old guard agreed with them. Recitations might be a useful way of instructing children, Joel Parker thought, and might be just barely useful in college, but certainly could not make lawyers.[84] Emory Washburn expressed a similar view when he described the ideal preparation for lawyering as ''a judicious and discreet course of reading, supplemented and aided by lectures, and, upon, a few subjects, recitations.''[85]

The term ''recitation,'' however, covered a multitude of teaching techniques. The sort of recitation Parker mocked in his defense of the ancien régime was not the sort of interrogation or colloquy that Langdell, or Parker himself for that matter, brought to the classroom in Dane Hall.[86] Eliot described the traditional sort of recitation and its weaknesses in his presidential report for the 1879–1880 academic year:

> The main objections to the recitation, at which the students simply recite a lesson previously set in a book, are, that good scholars who have learned the lesson well, and could recite it readily, get little or no instruction from the exercise, and that the teacher examines rather than teaches.[87]

This type of recitation "has well-nigh disappeared from the University." The term remains "perhaps, because a text or treatise affords a basis for the instruction," but the substance has changed greatly. It is now an opportunity to instruct by asking questions, "with a view to correct misapprehensions and to bring out the main points of the subject clear of the details." It is also an opportunity for the student to ask questions and to test his own powers of analysis. Eliot described this new type of recitation as used in the law school as an exercise "at which the instructor is the principal disputant in a discussion intended to elucidate and enforce a legal principle."

The other main tool of university instruction, the lecture, had also been transformed. According to Eliot, the lecture now included "a large admixture of the Socratic method." "In subjects which deal with chains of reasoning,—like mathematics, logic and law,—the skilful lecturer may draw from the class by successive questions the whole process of a long argument, getting a step from each student called upon." This change in the lecture led in turn to a different attitude toward references to printed authorities. Since the lecture no longer served as the primary conveyance for basic information, students are often "advised to use a book, or books, for parallel reading, or are required to read specified selections from a variety of books." The need to consult a number of sources that are not owned by the students but can be found in the library "presents grave inconvenience." There are often insufficient copies of the materials to allow all students timely access, and excessive wear and tear on the copies that do exist means they will be destroyed from overuse. The answer to this problem in the law school has been the creation of the casebook in which the principal cases are reprinted "with the addition of summaries or elaborate indices." "It is a good indirect effect of this method that it facilitates the study of original sources, and thereby tends to emancipate the student from treatises and other second-hand authorities."

To Eliot using the case method in law school was simply one facet of the general reform of teaching in institutions of higher education, the aim of which was to promote thought rather than rote memorization. The casebook was a convenient way to put before students the raw material for thought, the primary source for any analysis. However new the sort of recitations and lectures Eliot described were to college instruction, they were familiar in legal education long before Langdell began to teach. However "dull and inert" day-to-day teaching at Harvard Law School had become in the late 1850s and 1860s, a lively interchange between student and teacher had long been the ideal.[88]

If Langdell's classroom technique clearly had precedents, why did his advent so shake Harvard and eventually all American legal education? Why did his "case method" create so much controversy? The short answer is contained in its very name—it was a *case* method. Langdell made his classroom revolution by organizing his teaching around cases rather than treatises and around the search for principles rather than their explication, illustration, and application. His predecessors started with the principles; Langdell required his students to extract them.

The novelty of Langdell's approach and the extent of its departure from current practice at Harvard is illustrated by Emory Washburn's discussion in his *Lectures on the Study and Practice of the Law*, which was published in the summer of 1871, just after the end of the first academic year in which Langdell taught according to his new method. Washburn lectured "vividly and eloquently,"[89] and it is possible that this additional course was prompted by dissatisfaction with Langdell's teaching. In any event, Washburn's ideal legal education consisted of lectures that "illustrate and explain" for the student what he found in his books "by presenting the matter in a new light, or developing more clearly the principle which the author is attempting to establish." In addition, some subjects, such as the technical forms of pleading and the rules of evidence, require "a precise use of terms, and an accurate knowledge of the rules by which they are applied." This sort of learning can best be acquired through the drill and repetition of the recitation, which here seems to be the "old style" college recitation. The key to Washburn's ideas, however, lies in what sort of books the student is to be reading.[90] Since the object of the study of law preparatory to admission to the bar "is to treasure up, in a clear and intelligible form, the principles of the law for future use" and to discipline the mind, the student should begin with "good elementary treatises" which "state principles in a clear, orderly, and distinct manner." To begin by reading cases is a mistake. Cases are often full of extraneous matter, and the student will often fail "to possess himself of the principle which it is intended to illustrate or establish." Even if he reads the case correctly, he is then possessed of but a single fact which is meaningless until "its relations to other facts have been ascertained." In short, while "learning how to read reported cases with ease and advantage is, indeed, a part of the requisite training of a student, . . . the best time to do it is after he shall have made considerable progress in understanding what law is, and the elements of which it is composed."

This approach to teaching was also that of newer members of the faculty. After his first term as a lecturer, John Chipman Gray wrote to Eliot that his experience in the classroom had convinced him that lectures were the best means of teaching beginning students. Like Washburn's ideal lectures, Gray's would restate and illustrate principles the students would already have encountered in their reading.[91] James Bradley Thayer had similar thoughts at the beginning of his teaching career. On April 25, 1874, he confided to his memorandum book his disagreement with Langdell's methods. It was far better to give the student "as quickly as possible the outfit of a general and cursory view of the whole field of law."[92] A few days later he described his version of the ideal lecture:

> How if one should take 25 pages, say, of a text book, illuminate it, get to the bottom of the principles, discriminate, bring up the cases, cheer up

> the mind by anecdote, connect great names with subject, &c &c; then the next day question on all this pretty fully first, and go on to another 25 pages &c?[93]

Cases would be read and analyzed in the course of the lectures, but the heart of the work would be the textbook or elementary treatise.[94] Langdell flew in the face of accepted wisdom when he made his students do legal science in the course of their studies rather than giving them the results of legal science as recorded in treatises.

For Eliot, whose unwavering support was crucial to the successful transformation of the school, Langdell's love for the primary sources was not dangerous innovation but intelligent progress.[95] As the president implied in his discussion of teaching techniques, Langdell was doing in law what good teachers did in general: give students the raw materials, the original sources for analysis.[96] Such a vision also lay behind Eliot's reformation of the Harvard Medical School through the addition of laboratory and clinical work.[97] The advocates of scientific history had similar goals. Recitations made students dependent on the ideas of others and thus unfit to pursue "the scientific search for truth": "What they did believe was that first hand experience was the only way to learn the basic skills of historical investigation."[98]

In short, students learned by doing what professionals did in practice. Langdell's use of this method to teach law was a step beyond the sort of legal education carried out by the old method of expository lecture and more or less sophisticated recitation. The goal of that system was to lay a foundation of elementary knowledge that could be applied in practice. The new system trained students to understand the sources as a practicing lawyer must understand them.

Whether consciously or not, then, Langdell was in tune with new theories of pedagogy that emphasized doing rather than memorizing.[99] These ideas of how to teach and learn were in turn related to changing ideas about the professions and the role of education. Placed against this background, the significance of Langdell's reforms, both in teaching and in the administration of the school, is easy to understand. In a word, Langdell made legal study difficult: first, the institutional reforms made it more difficult to get in and stay in; then his new method of study made things more difficult once you were in. "His first lectures were followed by impromptu indignation meetings" of students desperate to be told what the law was. They were not pleased with a regime of questions: "Most of the class could see nothing in his system but mental confusion and social humiliation."[100] A similar reaction swept Columbia when Theodore Dwight was forced into retirement to make way for the case method in the person of William Keener. Dwight was proud to teach the "great and important class of men of average ability, who fill most respectably and usefully the humbler avenues of professional life."[101] Nor was Dwight unique in this boast. "To smooth the way of the law for beginners," wrote

W. W. Story of his father, "to help the weak through its doubtful and intricate passes, to stimulate the uninterested, and to partake in the zeal of the ardent was to him an endless joy."[102] Keener, however, who seems to have taken the adversary aspect of the method to an extreme, "was quick as a cat in discussion, pick you right up on a thing, get you into an argument about it, and he'd have you all twisted up like this—in no time." He was fondly known by his students at Columbia as "the red-bearded son of a bitch."[103]

In a less vehement vein, the *American Law Review* in its reviews of Langdell's early casebooks consistently noted that learning law through cases was not for the uncommitted, for "those students who desire to pick up in a few months enough law terms to enable them to pass the superficial examination which almost everywhere in the United States will admit to practice at the bar," but for those "who desire to know what the fundamental principles of law are, and the method in which they have been worked out and applied."[104] As James Carter, trained in the old Harvard Law School, pointed out, this method of study "is no royal road,—no primrose path":

> [I]t requires struggle. If there is anything which is calculated to try the human faculties in the highest degree, it is to take up the complicated facts of different cases; to separate the material from the immaterial, the relevant from the irrelevant; to assign to each element its due weight and limitation, and to give to different competing principles and rules of law their due place in the conclusion that is to be formed.[105]

The eventual success of this tough-minded approach to law teaching can be best understood if it is seen against broader social and intellectual transformations. Burton Bledstein emphasizes changes beginning in the colleges before the Civil War. A new sort of student was emerging: "The earnest young man regenerated himself during his college years; he purified his character and reformed his intelligence in order to fight out the battle of an American life on the terms of his own permanent choosing."[106] George Fredrickson dates a similar change from the war itself: "What was occurring was the transformation of the ideal of the 'strenuous life'—which had previously meant a retreat into the wilderness—into a social ideal."[107] Langdell tapped the desire for the strenuous life. After fifty years Franklin Fessenden remembers the new atmosphere vividly: one of "Kit's Freshmen"—those faithful few who stuck with that first contracts course—"when asked why he so decidedly preferred the new way, . . . replied that he felt freer, stronger, and better." Not content with the tests of the classroom, these same men formed the "Pow Wow," a club devoted to the arguing of cases:

> The deepest interest was taken. Able arguments were made, some of them equal to the best made in highest courts; and apparently as much was felt to be at stake as if the case were real. This practice, coupled with the

> mental discipline gained in Langdell's lectures, brought out the best there was in the men. A slovenly pleading or a careless argument—rare indeed—occasioned a sharp rebuke from the [student] court through the chief justice. This developed a thoughtful and studious set of men, and formed in them habits of industry which followed them in their later years of active work in practice at the bar and on the bench.[108]

The most famous of Kit's Freshmen, James Barr Ames, summed up the advantages of the new in condemning the old: "But the fundamental criticism to be made upon the recitation method of instruction, as generally handled, is that it is not a virile system. It treats the student not as a man, but as a schoolboy reciting his lesson."[109]

By creating a school that required students really to work to succeed, Langdell gave at least some of the students what they wanted in the classroom. He also helped give Eliot the type of law school he wanted for his university. President Eliot believed in the new world Christopher Columbus Langdell had discovered—at least he found certain regions pleasing for permanent settlement. The scholarly ambition of the inhabitants specializing in teaching satisfied Eliot's concern for the state of the learned professions. The dean's concern for the orderly life of the library and the emerging institutional structure of the school gave it legitimacy as part of the university. The very training of practitioners in this scholarly atmosphere appealed to Eliot's desire to have education serve a useful purpose in life. Finally, the rigor of the case method and of professional academics probably spoke to something in a man who wrote that "the common amusements of society have no charm for scholars. No man can be a successful student who does not devote his evenings to work; and the ordinary university teacher counts an evening given to the theater or to social amusement, as an evening lost or wasted."[110]

Langdell's case method as a method of teaching was indeed new because it emphasized instruction from the original sources and because it made the study of law a demanding intellectual enterprise. Both these qualities comported well with the plans of President Eliot to create a modern institution of higher learning dedicated to inquiry in the name of advancing knowledge. Less than novel was Langdell's conception of the nature of the legal science, which justified his approach to the teaching of law. Assessing the contributions to American legal education and legal thought of Langdell and the other members of the reformed Harvard faculty requires an investigation of what had gone before.

3

Antebellum Legal Education

Perhaps the most honored of all antebellum legal scientists, Joseph Story, defined common law in this way: "It is rather a system of elementary principles and of general juridical truths, which are continually expanding with the progress of society, and adapting themselves to the gradual changes of trade, and commerce, and the mechanic arts, and the exigencies and usages of the country."[1] The first part of this definition is the reflection in the law of a central idea in early and mid-nineteenth-century culture. The second played an important role in the rhetoric of justification often used by antebellum lawyers. Taken together, however, these two elements do not create a complete picture of the antebellum view of law. Law is a profession, as well as a science; it is practiced, as well as analyzed. The practical aspect of law was bound up with procedure, the part of law that governs practice in the courts. The science of principles and the practical study of procedure together formed an amalgam that defined American legal education before the Civil War. The first section of this chapter outlines the nature of the science of principles; the second section does the same for procedure. The consequences for antebellum legal education are set out in the third section.

A Science of Principles

For serious legal thinkers like Story, law was a science because like other sciences it was a system of principles. That definition in turn came from Francis Bacon, and the prestige of Bacon in antebellum America was immense.[2] Allegiance to "Baconianism" was "a mark of scientific orthodoxy."[3] The orthodox, however, did not adhere to a single creed. George Daniels has identified three different versions of faith in Lord Verulam. For some, Baconianism meant empiricism, a belief that all science rested on observation and that generalizations were formulated out of the facts that were so observed. For others, it meant the avoidance of hypotheses, a flight from the theoretical to the real world of what could be observed. Finally, it could also mean classification, an identification of science with taxonomy. The second and third meanings were the most often asserted by Americans. "In other words," Daniels writes, "nineteenth-century Baconianism, as most American scientists used the term, implied a kind of naive rationalistic empiricism—a belief that the method of pure empiricism consistently pursued would lead to a rational understanding of the universe."[4]

Such a view of science could easily encompass the common law. What are individual cases but the data to be observed? What is to be drawn from an observation of all cases but legal principles, the ordering of which should lead to rational understanding of the legal universe? Again and again in their public pronouncements, antebellum lawyers involved in legal education portrayed law as a science that conformed to the Baconian model. One of the new nation's first law teachers, James Wilson, made explicit for his auditors the common law's status as a Baconian science. A science, according to Wilson, is "best formed into a system, by a number of instances drawn from observation and experience, and reduced gradually into general rules" because "the natural progress of the human mind, in the acquisition of knowledge, is from particular facts to general principles." This is the only method "by which real discoveries have been made in philosophy." Progress is made in the field of natural philosophy by observing the phenomena of the material world; in law by observing the "phenomena" of men and society. The consequence is the regime of principles: "Hence, in both, the most regular and undeviating principles will be found, on accurate investigation, to guide and control the most diversified and disjointed appearances."[5]

In 1831 Daniel Mayes told his class in the law department of Transylvania University that the way to safe conclusions lay in the "decomposition" of complex ideas into separate parts and their examination in the light of every fact. He cautioned them never to "select facts to support a theory" but rather to "make sure of every fact and then search out a theory that rightly explains them." The following year he was more explicit, telling his charges that "cases are useful, but their greatest use is, that they serve to illustrate principles," which must then be subject to "analysis and classification."[6]

While Mayes was welcoming his class, James Gould was teaching for almost the last time at the law school in Litchfield, Connecticut, where he had been lecturing, first as an associate of Tapping Reeve and later as principal instructor, since 1798.[7] On the verge of retirement, in 1832 Gould published his lectures on pleading in treatise form. It was, he boasted, better than any other work on the subject because it exhibited the doctrines of pleading not as "as compilation of *positive rules*; but as a system of *consistent and rational principles*" in other words, as a science.[8] The growth of that science was given an exemplary exposition by Joseph Willard, who addressed his remarks to the assembled bar of Worcester County, Massachusetts, in fall 1829. According to Willard, the common law grows as the cases, the raw material of science, "are arranged, divided into classes and embodied with all the philosophy of induction." General principles are formed, "which are illustrated by cases, and the law then becomes a science."[9]

These views were not peculiar to the older generation. In his 1838 inaugural lecture at the University of the City of New York, William Kent, one of three professors in the new school, explained the growth of the law as a series of deductions from case to case and from principles to decisions, a process which, having gone on for a long enough period, had created a science "to a casual and superficial observer, vague and undefined, but known to those, who thoroughly studied it, to excel every other system in the rigidly logical connexion and dependence of its parts."[10] That same year Simon Greenleaf opened the academic year at Harvard Law School with a lecture in which he presented law as a Baconian science:

> Adjudged cases, are, to the philosophical student of law what facts are to the student of natural science. They are the elements from which, by the process of induction, his mind ascends to the higher regions of the science, scans its boldest outlines and familiarises itself with its great and leading principles.[11]

The language of principles was not limited to those who made a career of teaching law. Since 1821 the bar of Philadelphia had supported a law academy that provided lectures and the opportunity to participate in moot courts to young men who also pursued their education as clerks or apprentices. The practicing lawyers involved in the academy's activities acknowledged to their charges that the exercises of the law academy would not necessarily fit them to apply their knowledge "to the conduct of a *nisi prius* cause" but rather were designed to help students evaluate their progress "in acquiring the principles of law."[12] Indeed, students were counseled not to spend their time cramming their memories with the details of cases and treatises. Their task was to absorb principles and make them their own so that they could address problems through the exercise of their own powers.[13] However, the use of one's own powers was not a license to speculate at large because law is an exact science: "Its rules are not derived from speculative reasoning, but from the relations of things that exist."[14] Students of the Law Academy of Philadelphia were to be initiated into the workings of empirical science.[15]

Joseph Story died on September 10, 1845, while Christopher Columbus Langdell was still a student at Exeter. Langdell's generation, however, continued to repeat the language of law as a system of principles, especially when discussing legal education. Both in set pieces like commencement addresses and apparently in the classroom, law students of the 1850s and 1860s heard words that would not have sounded out of place coming from Story or other law teachers of his generation.

Before the graduating class of 1856 at the Albany Law School, George Van Santvoord, a practitioner from Troy, proclaimed law one of the "exact sciences" that start from "a few simple axioms and definite elementary truths, [and] proceed, by the process of demonstration, to the establishment of abstract principles, which remain unchanged in every age of the world'' and which are to be drawn out by Baconian induction.[16] On a similar ceremonial occasion in 1869, Henry Nicoll, a leading lawyer in New York City, assured the graduating class of Columbia Law School that they had received a sound education: ''You have been taught to discriminate cases, to apply the analogy derived from one to another; to trace principles from the first appearance of the germ in a rude age, to its full and perfect expansion in later and more refined times.''[17]

Indeed, the explication of principles was a crucial part of legal education as carried on in law schools. At Columbia, Theodore Dwight was adamant in his belief that principles were the guide through the thicket of reported cases, and his emphasis on principle would become synonymous with his style of teaching.[18] At Harvard, Joel Parker, whose teaching Langdell experienced, had as his goal ''to show that the law was a complete and homogeneous organism, with all its parts linked and capable of being understood in the dry light of reason.''[19] At least one of his students carried away just that impression:

> The lecturer's hour was given to the clearest statement of legal principles, the keenest dissection of cases, and oftentimes to the warmest discussions of what he deemed heresies of the law. Judge Parker fought for a principle of law as other men fight for life, or family, or for a nation.[20]

Parker himself could see value only in ''that course of instruction which leads the student to the acquisition of a knowledge of the great principles which lie at the foundation of jurisprudence—to an investigation of the relations of the different principles to each other—and to their practical application.''[21] At the very beginning of Langdell's deanship, fifteen years later, one of his colleagues who had been at the school since 1855, Emory Washburn, declared his own allegiance to the rule of principle. Law teaching must first put principles before the student since ''it is more in accordance with the laws of philosophy to become an adept in the *principles* of a science'' before attempting to use them. The student must be satisfied with learning principles ''which he may have occasion to use and apply as occasion may require.''[22]

The proper classification, systematization, and arrangement of these principles created the science of law.[23] Even though legal scientists induced the principles from decided cases, they did not contribute to the substance of those principles. Unlike scientists of the late twentieth century who acknowledge that their own subjective views enter into their understanding of scientific knowledge, the Baconian scientists of the first part of the nineteenth century believed that their research revealed truth.[24] Indeed, their work was revelation. The principles they adumbrated were real and true because, in the end, they were expressions of the Creator. The result of Baconian science, properly done, was a better understanding of God: ''Since the natural world was a Divine construct, its investigation could only advance the cause of belief.''[25]

Legal science was no different, and not solely because, as John Milton Goodenow put it, "natural justice and right reason are the foundation of all our private rights," which the common law upholds, and "natural justice and reason are the same in all countries and in all ages."[26] Law also depends on circumstances of a particular society. Municipal laws, a writer in the *American Jurist* observed in 1833, vary with the state of man which, in turn, depends on all the circumstances that surround him:

> But even this group of the laws, let it be remembered, are not arbitrary. Those which suit one people or age are not fit for another people or age. Far otherwise. The actually governing institutions of any people must conform to the nature of man, as it is modified by the accidental state of that people.[27]

In his treatise on the conflicts of law, Joseph Story described the ingredients creating that "accidental state" which led to variations in law. Some variations are caused by the physical world: "Climate, and geographical position, and the physical adaptations springing from them, must at all time have had a powerful influence in the organization of each society, and have given a peculiar complexion and character to many of its arrangements."[28] One rule resulting from these factors is that which governs the age of majority. Story noted that most writers prefer that the law of a person's domicile of birth shall control questions of capacity because "each state is presumed to be the best capable of judging from the physical circumstances of climate or otherwise, when the faculties of its citizens are morally or civilly perfect for the purposes of society."[29] Other differences are attributable to "peculiarities of religious opinion or conscientious doubt."[30] Differences also arise from the economic character of nations:

> Nations inhabiting the borders of the ocean, and accustomed to maritime intercourse with other nations, would naturally require institutions and laws, adapted to their pursuits and enterprises, which would be wholly unfit for those, who should be placed in the interior of a continent, and should maintain very different relations with their neighbors, both in peace and war.[31]

The commercial nature of certain nations makes certain rules appropriate for them. Law must then reflect the needs of these commercial societies since "it is obvious, that the law must fashion itself to the wants, and in some sort to the spirit of the age."[32] Other sorts of societies have other sorts of spirits, however, and their law would presumably be different from that of commercial societies.

Story has been described as a creature of the American Enlightenment,[33] and in his description of the sources of differences among nations, between their spirits, he reflects a form of the Enlightenment belief in the existence of stages of human development. This idea, which appears in Anglo-American jurisprudence as early as the lectures of Adam Smith, has in turn been traced to Montesquieu, whose *The Spirit of Laws* was an important influence on American notions of nationhood.[34] At the beginning of his work, Montesquieu explained the relationship between law and society in terms that Story would echo in his work on conflicts:

> [Laws] should be relative to the nature and principle of the actual, or intended government; whether they form this principle, as in the case of political laws, or whether they support it, as may be said of civil institutions.
>
> They should be relative to the climate, whether hot or cold, of each country, to the quality of the soil, to its situation and bigness, to the manner of living of the natives, whether husbandmen, huntsmen, or shepherds; they should have a relation to the degree of liberty which the constitution will bear; to the religion of the inhabitants, to their inclinations, riches, number, commerce, manners, and customs. In fine they have relations amongst themselves, as also with their origin, with the object of the legislator, and with the order of things on which they are established, in all which different lights they ought to be considered.[35]

Montesquieu had great influence on the Revolutionary generation, and it is tempting to see Story's echo of his thought as yet another sign of the jurist's deep personal attachment to the legacy of the Revolution.[36] But the Frenchman's influence was not limited to Story. Montesquieu's lack of a theory of development—his stopping short of a theory of legal evolution—may play some role in the absence of a sense of evolution in antebellum legal thought noted by Perry Miller and generalized to the entire early nineteenth-century intellectual scene by Dorothy Ross.[37] Ross draws an important distinction between a "static" sort of historical consciousness that emphasizes "long-standing and universal" processes as opposed to a view that sees change as "the product of merely local, temporary condition." She traces the strength of the former to its link to the ideology of republicanism and to Protestant religion, both of which helped invest America with millennial significance. Thus it is possible to see antebellum expression of belief in the progress of nations or peoples through various stages of development, culminating in the passage from a feudal to a modern, liberal, and commercial society, as compatible with a belief in universal principles and in a divine hand behind the historical process.[38] Without a clear link between legal change and specific concrete changes in society, the sovereignty of relatively unchanging universals is easier to sustain.

Belief in a law of principles which transcends human attempts to discover and elucidate those principles explains the oft-repeated statement that cases are the mere evidence of law and not law itself. Perhaps the most famous and most controversial statement of this view was made by Story himself in his opinion in *Swift v. Tyson*: "[Cases] are, at most, only evidence of what the laws are; and are not of themselves law."[39] It seems to have been a commonplace, in fact, to admit that judges did fall into error and to warn against reliance on a case rather than on the principles on which the decision should rest.[40] Daniel Mayes told his students just that, asserting, like Story some ten years later, that decisions are only evidence of the law.[41] James Kent's discussion of the authority of judicial reports in the first edition of the *Commentaries* is based on the idea that "even a series of decisions are not always conclusive evidence of what is law."[42] Nathan Dane found it necessary in his great *Abridgment* to often caution his readers "against admitting judicial decisions as authorities, where the remote principle, on which they are made, is not admitted."[43] An anonymous author in the *American Jurist* stated much the same thing in arguing for a limited sort of codification of the common law: it is no wonder that decisions conflict with each other since precedents can be overlooked and judges sometimes simply lack capacity.[44] Yet another interesting statement of this idea comes in a lecture by William Curtis Noyes to the Law Association of New York in 1840 on the subject of "The Legal Rules Governing the Enjoyment and Use of Light." The question of acquiring rights to light through prescription was an important one in the growing towns of early nineteenth-century America.[45] Noyes pleaded for a principled resolution of the issue and told his listeners that they should not hesitate to point out judicial errors like the assertion that the doctrine of ancient lights existed in America. As long as the lawyer's mind "be well stored with legal principles, . . . there is little danger of being lost or long led astray among the mass of cases, with which we are and I fear will continue to be overburdened."[46]

It fell to the anonymous author of the 1833 article in the *American Jurist* to most clearly link the denigration of cases and the science of principles. If law were not a science (that is, "if the subjects of law,—the nature of man, the situation, wants, interests, feelings, and habits of society,—cannot be classified upon general resemblances"), then the judge's opinion "is absolutely law." The judge would then be the maker, not the interpreter, of law, and in him would reside "that despotic power, which some political writers imagine must be committed to some body of magistracy. The only sort of classification that would be possible would be one based on the facts of the cases, "so that the beating of a neighbor, or a wife, or child, or slave, or beast, would fall into the same class, because the main circumstance is *force*." A case would then be decided not on principle but because "some other case, resembling it in facts, had been so decided."[47] Law would not be a science.

The link between the science of principles and the denial of judicial creativity was explicitly made by Story:

> With us the notion that courts of justice ought to be at liberty from time to time to change established doctrines, to suit their own views of convenience or policy, would be treated as a most alarming dogma, subversive of some of the best rights of a free people, and especially of the right to have justice administered upon certain fixed and known principles.[48]

At heart, such language is the reflection of the idea, basic to the Whig tradition that contributed so much to the Revolution, that the common law is the ultimate repository and defense of the liberties of the people. To allow anyone—king or executive; parliament or legislature; appointed or elected judge—to meddle with it could in the end only subvert the entire polity. As Story himself put it: "It is the law of liberty, and the watchful and inflexible guardian of private property and public rights."[49]

The common law, however, was undeniably English. Not all Americans were willing to accept English law as the basis of American freedom.[50] Judges' and lawyers' attempts to draw a distinction between the decision in a particular case and the principles of the common law helped harmonize the undoubted existence of the common law as part of American jurisprudence with the fact of the Revolution and to find an appropriate role for English decisions rendered after that event. Sitting on circuit in 1808, John Marshall drew a distinction between the principles of law and authority, which is clearly made up of cases. English cases decided after the Revolution

> lose that title to authority, which was conferred by the appellate character of the tribunal which made them, and can only be considered as the opinions of men distinguished for their talents and learning, expounding a rule, by which this country, as well as theirs, professes to be governed.[51]

Marshall's contemporaries who sat as state court judges in Virginia held much the same view. Judge St. George Tucker cited a post-Revolutionary English case in an opinion in the Virginia Supreme Court of Appeals not as authority but "as an apposite case decided by able Judges upon the same law which as to this point prevails in this county."[52] In his concurring opinion in the same case, Judge Spencer Roane also looked to modern English cases, again not as authority, but "merely as affording evidence of the opinions of eminent Judges as to the doctrines in question, who have at least as great opportunities to form correct opinions as we have."[53] Chancellor Creed Taylor, however, expressed this attitude most succinctly: "[I]t was the common law we adopted, and not English decisions."[54]

Senator John C. Spencer, rendering an opinion in 1825 as a judge of the New York Court of Errors, then the highest court of the state, described the authority of English cases in much the same way. Referring to the New York Constitution's declaration that the common law continued to be the law of the independent state subject to legislative alteration, he said that, in the absence of such alteration, he felt himself "as much bound to adhere to that law, as if it were engrafted in the Constitution in so many words." He cautioned, however, "that when the judges of England have applied the principle of the common law erroneously," New York judges were free to "correct the application, and restore those principles to their original purity."[55] In the decade before the Civil War the Georgia Supreme Court reiterated this view. In an opinion dealing with a complicated question of will construction, Judge Ebenezer Starnes turned to the common law for direction. He first recognized that Georgia had adopted the common law as of May 14, 1776, but that conclusion did not end the inquiry. It was perfectly permissible to "consult the decisions of Courts in England, previously made." Such decisions, however, "are to be received as evidence of the Law, and not the Law itself."[56] On the level of theory, then, the distinction between cases and the law played a useful role in allowing the common law to function while preserving the reality of American independence.

This science of principles was not merely a matter of theory and abstract argument. Judges had to use the principles induced from cases to answer the concrete questions brought before them. This intellectual task involved deduction, but always as the servant of inductively established principles.[57] Sometimes judges described the application of principles as the formulation of "rules" which actually provided the decision for the case at hand. In 1855, for example, Judge Benjamin Greene of the New York Supreme Court clearly described the intellectual process of judging as applying the principles, maxims, usages, and rules of action of the common law to particular cases. The common law, however, is not the product of "positive legislative enactment." Its constituent rules are those "which observation and experience of the nature of man, the constitution of society and the affairs of life have commended to enlightened reason, as best calculated for the government and security of persons and property."[58] A generation earlier, John C. Spencer, again speaking as a judge of New York's highest court, described the flexibility of the common law as consisting not in the alteration of its principles "but in the application of old principles to new cases, and in the modification of the rules flowing from them, to such cases as they arise, so as to presume the reason of the rules and the spirit of the law."[59]

Such application, however, was seldom certain; at least, it was not as certain as was the truth of the principles of the common law. In short, it was an art rather than a science.[60] The author of the 1833 *American Jurist* article summed up the intellectual construct quite well:

> Although the definitions of moral science are as accurate, its postulates as admissible, its axioms as self-evident as those of mathematics, it does not, therefore, follow that the resolution of every question which arises, will be equally feasible to every intellect to which society, from time to time, entrusts the administration of the laws.[61]

The appellate system exists to correct these errors of application and to ensure that justice is done. The system of civil procedure exists to accomplish the same end. All the complexity of special pleading and of the various writs in the end helps a court focus on the exact questions presented by the case before it and thus helps it apply the principles properly.[62]

Armed with the thorough knowledge of a noble science, Story, Dane, Mayes, the editors of *American Jurist* and their like-minded brethren, including properly trained young lawyers, could both boast of and console themselves with their membership in the intelligentsia of their day. Their attempts to stake out and maintain that position are well-chronicled in Perry Miller's *The Life of the Mind in America*.[63] One of Story's biographers described the sort of lawyer who aspired to intellectual preeminence:

> The learned and successful lawyer was a student not only of existing law but also of legal history and legal philosophy. In the course of his private search for correct precedents and principles, he had examined all the original sources—the *Corpus Juris Civilis*, the writings of the great legal thinkers, and the statutes and reports, both English and American. He was privy to the subtle workings of jurisprudence and to the ideas and practices which had contributed to its downfall and success. He knew where he was going because, in a sense, he knew where he had been.[64]

Not every American lawyer, however, met the standards of the intellectually oriented elite. Indeed, many did not even aspire to membership in that select group. The vast majority studied law only through apprenticeship and were never exposed to systematic instruction in the science of principles. In his study of the image of the legal profession before the Civil War, Maxwell Bloomfield has identified another sort of professional model, one that emphasized technical competence and a workmanlike approach to the business of lawyering. He finds this model of lawyering expounded especially in the new law magazines that appeared in America after 1830. However devoted some American lawyers may have been to the high intellectual road, "a different view prevailed among the rank and file who patronized the law magazines. For them legal practice was a bread-and-butter concern, a daily business in which intellectual refinements found little place."[65]

A Practical Science of Procedure

These "workingmen of the profession" possessed an organizing system of principles to guide their understanding of the common law.[66] This, however, was not the intellectually refined system of Story and his confreres, based on universal, or all but universal, principles from which the legal profession had to choose in creating a truly American law. Rather, it was particular to Anglo-American common law and intimately connected with the actual conduct of business in the courts. These lawyers used a thorough understanding of the system of common law pleading and of the ancient forms of action with which such pleading was linked to organize knowledge of the substantive law.[67]

Whatever untutored simplicity may have marked administration of the common law in the American colonies in the seventeenth and early eighteenth centuries, by the mid-1700s growing numbers of lawyers were applying an increasingly sophisticated system of pleading—one closely approximating that of the mother country—in their daily practice.[68] Herbert Johnson has written that

> civil practice in New York in the last decade of the colonial period was fairly close to the English pattern, both in common law and equity courts. . . . To properly plead a case and bring the matter to issue in any of the above courts required a thorough knowledge of procedure, which then, as now, was drawn from a variety of court rules and statutes.[69]

An impression of the effect of these changes can be gleaned from an examination of William Wyche, *Treatise on the Practice of the Supreme Court of Judicature of the State of New-York in Civil Actions*, published in 1794. For more than 300 pages Wyche expounds the ins and outs of carrying on a civil trial in the young state. While actual practice may not have lived up to Wyche's model, his work indicates that aspiration had reached a high level.

According to Chief Justice Roger B. Taney, after independence the importance of proper pleading grew in the eyes of members of the Maryland bar. In describing his own apprenticeship in the late 1790s, Taney lamented his lack of practical experience with drawing pleadings but admitted it did force him to study more carefully, which was an advantage "for in that day strict and nice technical pleading was the pride of the bar, and I might almost say of the Court." In fact, a victory achieved on a point of pleading "was much more valued than one obtained on the merits of the case."[70]

Addressing the bar of Worcester County, Massachusetts, in 1829, Joseph Willard praised the members of the pre-Revolutionary bar for their technical competence which actually improved upon the English models: "Consider the clear and concise forms of declarations [the opening pleadings in a suit at law], and of special pleadings, in which all the English redundancy is, with singular boldness, cut off."[71] Of course, what Willard saw as admirable terseness might have been regarded by some contemporaries of his heroes as the result of insufficient knowledge.

Writing in 1840 of Massachusetts law from the late seventeenth century to the Revolution, Emory Washburn found that "towards the latter part of the period of which I have been speaking, the forms of pleading and practice became generally as correct as they have ever since been." He also testified to the accomplishments of the pre-Revolutionary generation in the realm of pleading: "Those who are familiar with the forms of legal proceedings in Massachusetts will recal [*sic*] the great number of precedents that are now in use, that were originally drawn by leading members of the bar before the revolution."[72] Modern scholarship agrees with the implications of Washburn's assessment of his professional ancestors. After an exhaustive study of the surviving Massachusetts court records, William Nelson concluded that "except in actions to try title to land, the common law forms of action were in full vigor in the prerevolutionary period."[73] Even at the lowest levels of the colonial legal system proper procedure seems to have been honored, if perhaps not always practiced. For example, the mid-eighteenth-century *Conductor Generalis*, a popular manual for justices of the peace, included explanations of eleven common law actions. This sort of material was not included in the English models on which this and similar colonial manuals were based. John Conley, a recent student of this literature, found this a conscious attempt to preserve common law forms "in the absence of a fully developed legal system and the general availability of law books."[74]

The state of pleading in colonial American courts is probably not susceptible to simple explanation. The expanding commercial life of the colonies both increased legal business and brought practitioners into increasing contact with English ways of doing things.[75] A more general desire to adopt English ways seems to have appeared in many aspects of colonial life after mid-century and certainly had its effect on the legal profession.[76] The desire to belong to a truly learned profession led many lawyers to form bar associations and regular study groups and to attack pettifoggers and other unlearned practitioners.[77] Practicality and fashion may have marched hand in hand, leading a parade of colonial lawyers to examine more closely English precedents of pleading and of substantive law as well.[78]

Whatever the reasons for the increased importance of pleading and the traditional forms of action, the effect of the change on law students was marked. John Adams studied Roman law to impress established lawyers whose patronage he needed and certainly won the aid of at least one, Jeremiah Gridley; but Adams lost his first case because he was unable to draw properly the necessary pleading. Unable to find a precedent, he had done his best with what was at hand. His resolution in the face of this disaster illustrates the amount of effort needed to master the system: "Let me never undertake to draw a Writt, without sufficient Time to examine, and digest in my mind all the Doubts, Queries, Objections that may arise."[79]

Students in the early national period had an easier time than young Adams in resolving doubts, queries, and objections about the proper form of pleadings. First, they had access to printed books of precedents, such as Joseph Story's, which put into print model pleadings previously available only in manuscript notebooks.[80] Projects like Story's separated access to the tools of practice from the patronage of established practitioners. Second, a completely new tool for apprentice practitioners appeared in the form of nisi prius books. David Hoffman's definition of this new type of treatise indicates its usefulness to students:

> It deals principally with the forms of actions,—the pleadings and evidence appropriate to each,—the modes of trial,—the proceedings of practice,—and finally, with every matter relating to the trial of issues of fact and of law, and the removal of points to the superior courts, for final adjudication.

He listed six examples of the genre, which was "wholly unknown to the *bibliotheca legum*, prior to the year 1760."[81] Not only did such works provide models for the practice of law, they also seem to have been important pedagogical tools, providing an organizing scheme for students confronted with the complexities of Sir Edward Coke and the English abridgments which were forced to serve in the absence of extensive American reports.[82] Daniel Webster's account of his discovery of one of the most popular nisi prius volumes can stand for the probable experience of many students:

> I read Coke['s] Littleton through, without understanding a quarter of it. Happening to take up Espinasse's Law of Nisi Prius, I found I could understand it, & arguing that the object of reading was to understand what was written, I laid down the venerable Coke *et alios similes reverendos*, & kept company for a time with Mr. Espinasse, & other [of] the most plain, easy & intelligible writers.[83]

Story, too, was driven to distraction by the

> dry and technical principles, the dark and mysterious elements of the feudal system, the subtle refinements and intricacies of the middle ages of the Common Law, and the repulsive and almost unintelligible forms of processes and pleadings, for the most part wrapped up in black-letter or in dusty folios.[84]

The obscurities of Coke on Littleton made him weep. He found pleading, however, to be refreshing and, once mastered, "it became for several years afterward my favorite pursuit."[85]

The fruit of this enthusiasm was his first published work, *A Selection of Pleadings in Civil Actions*, published in January 1805.[86] Diligent search in English books and in records of the Massachusetts courts, along with examination of manuscript collections of some of the leading lights of the Massachusetts bar, resulted in a book that was more than a collection of forms. Story provided numerous citations to authorities and principles elucidating the use of particular forms, thereby, he hoped, increasing their usefulness to students.[87] Apparently the work fulfilled its purpose, and was still consulted as a reference at least until the time of Story's death forty years later.[88] Perhaps more telling evidence of its influence comes from a remarkably hostile review in a Boston magazine: an anonymous reviewer derided the book as a mere compilation of knowledge, which any student who has read Blackstone should be presumed to possess. The only effect of the book would be pernicious, convincing the uneducated that, having read it, they knew more than they truly did.[89]

The appetite for works such as Story's, however, was undiminished by such slights. Joseph Chitty's famous treatise on pleading and the accompanying collection of model forms went through eight American editions from 1809 to 1840.[90] James Gould's treatise on pleading, taken from his lectures at the law school in Litchfield, Connecticut, was published first in 1832, again in 1836, and then several times after his death in 1838.[91]

The profession's need for clear guides to pleading is not surprising.

What is at least a bit surprising, given the unremitting praise of the science of principles, is the leading role the system of pleading took in organizing legal knowledge. The popularity of nisi prius books, for instance, hints at the importance of the forms of action for practical understanding of the legal system. Legal scientists, not surprisingly, frequently lauded the "science" of pleading and the structure provided by the forms of action as the key to understanding the common law, an example of the highest attainments of logic and even something of aesthetic appeal.

James Wilson told his auditors in Philadelphia that the existence of abuses of the system of pleading which caused delay and frustrated justice did not lessen the glories of the subject. In fact, "the history of a suit at law" is full of "the beauty of strict and accurate arrangement."[92] For Gould, whose law teaching was of more practical effect than Wilson's, pleading was not only a thing of great logical beauty, it also was "the most important *single* title in the law." It was

> necessarily and closely *interwoven*, both in theory and practice, *with those of every other title of the law* . . . because even the most simple of judicial remedies, which the law affords, and without which it would be, practically, a dead letter, cannot be obtained, without the aid of *pleading*.

In the best scientific fashion, Gould claimed to present pleading not as "a compilation of *positive rules*; but as a system of *consistent and rational principles*."[93] David Hoffman told the readers of his course of legal study much the same thing, quoting the praise offered by leaders of the English bar and summing it all up quite well: "[The system of pleading is] a most ingenious, beautiful and wonderful system;—a system entitled, when well comprehended, honestly practiced, and reduced to its real elements, to rank with the sciences most worthy of being studied."[94]

The study of procedure, however, was emphatically the study of the practical application of the law. In spite of all the praise and glorification heaped on the science of principles, a thorough knowledge of its precepts would not get a client's case before the court, as the young John Adams painfully discovered. There were attempts to organize formal legal education around an understanding of procedure. In the 1820s Virginia was the site of a thoroughly practical experiment in training young men for the bar. Chancellor Creed Taylor began a law school in his home at Needham in 1822. His method of instruction centered not on lectures but rather on a moot court in which all students would "practice" and receive intensive training in drafting papers which the instructor would then review. Taylor planned to publish the records of these moots in journal form so that

> should I live to complete four volumes of the journal of the *law-school* . . . there will not be an order in the common course of proceedings, which a court can be called upon to make, but a precedent of it will be found in one of the volumes: and so, as to all the usual pleadings in the courts of law or equity: for there will not be in either a useful precedent omitted.

Taylor advised his students not to ignore the science of the law, the study of "the law of nature and nations: civil law: admiralty law: mercantile law:" as well as criminal law and reports of the American and English courts. He contented himself, however, with the effort "to bring the noble profession of the law to something like a correct system of pleading, and that very meritorious and distinguished class of gentlemen, the clerks of our courts, to a uniform method of entry, and of making out complete records."[95] Producing competent workingmen of the profession was challenge enough for the Virginia chancellor.

Taylor's experiment was short-lived. Most training in procedure probably came through a student's individual enterprise of reading law. Some hint of how the student approached that task is given by the suggestions for legal study with which William Wirt favored his young kinsman Francis Gilmer. Wirt suggested that Gilmer work his way through the headings in Bacon's *Abridgement*, paying attention first to the related pleadings. For example, the first head in Bacon is abatement:

> The course which we propose is, first, to see what Blackstone says on that subject throughout, which you will easily do by the aid of his index. Consult Tucker's Blackstone, with the editor's notes, to see the changes superinduced by our state law. You will thus have gotten the chart of the coast, at least in outline, and know were [*sic*] you are; next Chitty,—in his first volume you will see his learning on the pleas of abatement. In his second, you will see the forms of the plea itself, which you must be able to draw before you lay him down.[96]

Only then should the student read the cases referred to by Bacon, adding to those subsequent English and leading American cases. Pleading came first and provided the structure.

One judicial expression of the importance of pleading in providing usable knowledge of the law is clearly worth noting because of its source. In 1857 Justice Robert C. Grier of the United States Supreme Court defended the traditional system of pleading. The justice found utterly irresponsible the attempt to abolish "this system, matured by the wisdom of the ages, founded on principles of truth and sound reason." Grier wrote: "The distinction between the different forms of actions for different wrongs, requiring different remedies, lies in the nature of things; it is absolutely inseparable from the correct administration of justice in common-law courts."[97] Grier's outcry was provoked by the growing movement to abolish common law pleading and the accompanying forms of action in favor of codes of pleading, many modeled on the first code, that of New York, adopted in 1848. The justice's assertion that the forms of action and the pleadings connected with them are somehow rooted in the nature of things and beyond legislative alteration is striking evidence of the extent to which common law pleading penetrated antebellum legal thinking and organized understanding of substantive law.[98]

If pleading was so important, then, to both understanding the law and actually earning a living through practice, what was its relationship to the science of ordered principles that dominated discussions of legal science and legal education? The workingmen of the profession were not necessarily the sorts of lawyers scientific legal educators hoped to train. The nisi prius book and the sort of instruction Wirt suggested to his nephew were emphatically out of place in antebellum law schools. Understanding law through the writ system in some degree contradicted the tenets of the science of principles. In fact, formal academic legal instruction found its worth in separating scientific lawyers from lawyers who were merely adept at manipulating the procedural system.

Education in Legal Science

The division between the science of principles and the practicalities of the procedural system had important implications for legal education. Legal science was important for maintaining the self-image of the profession, and law schools were critical for the perpetuation of the scientific enterprise.[99] Mastery of legal science set lawyers apart from mere pettifoggers, and the need to distinguish accomplished members of the profession from charlatans is a long-standing theme in the history of the profession in America. As far back as 1762 Thomas Hutchinson, newly appointed chief justice of Massachusetts, decided that only "barristers" could argue before the province's highest court and had lawyers who attained that grade attired in the traditional wigs and gowns of the English profession.[100] Hutchinson was not a lawyer, and his formalization of a graded profession may have been an attempt to "placate trained lawyers by aiding their efforts to create a stratified profession."[101] Whatever Hutchinson's skills as a politician, in this instance he was astute. The desire to distinguish trained advocates who were worthy to appear before the highest courts from mere attorneys, or, more disparagingly, pettifoggers, whose mechanical knowledge of forms and pleading fitted them, at most, for appearance before lay justices of the peace, burned brightly in the hearts of trained lawyers throughout the Revolutionary and antebellum periods. John Adams carried on a personal crusade against the lowly tribe.[102] Young Joseph Story was roundly criticized for producing his book of pleading forms because, at least in the view of one anonymous reviewer, it would only enable "some men to get a living in the character of lawyers, whose knowledge and whose moral delicacy are far removed from being subjects of commendation."[103] The disgust that trained lawyers felt at the presumptions of these troublemakers was well summed up by Aaron Barlow Olmstead, a young graduate of Yale's law school who went on to clerk in an office in Saratoga Springs. In January 1842 he confided to his diary his definition of a pettifogger:

> Pettyfoggers are those who without any preparatory study enter our lower courts with a few snatches of what they call *law* picked up at the

> Corners of Streets. These they rant & rave—quibble upon words—stammer & quarrel & raise often not a petty fog, but a great one—to the total eclipse of Common Sense & the discomfiture of justice.[104]

Olmstead, in contrast, was a real lawyer since at Yale he had studied principles, the "reason of the law."[105]

Young Olmstead was set apart from pseudolawyers by more than his preparatory studies. Just as Story's anonymous reviewer was certain that the only audience for his book lacked the moral fiber needed for real accomplishment in the legal profession, Olmstead was certain that pettifoggers lacked decency as well as knowledge:

> These men are mostly well schooled in vice before they enter the *Legal Profession*—men who have tried other means of cheating & who, being met on every side by the Law—have at last become familiar with its face—got tired of cursing it—Come to a Compromise with the Devil & turned Lawyers.[106]

The double challenge of ignorance and vice did not go unanswered. Even in the late colonial period lawyers had attempted to control admission to their ranks in an effort, as they saw it, to preserve both educational and moral standards.[107] These attempts often included the preservation of varying grades within the profession on the English model. Gradation and the accompanying long period of preparation usually needed to attain the highest status began to wither in the increasingly democratic ethos of Jacksonian America. One by one many states adopted legislation abolishing all educational requirements for admission to the bar and effectively destroyed lawyers' attempts at formal self-regulation.[108] For example, New York's Constitution of 1846, which so thoroughly reformed the organization of the courts and the procedure governing actions in them, also provided that "any male citizen of the age of twenty-one years, of good moral character, and who possesses the requisite qualifications of learning and ability, shall be entitled to admission to practice in all the courts of this State."[109] Section 75 of the Judiciary Act of 1847, which governed admission under this provision, provided for public examination of applicants and for the adoption of rules by the New York Supreme Court prescribing "what shall be sufficient proof of good moral character" but also flatly stated that "no term of clerkship or period of study shall be required."[110]

Lowering the formal barriers did not end all educational standards for admission to the bar. Informal pressure, "the simple device of professional ostracism," and a certain amount of cooperation from the judiciary all helped sustain the ideal of an educated bar.[111] In his detailed study of the Massachusetts legal profession in this period, Gerard Gawalt went further. He argued that the legislation of 1836, which provided for automatic admission of those who had studied for three years in either a school or an office, and admission by judicial examination for those without the educational credentials and also abolished the distinction between attorney and counsellor, was emphatically not a defeat for the profession.

While the role of bar associations in the admission process was ended, control "had only been transferred to other institutions that were controlled or greatly influenced by lawyers." Most of the judges charged with examining those without educational qualifications were professional lawyers, "[a]nd lawyers controlled the law school at Harvard, which remained the chief alternative to law office apprenticeship in the state."[112] In fact, even before the formal abolition of corporate control over admission, "'enlightened' and scientifically minded lawyers had already transferred their hopes for maintaining professional excellence to the university law school." Finally, the social position of Massachusetts lawyers was secure. "By the early nineteenth century," Gawalt concludes, "lawyers had become part of an exclusive, prosperous, and expanding professional elite, part of the upper-middle class." As the formal barriers diminished, "entrance into the profession was increasingly restricted by the invisible barriers of family connection, the cost of education, and the expenses of beginning a professional practice."[113] Other states witnessed similar changes, especially with regard to the role of legal education: "The best place for legal training had been judged by the profession's leaders to be a university-connected law school designed in the tradition of Blackstone to produce attorneys who were also gentlemen of the law and men of public affairs."[114]

Of course, graduates of antebellum law schools did not immediately enter practice. They spent some time as clerks to established members of the bar. Their apprenticeship involved more than learning practical skills. Before the Civil War, the dominant tone of commentary on the task faced by beginning practitioners emphasized the difficulty of acquiring clients and the monopolistic nature of the established bar. Even in the eighteenth century one can discern the familiar theme. The young John Adams was counseled by Jeremiah Gridley, the "dean of the Massachusetts bar," to study law rather than expect to make a fine living from it, at least for the first few years.[115] Adams found Gridley's advice all too accurate as he struggled to impress upon his neighbors in Braintree his superiority to the local pettifoggers. Similar difficulties for young lawyers existed in Baltimore just before and after the War of 1812, when that city was one of the leading commercial, and thus legal, centers of the United States.[116] In 1808 Henry Marie Brackenridge arrived in the city in search of a legal career. He had been counseled by his father, one of the most distinguished lawyers of the period, that law was indeed "the road to honor and preferment in this country," but "in a city you cannot expect to succeed without the utmost diligence and application to business."[117] That was good advice for Baltimore, where the profession was dominated by a few, and two-thirds of the bar could not make a living from practice. After 1815 John Neal found Baltimore to be unchanged.[118] In New York City seven or eight lawyers dominated the bar and were determined to maintain their place. "They were jealous of their magic circle"; according to the recollections of one observer, they "allowed no rising man, if possible, to enter it, and frowned down him who was bold enough to try."[119]

The situation may have been better outside the commercial centers as the practice of circuit riding brought bench and bar as a unit to outlying communities. In the 1760s circuit riding was financially profitable for John Adams, although he sometimes found himself hurrying from one town to another in order to beat the competition. Some business was acquired at the courthouse door.[120] In his study of the circuit system in western Tennessee in the early nineteenth century, Daniel Calhoun found that "it worked to preserve or find opportunities for those of lesser rank, and in a way that dissipated the sharpness of competition between practitioners."[121]

The effect did not last long. The circuit system was dying in western Tennessee as early as the 1820s, by which time a small group of practitioners had come to dominate much of each county's legal business.[122] From the 1830s through the 1850s the bars of Sumner, Davidson, and Gallatin counties came to resemble the bar of Baltimore before which the ambitious Henry Brackenridge and John Neal despaired. The rigid nature of the resulting structure is exemplified by David Hoffman's "Fifty Resolutions in Regard to Professional Deportment" of 1836.[123] Resolutions 17 and 38 portray a bar in which the "senior brethren" take precedence of a powerful sort. The ethical lawyer resolves that, upon reaching such a position, he will not make life miserable for his juniors, remembering "the days of my youth, when I too was feeble in the law, and without standing." He will not blight a young man's aspirations by "inconsiderate, or rude and arrogant deportment." It was clearly taken for granted that established members of the bar successfully made life as difficult as possible for the neophyte.

Starting a practice seems to have required the good will of established lawyers, and one of the ways to acquire it was to spend time as their clerk. Aaron Olmstead did just that after graduating from Yale. Joseph Hodges Choate spent a year with a Boston firm after completing Harvard's two-year course, three years of study being generally required for admission to the Massachusetts bar.[124] After admission in Massachusetts, Choate went to New York City armed with a letter of introduction to William Evarts written by his kinsman Rufus Choate. Joseph Choate began by copying documents and attending calendar calls in the courts, learning document preparation along with the workings and personalities of the court system.[125] While the prevailing ideology of professionalism would not have admitted such office work as sufficient preparation for the bar, it was a necessary adjunct to formal legal education and usually the only training a prospective lawyer received. By far the overwhelming majority of American lawyers received whatever training they had prior to admission to practice outside the classroom.[126] This was due to the importance of the system of procedure and the mechanics of drawing writs and other papers to the functioning of the legal system and the difficulty of acquiring business. It might be said, then, that the most important training for practicing law happened outside school. What then did antebellum law schools teach? They provided some instruction in legal principles through lectures and recitations to a student body, which, on the whole, seems to have been lackadaisical at best. The entire enterprise sometimes seems to have been something of a half-hearted charade. Such a characterization may seem far too harsh, until it is put beside student recollections.

The aims and hopes of antebellum legal educators were far from foolish, however. They tried to inculcate the science of law as best they could using the standard educational techniques of their day. Contrary to what is often assumed about the world of legal education before Langdell, those techniques did involve at least some form of colloquy between student and teacher.

A typical example of pedagogical aspiration can be found in Joel Parker's description of his own preparations for his debut at the podium in the lecture room in Dane Hall in 1848. He was expected to lecture, yet the textbook formed the basis of the lecture and the students were supposed to have read the relevant portion before entering the lecture room. He decided that by asking questions of the students he could escape the twin pitfalls of merely repeating what the textbook had to say or of engaging in "a 'departure,' which lawyers well know is, in pleading, obnoxious to a special demurrer." The experiment worked well, and "we had for some time a lively interchange of interrogatories." Parker also employed hypothetical cases in his teaching, since "in this way the student made a practical application of what he had read and heard."[127]

Parker's method of teaching was not without precedent. William Wetmore Story described his father's teaching in terms that resemble Parker's account of his own work. Like Parker, the justice began with general remarks on the subject and then questioned his students in the course of making "a full and free commentary" on the "general principles" laid down in the textbook. Like Parker, Story used hypothetical cases to illustrate a general principle. Having established the main point, he would shape its circumstances to expose the various modifications and exceptions to which it was subject. The question constantly changed "like the pattern in the kaleidoscope." To an Irish correspondent Story described "our system of instruction" in terms that clearly indicate the importance of a classroom dialogue much like the joint effort of student and teacher that Langdell brought to his classroom:

> Our system of instruction is not founded upon written lectures, (which, I am persuaded, is a very inadequate mode,) but upon oral lectures connected with the daily studies of the students in the various works which they study, and in the lecture-room where they are all assembled in classes, and where they undergo a daily examination; and every lecture grows out of the very pages of the volume which they are then reading. In this way difficulties are cleared away, additional illustrations suggested,

> new questions propounded, and doubts raised, and occasionally criticized, so that the instructor and pupil move along pari passu, and the pupil is invited to state his doubts, and learns how to master his studies.[128]

A similar description of the methods at Harvard appeared in the *American Jurist* shortly after Greenleaf's appointment to the faculty. In contrast to the public lectures of English universities, instruction at Harvard consisted of "private lectures" which involved

> examinations of the students, . . . calculated to test the accuracy of their knowledge of the books read, accompanied by oral explanations and illustrations, which shall throw light upon the text, and assist in its application to practical cases, besides enlisting the attention of the student.[129]

It seems clear that the method of teaching which preceded Langdell at Harvard did indeed involve some form of dialogue between teacher and student.

The contrast Story drew between this method and that of "written lectures" indicates that the teaching method he and his successors used was an innovation on the methods followed at the first true American law school, that founded at Litchfield, Connecticut, by Tapping Reeve. Reeve and James Gould, who later joined and then succeeded him, lectured from written notes that were meant to be copied verbatim. Citations to leading cases were also provided, but these apparently were meant to be read outside the classroom. While Reeve would occasionally deviate from his text to add "off-hand remarks of a colloquial nature, explanations and illustrations," Gould did not indulge in even that degree of spontaneity, and neither man seems to have interrogated his students.[130] So polished were the lectures that they appeared in print without many changes: "A comparison of the manuscript [of Gould's treatise on pleading] with the printed work shows that the latter must have been printed almost verbatim from the lectures."[131]

Other antebellum discussions of the techniques of legal education also distinguished written lectures, or the reading of a polished text, from oral lectures. In his 1835 plan for the law school of New York University, Benjamin F. Butler confidently asserted the superiority of the oral over the written lecture. The latter is really only a treatise or dissertation, and "if treatises or dissertations are to be read, the pupil had better do it for himself, and under such circumstances as to enable him to peruse and digest them at his leisure." The oral lecture, being more informal and not "a strictly scientific examination" of the subject, is "more attractive and inciting" and allows the lecturer to amplify and to reemphasize aspects of the reading. The readings in "the most approved elementary books, with references to the Statute Law . . . and to one or two more leading authorities from the Reports" are to be the basis of instruction. To ensure that students have read the assigned material and thus are ready to profit from the lecture, Butler suggested the use of "personal examinations," the professor putting one question to each student during the course of the lecture. Butler seemed to have intended that these questions be more than a recitation of the assigned reading. At least he hoped that "the use of occasional interrogatories" would animate and excite the lecture and compel students to prepare carefully. To give an answer, the students would have to think about what they have read and "will frequently be obliged to reflect, to reason, and to judge."[132]

Similar hopes motivated the plan for a law school at Hamilton College put forward almost simultaneously with Butler's effort by his friend John C. Spencer. Indeed, the two men had discussed the entire subject and found themselves in general agreement.[133] Spencer made it clear that the law school's method of instruction would be the same as that used in colleges: "Textbooks will be prescribed, which the pupils will study and recite in the same manner as, for instance, treatises on metaphysics are recited in colleges."[134] After each student has recited, the instructor will give an oral lecture, explaining what the recitation has revealed the students do not well understand, reconciling contradictory views and authorities when possible and stating his opinion as to the correct view when it is not, adding references to the latest cases and statutes, and illustrating "the whole by such analogies in the law, and by such references to moral and natural philosophy, and to metaphysics, as the occasion may permit."[135]

The ideal model of the antebellum law school, therefore, provided for close interaction between instructor and students. Even at Harvard under Story, however, reality seems to have fallen short of the goal. On September 1, 1843, Rutherford Hayes recorded in his diary his impressions of his law teachers. Greenleaf he found "very searching and logical in examination. It is impossible for one who has not faithfully studied the text to escape exposing his ignorance." Story, "on the other hand, is very general in his questions, so that persons well skilled in nods, affirmative and negative shakings of the head, need never more than glance at the text to be able to answer his interrogatories." The judge was also "fond of digressions to introduce amusing anecdotes, high-wrought eulogies of the sages of the law, and fragments of his own experience."[136] As Hayes's observations indicate, realization of the ideal depended completely on the skill and effort of the professor, and there is evidence that at Harvard, at least, the ideal of colloquy between student and teacher and the resulting rigorous investigation of the law became just that: a counsel of perfection seldom attained in practice. Parker, for instance, found that his method of teaching by discussion worked well for only a short period:

> There came, in time, a new difficulty respecting questions of any sort,—and that was in obtaining answers to them without consuming too much of the time assigned to the lecture,—arising mainly from a fear, on the part of the student, that the answer might be wrong,—and an erroneous answer, made in the face of the whole School, was a subject of dread.[137]

The teacher was not himself without fault. His students recalled his classroom manner as uninspiring. "Parker," a member of the class of 1856 recalled, "was as dry and uninteresting as a mummy." Forty-seven years later John D. Long condemned Parker's lectures for being "as inspiring as a Puritan sermon on the metaphysics of the freedom of the will."[138] Of course, Professor Parker had perhaps been led to believe that he really did not have to make much of an effort to be a successful law professor. "I would observe," President Edward Everett of Harvard wrote then Chief Justice Parker in an attempt to persuade him to come to Cambridge, "that the duties of the office are perhaps less onerous than you suppose," involving as they did "but an oral commentary upon the text book; requiring, I suppose, no more preparation, than an ordinary charge to the Jury in cases where no nice point of law is to be discussed."[139]

Whatever Parker finally came to believe about the requirements of his new job, there is ample indication that the school he, Parsons, and Washburn ran had its difficulties.[140] In his memoir of "The Harvard Law School in 1857," Everett P. Wheeler, a leading member of the New York bar, portrayed a rather undemanding institution. There were no recitations, and while questions were sometimes asked during lectures, no specific topics were assigned and the professors made "no attempt to ascertain how thoroughly a student had studied the textbooks which were supposed to be used outside the lectures." All that was needed to obtain the degree was reasonably regular attendance at the lectures and the payment of fees.[141] Joseph Choate entered Harvard Law School in 1852 and found conditions much the same. "The standard at the school was very low at that time," he wrote in his autobiography, and "there were absolutely no examinations to get in, or to proceed, or to get out."[142]

Choate's memory seems to have been accurate. As a student he recorded moot court exercises in a notebook. Students regularly argued motions for new trials based on records created by the professors. For each exercise Choate recorded facts, pleadings, and points of law with supporting references. It is not clear whether the pleadings and points were supplied by the instructors or by the students. After argument, the professor-judge gave a lecture on the legal points implicated in the case in the form of an opinion. During the course of the year (1853–1854) Choate's notes become less and less detailed, perhaps a sign of boredom. On October 13, 1853, he simply wrote "at this point *Parsons* became *Pathetic*!" and ceased notetaking. The later entries in his notebook are almost bereft of substantive notes.[143]

Wheeler and Choate were not alone in remembering the laxness of their legal education. The reminiscences collected by Charles Warren testify to professorial attempts at classroom interrogation in Langdell's student days and give an even more vivid picture of students' ability to avoid even this less than demanding form of rigor. Wrote Alexander Wilson:

> In the lecture room in Dane Hall there were three tiers of seats. Students who sat in the third block were never questioned by the professors during the lectures, but those in the other seats were often called upon to answer questions upon the subject matter of the lecture.

Gregory Noble added that this raised section "where the loafers congregated" was called "Oregon."[144] Even the official history of the school frankly notes the lack of discipline: "Neither attendance nor preparation was required for recitations or lectures, and as a considerable part of the class sat in the seats of the unprepared, the exercise furnished no test of the work done by a student."[145]

Yet another alumnus who was a contemporary of Langdell remembered that the school was untouched by the spirit of legal reform current at the time: "The atmosphere was still charged with the complacent optimism of Sir William Blackstone and the other 'venerable sages of the law.'" All in all, the contrast between the school Langdell attended and the one he created was summed up by another of his contemporaries, who remembered the school of Parker, Parsons, and Washburn as "dull and inert," a place where students wished either to shine or to learn, "but there was nothing very earnest about it."[146]

In addition to the failings of individual teachers and students, there may have been structural reasons for the failings of antebellum law schools. The law school in antebellum America was clearly an adjunct of office training. It supplied what offices could not, it is true, but what offices supplied was absolutely essential to the practice of law. As Butler candidly observed, there was little place in America for legal specialization. Lawyers found themselves doing every sort of legal work and therefore had to know something of conveyancing and of the practice of all of the courts. Such knowledge, Butler admitted, "is only to be acquired, by spending the whole, or nearly the whole, term of study, in the office of an extensive and accurate practitioner."[147] Butler hoped to accommodate his planned school to this reality by accepting the fact that most students would be simultaneously clerking and scheduling lectures accordingly.[148] He went further, however, much further. Although he believed in the inductive legal science of principles, Butler also knew what a lawyer needed to know in order to make a living. He thus proposed that entering students begin not with the foundation of properly systematized legal science—the law of nations and constitutional law, only then turning to municipal law and the rights of persons—but, rather, with the most mundane aspect of legal knowledge: practice. Training students in practice, at least as far as it could be done from books, would make them better clerks and more able to profit from their work in the law office. This was heresy; at least, it must have seemed heresy to dismiss "the first and second volumes of Blackstone, and the whole of Kent's Commentaries" as inappropriate to beginning legal study "because they have little or no connection with the practical business of the office."[149] In fact, the one syllabus of lectures prepared for the school indicates that the matters treated in Blackstone and Kent—the rights of persons, especially as regards status, the rights of property and the law of real property—were to be taken up in the second and third years of study.[150]

Butler's inversion of the usual order of the scientific study of law was not arbitrary or whimsical, but it may have contributed to the failure of the school. Ronald Brown's brief study of the attempt to found a law school at New York University with which Butler was so intimately involved canvasses several reasons for its failure. The panic of 1837 often interfered with collecting all the pledges made to support the new school, and the resulting difficulties disrupted the university's administration.[151] Butler's politics—he was an active supporter of Jackson and Van Buren, both of whom he served as attorney general—made him anathema to at least some of the New Yorkers whose sons could have been expected to patronize the school.[152] The professors themselves—Butler; William Kent, son of the chancellor; and David Graham, Jr.—were not prepared or expected to devote full time to the teaching of law. The understandable pressures of faithfully attending to their clients' business impeded that "persistence of purpose" which Brown notes was a prerequisite for the success of an antebellum law school.[153]

All these reasons, however, seem to be subordinate to the antebellum law school's "weak foundations in legal culture."[154] Brown notes that in 1839 William Kent wrote to Story that he had no hope of reviving the New York school because of its inability to compete with Story's own institution. "The Cambridge Law School," he wrote, "sold vastly better Law at the same price." The New York school's emphasis on New York law, in other words, could not compete with "Harvard's projection of a national jurisprudence." In addition, Butler's emphasis on teaching practice put his school in direct competition with the education gained in law offices where face-to-face encounters between established practitioners and neophytes allowed the former to control access to the profession. Academic training was not yet seen as sufficient preparation for lawyering.[155]

If this view of antebellum legal education is accurate, why did Harvard under Story prosper so mightily? In part, Harvard succeeded because it served the dominant interest in New England society by fostering "a unified body of national commercial law to facilitate the growth of the national economy."[156] More broadly, the school helped promote New England culture and was in fact the principal weapon in the struggles of Massachusetts conservatives like Story, Nathan Dane, and Josiah Quincy to preserve a deferential social order against the rise of Jacksonian democracy.[157] The legal science that was Harvard's, and especially Story's, stock in trade would bring order not only to the increasing confusion of case law but also to the entire polity.[158]

By insisting that the "[s]trict philosophical method must therefore give way to the necessities of the case," Butler robbed his school of the principal excuse for its existence.[159] Legal science was not totally a matter of professional polish and high culture separate from the courtroom. Story's scientific commercial law provided a way of answering important practical questions.[160] Far more practical, however, was that science of procedure which the school did not teach—that knowledge of the writ system and the intricacies of common law pleading without which the most scientifically learned lawyer could not win the simplest case. On the whole, the antebellum law school was an institution devoted to the exposition and inculcation of legal philosophical truths through a system of rote learning that emphasized the passive assimilation of authoritative statements of the law. Story's occasional frolics and diversions did not detract from the educational purpose of the school. Through it all, students basked in the benign influence of Story's superior learning and morality; by his example he would help make his students proper members of the profession. It should not be surprising that a far from indifferent student, Charles Sumner, would find Story's school less than demanding:

> Come, [he wrote a friend] and we will have an evening's chat. You will not disturb me; for, though I try to seize every moment of time, yet our law-studies are so indefinite that no number of hours cut out will be missed. We recite but three times a week; and one forenoon will master our lesson, though days can be given to it with profit.[161]

Indeed, there was nothing very earnest about it.

4

Case Method and Legal Science

The legal science of the antebellum period and the antebellum law school were closely related. A science of ordered principles based ultimately on the truths of revelation was inculcated in institutions designed as much to strengthen their students' resolve to be proper lawyers as to teach them what they would need to know as practitioners. The law school Langdell helped create was also a reflection of his idea of legal science. What that idea was has been a source of scholarly debate for some time. Recent work has begun to recognize the connections between Langdell's vision of legal science and that of his antebellum forebears.[1] The dean's talk of principles to be extracted from cases is the old language of Baconian science applied to a new subject matter. The legal science of the antebellum law school subordinated cases to great principles of law based on universal truth. Cases were the material from which the principles to be taught could be induced; they were not the substance of teaching. Langdell's science and his teaching looked to the cases themselves as the law.

A Science of Narrow Rules

What Langdell meant by legal science is easier to paraphrase than understand. Perhaps moved by the spirit that prevented him from aiding the campaign for his appointment to the Dane Professorship, Langdell seldom spoke to support or even to explain the theory of his teaching. The preface to *A Selection of Cases on the Law of Contracts* and his brief speech before the Harvard Law School Association in 1886 embody the sum total of Langdell's direct statements of his ideas outside his annual reports as dean. In the preface Langdell recounted his conviction that making "a series of cases, carefully selected from the books of reports, the subject alike of study and instruction" provided the best answer to the question of how to teach. Another question was implicit in this statement: Which cases were to be selected? The answer was clear. Because "law, considered as a science, consists of certain principles or doctrines," one need only select the cases that illustrate the growth of these doctrines or principles. Fortunately, only a small number of cases are necessary: "The vast majority are useless, and worse than useless, for any purpose of systematic study." Indeed, a proper system of classification in which each doctrine would "be found in its proper place, and nowhere else," would show that there are really very few fundamental doctrines. A collection of the appropriate cases would be of value to all who wish to study contracts "systematically and in the original sources."[2]

The speech before the alumni in 1886 emphasized both law's status as a science, and thus its worth as a subject of university teaching, and the importance of printed books as the ultimate repositories of all law. Since books are so important, Langdell said, the university is justified in teaching law and in supplanting every other method of legal instruction—especially the office. The library then is seen as "the proper workshop of professors and students alike; that it is to us all that the laboratories of the university are to the chemists and physicists, all that the museum of natural history is to the zoologists, all that the botanical garden is to the botanists."[3] It is, in other words, the repository of the original sources. Langdell was still the Baconian scientist, examining the cases, discriminating between the well and the poorly reasoned, extracting principles from them through inductive reasoning, and then ordering the principles to aid understanding. References to the natural sciences in the 1886 speech did not represent an experimental view of legal science. Rather, they acknowledged that the university is the place to do all science, that law is at least as much a part of the life of the mind as it is of the life of the courtroom.

In fact, according to Langdell, the life of the courtroom is not usually conducive to scientific understanding. Busy with the details of practice, the ordinary lawyer cannot approach the subject scientifically because there is no easy route to order. Langdell made this view clear in a remarkable passage of his annual report for 1876–1877 in which he attacked the use of the bar examination, set by state officials, as the sole criterion for admission to practice:

> The difficulty of examining in a given subject is in proportion to the difficulty of teaching it; and there can be no doubt that English and American law is one of the most difficult subjects to teach. The opinion has, indeed, been prevalent that it is incapable of being taught as a science; and, though the correctness of this opinion will not be admitted by those who represent this School, it may be supported by plausible arguments. Law has not the demonstrative certainty of mathematics; nor does one's knowledge of it admit of many simple and easy tests, as in case of a dead or foreign language; nor does it acknowledge truth as its ultimate test and standard, like natural science; nor is our law embodied in a written text, which is to be studied and expounded, as is the case with the Roman law and with some foreign systems. Finally, our law has not any long-established and generally recognized traditions which will indicate to the examiner what his examination ought to be, and to the student what it will be; and the whole field of law is so extensive, and so much of it is unfit for the purposes of systematic study and instruction, that one who attempts to cultivate the whole of it indiscriminately will not cultivate

> any of it to much purpose. Hence, an examiner who examines without reference to any particular course of study or instruction (and such is the character of nearly all examinations for admission to the profession) can have no other standard than the state of his own knowledge; and the success of the persons examined may, therefore, depend less upon what they know than upon what the examiner knows.[4]

At first glance, the Langdell of this passage hardly seems to be the same man as the father of the case method. It has been argued that here "Langdell seeks to downplay the presumed identity between law and science sufficiently that no argument can be advanced in behalf of passing 'scientific' examinations as the exclusive prerequisite to admission to the legal profession."[5] Yet he did have complete faith in the validity of the examinations administered by the faculty of Harvard Law School, and, in the portion of his report just previous to the quoted passage, he elaborated at length on the time, care, and thought the faculty lavish on examinations.[6] These examinations are useful, he said, because they are part of an "effective system of legal education" to which three conditions are "indispensable":

> [F]irst, that a scientific course of study be prescribed; secondly, that systematic instruction be given upon the prescribed course of study; and, thirdly, that the student's diligence and success be tested by examinations based strictly upon the course of study and instruction.[7]

Thus, examinations were meaningful only when they examined something meaningful. Most lawyers, including those who set bar examinations, had no systematic knowledge of the law. The Langdell who found much of the law unfit for systematic study is the very same man who found "the vast majority" of cases "useless, and worse than useless, for any purpose of systematic study."[8]

The importance of the long passage on examinations lies not in any rejection of academic legal science but in the rejection of some of the traditional bases of legal science. First, law is not like mathematics, a science of axioms easily applied by deduction. The mathematical model was widely alluded to in antebellum legal thought as the means for making law clear. It was often connected to admiration for the deductive method of Roman law studies.[9] Neither aspect of this point of view was acceptable to Langdell; the common law lacked both authoritative texts and easily provable answers. Not surprisingly, then, Langdell did not see legal science consisting of propositions that can be easily tested like the grammatical rules of the classical languages. Finally, and most important, it was impossible to test legal propositions against some external standard of truth, a role that nature performs for the natural sciences.

What content, then, can be found in the statement that law is a science? The importance of the case method of teaching to the definition of the new model law school provides at least a partial answer. Only full-time scientists can properly pursue legal science. Their task is to find principles in the original sources of the law, which are the cases. Understanding the opinions of the courts will reveal the true basis of the law. That basis is not grand principles related to the ultimate ordering of society, but the narrow, technical principles that make up the real work of the lawyer, which courts use to decide real cases. The importance of the decided case is made startlingly clear by Langdell's defense of one of the principles of contract law he extracted from the cases.

In 1894 Samuel Williston published in the *Harvard Law Review*, volume 8, an article entitled "Successive Promises of the Same Performance" in which he attacked a proposition advanced by Langdell in his discussion of bilateral contracts and the status of mutual promises as consideration for one another. In 1901 Langdell published his reply. The subject of the disagreement is not as important as the nature of Langdell's defense. He maintained that he could not understand Williston's "line of reasoning" and thus was reduced to simply asserting the contrary position. Therefore the only way to show the truth of his position was "to show how the proposition . . . is to be established in a court of justice, whenever the decision of a legal controversy shall involve the question of its truth." He then showed how the courts would decide hypothetical cases involving the question which, he noted, "can be put in issue, tried, and decided in the same manner, and with as much facility, as any other question which will be decisive of the cause." Using principles of contract law and pleading, he then showed that the question, if properly isolated for decision, would be decided in accord with his views.[10]

It is a remarkable demonstration, full equally of self-confidence and circularity. What is important for the idea of legal science, however, is the attempt to test the proposition in question through the experiment of putting it to a court. Acquaintance with the contents of those printed books of reports will provide the raw material both for the induction of principles and for the experimental testing of their deductive application to questions arising in practice.

In Langdell's thought the two realms of legal science of the antebellum era merged, but they are unequally represented in the resulting amalgam. The scientific aspirations persisted, though without the assertion that there are those great universal principles, which, once understood, will reveal to the scientist the nature of the world and, indeed, the very mind of its Creator. Rather they are principles of a narrower sort, rules of substantive law whose formulation and organization will create a substitute for the structure once given by the forms of action, the absence of which Langdell experienced as a practitioner of New York law under the reforms of the Field Code of Civil Procedure. The rules he struggled to establish are oriented to the practice of the profession as a technical undertaking.

A Technical Science of Contracts and Equity

The technical nature of Langdell's science of principles can be illustrated by a comparison of his views of contract law and equity—the two fields on which he staked his academic career—with those of earlier treatise writers.

Recent writing on American legal history commonly asserts that Langdell's work on contracts inaugurated a body of thought that would become the "classic" or "orthodox" view of law in America in the last third of the nineteenth century.[11] Whatever the merit of that assertion, it is clear that Langdell's *Summary of the Law of Contracts* stood for an important change in treatise literature of contract law.[12] One of the first American treatises on the subject, William Wetmore Story's *A Treatise on the Law of Contracts Not under Seal* published in 1844, not only dealt with topics which would eventually be seen as separate from contracts but moreover was concerned less with contract law than with the law of many different kinds of contracts.[13] For Story (the son of Justice Joseph Story and eventually a sculptor),

> there were as many types of contracts as there were classes of people to enter into them: contracts of factors, brokers, auctioneers, executors and administrators, trustees, seamen, corporations, guardian and ward, masters of ships, guarantors, landlord and tenant—and on and on in a never-ending list.[14]

The next significant American treatise was written by Theophilus Parsons, to which a youthful Langdell contributed as Parsons research assistant. Like Story, Parsons wrote much more about particular types of contracts than about what was common to them. His discussion of the two most important common elements, consideration and assent, occupied only fifty-seven pages. Exposition of the law regarding parties to contracts filled six times the space, dealing in turn with agents, factors, servants, attorneys, trustees, executors, guardians, corporations, partnerships, novation, assignment, and indorsement (all ways of substituting parties) and with infants, women, bankrupts, those of weak mind, aliens, slaves, and outlaws (those whose capacity to contract is limited). An even greater number of pages was devoted to the subject matter of various contracts, with separate discussions of the purchase and sale and hire of real estate, sale of personal property, warranty, guaranty, hire of persons, marriage, and bailment.[15]

There is almost a generation between the work of the younger Story and that of Langdell and some twenty years from the publication of Parsons's work to Langdell's assumption of the deanship at Harvard. Interestingly enough, two other treatises on contract law were published more or less contemporaneously with Langdell's work: Francis Hilliard's in 1872 and Joel Bishop's in 1878.[16] Like Story and Parsons, Hilliard and Bishop lived and wrote in Massachusetts, and their work resembles that of their fellow Bay Staters more than it does that of the New York practitioner Langdell. Both stressed the particular.

The clearest differences between Langdell and his two contemporaries lie in their use of authority. The books by Bishop and Hilliard overflow with citations of hundreds of cases from many American jurisdictions, as well as from England. Langdell discussed, or cited without discussion, far fewer cases, almost always English and reproduced in his casebook. Bishop told his readers that he included numerous citations in order to provide practitioners relying in argument on a proposition in the book with the cases that can be used to support it. As a result, however, in spite of his expressed desire to reduce the law of contracts to its "skeleton," Bishop, in direct contrast to Langdell, concentrated more on amassing authority than on elucidation of principles.[17]

Bishop's treatise, however, does appear skeletal in comparison with Hilliard's two volumes. Not only did Hilliard include large numbers of citations to American cases, but also, like Story, he discussed subjects that for Langdell were separate from the realm of contract.[18] Unlike Langdell, Hilliard discussed the facts of cases at great length and even reprinted recent opinions in full in the footnotes. Like Bishop he seemed implicitly to accept the notion that his work should help practitioners with the practical chore of hunting up cases from the relevant jurisdiction with which to make the winning point.

The differences between Langdell and his predecessors go deeper than varying criteria for the selection of cases and subjects to be included in a treatise nominally concerning the law of contracts. Langdell believed in and explicated a theory of contract law that explained the results in decided cases and provided the key to understanding all contract problems; the other authors wrote about fact patterns and recurring situations in life, not all of which could be confined within the bounds of general theory.[19] These differing approaches can best be illustrated by considering the treatment in the four earlier works of two aspects of the subject of "consideration," the single most crucial element in that traditional or classical theory of contract law which Langdell helped develop. Consideration is important because it is the legal concept fashioned to answer the question of what promises shall be enforced by the courts. Whether or not moral obligation and mutual promises could serve as consideration was an important question in nineteenth-century discussions of contract law. The different answers the four authors presented clearly reveal the extent of Langdell's desire to develop and to apply a systematic theory. The history of the moral obligation question also helps explain the novel elements of Langdell's thought.

The notion that "a promise to discharge a duty which was morally but not legally binding on the promisor could be a valid consideration" was recognized in the nineteenth century as having been first expressed in the decisions of Lord Mansfield, and it came to be regarded as a dangerous innovation.[20] At first blush, it seems inherently just to invoke the power of the law to *require* the performance of something one has promised to do. Professor A. W. B. Simpson showed that indeed, before the eighteenth century, contract law conformed to this idea.[21] In this light, Lord Mansfield's decisions were anything but innovative. They were followed, in fact, after his death, and by 1813 the doctrine they established "was so firmly rooted as to be impervious to argument."[22] In 1802, however, two law reporters, Bosanquet and Puller, wrote an essay on the subject, which they printed as a note to the decision in *Wennall v. Adney*. First, they asserted that "an idea has prevailed of late years that an express promise, founded simply on an antecedent moral obligation is sufficient to support an assumpsit." Second, they suggested that the idea was based on false inferences from "some expressions of Lord Mansfield and Mr. Justice Buller."[23] Finally, the two reporters set forth their explanation for the cases that allegedly validated moral obligation as consideration. They argued, not without some strain, that every case involved the revival by an express promise of "a precedent good consideration, which might have been enforced at law through the medium of an implied promise, had it not been suspended by some positive rule of law," such as the statute of limitations or the lack of capacity attendant on infancy.[24] This explanation led to the obvious question: What sort of good consideration might be "enforced at law through the medium of an implied promise"? Their answer was that consideration which could be enforced through the action of assumpsit, which has at its heart the willingness to say that, given certain circumstances, defendants can be required to do something on the theory that they promised to do it. Because of the way the action of assumpsit was pleaded, the "promise" was often "implied as a matter of law" and was not really something to be proved.[25] In such a system the only control on bringing lawsuits to enforce promises was the doctrine of consideration, which sought to define the kind of transaction between plaintiff and defendant that would allow a promise to be implied. Bosanquet and Puller then went all the way back to Coke to show that "to support an assumpsit the party promising must derive a benefit, or the party performing sustain an inconvenience occasioned by the Plaintiff."[26] In other words, mere "natural affection" and unsolicited "curtesies" are not good consideration.

This formulation directly contradicted Mansfield's views. He believed that the function of consideration was to indicate that a promise was made seriously and thus ought to be enforced. This indeed is the traditional explanation of consideration, and it is related to the different treatment common law gives to agreements under seal (which do not need consideration because the seal imports the requisite solemnity) and to all other agreements, written and unwritten.[27] Bosanquet and Puller, by contrast, seem to want to limit the appellation "consideration" to transactions that involve economic benefit and detriment.

Under the influence of ideas like those expressed by Bosanquet and Puller, Mansfield's views were attacked. By 1831 Lord Tenterden in *Littlefield v. Shee* had cast doubt on Mansfield's formulation.[28] Finally, in *Eastwood v. Kenyon* in 1840 Lord Denman sitting in the Queen's Bench cited Bosanquet and Puller's note with approval and decided that moral obligation would not sustain a suit for the enforcement of a promise to perform it.[29]

Since *Eastwood* became the leading case on the matter, dealt with by all five writers we have been considering, a statement of its facts and reasoning is worthwhile. P. S. Atiyah described *Eastwood v. Kenyon* as "one of the most puzzling of all nineteenth-century decisions on contract law," especially because of the appealing nature of the plaintiff's claim.[30] Eastwood was Sutcliffe's executor. Kenyon had married Sutcliffe's daughter and heir, Sarah. After Sutcliffe's death and while Sarah was an unmarried minor, Eastwood spent money of his own for Sarah's maintenance and on the upkeep of some cottages that formed part of the estate. In order to reimburse himself (available assets of Sutcliffe's estate being insufficient), he borrowed the sum—£140—from Blackburn, giving Blackburn his own promissory note for the amount. When she came of age Sarah promised Eastwood that she would pay the promissory note, and after her marriage Kenyon repeated the promise. The promises of repayment were never carried out. Eastwood sued, won at nisi prius, but found his victory overturned because the promise lacked consideration.[31] In Denman's view, to hold otherwise would turn every good deed done into grounds for a lawsuit, just as Bosanquet and Puller and the authorities of the "old common law" (that is, the law imagined to have existed before Mansfield's innovations) all feared, because "the mere fact of giving a promise creates a moral obligation to do it."[32]

Both Bishop and Hilliard dealt with the problem of moral consideration rather summarily, relying on *Eastwood v. Kenyon* to show that moral obligation would not sustain a promise. To the extent that they explained why, both authors agreed that the contrary doctrine would involve the courts in determining matters of morality that are beyond their competence. Story went a bit further. He, too, believed that courts could not enforce every moral obligation, the performance of which "must be left to the good faith of the individual, and it is neither within the province nor the policy of the law to apply a metaphysical standard of morality to the conduct of men in their common relations of life."[33] He also found, however, two exceptions to the general rule, both of which rest on the notion of the ratification of voidable contracts. The first exception involved enforceable promises, liability on which was barred "in consequence of some statute or positive rule, growing out of general principles of public policy." In Story's view, the moral obligation represented by the original liability would support an express—but not implied—promise to perform obligations barred by the statute of limitations or a discharge in bankruptcy or to make good on obligations contracted during infancy. The second exception concerned "gratuitous bailees or trustees, holding the goods or property of another," on whose part the law raised an implied promise to perform the trust or bailment undertaken, although, if the undertaking were truly gratuitous, such bailees were liable only for gross negligence.

Story recognized that *Littlefield v. Shee* "abridged and modified" the doctrine "that a moral obligation is a sufficient consideration to support a subsequent promise" and the *Eastwood v. Kenyon* decision denied it. He was confident "that the modern cases have, however, perfectly established the doctrine,'' as he described it, citing lower court cases from Pennsylvania and New York.[34]

Parsons, too, noted the insufficiency of moral consideration and added that the refusal to enforce duties dictated by sound morality did not ''appear at first sight very creditable to the common law.''[35] It is, however, a sound position, he said, because the difficulty in deciding which moral considerations would and which would not sustain an action at law is ''extreme.'' He then stated a brief version of Story's exceptions, calling it a ''rule'': ''A moral obligation to pay money or to perform a duty is a good consideration for a promise to do so, where there was originally an obligation to pay the money or to do the duty, which was enforceable at law but for the interference of some rule of law.''[36] In the notes he cited forty-nine cases, English and American, in support of his rule and quoted almost the whole of Denman's opinion in *Eastwood v. Kenyon*.[37]

Langdell's discussion of moral consideration, by contrast, was predicated on a theory of what contract was all about, which dictated his conclusions. He began, conventionally enough, with an invocation of Mansfield: ''Lord Mansfield appears to have entertained the opinion that a mere promise to do what the promisor was already under a moral obligation to do was binding.''[38] He went on to state that it is not clear whether Mansfield meant that a moral obligation was good consideration or that such a promise did not require consideration to be binding. The latter theory

> would have been less untenable, and less mischievous in its tendency. It would indeed have been liable to the serious objection of involving judicial legislation, but the theory of moral consideration was liable to the much greater objection, at least in a scientific point of view, that it could only succeed at the expense of involving a fundamental legal doctrine in infinite confusion.[39]

In a sense, Langdell's entire approach is summed up in this criticism of moral consideration. His identification of two possible rationales for Mansfield's position opens the door for discussing the role of consideration as a validation device, as simply one way of making sure that only serious promises are enforced. In other words, Langdell seems, at least in part, to have recognized Mansfield's analysis. Yet he ignores the potential of his own insight because he believes that courts can only enforce those promises for which there is consideration, the nature of which is dictated by ''fundamental legal doctrine.''

That ''fundamental legal doctrine'' seems to be, in fact, a congeries of principles which together made up Langdell's view of contract law. The most important is a statement he described as a ''definition'': ''The consideration of a promise is the thing given or done by the promisee in exchange for the promise.''[40] He continued: consideration, in turn, comes in two varieties, best distinguished by the forms of action that enforce contracts based on them. One type of contract is enforced by the action of debt, and the consideration necessary to sustain that action of debt must be something actually given to or done for the obligator directly. The other type is enforced by the action of assumpsit, and the consideration necessary to sustain that action

> may best be described negatively, namely, by saying that it need not satisfy any one of the requirements [necessary in order to support an action of debt]. If anything whatever (which the law can notice) be given or done in exchange for the promise, it is sufficient; and therefore, if one promise be given in exchange for another promise, there is a sufficient consideration for each.[41]

Finally, the consideration and the promise must be simultaneous. A debt is created "the moment the consideration is given and received." When the second sort of consideration is involved, that which can only support a promise, "the promise must be made in legal contemplation the moment that the performance of the consideration is completed." And why is all this so? Were it not, "it would not be true according to the definition, that the consideration is given in exchange for the promise."[42]

Having established all this, Langdell then explained all the classic cases involving moral consideration. Cases involving infancy, discharges in bankruptcy, and the statute of limitations result in recoveries, he said, not because plaintiffs have an action based on the subsequent promise to pay, but because that promise ratifies or waives the protection otherwise offered to the defendant by the law.[43] Such a theory is particularly difficult to apply in the case of debts barred by the statute of limitations since waiver of a rule of positive law is an anomalous concept. Langdell's ingenuity rose to the occasion, however, and he explained the cases allowing such recovery as proceeding on an admittedly "highly artificial doctrine." For example, the plaintiff (the person to whom the debt more than six years old is due) brings an action of assumpsit, based on the implied promise of the debtor to pay the debt. In response, the defendant debtor proves that the debt is more than six years old and that therefore he is entitled to the protection of the statute. The plaintiff then proves a new promise to repay the debt made less than six years before, which sufficiently repels the effect of the statute to allow the implication of a new promise to pay the debt. Finally, "as this new implied promise supported the declaration equally well with the old one upon which the plaintiff was supposed to have declared [to begin with], the issue had to be found in the plaintiff's favor." "Artificial" though this may be, it is a true theory because it bases recovery not on the only promise the defendant actually made, the "new" promise to pay the old debt, but an implied promise which the law understands as having been made simultaneously with the incurring of the debt. Only this implied promise can serve as the basis of an action because of the requirement that promise and the consideration for it be exchanged simultaneously, which, in turn, is required by the very definition of consideration.[44]

Langdell explained cases dealing with the sort of situation involved in *Eastwood v. Kenyon* in the same way. According to Langdell, no action will lie on a promise to pay for services rendered to or to repay money paid on behalf of a promisor without his or her authority. The promise, however, does create liability because it cures the lack of authority and makes the promisor the promisee's debtor from the time of the original transaction, all in conformity with Langdell's general theory. The debt can then be recovered by an action of assumpsit on the strength of the implied promise to repay the debt, which is the basis of the action. Therefore, Eastwood would have been able to recover if he had joined Sarah as a defendant along with her husband. Her promise would supply authority for Eastwood's expenditure and also waive her defense of infancy.[45]

The difference between this treatment of the moral consideration question and that of the other writers is clear. Each made the difficulty of deciding questions of morality the cornerstone of his discussion. Langdell, however, was concerned with a coherent system of rules directly connected to the procedural system that provides logically consistent answers to problems posed by cases. His solutions existed within a legal system that was totally self-contained.

Another example of Langdell's propensity to theorize also helps explain his place in the history of thought about contract. He treated mutual promises as consideration in a way that strikingly contrasts with treatments by Story, Bishop, and Hilliard. Story devoted three brief paragraphs to the subject. He maintained that two valid promises could support each other as concurrent consideration as long as they were made simultaneously, for otherwise there would be lack of reciprocity; he acknowledged that reciprocal promises to marry and promises to sell and deliver goods and pay for them are valid and binding.[46] Bishop also recognized mutual promises as good consideration, noting that the resulting contract had to bind both parties or it would bind neither, and he agreed with the idea that the promises must be simultaneous.[47] Hilliard was even less systematic. Confining his treatment to the bald statement that mutual promises were good consideration, he briefly stated the holdings of some seven cases on the particular facts there involved.[48]

Parsons's treatment of this topic, however, started down the road his former student would follow twenty years later. He began by describing particular situations in which a promise for a promise is good consideration, producing a discussion much like those already described. He broke new ground with his discussion of mutuality. According to Parsons, a party making a promise to another party, which will be fulfilled when that party does something, is bound once the promisee "engages to do, or else does or begins to do, the thing which is the condition of the first promise." Most common contracts illustrate this principle, according to Parsons, and he went on to analyze the ordinary retail sale in terms of the exchange of promises.[49]

Seeing far more that needed to be explained, Langdell went beyond his old teacher. He presented the historical background. Before the action of assumpsit was introduced, no mere promise could create a debt and therefore could not be consideration. Once assumpsit was established, however, anything of value could serve as consideration, and "the courts were not long in perceiving that the making of a binding promise was giving or doing something of value." Since a promise is good consideration, said Langdell, it is subject to all the rules that govern any other sort of consideration. Therefore, mutual promises must be simultaneous and both must be binding if there is to be a contract.[50] Keeping these rules in mind, Langdell again explained a great number of cases in terms of his theoretical understanding of what was becoming to be known as the bilateral contract.[51] He concentrated most of his effort on cases involving compromises of existing claims, situations that caused a great deal of confusion in English law in the eighteenth century.[52] In Langdell's view, all these cases involved bilateral contracts, and the validity of each alleged agreement was to be measured by the rules applicable to the exchange of mutual promises.[53]

The elaborate nature of Langdell's treatment of consideration and its centrality to his discussion is even more striking when compared with what the other four writers had to say about the subject generally. Story began with an assertion that comes the closest to being a fact of common law—that any contract not a specialty, that is, not under seal, must have consideration if it is to be enforced. The subject "naturally divides itself into, 1st. Valuable Considerations; 2d. Insufficient Considerations." Valuable considerations, in turn, can be divided into five classes: benefit and injury, forbearance, assignment of a chose in action, mutual promises, and consideration moving from third persons.[54] The discussion of each class was similar: rules were stated and illustrated by setting forth what amount to the briefest of statements of the holdings of the cited cases. Bishop and Hilliard a generation later proceeded much the same way: rules were spun out and illustrated by greater or lesser discussion of decided cases, usually greater in Hilliard's case. Parsons did note Blackstone's use of a civil law scheme for the classification of consideration, but he admitted that it was of little use when applied to the common law.[55] It is clear that what is lacking in all these discussions is any sense of a coherent theory.

Perhaps enough has been said of Langdell's method of discussion to illustrate the coherence of the system he promulgated.[56] Perhaps, too, enough has been said to exhibit the main elements of the classical theory of contracts that Langdell is supposed to have helped establish. The substance of his system is an example of the new view of contract law prevalent in the first half or so of the nineteenth century, at least in the English courts. The elements of this new system are all evident in Langdell's *Summary:* the belief in consideration as the crucial element in contract, signifying something more than just the solemnity of the undertaking, along with the importance of promises as consideration and the related emphasis on the bilateral contract, which, in turn, leads to elaborate rules about the formation of contracts stated in terms of offer and acceptance and the eventual articulation of the will theory of contract.[57]

Story, Bishop, and Hilliard do not approach Langdell on the theoretical level. While Parsons's work shows some foreshadowings of this classical system, Langdell in all areas goes beyond his teacher in the direction of greater generality and clearer articulation of theory. Parsons lacks any idea of an "explanation" such as the one Langdell creates out of the supposed history of the actions of assumpsit and debt. Parsons only hints at the scheme of classification based on bilateral and unilateral contracts; Langdell puts it at the center of his discussion. Parsons discusses assent and the importance of time in contracts; Langdell raises the requirement of simultaneous agreement to a universal principle.[58] Parsons discusses common fact patterns at great length; his student subsumes them under theory.[59] In short, Langdell's new theory is best summed up in his statement that assumpsit "was founded upon the theory that the defendant's obligation was created by his promise, and not by a consideration received."[60]

Langdell did not limit his scholarly writings to the field of contracts. Indeed, he devoted most of his academic career to the study of equity. The dean published the results of his studies in a series of articles in the *Harvard Law Review*, which appeared from 1887 to 1905.[61] A comparison of these works with Joseph Story's *Commentaries on Equity Jurisprudence, as Administered in England and America*, published in 1836, reveals the same sort of contrast as that found in the comparison of contracts treatises.[62] First, Story's work is much longer and cites far more cases than Langdell's. Again and again the justice amassed authorities for his readers' use. Like the contract treatises, Story's work is organized around typical fact situations falling under the jurisdiction of the equity courts. His chapters bear titles such as "Constructive Fraud," "Administration," "Legacies," and "Confusion of Boundaries." Langdell's articles, on the other hand, deal with specific types of equitable proceedings: "Bills for an Account," "Creditors' Bills," "Bills of Equitable Assumpsit." The discussions of these topics are finely detailed expositions of the mechanics of a suit in equity which pay careful attention to the technical workings of the court.

The difference between the two approaches can be clearly seen in the two discussions of the role of equity courts in the administration of decedents' estates. In present-day American law, probate and administration of wills and intestate estates are the province of statutorily created probate, orphans', or surrogate's courts whose procedure is likewise set out by statute. In nineteenth-century England, and to a certain extent in the antebellum United States, proper administration of the estate of a deceased person could only be accomplished through the powers of the equity court, especially the power of the court to order discovery of the facts relevant to the case before it.[63] The process was set in motion when a creditor of the deceased initiated a suit in equity court by filing a bill, the equitable equivalent of the common law declaration or complaint. The creditor asked for a discovery of the decedent's assets and payment of his debt from them. The court then issued a decree directing a master (an official of the court, not a judge, sometimes appointed ad hoc) to, as Story puts it,

> take the accounts between the deceased and all his creditors; to cause the creditors, upon due public notice, to come before him to prove their

> debts, at a certain place, and within a limited period; and also directs the master to take an account of all the personal estate of the deceased in the hands of the executor or administrator; and the same to be applied in payment of the debts and other charges in a due course of administration.[64]

To further this process, the court utilized another special equitable remedy, the injunction, to prevent the commencement or prosecution of actions at law against the executor or administrator for the payment of debts.[65] This brief description is fleshed out with numerous footnotes of string citations to cases that illustrate the workings of this procedure.

Langdell's treatment was far more detailed. Story justified equitable jurisdiction in this case by noting that, first, the fiduciary duty of the executor or administrator was a traditional subject of equity jurisdiction and, second, that the equity procedures, outlined above, were more expeditious than those available at law.[66] Langdell agreed, observing that "[i]t would be difficult to devise a course of proceeding more perfectly adapted to the exigencies of the case, more simple, more direct, or more conformable to justice," than that available at equity for the administration of an estate. It is not enough, however, to sustain the jurisdiction of equity simply because "the remedy furnished by the common law was not as good as it might be." Equitable jursidiction should be sustained only where "the case is one for which the common law cannot furnish an adequate remedy."[67] The conduct of that inquiry gives a revealing insight into Langdell's thought.

The problem with the legal action available to the creditor of a decedent, said Langdell, involved the executor's or administrator's defense of want of assets.[68] The only way to deal with such a defense was to have the executor account for the estate. A common law court, however, could take an account only through the action of account, which did not lie for the recovery of a debt. The only actions that were available—debt and *indebitatus assumpsit*—had no mechanism for taking an account. They involved only a trial before a jury on whose verdict judgment is rendered. "If any account was to be taken," Langdell wrote, "it must be taken at the trial, and yet it was never claimed that an account could be taken by or before a jury."[69]

Even this objection was secondary, he continued. The more basic problem involved the difference between an accounting and an affirmative defense. An accounting was rendered as a result of a suit whose primary object was to secure the accounting. The executor's defense of want of assets to an action of debt or *indebitatus assumpsit* would lead, through the rules of common law pleading, to a single issue, which would, in turn, depend on exactly how the executor pleaded. The mechanism of pleading was such that the only three results were possible: the plaintiff receives judgment for his entire debt; or for nothing at all; or for so much his debt as the executor could pay with assets on hand, the remainder to be paid when further assets come to hand. According to Langdell, "such . . . is the true theory of the common-law defense of want of assets, pleaded by an executor to an action brought against him by a creditor of the testator.''[70]

The ''true theory,'' however, was abandoned in practice as early as the reign of James I, when, in a case where the executor pleaded no assets on hand, the jury found assets less than the amount of the debt. The court gave judgment for the entire debt, but granted execution only for the amount of the assets and required the plaintiff to obtain a writ of *scire facias* to collect the remainder should the executor acquire further assets. To Langdell this disparity between judgment and execution, requiring the plaintiff to in effect start a new action to secure the remainder of his judgment won in the first, was ''extraordinary'' because it ''involve[s] a plain contradiction.'' Judgment and execution must correspond. It remained for Lord Mansfield to restore the harmony of the system, making the execution conform to the judgment by changing the judgment to one for the amount of the debt equal to the assets on hand with a further judgment for the balance as assets should come to hand.[71]

Mansfield's solution caused further problems, however. By giving the creditor judgment only in the amount of the assets in the executor's hands, Mansfield in effect required the jury ''to inquire, and to find by their verdict, how much assets was in the executor's hands,'' which could only be done by taking an account. That a jury was not competent to do.[72] Furthermore, once the proceeding was under way at law, the burden of proof involved complicated any sensible resolution. The plaintiff creditor was required to go forward by proving the receipt of assets by the executor, something totally within the knowledge of the defendant. The mechanisms for doing so at law were notoriously deficient, but such proof was necessary before the executor would be required to show what became of those assets and why they were not available to pay the plaintiff's debt.[73]

Only after outlining in painful detail these procedural considerations did Langdell feel confident in concluding that equitable jurisdiction over the administration of decedents' estates was justified. First, fairness to the parties required that the executor account for all assets received, and equity was the preeminent forum for accounting. Second, although the common law attempted to frame creditors' actions as accountings, ''the form of action, the nature of the pleadings, the question to be tried, and the mode of trial'' all doomed the attempt. Finally, the creditor needed some way to take the executor's accounting under oath, something easily done in equity and impossible at law.[74]

The similarities between Langdell's vision of contract law and his analysis of equity jurisdiction are striking. In both cases he eschewed collecting cases in favor of spinning theory from a small number of leading opinions. In both cases his explanations of the workings of the law are intimately tied to the peculiarities and technicalities of procedure. Even his justification of equity jurisdiction—in a field where the superiority of equity procedures over those available at law is both clear and long acknowledged—depends totally on a painstaking and minute analysis of the failings of common law procedure. His argument for his theory of contracts similarly depends to a great extent on his view of the proper workings of the common law actions. At the heart of Langdell's scholarship is a reverence for the decided case, the judicial opinion, as the root of all Anglo-American law and the source of principles rather than as a more or less accurate illustration of them. For all the citation and discussion of cases by the other treatise writers, they did not draw the law itself out of the reports. The multitudinous situations of fact provided by cases were subordinated to the great overarching principles, which presumably could best be found in treatises and texts. For Langdell, in contrast, only what could be learned by analyzing the cases had any value.

Changes in Procedure and Legal Thought

Langdell's legal science exemplifies the shift from the idea of legal order based on principles inherent in the constitution of a divinely created universe to one based on proper understanding and arrangement of technical principles inherent in the historically produced legal system. The roots of his participation in this intellectual transformation go back at least to his studies at Harvard Law School. Although he received his legal education in an institution designed to inculcate the inherent principles at the foundation of the law, his habits of study were centered on the case. Because of poor eyesight, which was to fail completely at the height of his teaching career, Langdell had other students read to him. One of them was the future Episcopal bishop of Fond du Lac, Wisconsin, Charles Grafton:

> He used to get me to read aloud with him evenings, along with [George Otis] Shattuck, for I had the small accomplishment of reading well. He taught us how, from his point of view, to study law. He began with the cases of leading import. We had to read them, and then state the points to him. Then he made us read all the leading authorities on such cases, and so he pounded certain principles of law into us.[75]

These habits were probably reinforced by his experience as research assistant to Theophilus Parsons. During the latter part of his study at Harvard Law School, Langdell was the school's librarian and also aided Parsons in writing his treatise on the law of contracts, first published in 1853.[76] According to Parsons's preface to his work, his assistants undertook a specific task, dictated by his decision to exclude references to cases in his text. To discuss cases supporting his assertions in the body of his work, Parsons feared, would inevitably lead his readers to slight or even ignore cases opposing or modifying the principles in the text. The result would be unpleasant surprises should they ever find themselves arguing in court a question involving those principles. He therefore relegated all discussion of cases to notes, some of which extensively quoted and abstracted cases that contradicted or modified the text. Langdell and his fellow assistants aided in preparing the notes, and their work was certainly thorough. They read and considered more than 6,000 cases. Nothing was taken second-hand from digests or indices.[77] Langdell's understanding of the law of contracts was formed by this careful explication of decided cases. Under the direction of a respected teacher he learned to look for the law in a rigorous dissection of the original records of judges' reasoning.

Langdell's exposure to the importance of decided cases continued after his student days when he became a member of the bar of New York City. After a slow start, he formed a partnership with William Stanley. Between 1860 and 1864 Stanley and Langdell were joined by Edwards Pierrepont and between 1864 and 1870 by Addison Brown. Throughout these years "Langdell did not appear in court, and leading a secluded life, was not generally known even by lawyers. . . . In the almost inaccessible retirement" of his private rooms above the office of his firm and in the library of the law institute, "he did the greater part of his work."[78]

Despite Langdell's relative isolation, he managed to argue at least one case before the New York Court of Appeals, the state's highest court, and his partners argued seven others.[79] Two of his partners were distinguished members of the profession. Pierrepont interrupted his partnership with Langdell and Stanley to take a seat on the Superior Court of New York City, and after leaving for good in 1864 represented August Belmont in litigation of the "Erie War." He served as United States attorney for the southern district of New York and attorney general of the United States and capped his public career by being appointed minister to Great Britain. All these positions he owed to the patronage of President Ulysses S. Grant. He died in March 1892.[80] Addison Brown, who succeeded Pierrepont in the partnership in 1864, went on to become a federal judge.[81] Although the evidence is slight, it is reasonable to conclude that Langdell and his partners had experience and active practice at the New York bar.

Langdell's practice should have made him as familiar with the practicalities of the procedural system as his formal education had familiarized him with the science of principles. By the time Langdell began to acquire practical experience, however, lawyering in New York had been transformed in fundamental ways.

In the year that Joseph Story died, the voters of the state of New York approved calling the state's third constitutional convention. The document that emerged from its deliberations was approved by the voters on November 3, 1846, by a better than two-to-one margin.[82] The new constitution drastically reorganized the judicial system of the state. The separate equity courts were abolished, and jurisdiction in both law and equity was vested in a single New York Supreme Court. The Court for the Correction of Errors, composed of the judges of the old supreme court, the chancellor and the senate of the state, was replaced by a new New York Court of Appeals. All judicial offices became elective.[83] Finally, the Constitution of 1846 contained a provision that had great impact on what went on in the newly reorganized courts. The legislature was required to appoint three commissioners to simplify the law of pleading and procedure. Commissioners were duly appointed in April 1847, and a new code of procedure was enacted on April 12, 1848, to become effective on July 1. The code was reenacted on April 11, 1849, with amendments. Amended again in 1851 and 1852, the code governed the practice of the New York courts until it was repealed in 1877.[84]

The basic alteration in legal practice worked by the code was the abolition of the old forms of action and the substitution of a single "civil action."[85] The forms of action had once provided the framework for the organization of the principles of legal science. Because the resulting schema was intimately related to the actual practice of law, practice and theory were well integrated. The workingmen of the law could be part of professional culture, no matter how narrow their practice. The Field Code smashed that world, first in the state of New York and later elsewhere as code pleading spread.[86] The results, however, were not totally new. Whatever David Dudley Field, principal drafter of the legislation, hoped the changes would accomplish, the New York courts managed to limit the effect of the code to the abolition of the forms of action as verbal formulas only, not as legal concepts. More than a decade of judicial hostility to the code culminated in an 1860 opinion of the court of appeals in which Judge Samuel Selden declared that "there are intrinsic differences between [actions] which no law can abolish."[87] Because the stock allegations and fictions of the forms no longer meant anything, however, lawyers and courts were forced to articulate clearly the legal principles that underlay concepts like trover, replevin, assumpsit, and debt.

The description of the new system given in one of the first treatises on New York code pleading explained the change quite clearly. George van Santvoord, author of that treatise, was a successful lawyer in Troy and after the passage of the code quickly became a leading authority on its interpretation. At the beginning of his work, first published in 1852, he noted that "in order to frame a pleading correctly under the new system, not only the rules of pleading, properly speaking, but the legal principles involved in the action, and upon which the relief depends, must be thoroughly understood" because judicial interpretation had made it clear that the principles behind the old forms of action remained intact.[88] For example, the traditional form used for the action of trover alleged that A was possessed of his property which he lost and which B found. It went on to allege that, although he was requested to return it, B retained the property and converted it to his own use. These allegations, however, were not necessarily true: "No request was, perhaps, ever made, and no loss or finding was necessary to be proved, and yet the pleading was theoretically good; and the plaintiff was allowed to show any state of facts to prove that the defendant had converted, or sold, or destroyed, or was exercising unlawful dominion over the property." Such a disparity between the allegations of the pleading and the plaintiff's grievance were not tolerated under the code, which required that the plaintiff plead only the facts "constituting the cause of action.'' The result of this requirement to plead facts was clear:

> In what cases, therefore, it may be asked, is a demand necessary to be alleged in an action which would have been formerly trover, or an action to recover personal property? This question, often a nice and difficult question of law, it will be seen, must be first satisfactorily solved before the pleading can be correctly drawn; for no general form of pleading can meet every variety of case, particularly where it may be desirable to verify it by the oath of the party.[89]

A similar result obtained where the common counts, the traditional method of dealing with contract actions, were involved. The various promises and requests for payment or performance involved in the actions of *indebitatus assumpsit, quantum meruit, quantum valebant*, and the account stated ''were scarcely anything more than mere legal fictions.'' Both implied and express promises were stated positively, with the implied promise proved by showing the facts from which the law implied a promise. Under the code, however, implied requests or promises cannot be pleaded: ''The facts raising the implication, and they alone, should be stated, because they alone are to be proved.''[90]

These changes meant that successful practitioners could no longer depend on a book of form pleadings. van Santvoord wrote:

> Under the Code precedents are, in general, to be invented, and cannot in all cases be prepared beforehand for use. The pleader is required to understand the legal principles on which his action is based, the evidence necessary to support it, the general rules of pleading, and make his forms for himself.[91]

Research which in the past might be limited to a search of precedents, such as those collected in Chitty or in Story's first work, with perhaps a reference to digests such as Nathan Dane's in order to find statements of general principles, would now have to concentrate on a close reading of earlier cases in order to find a narrower sort of precedent, one whose facts resembled the case at hand. Somehow the lawyer had to find the legal essence of the actions represented by these earlier cases and express them in the complaint. The premium put on a particularized, close reading of previous cases is shown by the additions made by Nathaniel Moak to the new edition of van Santvoord's treatise published in 1873. Almost all the additional material is a recitation of the facts of individual cases, culminating in a new chapter IVA, ''Complaint in Particular Cases,'' 200 pages of short synopses of cases grouped by broad subjects, such as ''illegal contract,'' ''infants,'' ''mistake,'' and even ''milk''—an entry that reads in full:

> An action for fraudulently adulterating milk may be brought in the name of the owner of a cheese-manufactory and its patrons, where the cheese is to be divided in proportion to the quantity of milk furnished by each; and so by the treasurer of such association.[92]

It is unlikely that a legal world dominated by the organizational framework provided by the forms of action would have found room for such a classifactory heading.

Determining the meanings of provisions of the Field Code was a matter of daily professional life to Langdell and his partners. Having dealt perhaps on a daily basis with the need to understand the code and therefore with the sort of research necessary to formulate proper pleadings, Langdell left New York. As a student at Harvard, Langdell had been exposed to teaching law as a system of principles. His work after assuming the deanship at his alma mater shows a strong commitment to order and coherence in the law. It is tempting to imagine Langdell as agreeing with the conservative interpretation of the code—seeing the principles of the forms of action as still alive and finding them best expressed in a small number of older English cases dating from a time of procedural purity. All of Langdell's theory of consideration, as has been noted, rested on the distinction between the sort of consideration necessary to support the action of debt and that necessary to support the action of assumpsit.[93] The research techniques required to find these principles, the careful searching of past cases for particular circumstances that may provide analogies to the matter at hand and provide raw material from which to induce general principles, might also have been reinforced by Langdell's habit as a law student of focusing on cases.

Other aspects of mid-nineteenth-century American intellectual life may also have helped form Langdell's idea of law and legal science. The effect of those influences is harder to establish than that of Langdell's experience at Harvard Law School or even than that of his posited experiences at the bar under the reformed procedure. In this case there is only the possibility of inferring from similarities of expression a certain degree of influence on the shy but intellectually alert young lawyer. A general change in legal attitudes may have occurred in the period after the death of Joseph Story. For example, a great gap separates Gulian Verplanck, who wrote in 1825 *An Essay on the Doctrine of Contracts: Being an Inquiry How Contracts Are Affected in Law and Morals by Concealment, Error, or Inadequate Price*, from the writer of a three-part essay on consideration in contracts that appeared in the March, May, and June numbers of the *American Law Register* for 1854, and which Theophilus Parsons, Langdell's patron and teacher, cited with approval in his own contracts treatise.[94]

Verplanck was troubled by the question posed in the title of his book. He began by recognizing the reality of the moral revulsion felt by many at decisions that seemed to sanction cheating by one party to a contract, a revulsion which was "spontaneous result of the moral observations and experience of our whole lives."[95] As a conscientious Baconian scientist, he set for himself the task of resolving the various cases on the subject into "a few fixed and broad rules, founded in nature, conscience and reason" which "would be fitted alike for the guidance of private conscience, and the direction of public justice; would be in unison with the great laws of universal jurisprudence; and not inconsistent with the habits, wants, and true policy of an enlightened age and a commercial country."[96] Verplanck acknowledged that certain moral duties cannot be enforced by law; benevolence, gratitude, liberality, and the like must be left to the individual conscience.[97] He believed, however, that the degree of fair dealing necessary in ordinary transactions is "perfectly well understood" and that "the doctrines of sound legal ethics, and those of a strict and enlightened private honesty, must always run together, except so far as the former are modified by necessity," which does not happen often.[98] The principles he derived from these beliefs were meant to allow sagacity and superior knowledge gained though honest application their true reward, while frustrating chicanery.[99]

Almost thirty years later the author of the articles in the *American Law Register* based the doctrine of consideration on "the right of property and the functions of civil government." The purpose of law is to make people secure in what is theirs, be it "life, limb or estate." In short, "the protection of persons, and of their rights of property, and the conservation of social order, and not the enforcement of the decalogue is the business of the civil magistrate." The promise to give something in exchange for someone's property must be enforced. To do otherwise injures that person's right of property "to as great an extent as if it had been seized by force." The force of this reasoning is not vitiated by the allowed disparity in value between the consideration and the property given: "It must be remembered that the law abides by general principles with wide boundaries, which on the whole work out their intended results."[100]

It is true that Verplanck recognized the subjectivity of value and sanctions the legal recognition of some sorts of superior bargaining power.[101] He clearly accepted the existence of the market economy.[102] He also, however, believed in the existence of moral principles to which law must and really can conform. Law is based on universals, and it is no surprise that Verplanck asserted the existence of a "common commercial and maritime law of the civilized world" based "partly in convenience, and partly in natural equity."[103] Because he believed the applicable moral rules were so evident that they really would prevent overreaching, Verplanck could assert the subjectivity of price, support the resulting refusal to interfere with contracts because of disparities in value, and sanction giving free play to superior abilities.

By 1854 the rhetoric of moral universals seems to count for little. Why that occurred cannot be fully investigated here, but work on the relationship between law and the agitation over slavery is suggestive. Between the publication of Verplanck's book and the articles in the *American Law Register*, the controversy over slavery came to dominate American politics. The moral discord created by the competing arguments of the abolitionists and their opponents, especially as they confronted each other in the legal system, may have rendered a belief in universal—or even widely held—moral values both more difficult to accept and hence less useful to lawyers.[104]

The legacy of Jacksonian democracy also fostered the limitation of moral rhetoric in legal argument. The battle to limit government intervention in the economy in order to preserve for all the opportunity to prosper was an important tenet of the "Jacksonian persuasion," whatever the actual experience of workers in the mid-nineteenth-century United States.[105] Favors for none and an open field for all were promoted by restricting government activities designed to limit human action in the name of a higher law.[106]

It is apparent, moreover, that at least some of the legal doctrine coming from this era should reflect the influence of classical theories of economics and political economy. In *The Rise and Fall of Freedom of Contract*, Professor P. S. Atiyah offered an elaborate intellectual pedigree of the English equivalent of classical contract law, which is relevant to Langdell because he spent so much ingenuity on the very English cases Atiyah discusses. Broadly put, Atiyah traced freedom of contract to ideas such as the free market, individualism, positivism, and utilitarianism—in short, in all the intellectual fellow travelers of the great social changes that occurred during the industrial revolution.[107]

Application of this analysis to a case of classical contract law can be clearly seen in Atiyah's discussion of *Eastwood v. Kenyon*. Three factors are responsible for the decision, he said. First, "there was the growing strength of positivism, which stressed the line between law and morality far more than had ever been the case in Mansfield's time." John Austin contributed greatly to its application to legal questions, and it even appears that Thomas Denman, in spite of his reputation as a legal conservative, was open to new ways of thinking about law. Second, around the time of the decision in *Eastwood* the courts were showing themselves more hostile to quasi-contractual duties, that is, to "liabilities not based on consent." Finally, the idea "that the binding nature of a promise rested upon some preexisting obligation" was disappearing.[108] In short, the decision took its place in a world dominated by a specific idea of freedom of contract, an idea which would have an important career in America after the Civil War and whose roots go back to Jacksonian ideas. The attitude toward unrequested benefits described by Atiyah appeared clearly in at least one case decided in 1825 in the highest court of New York. In his dissenting opinion, Senator John C. Spencer maintained that the only possible basis for liability to pay for benefits is a request, because "every man is permitted to regulate his own affairs in his own way, and he is the best judge when and where he will have services performed or money advanced for him."[109]

Yet another strand in the complex tapestry of Langdell's thought may have been provided by John Austin. Austin's thought is subtle and is often expressed in convoluted prose.[110] In addition, he never finished his great project to reformulate the science of law. Posthumous publication of his work in the early 1860s, however, set loose upon the common law world two important ideas: first, law could and should be separated from morality, at least for purposes of study; second, all law is directly or indirectly the command of the sovereign. Both ideas have long reverberated in American legal thought and were prominent during the formative era of modern legal education. It is clear that for Austin, the study of the science of law meant the study of law as it is without consideration of what it should be. Determining what law ought to be is the province of the science of legislation.[111]

There is one remarkable piece of evidence that Langdell held similar views. At the very beginning of his teaching career he was appointed, perhaps through the influence of Eliot, secretary of a "committee on jurisprudence," probably a subdivision of the American Social Science Association. Landgell was not particularly honored by the appointment and wrote to Theodore Dwight Woolsey of Yale, who seems to have chaired the committee, expressing his bewilderment at exactly what he was expected to do, as well as "to offer for your consideration the following suggestions in regard to the study of jurisprudence":

> [I]t [the study of jurisprudence] does not specially concern lawyers or those intending to become lawyers, but other portions of the community as well; some perhaps more, e.g., those aiming at public life or a high order of journalism. The chief business of a lawyer is and must be to learn and administer the law *as it is*; while I suppose the great object in studying jurisprudence should be to ascertain what the law *ought to be*; and although these two pursuits may seem to be of a very kindred nature, I think experience shews that devotion to one is apt to give more or less distaste for the other.[112]

In fact, the study of jurisprudence does not even belong in the law schools but rather should be part of the postgraduate studies available in the university and should be carried on by "University men who devote themselves to the higher education, and not lawyers, whether on or off the Bench, not even professors in Law Schools."[113] Langdell thus clearly articulated the division between the study of law as it is and as it ought to be which is the heart of Austinian positivism.

Whether or not Langdell was directly influenced by the English thinker is impossible to determine definitively. There is a lone reference to Austin in the discussion of moral obligation as consideration in the *Summary*. Langdell noted that the moral obligation created by a promise is even less serviceable as consideration than a preexisting moral obligation because every binding promise "excites in the promisee an expectation of performance." The only difference between promises in this regard is in the degree of expectation generated, a proposition in support of which Austin is invoked. To allow such an expectation to lead to enforcement of the promise would destroy the need for consideration.[114] Austin for his part had criticized the "vagueness and indeterminateness of 'moral obligation,'" a position clearly consistent with his statements about the need to separate the "is" and the "ought" in studying law.[115]

While this reference may be taken as evidence that Langdell was at least familiar with Austin's work, it must be remembered that Austin's writings remained obscure until the early 1860s. *The Province of Jurisprudence Determined* was republished in 1861, and the *Lectures on Jurisprudence*, the lecture notes for his unsuccessful course taught at the University of London, were published for the first time in 1863. Thereafter Austin was widely recognized as an important contributor to the Anglo-American study of jurisprudence.[116] American interest in his work may have been heightened by its appearance during the Civil War. Austin had much to say about sovereignty, a subject of importance to thinkers who were considering how to remake the Union. Langdell almost certainly encountered Austin after the foundations of his view of law and legal science had been set. It is possible, however, that Austin's insights helped clarify Langdell's narrow, technical view of legal principles, which comports well with Austinian positivism.

Many factors may help explain Langdell's unique contribution to the intellectual history of American law. If the methodology of his science of law was that of the science of law of his predecessors, the subject matter of his science was different. Langdell studied and taught law not as a system of principles whose validity could ultimately be traced to the Creator, but as a logically coherent system of technical rules, principles that are applicable only to the decision of cases in the courts and which come from those cases.[117] The case method of teaching law was also the case method of studying law. It would give birth not only to a new model law school but also to a new model legal science. Both these offspring were intimately related; the one provided a home for the other. In retrospect it seems that a new legal science could not succeed without an institutional home.

5

Harvard and the Legal World

The success of the reformed Harvard Law School was no foregone conclusion. The creation of a new sort of law school caused internal stresses that lasted for much of the 1870s and 1880s. Even when the school could present a united front to the world, it was not always attractive. The academics' claim to a monopoly on understanding legal science, evident in Langdell's criticism of bar examinations, could ruffle the feathers of the profession. The bar, however, eventually learned to accommodate the new school with its claims to superiority in training lawyers. Moreover, doubts about the traditional system were not limited to academics. Some practitioners, especially in New York City, came to believe in the 1860s and 1870s that something had to be done to raise the standard of the bar, to put stricter controls on entry into the profession. Langdell, Eliot, and the reformed Harvard eventually proved to be allies.

The Struggle for Standards in New York

A typical lament about the current state of affairs can be found in Langdell's annual report for the 1876–1877 academic year. The dean berated the state for its role in regulating admission to the bar. Langdell first drew a distinction between the "counsellor," the accomplished master of legal science who argues before the higher courts and assists the judges in the elucidation of the law, and the "attorney," who deals with routine legal business. The formal requirements for admission are based on the idea, which Langdell maintained was widely held by the bar itself, that "age and experience alone are a sufficient warrant for assuming the position of a counsellor" and that the most that can be expected of new lawyers is that they be trained as attorneys.[1] Langdell seems to have accurately portrayed the antebellum system, when formal requirements for admission set by the state were the lowest common denominator. The prestige and quality of the profession was preserved through lawyerly control of the institutions important to admission—the courts and the schools—and by the identification of the profession with social class. These two mechanisms of control helped maintain the intellectual and moral tone of the profession, the two areas in which the pettifogging attorney was deficient.

By the 1870s, however, this careful construct had severely eroded, and nowhere more obviously than in the City of New York. An attempt by some New York lawyers to restore a degree of control over recruitment to the profession led Langdell to criticize bar examinations. The importance of New York as a market for the school's graduates was great and would become greater. It was important, therefore, for Harvard Law School and those who set the requirements for admission to the New York bar to come to terms. The specific problem faced in 1876 was settled favorably to the school, but this victory was not the most important result of the controversy. The entire debate over standards for admission to practice reveals the way in which the school of Eliot and Langdell better served the profession than schools run on older models, specifically, in this case, the law school associated with Columbia College.

The turmoil in the New York legal profession during the 1860s and 1870s was a consequence of rapid social change. Ever since the Erie Canal was completed in 1825 the city had been the dominant force in American economic life. Its diverse and growing economy fed dreams of success and made the city a magnet for ambitious people, native-born and immigrant alike. It also was a center for legal work. When Langdell came to New York at the end of 1854, the ancestors of some of the greatest law firms of late twentieth-century New York could be found among the partnerships and small firms busying themselves with work growing out of the need to raise capital for the economic development of the United States.[2]

The increase in business and opportunity coincided with the loosening of requirements for admission to the bar mandated by the New York Constitution of 1846. An examination by the justices of the New York Supreme Court had to precede admission, but whether conducted by the judges themselves or, as commonly occurred, by lawyers appointed for that purpose, "this examination was necessarily brief and cursory," and "at length came to be regarded as a mere technical ceremony that the most stupid and ignorant need not fear."[3] The result, of course, was that often lamented phenomenon—the degradation of the bar from the glories of the past.[4]

Whatever the state of the morals and behavior of the bar under the post-1846 regime, many perceived them to have decayed. The situation could only have been exacerbated by the effects of the panic of 1857, which not only considerably diminished economic activity but also seems to have brought a new brazenness to the world of business.[5] The panic swept away the older generation of New York businessmen. A new group emerged, of whom the most prominent—or infamous—was Jay Gould. Gould's biographer sees in these "new men" the harbingers of real change in the business ethos of New York: "The traditions of the Street meant nothing to them. Where the older generation at least paid lip service to rules they often violated, the new breed simply ignored them."[6] While lawyers survived the panic and busied themselves with cleaning up the rubble it left, newer men, unconnected with polite New York, must have found a position at the bar as well as in the business world.[7] Even more opportunities sprang up in the wake of the Civil War, and by the beginning of the 1870s the editors of the *Albany Law Journal* observed that "thousands have taken up the law as a means of livelihood, spent as short a time as possible in preparation, . . . immediately upon admission, opened for business," and some of them "thrive most miraculously, . . . especially in our cities."[8]

Once the profession had been cohesive enough and business scarce enough to raise at least some barriers to the entry of the unsuitable.[9] In New York City on the eve of the Civil War, however, prosperity was not the monopoly of the few, and abundant opportunities attracted many indifferent to the disapprobation of the established bar. For one of the most proper of proper New York lawyers, George Templeton Strong, the resulting state of the bar was dismal to contemplate:

> About one hundred ornaments of our liberal and enlightened profession—one hundred "gentlemen of the bar"—were congregated in the Special Term room this morning [December 19, 1859]. I scrutinized the crowd, to determine how many there were whom I would be willing to receive as visitors at this house, or rather whom I would not be annoyed and disgusted to receive. There were really not more than *three* who were not stamped by appearance, diction, or manner as belonging to a low social station, and as having no claims to the conventional title of "gentlemen." It was manifestly a mob of low-bred, illiterate, tenth-rate attorneys, though it included many successful and conspicuous practitioners. Such is the bar of New York.[10]

The power of upper-middle-class status, which helped preserve the professionalism of the Massachusetts bar, was far more tenuous in New York City. All the more significant then is the hope Strong voiced at the end of his dismal assessment of the New York bar: "May our Columbia College Law School do something to elevate it."[11]

Strong had played an important part in creating Columbia Law School. Elected to the Board of Trustees of Columbia College on December 5, 1853, at the comparatively young age of thirty-three, his addition to that distinguished group was considered a victory for the "progressive" members of the board whose program included both moving the institution uptown and expanding the college into a university.[12] Legal instruction had been given at Columbia in times past, and establishment of a law school became one of the first goals of those who wished to institute university instruction. The goal was accomplished in 1858. On November 1 of that year Theodore Dwight gave his introductory lecture as professor of law.[13]

The new school was designed to offer the sort of instruction that would be of use to practicing lawyers. As the committee of trustees charged with organizing the new school reported:

> A greater probability of success will attend this Department, should it be organized with a view of actual admission to the Bar: and that instruction in other and higher branches not absolutely necessary for such admission, may be superadded to the course, and placed within the reach of the Students.[14]

Strong was certain that was the best way to proceed. There was little demand, he felt, for higher education that would attract students only by offering scholarships which Columbia could not afford. The way to begin, therefore, was to create schools designed to "plainly produce thoroughly trained lawyers" and other professionals. "Exhibit a seductive bait of tangible material advantage," he wrote in his diary, "and you will catch students." Once caught, they can be pushed into more liberal studies as the price of acquiring "all the armory of the mere lawyer."[15]

The trustees hired as their professor the man who became probably the most renowned law teacher in the United States, at least until Langdell. Born in 1822 in upstate New York, Theodore Dwight was by ancestry a New Englander and related to the Dwight family that provided Yale with two presidents. He attended Yale Law School but left without completing the course to take the position of tutor at Hamilton College, his alma mater. There he taught law among other subjects, but eventually made it his main pursuit, organizing a department of law and obtaining incorporation from the New York legislature in 1853.[16]

The mission Dwight framed for his school in New York resembled Langdell's aim in Cambridge. He hoped to correct the deficiencies in the usual preparation for the bar by exposing his students to the study of law as a science of principles. Without the knowledge of principles these young lawyers "make the law a trade, a mere mechanical employment; that instead of being artists in their profession, they are content with being artisans."[17] Here then was a school dedicated to producing properly professional lawyers and associated with an educational institution whose leadership reflected the best part of society.[18] The profession itself played an important role in forming the new school. Lawyers were the most numerous occupational group among the Columbia trustees, and prominent New York practitioners lectured on special topics beginning in fall 1859.[19] All in all, Strong had good reason to hope that the institution he had done so much to help create would uplift the profession.

In 1860 the young school even won a signal victory: through Dwight's vigorous advocacy before the court of appeals, legislation was passed granting the school the privilege of admitting its graduates directly to practice.[20] This "diploma privilege" had first been given to the law department of Hamilton College in 1855 when Dwight taught there.[21] Similar grants were made to the law departments at the University of Albany in 1859 and at both Columbia and the University of the City of New York (now New York University) in 1860.[22] The legislation for Columbia stated that the professors of the law school and the members of the Law Committee of the Trustees who were lawyers could examine the school's students and recommend them for admission. Examination and recommendation for the diploma sufficed to admit students to the bar, as long as they had completed a course of study of at least eighteen months. Thus examination by officers of the school replaced examination by the supreme court, which until then was the usual route to the New York bar.

Despite the legislative sanction, at least some judges of the supreme court were displeased with this usurpation of their function. When the admission of graduates of New York University was moved before the court under the statute applicable to that institution, the motion was denied.[23] The admission of Columbia graduates was moved the next day and denied on the same grounds.[24] The denials were appealed to the court of appeals, Dwight arguing successfully for the admission of the graduates.[25]

The decision of the court of appeals would seem to have been a triumph for the infant school. Strong certainly saw it that way, and even accepted the original defeat cheerfully, believing it would be reversed. In the meantime it was "generally discussed and condemned" and also "advertises us [Columbia] most effectively."[26] Strong confided to his diary his contempt for the judges who made the original ruling:

> I have the opinion of the court on the [New York] university application, and a most shallow and flippant production it is. The legislature is bad enough, but our courts are little better. Witness the arrogance with which these three judges, two of them second-rate lawyers, and the third (Leonard) a tenth-rate, groggy attorney, overrule and nullify an act of the legislature, without even hearing counsel. They ought to be impeached. . . . A bench adorned by Leonard and others naturally dreads an educated bar, and instinctively discourages whatever tends to raise the professional standard from its present zero point of utter degradation.[27]

In New York in 1860 legislative control of admission to the bar and the diploma privilege granted by the legislature encouraged law schools. Lawyers like Strong saw it as a positive element in the struggle to upgrade the bar, at least in part because it removed power over admission from a corrupt and stupid judiciary. Sixteen years later, however, Langdell clearly regarded the power of the state over entrance to the profession as inimical to his task and that of his school.[28] At the same time, the newly organized Association of the Bar of the City of New York was vigorously attacking the diploma privilege in the name of professional betterment. To the self-styled reformers of the legal profession in New York, Columbia Law School had become, if not the enemy, at least an obstacle to the accomplishment of their aims. The school of Langdell and Eliot, in contrast, fitted their plans quite well.

The erosion of the Columbia school in the eyes of the very men who had helped found it seems to have begun with the amendment of the New York Constitution in 1869. On November 2 of that year the voters approved a new judiciary article.[29] It omitted the language of Section 8 of the former article relating to admission to the bar. In April 1871 the legislature passed a statute allowing the court of appeals to govern admission through rules of court. While there was some concern that the failure to repeal section 75 of the Judiciary Act of 1847 would prevent the high court from requiring a specific period of study for admission, those fears proved to be unfounded.[30] No challenge on that ground was mounted to the court's rules promulgated on May 1, 1871.[31]

Those rules continued to permit admission on examination by the New York Supreme Court and the requirements of legal majority, citizenship, and good moral character. They also added what the 1847 Judiciary Act had specifically prohibited—a period of study. Every candidate for admission was obliged to have served "a regular clerkship of three years in the office of a practicing attorney of the supreme court, after the age of seventeen years." While the clerkship requirement harked back to the notion of an apprenticeship, formal legal education in a school was not ignored. Rule 7 allowed the substitution for one year of clerkship of one year

> actually spent in regular attendance upon the law lectures in the university of New York, Cambridge university [Harvard], or the law school connected with Yale college, or a law school connected with any college or university of this state, having a department organized with competent professors and teachers, in which instruction in the science of law is regularly given.[32]

The provision aimed to improve the state of the profession, and Strong for one was pleased with the restoration of a period of study.[33] The *Albany Law Journal* offered frequent editorial comments supporting the new rules as the best hope for restoring the position of the bar to what it had been a generation before.[34] The nature of that fondly remembered position is difficult to understand. The editor of the *Journal* described a golden age in which lawyers filled the offices of public trust, while at the same time earning good livings at a bar free of "great numbers of uneducated men" who bring on a regime of "over-competition."[35]

The judgment that legal practice in New York was marked by overcompetition depends, of course, on the observer's view of what is legitimate business. In the age of Gould and Fisk, of the Erie War and the gold corner, of Tammany Hall and Boss Tweed there was business aplenty, but much of it, at least in the eyes of some, was far from honorable. The techniques used in the struggle to control the Erie Railroad especially aroused the ire of observers of the profession. Injunctions and counter-injunctions flew, along with criticisms of the judges who issued them and the lawyers who prepared the papers on which they were granted. The *locus classicus* of the criticism is Charles Francis Adams, Jr.'s, "A Chapter of Erie":

> No portion of our system was left untested, and no portion showed itself to be sound. The stock exchange revealed itself as a haunt of gamblers and a den of thieves; the offices of our great corporations appeared as the secret chambers in which trustees plotted the spoliation of their wards; the law became a ready engine for the furtherance of wrong, and the ermine of the judge did not conceal the eagerness of the partisan; the halls of legislation were transformed into a mart in which the price of votes was higgled over, and laws, made to order, were bought and sold; while under all, and through all, the voice of public opinion was silent or was disregarded.[36]

At least some segment of the public was aroused. Describing the oratory at the Columbia Law School commencement in May 1869, Strong found it notable that all four speakers had independently chosen the theme of the need for "revolutionary action" should no legal remedy be found for the increasing corruption "in our legislative bodies, our great corporations, and now even in the state judiciary, and in the sheriff's office." "Such things," he wrote, "are 'in the air.'"[37] One of the speakers, Henry Nicoll, after lamenting "the surging tide of corruption which threatens to overwhelm us" and the degeneration of the bar "into a merely sordid vocation, whose highest aspiration is the acquisition of wealth," suggested a remedy. An organization of the good men of the profession, he asserted, "would largely prevent fraud and crime" by "terrifying" the evildoers and thus become the nucleus for sound public opinion.[38]

Such an organization came into existence on February 1, 1870, with the founding of the Association of the Bar of the City of New York.[39] It was clearly designed to bring together the "best men" of the profession in an organization that would help stem the tide of corruption and, more particularly, help purify the bar and the bench. As an organization, it took part in the prosecutions of the judges most closely associated with the machinations surrounding the railroad controversies. Many of its members took the lead in prosecuting Tweed and in the efforts of the Committee of Seventy to reform city politics.[40]

The participation of the association in such activities was less than that of its individual members. The decision to further the investigations of the judges was opposed by some members who felt that the organization should limit itself to the reform of the bar.[41] When the flurry of prosecutions ended, the reform impulse seems to have diminished generally, and many of the members once prominent in the reform movement gave up active participation in the association.[42] Those who assumed positions of influence were concerned with more narrowly professional projects, especially stiffening the qualifications for admission to the bar.

Ironically enough, the reforms of 1871 precipitated the struggle over standards for admission to the bar. The rules promulgated in that year had required for the first time since the adoption of the Constitution of 1846 a definite period of study before admission. There was, however, a loophole which Strong glimpsed: "I believe our law school retains its privileges under the Act of April, 1860."[43] The statute empowering the court of appeals to make rules governing admission preserved the diploma privilege of Columbia and Albany.[44] Suddenly the schools had become the easy route to the bar.[45]

During the 1860s and 1870s Strong remained a faithful member of the law committee of the Columbia trustees. He regularly participated in the annual examination of the graduates, which gave them their degree and the right to practice. As the years wore on, his optimism about the school declined. By 1873 he was clearly disillusioned. Dwight was too kind to the students. "Under fairly strict examiners," Strong confided to his diary, "I believe a third of every graduating class would fail."[46] Dwight was the source of other problems as well. He adamantly opposed adding faculty, appointments which in Strong's view were needed "to render the school an institution not wholly dependent on [Dwight's] life and health." "Were he laid up for a month with a bad cold or a broken limb," the worried trustee wrote, "the School would collapse and disappear."[47] Strong believed that Dwight's opposition to new appointments arose from his fear of losing income. Dwight received a portion of the fees paid by the students, and Strong concluded that "he thinks more than so able and so rich a man ought about the diminution of his income by the introduction of an adjunct paid out of the fees."[48] John W. Burgess, who came to Columbia in 1876, made the same observation: "It was to the pecuniary interest of Professor Dwight to have as many students as possible, and as few instructors as possible unless he could throw the paying of their salaries on the trustees of the college."[49] Presumably, the professor's generosity as an examiner rested at least in part on similar sentiments. If everyone passed, everyone would be admitted to practice, and enrollment and the total fees would remain high.

Paradoxically, then, the very success of the school was endangering the integrity of the bar. The problem was partly met in 1874 when the trustees voted that, beginning with the 1876–1877 school year, candidates for admission who were not college graduates would have to pass an examination that included Latin translation. Strong was certain that the new test would greatly improve the character of the students: "This will keep out the little scrubs (German Jew boys mostly) whom the School now promotes from grocery counters in Avenue B to be 'gentlemen of the bar.'"[50]

Strong's prejudices are quite freely expressed in his diary and extended widely. The talk of overcrowding at the bar and excessively easy access to the profession through the law schools may very well have been based in part on dislike of those who were doing the crowding, the people who were unlike George Templeton Strong in religion and ethnicity, the immigrant newcomers to the bustling world of New York. Increasing the formal requirements for admission would exclude them. Presumably those who were not the "right sort" had little opportunity to learn Latin.[51]

In spite of these efforts by the trustees, Columbia was still, in the words of Justice Noah Davis of the New York Supreme Court, "a cheap, easy and *secure* road to the bar."[52] The diploma privilege did not finally come to an end until 1882. The struggle was intense. It began on June 1, 1875, when the supreme court justices adopted a resolution urging the legislature to repeal the diploma privilege and to require an examination of all candidates.[53] In November the Association of the Bar appointed a committee to consider the matter and received its report a month later. The committee lamented the increase in lawyers and the resultant "crowding" of the profession; it blamed this condition on the schools that advertise themselves as the easy way to the bar. The schools' attitude "fosters the spirit of cramming, of superficial knowledge and undigested reading."[54] It lauded the move toward a preliminary examination, but found Columbia's inadequate. The report ended with a series of resolutions, the most important of which called on the legislature to require all candidates seeking admission to undergo a period of clerkship.[55] In the end, however, Dwight and his allies on the committee prevented the association from taking any action on the report. The committee made no further reports, and the role of the Association of the Bar in the debate over standards of admission to the bar ended.[56]

The struggle then shifted to the New York legislature, which in 1876 revised the laws organizing the courts and gave the judges of the court of appeals the option of preserving the privileges granted to the law schools. Before the judges could act, however, the friends of the law schools persuaded the legislature to pass an act preserving the diploma privilege for those who had entered law school before April 1, 1876. The privilege was extended from year to year, to the increasing consternation of its opponents, who now included the newly formed New York State Bar Association.[57] Individual lawyers often appeared as *amici curiae* to oppose the admission of law school graduates, and succeeded in blocking at least one graduate on the grounds that his supporting documentation showed that he had attended Columbia only seventeen and one-fourth months rather than the eighteen months required by the statute.[58] The yearly extension of the diploma privilege finally ended in 1882, when the legislature refused another year's extension. Dwight and the chief judge of the court of appeals in effect negotiated a treaty that preserved the idea of a year's clerkship for admission of law school graduates but allowed the candidate to count toward the requirement work in an office done during summer vacations.[59]

The long history of tension and conflict between the leading representatives of law schools in the City of New York and prominent attorneys who professed to desire only to improve the profession contrasts with the generally favorable response of Eliot and Langdell to the efforts of these New York lawyers. The rules the court of appeals promulgated in late 1877, which excluded the diploma privilege, mandated a period of clerkship before admission.[60] Up to one year of legal study in a law school in New York State could be applied to replace one year of the required clerkship.[61] This discrimination in favor of New York schools annoyed Langdell and led President Eliot to intensive lobbying of Chief Judge Sanford E. Church.[62] The court of appeals responded the following year by amending the rules to allow an applicant holding a degree from any law school outside the state to apply the time spent in that school to the clerkship requirement.[63]

That modification of the rules of the court of appeals was all Harvard needed. Superficially, New York schools appeared to enjoy an advantage: candidates who attended out of state law schools had to be graduates if their time in school was to be counted toward the clerkship requirement.[64] In fact, this resolution may have been more advantageous than strict equality since it encouraged New Yorkers who chose to come to Harvard to stay for the degree. Harvard's equanimity in the face of the bar's efforts is telling. Eliot and Langdell simply wanted to avoid invidious discrimination. Eliot himself specifically rejected the diploma privilege.[65] Together, the dean and the president resolutely implemented a program to stiffen requirements that was compatible with the views of the reform-minded bar.

During the 1870s Harvard transformed the structure of legal education. The course of instruction was reorganized into a "graded curriculum" with specific courses ending with exams that had to be passed before students could continue their studies. Entrance standards were raised, and an entrance examination, including Latin, was required of those who were not college graduates. A third year of study was established.[66] Eliot summed up the effect of all these changes in his report for 1874–1875: "[T]he whole tone of the School [has] changed from laxity to strictness."[67] Meanwhile, Dwight was carrying on at Columbia much as he had in the 1860s. He may have been more dynamic than Parsons, Parker, and Washburn, but the lectures and recitations and oral examinations of his Columbia recalled their vanished Harvard.

There was another striking difference between the two law schools. Until 1878 Columbia was still in effect a proprietary school. Dwight's compensation depended on the fees of the students he could attract. Attempts to increase the size of the faculty and to tighten standards threatened Dwight's income. At Harvard, in contrast, the school was clearly part of the university and the faculty were paid salaries.[68] In addition, neither Eliot nor Langdell, at least in their more confident moments, had any qualms about the loss of revenue that might result from increasing standards.[69] In Eliot's view, the eventual consequence would be greater prosperity. As the school demands "greater attainments on the part of its students," its degree will become all the "more valued and more valuable."[70]

Eliot's acceptance of the blame for the low standards afflicting the professions was just as striking as the changes wrought at Harvard, and perhaps even more gratifying to those lawyers determined to enhance the profession's status. Assessing Harvard's decision in early 1875 to require a college degree for admission to legal or medical studies (a requirement softened by providing "for the present" for admission by examination), Eliot claimed the university was "only doing its duty to the learned professions of Law and Medicine, which have been for fifty years in process of degradation through the barbarous practice of admitting to them persons wholly destitute of academic culture." Had the schools demanded preliminary academic training, "most of them could have procured it from a large proportion, at least, of their pupils." "It is not the young men of the country, or their parents, who are responsible for the present degraded state of professional education," he wrote, "but the Faculties and the Governors of the modern American professional schools," who, fearful of diminishing enrollment, have failed to require serious preliminary training. Eliot linked this momentous decision with the changes in methods of teaching and evaluation at both professional schools. "So long as lectures were the only means of teaching in the Law and Medical Schools of this University," lack of preparation did not have much impact on "the efficiency of the instruction." But with the adoption of "catechetical methods in both Schools," the questioning of students on the original sources, the presence of untrained students in the classroom "became at once a serious impediment."[71]

Here then was a university president who gave his full support to the efforts of the dean of his law school to put into effect a program of raising standards, which closely paralleled that put forward by lawyers like Strong and others who hoped to strengthen the bar through better education. Nor was it unimportant that Eliot's own criticisms of the recent history of professional education often echoed what the lawyers were saying. Eliot's strictures could easily have been turned into criticism of Columbia. Whatever the profession thought about the courses and methods of Harvard, the organization of the school and the structure of professional education offered there met its demands. Eliot and Langdell had transformed the law school from the enemy of stricter professional standards to one of its strongest allies.

The appeal of the reformed Harvard to those who wished to better the profession had a wider basis than raising standards. The mission of the school to investigate and propagate legal science also may have attracted self-consciously professional lawyers, especially in Eastern cities.

Oliver Wendell Holmes, Jr.'s oration on "The Use of Law Schools" to the founding meeting of the Harvard Law School Association in 1886 illustrates the nature of the relationship between the new model of legal eduation and professional aspirations."[72] The chief justice of the Massachusetts Supreme Judicial Court duly celebrated the advantages of the new methods. When he had taught torts in the law school, he "plunged a class of beginners straight into Mr. Ames's collection of cases, and we began to discuss them together in Mr. Langdell's method." The result was gratifying—"my class examined the questions proposed with an accuracy of view which they never could have learned from text-books, and often exceeded that to be found in the text-books." As a judge, he had seen that young lawyers brought up on the Harvard method are better served by their education than the lawyers of his own generation were served by theirs. He also acclaimed the Harvard practice of taking students "to the bottom of what they seek to know" as the most practical form of legal education.[73]

Holmes's words of comfort for the current regime were tacked onto the end of his talk.[74] The bulk of the address was devoted to an exposition of the school's task, which was both abstract and perhaps remote from the "practical" lawyer's daily work. Holmes began by observing that "all the education which man can get from others is moral, not intellectual"; it should shape interests and aims. The law school, therefore, must "teach law in the grand manner" and thereby "make great lawyers." To ensure these results, the law school "should be at once the workshop and the nursery of specialists." A specialist is simply the master of a particular branch of human knowledge. A specialist is also a man of power and of great social responsibility. His task is to correct the excesses of equality which play havoc with the true hierarchical order of things. "When the passion for equality is not content with founding social intercourse upon universal human sympathy, and a community of interests in which all may share, but attacks the lines of Nature which establish orders and degrees among the souls of men," the times are badly out of joint and specialists must apply traction by compelling to "obedience and respect" those who can only conduct their affairs with the help of their superiors. Fortunately, all lawyers are specialists, although some members of the profession have imbibed the "spirit of the times" and become intoxicated with "'smartness' as against dignity of moral feeling and profundity of knowledge." The law school must set its face against such error. It has done so in the past, but the past cannot be a model since "Story's simple philosophizing has ceased to satisfy men's minds." A new age has dawned and under the German sun "science is gradually drawing legal history into its sphere. The facts are being scrutinized by eyes microscopic in intensity and panoramic in scope." With new intellectual tools the law will be refashioned and restated, its rules and principles generalized, and the professors of the Harvard Law School "will be found to have had a hand in the change not less important than that which Story has had in determining the form of the text books of the last century."

Holmes was to repeat elements of his brief oration at the opening of Boston University's new law school building in 1897.[75] The exaulted professionalism of the Harvard address was sharpened. He told his audience: "To an imagination of any scope the most far-reaching form of power is not money, it is the command of ideas. And happiness . . . cannot be won simply by being counsel for great corporations and having an income of fifty thousand dollars." The only practicality lies in "going to the bottom of the subject." In some ways, Holmes's approach to greatness for his calling is a reflection of that fascination with rigor and the strenuous life that was his and others' legacy from the Civil War. More intimately, it may have been a reflection of his own strong desire to carve out a life of influence and power and also a severe judgment on what he saw as his father's failure to accomplish great work. Certainly, during his speech to the law school association he seemed to depreciate his father's part in the Harvard anniversary celebrations: "Perhaps, without revealing family secrets, I may whisper that next Monday's poet also tasted our masculine diet before seeking more easily digested, if not more nutritious, food elsewhere."[76]

One did not have to be a veteran of the Civil War or Dr. Holmes's son to appreciate the justice's rhetoric. He laid before his fellows a noble prospect, one which summoned lawyers to a commanding role in American life. Before the Civil War elite lawyers had occupied the ramparts of the Constitution and used in its defense their mastery of a legal science of transcendent principles, as well as their status as educated men whose oratorical talents were important to the functioning of the polity. Their descendants were embarrassed by the "smartness" Holmes attacked; growing commercialization threatened to rob the law of its dignity as a profession. The revival of the bar association movement after the Civil War was strongly influenced by the desire of some lawyers to foster the cooperation among right-thinking lawyers that was necessary for promoting professional self-regulation.[77] The exalted vision Holmes presented evoked comforting thoughts about the social role and position of the accomplished—or for younger men, promising—lawyer. The glorification of the lawyer as lawyer came to supplant the antebellum image of the great lawyer as cultured statesman. In 1809 William Wirt hoped to contribute to "opening, raising, refining and improving the understandings of my countrymen by means of light and cheap publications" which would bear favorable comparison to Voltaire.[78] Holmes found his model of greatness in the seminar of the German university.

Holmes's vision thus served a professional purpose, although it was erudite enough to alienate some. His deprecating reference to Story may have called forth the detailed praise of that great jurist in the after dinner speeches on that celebratory day.[79] By even suggesting that Story had limitations, Holmes affronted the ancestor cult which plays an important part in lawyerly celebration of social cohesion and indeed in alumni rites as well. Story was a particularly venerated figure. His great influence on the law through his treatises and activities on the Supreme Court was a comforting reminder of lawyers' power and an anodyne to fears of social change.[80] Holmes's emphasis on philosophizing also upset those who were most concerned with remodeling the school's image. John Chipman Gray hastened to assure his audience that Holmes "hit what I think is the merit of the School, so far as it has any merit, that we try to teach the law in a large manner, but not, on that account, in any the less practical way."[81]

Careful cultivation of a science of the law closely associated with the needs of practice could, however, provide a substitute for the broader cultural aspirations of earlier days. The growing complexity of lawyerly business in the large cities promoted such a substitution. Lawrence Friedman's summary of the story of the growth of the Cravath firm fairly depicts the nature of the new substance of elite legal practice:

> Between 1880 and 1900, the career of the firm was intimately bound up with Wall Street finance; it drew up papers merging businesses, it advised railroads on their legal affairs, handled stockholders' suits, floated bond issues . . . . It was a servant and adviser to big business, an architect of financial structures; it did not feed on lawsuits, rather it avoided them.[82]

Skill in oratory and public display counted for little. Routine legal business was far more complex and ad hoc than conveyancing and title searches had been. The growth of firms helped efface the individual lawyer, minimizing his opportunities for public display and blurring any single lawyer's contributions to a successful undertaking.[83] The knowledge of law itself and skill in applying it could appear to justify the claim to learned professional status. The ultimate appeal of the new Harvard Law School may have derived from the way new institutional arrangements fostered such a claim. It is not surprising that such should be the result. Eliot set out to restore the learned nature of the professions. A three-year course, real criteria for admission, rigorous examinations and standards of classroom performance, the intensive nature of study from the sources rather than from texts, the existence of a professional faculty devoting all its time to promoting hard work and demanding study—all these factors contributed mightily to the Harvard lawyer's self-image. The crowning touch was the status of specialist that the rigorous institution conferred, a status that would stand firm against attempts to erase the natural distinctions among the souls of men. Not only did it reveal a side of Holmes obscured by the adulation received in his later years, but it appealed to fears that many prosperous Americans, lawyers included, felt in the year of widespread labor unrest and the Haymarket riot.[84] The institution of the law school helped build the institution of the bar.[85]

Case Method Comes to Columbia

The reformed Harvard appealed not merely to those members of the profession who were concerned with professional standards. Professional educators, men who like Eliot sought to create the modern universities, could also find in Eliot's law school the example of the sort of law school they wanted. The first and most spectacular example of the spread of the model after its firm establishment at Harvard was the revolution that swept the law school of Columbia University. The changes at Columbia in 1891 created the first important reproduction of the Harvard model and helped fuel a wide-ranging debate about the importance of those changes for the future of legal education. The transformation in Cambridge had not passed unnoticed during the 1870s and 1880s. The founding of Boston University Law School derived from skepticism about the wisdom of the course pursued by Eliot and Langdell, and a small amount of commentary had appeared in print. After the Columbia upheaval, however, a debate was clearly joined and its arena began to widen. For the first time, the American Bar Association became an important forum, and the resulting committee reports, papers, and discussions reveal deep-seated clashes about the nature of American law that underlay the conflict over the proper conduct of legal education.

Before investigating the larger debate, however, it is necessary to examine the events at Columbia and the light they shed on the attitudes toward legal education of late nineteenth-century administrators and students of one important university. The story of the reorganization of the Columbia Law School resembles in many ways a reenactment of the events at Harvard twenty years before. Seth Low played the part of Charles Eliot, and William Keener, one of Langdell's students and colleagues, was the innovative teacher. William Chase and Theodore Dwight divided between them the role of defender of the old ways first filled by Joel Parker. The students seemed to have reacted much as Harvard's students did, recording their thoughts in the pages of the *Columbia Law Times*.

The Columbia Law School in 1889 was still the place that had angered and frustrated the aging George Templeton Strong. While it had been financially integrated into the university and was no longer a proprietary institution, it still lacked entrance requirements and had only recently lost the diploma privilege. Theodore Dwight, warden of the school, continued to dominate the entire enterprise, but agitation for change, specifically for extension of the course to three years and for requiring three years of college study for admission, had begun in 1881. Although supported by both John W. Burgess, who was responsible for the school's elective courses on public law, and the president of Columbia College, Frederick A. P. Barnard, seven years passed before a majority of the Board of Trustees and its law committee approved resolutions establishing a third year of study.[86]

The committee's rationale for the change exhibits the same belief in the academic nature of the degree and the corresponding deemphasis on preparation for admission to practice that marked Eliot's and Langdell's position in the controversy over requirements for admission to the New York bar. In its report to the trustees, the committee admitted that when the school held the diploma privilege and when opportunities for legal education outside the law school were few, the two-year course "was an important step towards elevating the standards, then very low, of legal requirements." "But that day is past," the committee wrote. Since New York required three years of study for admission to practice and accepted a certificate of attendance at law school as evidence that the period has been met, the time for change had come. The conclusion was clear: "The diploma, . . . should be restored to its purely scholastic value."[87] By adhering to rigorous academic standards set by its faculty, Harvard claimed to prepare students to be accomplished, scholarly, and, of course, competent professionals. Now Columbia expressed its desire to train students according to the same notion of what made a good lawyer and to make its degree representative of a more thorough understanding of the law rather than of the minimum knowledge necessary to begin practice. Once again a university law school was asserting its competence and power to govern professional education.

In spite of the unmistakable direction of the trustees, Dwight's law faculty dragged its feet. Delay was possible, at least in part, because the issue was caught up in the larger debate over the future of Columbia College. With Seth Low's appointment as president in October 1889, those who wished to see Columbia become a modern university gained the upper hand, and the days of the old Columbia Law School were numbered.[88] Low had no patience with Dwight's obstruction of the third-year curriculum. When the opportunity came to expand the law faculty, Low selected a man completely identified with the new methods, William Albert Keener, Story Professor of Law at Harvard Law School. Just as Eliot sought to appoint an ally to the Harvard law faculty at the time he began his campaign for standards, Low went looking for and found the man to remodel his law school along the lines of what was widely regarded as the leading university law school in the country. At least, that is assumed to have been his goal. As the official history of the school states: "Why President Low should have brought him [Keener] to Columbia is conjectural, but it seems clear that Low believed Dwight's school to be moribund."[89] "Moribund" is too strong a word. After all, in 1890–1891 the school had over 600 students and was the largest law school in the country.[90] What it was not was the newfangled university law school Harvard had become, complete with a graded course, rigorous admission standards, and a faculty devoted to research and publication, as well as teaching.

One aspect of the appointment of Keener to Columbia illustrates the degree to which legal education was already an academic enterprise rather than an extension of professional practice. Keener's appointment to the Harvard faculty after only a short time in practice had been controversial and had occurred at least as much out of necessity as out of a belief in the possibility of forming a professional legal academic class. Low apparently thought first of an academic lawyer for the new position at Columbia and sought out Keener as early as January 1890. The new president of Columbia seems to have planned his approach well, because with Dwight's cooperation in the matter of reserving a lectureship for his prospective colleague, Low was able to pay Keener slightly more compensation than he was receiving at Harvard.[91] The matter of salary was not a minor one. Keener explained his resignation from the Harvard faculty solely in terms of a dispute over salary.[92] Low meddled in these troubled waters and could be considered to have carried out an early academic raid to bring new talent to his law school. For the first time, it seems, a university president desiring to improve his law faculty had a pool of academic talent from which to recruit, recruitment made easier because the teachers depended totally on their academic salaries. The modern world of legal education was coming into being.

Whatever Low's plans when Keener was hired, his subsequent policy toward the law school shows that he considered the new professor to be his ally in the campaign for academic standards. When Dwight and the majority of the faculty resisted the president's plans, Low turned to Keener to draft a scheme to implement them. Soon after learning of Low's actions, Dwight announced his retirement at the end of the 1890–1891 academic year. Two months later, professors George Chase and Richard Petty resigned, effectively leaving Keener as the only full-time member of the faculty.[93]

The causes of the schism were many, although the slight to the venerable Warden implicit in the president's consulting with Keener on how to implement his plans seems to have played an important part. All of Low's actions, in fact, indicate that in his view it would be better for the school if Dwight were to depart. Dwight had several specific objections to Low's plans for the school, although he was adamant about the unsoundness of the graded curriculum and the futility of the attempt to bring political science courses into the law school.[94] The first of these changes was certainly the adoption of part of the Harvard scheme. The second was alien to the Harvard view of the content of proper legal education. As the curriculum emerged from the turmoil of the spring of 1891, it looked very much like the Harvard plan of study.[95] But neither aspect of Low's plan became the focal point of disagreement between the supporters of the old and the new regimes. The public debate pitted the case method of instruction against the "Dwight method."

Dwight's fame rested almost entirely on his ability as a teacher. Indeed, his distinctive method of teaching was as closely associated with the Columbia Law School as the case method was with Harvard. That method of teaching was as characteristic of the old regime as were the administrative arrangements at the school. In the words of the official history of the school, "Professor Dwight was still employing in the eighties the same methods of instruction he had introduced at Columbia in 1858."[96]

The technique was based on the recitation, that most characteristic feature of the old education. For Dwight, however, the old ways were tried and true. He described his methods in an article on Columbia written in 1889:

> The central idea in instruction has always been this: the student is assigned daily a certain portion of an approved text-book for his reading prior to listening to expositions of the subject involved. To make the assignment effective, he is asked questions upon the topic, mainly to make it certain that he has studied the subject and has in a measure comprehended it, and is thus in a position to listen with advantage to expositions.[97]

The method aimed to inculcate in students a knowledge of the principles of the law. Only a thorough acquaintance with them would enable a lawyer to deal with the intricate questions that arise in practice. As Dwight put it in 1890 in an article explaining the objects of the new three-year curriculum, the rules were many, but "these rules for the most part cluster around great and unchanging principles. He who is master of these has an invaluable clue to the labyrinth." Dwight did not slight the importance of training students to "think like a lawyer." In the same article he wrote that one goal of the first two years of study is "to teach the student *how to think*, and to work out by a mere course of reasoning cases that may be presented to him for solution."[98] In spite of the resemblance between Dwight's aims and those of the Harvard faculty who used the case method, he emphatically rejected their method. For him and for his supporters it put the cart before the horse, needlessly confusing beginning students by exposing them to the raw material of the law rather than to the final product created from that material by treatise writers. George Chase, one of Dwight's associates who left Columbia to help found New York Law School in an effort to perpetuate the Dwight method, compared teaching law by the case method to requiring the student of history to ignore Parkman's volumes in favor of attempting to reproduce the master's conclusions by rereading and reanalyzing all the original sources Parkman had consulted.[99]

Dwight even tried to appropriate one of the most prominent selling points of the case method. He maintained that his method, far from being merely a matter of lecturing, embodied the true Socratic method—that is, a method of teaching by oral colloquy adapted to the needs of each individual student.[100] Chase elaborated this point:

> [The student] is called upon to recite, not that he may repeat, parrot-like, the words of the book, but that he may show and develop his capacity to state in his own language the knowledge he has acquired. He is encouraged to ask questions, in order that his own individual needs may be met. And the professor's constant endeavor is, by teaching the law as a system of principles, by unfolding the reasons upon which these principles depend, by simplifying abstruse statements of doctrine, by illustrations drawn from the reports and from practical life, to give vitality and interest to the whole course of instruction, and to adapt it to the student's comprehension.[101]

Central to the argument for the older method of teaching is the emphasis on individualized instruction. This concern is, in turn, a reflection of one of Dwight's fundamental beliefs. The case method, Dwight wrote in 1889, has its advantages "particularly in reference to the superior class of students," but it is "inferior to true teaching in its effects upon those of average powers." Those of average powers, in turn, "fill most respectably and usefully the humbler avenues of professional life."[102] Dwight was proud to teach the great middling crowd of attorneys. In fact, in Chase's description of the Dwight method, all difficult analysis was left to the teacher. In Chase's view, the glory of the Dwight system was Dwight's grasp of all the difficult aspects of the law. Having himself come "out of darkness into light," he then stated the topic "so simply and clearly, that the veriest tyro in the law can comprehend it, if not in full measure, still up to the full limit of his own capacity."[103] Such an approach had no place in Cambridge where the difficulty of the case method was one of its most important virtues.

The Columbia students seemed to place high value on Dwight's method. Most of the complaints about the events of the spring of 1891, collected in the student-published *Columbia Law Times* under the title "The Law School Crisis," concerned the role of Dwight's teaching in drawing them to the school and their deprecation of the case method.[104] Predictably, the class of 1892 in its petition to the trustees requested an exemption from the requirements of the new regime which would govern them during their final year on the grounds that they had "entered the college upon the faith in and reputation of its professors and distinctive method."[105] In the same issue, the editors maintained that, while Dwight's resignation was the natural result of advancing age, the subsequent resignations of Chase and Petty implied that there was serious trouble and that Keener was behind it: "He and his method were the all-absorbing topics."[106] Given the students' attitudes, the question of teaching method dominated discussions of changes at the school.

To advocates of the case method, the failings of the old Columbia regime were almost too obvious. To some observers in Cambridge, Columbia under Dwight was simply a version of the decadent Harvard Law School before Langdell. The editors of the *Harvard Law Review* described the "old Columbia or so-called 'Dwight' system of instruction" as "little more that the discarded Harvard method as pursued by Professors Parsons, Washburn, and others."[107] Indeed, Dwight's and Chase's descriptions of their teaching method exhibit similarities to Parker's and Thayer's ideal classroom experience.

Once again, it is clear that the novelty of the case method did not lie in the activity of questioning students. Skilled use of questioning, whether described as a recitation or as a Socratic dialogue, could test students' understanding and, in the hands of a patient teacher, help even the most confused to grasp the important points. But, as Parker noted, students soon grew tired of demanding classroom work. Similar problems arose at Columbia. Starting in 1887 the *Columbia Law Times* published "officially revised" lecture notes for all law school courses. With the departure of Dwight and the installation of the new regime, the editors of the *Times* abandoned its support of the old policy: "The use in the lecture room of the books of cases," they concluded, "renders it unnecessary; and if a student properly digests the cases therein contained, he will have little use of other citations." Under the old system no one bothered to take notes and everyone waited to the end of term to rush through scores of citations. "The only notes taken by which a student profits are those taken by himself; and one case carefully studied is worth more than a hundred citations filed away and never read."[108] While most of the contemporary student reaction to the "law school crisis" recorded in the *Times* was adverse to Keener's new method, one anonymous student criticized the Dwight regime in terms that echoed the views of the Harvard students who first studied with Langdell:

> Let us face facts. Is there a thoughtful student who does not feel that much of the work here makes him mentally weaker, not stronger; that "cram" is too often the watchword, conceit often the chief result? Candidly, what is the net result of the brain-torturing hours spent over the text-books in contracts? . . . "Attorneyism" is rampant here, especially in the afternoon division, and has had things its own way. The school has tended to produce what most of us, it seems, desire to become, lawyers of memory and practical skill, attorneys in the English sense. I for one shall be glad to see it become a school for the few who wish to fit themselves broadly and deeply for the higher places, who wish to become counsellors, barristers, "jurists," or whatever you may choose to call the lawyers of thought and power. . . . Haste has been in the saddle; thoroughness seems to have seized the reins.[109]

Once the new regime was firmly established, the *Times* both editorially and in articles was even more emphatic about the benefits of rigorous study using the case method. By fall 1892 the editors were regularly lauding the three-year course and the scheduling of classes during the first two years so as to prevent office work. "By that action," they wrote, "Columbia bars out that large class of men who desire a legal education by the royal road of a short cut." The case method also contributed to tougher standards. As a result of these changes, Columbia had become unsuitable for those seeking a superficial education and a magnet to the serious-minded: "If you expect to obtain a degree by a small amount of work, we do not want you here. But if you come with a realization of the importance of the subject, if you are willing to do hard work and original work and steady work, you are welcome at this school." The editorialists saw practical advantages to the students in the new dispensation. It could make the Columbia degree "of more value than a like degree from any other law school in this country."[110]

Two students writing for the *Times* in the course of the 1892–1893 academic year expressed similar views. Both linked the demands of the case method with the formation of truly professional lawyers. For John Hill, Harvard and Columbia were the leading American institutions of legal education, because both "are most decidedly in favor of placing their stamps on future *lawyers*, not artisans." Their alumni would be "prepared for a broader field and a higher plane than the parrot-like quotation of the words of some legal luminary with an endless list of case references that may or may not apply to the case in hand."[111] Sounding the same note, Stanwood Menken in two sentences summed up the close relationship between the intellectual demands of the case method—the desire to strengthen the professional status of lawyers, and the desire on the part of those who governed the modern university to make professional education a respectable part of their educational enterprise:

> To give the student who has the intelligence requisite for the successful lawyer, not only the substantive rudiments, but that analytic feeling which distinguishes the attorney from his counterfeit, is an object of our school. We [students] feel that it cannot be acquired except by the comparative study of cases, and that the requisite effort is not beyond any who possess the ability that can justify a university maintaining the significance of the baccalaureate degree in recommending him to the community as legally competent.[112]

For these students, the important feature of the case method was not classroom interrogation, but the subject of the interrogation. The student of the case method had to do the intellectual labor necessary to extract the law from the cases; the student of the Dwight method was only learning to repeat statements of the law taken secondhand.

Adoption of the case method by Columbia Law School was simply the most conspicuous aspect of a reformation that created in New York the sort of university law school that Harvard had become during the preceding twenty years. The aftermath of the great changes of 1891 also had parallels in what had happened in Cambridge. Just as the Boston University Law School was founded in response to the changes at Harvard, Chase and Petty founded the New York Law School in reaction to the changes that had driven them from Columbia.[113] The case method had not been immediately triumphant at the reformed Harvard, nor was it at the renewed Columbia. Keener's three new colleagues followed their own inclinations in the classroom, although instruction primarily through cases increasingly became the norm.[114] It is clear that the two props of the Harvard Law School also supported Columbia: the desire of the university's president for a law school within the university and the belief of some students that more rigorous standards for admission, pedagogy, and retention would increase the value of their degrees. The measures would be for naught, however, unless the graduates of the reformed school found a place at the bar. Rigor alone was insufficient. The curriculum of the antebellum school had equipped the student with the ability to talk the language of scientific principle and thus participate in legal culture. What could the new model school provide besides the assurance that its graduates were socially acceptable and trained with rigor?

Case Method and Practice

Although the heightened standards and cultural claims of Harvard Law School eventually helped strengthen the self-image of the American bar, the success of the school depended immediately on the marketability of the education it offered. In several ways that education met the needs of the practicing bar, or at least of that segment that was changing in ways that were shaping the future of American legal practice. The case method itself, despite the controversy it provoked, advanced the school's success.

One aspect of a Harvard education which met the needs of the emerging modern profession took place outside the classroom. In fall 1886, fifteen students, several of whom—Joseph Beale, Julian Mack, John Wigmore, Blewitt Lee, and Samuel Williston—were to play important roles in legal education, became the first editorial board of the *Harvard Law Review*.[115] Hoping as they did to give "to all who are interested in the subject of legal education, some idea of what is done under the Harvard system of instruction," their statement of purpose indicated as much devotion to celebrating their school as to advancing legal knowledge.[116] Membership in the *Review*'s board of editors soon acquired special cachet. In 1902 the practice of limiting editorial positions to those students ranking highest at the end of the first year was formally established.[117]

Even earlier, however, the *Review* had served the useful institutional function of conferring distinction. In spring 1886 the faculty made all courses in the second and third year elective, thus destroying the honors course whose definition had so divided the dean and Ames from Gray and Thayer. The honors degree still existed, but it no longer signified a legal education that completely covered every principle and concept necessary to the properly prepared lawyer. Its gradual replacement as evidence of academic distinction by a seat on the board of editors of the *Harvard Law Review* is another illustration of the acceptance of the case method as a methodology and as a means of inculcating mental discipline. An editor of the *Review* spent his time criticizing articles submitted; writing notes of current decisions; and attending to the details of legal bibliography, printing, and perhaps office management. If to outsiders an editorship meant anything beyond good grades in the courses of the first year—themselves seen more and more as devoted to teaching the techniques of study by the case method—it meant training in the skills of written legal argument and legal criticism, in bibliographic conventions that were becoming normative, and in teamwork. Those habits grew in esteem as the advocate replaced the counsellor, written briefs and opinions replaced oratory as the characteristic form of legal communication, and the firm replaced the single practitioner and the two–three-member partnership. In 1886 their fruition lay in the future, yet experience on the law review appealed to the world that was aborning. The law school was evolving into an institution that taught the skills and techniques necessary to succeed in the changing world of metropolitan legal practice.

The case method was the most important means of training in those techiniques. As much as Langdell probably believed in the truth of the principles he extracted from the cases, he lost the battle to keep a prescribed curriculum designed to inculcate those principles. He eventually acquiesced in an elective system which was promoted by his colleagues in terms of the case method itself. Langdell's method of teaching through the use of original sources was promoted as a means of training students to think like lawyers, of introducing them to the sorts of intellectual endeavors they would undertake as practitioners.

The faculty felt obliged to defend the law school's methods in speeches presented as a contribution to the celebrations of the university's 250th anniversary in 1886. Occurring as the reformed school was still trying to find success, the occasion was of great symbolic significance. An uncharitable but acute observer likened the pageantry surrounding the feature event of the law school's observation of the anniversary to a revival meeting.[118] His analogy had a certain aptness. While knowledge of the tensions within the law faculty may not have been widespread, other problems were evident to all who could count. Attendance had declined since the mid-1870s, when a rush to seize the last chance to earn a degree in two years swelled enrollment to just under 200. The third year also failed to attract many students.[119] Thus, the external success of the modern law school was as much in question as was the nature of its internal structure.

In this situation some alumni practicing in Boston took the initiative in creating an organization of their own, the Harvard Law School Association. On July 21, 1886, Darwin E. Ware, John C. Ropes, Henry W. Putnam, Joseph B. Warner, Louis D. Brandeis, William Schofield, and Winthrop H. Wade met to plan the new group. On August 9 they issued a circular to their fellows asking them to come together as a "means of increasing the influence and usefulness of the school" through activities like those of the various Harvard Clubs.[120] This appeal was remarkably successful. By the time of the first general meeting on November 5, 1886, the association numbered 563 members.

The men who gathered in Cambridge on that day witnessed a carefully orchestrated attempt to establish a new image for Harvard Law School. James Carter gave a most effective performance as president of the association. He praised the school's methods as "a vast improvement over those with which I was acquainted when I was a member of the School" in the early 1850s.[121] Far from producing theoreticians, study of law through its sources produced young men "of a great amount of actual acquirement, and—what is of more consequence—an accuracy and precision of method far superior to anything which the students of my day exhibited." Present-day students know how to work hard, and it is hard work that is needed to sift complex facts, identify the most important, and interpret them in the light of the applicable rules and principles. Thus a successful practitioner and leader of the New York bar gave full approval to the product of the modern law school.

Other speakers took pains to emphasize the curriculum's requirement of sound learning and practicality. Eliot contributed to the apotheosis of Langdell by telling the story of the dean's selection while stoutly affirming that "this School has been converted into a scientific school of law without losing its best qualities as a practical school of law."[122] Professor Gray, too, emphasized the school's dedication to practical education and pointed to the examinations—themselves part of the great reform—as not at all theoretical but rather set in such a way as to ensure that the students who can answer the questions can also meet practical problems.[123] Gray emphasized the superiority of the case method as a method of study by recounting his own experience as a student: "When I was a law student," he told the assembled alumni, "I read twenty or thirty text-books through: I fear little of them remained in my mind. I had to begin again with the study of particular cases and learn my law in that way."[124]

Jeremiah Smith gave the fullest testimony, and perhaps the most convincing. Not yet a member of the faculty, Smith spoke as a respected practitioner. Having studied under the lecture system, he was sure of the superiority of the case method: "The mind of a listener has sometimes been compared to a sponge, but I agree with Professor Keener that a better metaphor can be found in a sieve."[125] Teaching by assigning portions of a textbook, hearing recitations, and assigning cases as supplementary work was better than lecturing, but unlike the case method "it does not sufficiently arouse the interest of the student, nor does it compel original thinking." In addition, the case method teaches students to deal with reported opinions, to understand how legal principles interact with the facts of life. Indeed, "the young man who studies and analyzes the cases is doing much the same thing as he will afterwards be called upon to do in practice. He is endeavoring to apply law to facts." He is learning skills of legal analysis, and "it is precisely here that many of us older lawyers make our most disgraceful failures." No more thorough defense of the Harvard methods could be made.

The claim that the case method provided a mental discipline of practical use at the bar became a standard response to criticism of the Harvard methods. In the wake of the controversy over the changes at Columbia, Gray elaborated the argument in his contribution to an unusual collection of articles on legal education in the first volume of the *Yale Law Journal*. He emphasized particularly the rigorous nature of study by the case method. "To the quicker witted," Gray wrote, lectures "are a bore and a waste of time."[126] The demands made on the student by the case method, however, the ability "to give a neat oral statement of the facts and the precise point of law involved, and to show how the decision has extended or modified the law as previously held, will give full occupation to all the faculties of the cleverest man." Gray added a further point to his argument for the case method's superiority. For Eliot the introduction of the case method to legal education was merely one facet of a general reform of the methods of higher education which replaced secondhand learning through textbooks with the study and analysis of original sources. In Gray's view, however, the case method surpassed all other pedagogical methods:

> Many bright young men in school and college develop an extraordinary capacity for having other people's ideas pumped into them, and win rank

> and reputation thereby, but they have never intellectually "labored" in their lives. Our mode of study is a sharp break in their habits and traditions. The result is at first perturbing, often amusingly so, but it is invariably salutary.

Finally, the case method replicates in the classroom what the practicing lawyer does every day in the office: "To extract law from facts is *the* thing . . . [T]o do it well makes the successful lawyer; to do it pre-eminently well makes the great lawyer; a student cannot begin it too early."

Other members of the Harvard faculty also praised the case method for linking pedagogy to what lawyers do in practice. Thayer's views, expressed in the preface to his *Cases on Constitutional Law* of 1895, were approved by both Langdell and Ames.[127] There was nothing new, Thayer maintained, in Langdell's method when considered as a "mere mode of investigation. . . . [L]awyers have always known well enough the necessity of following it in working out their problems." What was new was the application of the technique to instruction in law. Teaching methods might differ, Thayer wrote, but

> as to modes of study, a very different matter, Dean Langdell's associates have all come to agree with him, . . . in thinking, so far at least as our system of law is concerned, that there is no method of preparatory study so good as the one with which his name is so honorably connected—that of studying cases, carefully chosen and arranged so as to present the development of principles.[128]

For Ames, Langdell's greatest student, the case method was training in lawyering. He compared the well-organized casebook to the perfect law office in which clients with all sorts of cases would appear in the order in which "one would arrange the topics of a scientific law-book."[129] Finally, Samuel Williston, one of the first members of the Harvard faculty to be trained in the reformed school, described Langdell's method as the skills of practice brought to the classroom. The dean "sought simply to apply to the systematic study of law the methods habitually used by lawyers in the preparation of particular cases—namely, to study chronologically the previous decisions that seemed applicable to the question at issue, and to extract from them a guiding thread of principle."[130]

The likening of the case method to clinical instruction had been an important argument in favor of the new form of instruction. The argument that it also provided a superior form of mental training was an important addition to the rhetoric of the supporters of the new model school, although it did not originate with them. By the 1890s the emphasis on the practical value and rigor of the training the school provided helped it retain a national student body while the nation's law became more complex and diverse. The case method provided at least the hope of mastering a situation many practitioners saw as almost beyond hope: American law was drowning in reported cases. In 1878 the chief judge of the United States

Court of Claims, Charles D. Drake, gave the graduating class of the Cincinnati Law School a typical analysis of the situation. After observing that there were already some 4,000 volumes of American and British reports with more than 100 new ones arriving every year, he asserted that "this multiplication of Reports tends to diminish the discussion of cases on principle, and to control their decision by the mere club-law, so to speak, of precedents" to the detriment of reliance on principles.[131]

Such concerns are a staple of discourse in a common law system. The whole scientific enterprise of antebellum lawyers aimed to impose order on the numerous cases in which principles were applied to real problems by making the principles clear and well-known. Concern about sustaining order became more acute, however, with the gradual erosion of the framework provided by the common law forms of action. As the writs diminished in importance, successful litigation came to depend increasingly on matching the facts of the current controversy with a pattern of facts that had already been judged to give a cause of action. Langdell's fascination with cases seems to have been nourished at least in part by his experience in practice under the Field Code.[132] More and more states abolished the common law system of pleading, and the role of the individual precedent grew.

One by-product of the decay of the old system of pleading was the multiplication of reporters. With the advent of the Field Code, the number of reporters of the decisions of the New York courts increased, and some were dedicated solely to opinions dealing with matters of pleading and procedure under the code. Opinions of lower courts were now regularly printed, not because they were binding authority—only the decisions of the court of appeals, the highest court of the state, could have that status—but because lawyers needed access to opinions in which the procedural effect of different patterns of fact was considered. In 1866 one New York lawyer estimated that in the seventeen years of the code's existence the courts had rendered some 4,500 opinions interpreting its provisions.[133] Soon there was a market for an annual digest of New York law which tried to classify and summarize these numerous reported cases. By 1882 one commentator observed that the volume of the New York digest for 1881 included cases

> in two volumes of Abbott's New Cases, one of City Court Reports, two of Howard's Practice, three of the Supreme Court, five of the Court of Appeals, one of Civil Procedure Reports, one of New York Superior Court Reports, one of Surrogate Reports, besides the New York Daily Register, Monthly Law Bulletin, and Weekly Digest.[134]

He predicted that soon the law of other states would be in the same sorry mess.

In fact, the nightmare had already become a reality. In 1879 John West published the first of his regional reporters, which within a few years would make available to the profession every opinion of every court of last resort in the United States, as well as the decisions of the federal courts. The nature of the enterprise was clearly dangerous in the eyes of some observers. An anonymous reviewer of the first bound volumes of the West series was aghast at their promiscuousness. Since every opinion was printed in full, "we have a bushel of chaff to every pint of grain."[135] Two years later another observer made much the same point: "The volumes that are constantly falling from the press teem with cases of no interest to the profession or to the public, and are important only to the parties litigant."[136] Such concerns quickened in the mid-1880s as the rapid growth of indiscriminate reporting became a staple of discussion at meetings of the American Bar Association. In 1884 John F. Dillon, prominent judge and railroad lawyer, gave the annual address before the ABA and also noted the rapidly growing numbers of volumes of reports. The question of what, if anything, to do was referred to committee, and largely through Dillon's urging the association adopted a resolution deprecating the ungoverned use of precedent but urging that the publication of opinions in no way be limited by statute.[137]

The resolution of the ABA was a triumph of practicality over theory. Dillon and others believed that reporting cases could yield too much of a good thing, but while lawyers complained about the multiplication of cases, they also asserted that practice without them was impossible. In his address to the class of 1868 at Columbia Law School, Charles Tracy warned that searching all the reports to find a case in point was difficult work. It was effort well spent, however, because to be confronted with an unknown but relevant case meant disaster.[138] In 1886 the editors of the *Central Law Journal* dismissed the assertion that the great number of reported cases caused the problem: "It is idle now to talk of the practice of law at all, without the use of precedents, as indeed it would have been at any period within the life time of the common law; and access to the very latest decisions of the courts is an absolute necessity to a lawyer in active practice."[139] In the same year in an address before the Allegheny Bar Association, Harvey Henderson, a Pittsburgh lawyer, said much the same thing even more pithily: "The necessity of consulting many books is the penalty a lawyer must pay for exercising his profession in this extraordinary age."[140] There is also evidence that legal research was based on cases rather than on principles. An anonymous review in the first volume of the *American Law Review* criticized the author of a treatise on the law of titles to real estate in New York for not citing cases by name but only by volume and page and for not including in his work a table of cases cited. The way lawyers work dictated the need for full citations and for a table; experienced practitioners "habituate themselves in searching for a principle through the books to follow the track of a leading case," making a table of cases a necessity.[141] In 1884 the editors of the same journal asked whether tables of cases "did not occupy the same economical place in legal literature as the hair on the end of a man's nose occupies in the human anatomy."[142] Readers who responded favored appending a table of cases to every treatise. Their reasons were clearly summed up by Emlin McClain, at that time head of the law department at the University of Iowa:

> The secret of the whole matter is just this: the title of the case is a definite clue, having no dependence on the varying notions or whims of the different authors, while the heading and the sub-head under which the subject may be referred to in an index is a matter wholly indefinite and uncertain.[143]

Perhaps the most striking evidence of the profession's appetite for cases, however, was the success of John West's comprehensive reporters. As the editors of the *Central Law Journal* pointed out, the law of survival of the fittest would determine whether law books continued to be published or not.[144] There certainly was competition. In 1889 the *American Law Review* printed "A Symposium of Law Publishers," in which James E. Briggs of Lawyer's Co-op urged the selective reporters his organization published: "It had not occurred to us so forcibly until our experience drove us to study the problem, that so large a proportion of the decisions contained so little that was new as not to warrant even a bare publication of the opinion, to say nothing of full reports."[145] That observation might have been true. Certainly true was Briggs's assertion that

> there is a generally felt and frequently expressed regret, on the part of bench and bar here and in England, for the unlimited production of law books, whether of reports or text-books, which, instead of simplifying and facilitating a knowledge of the present state of the law on any given question, complicate and embarrass it by the very quantity of matter presented for examination and reconciliation.[146]

In spite of that "generally felt . . . regret," West's enterprise prospered. In his contribution to the publisher's symposium, he showed that he had separated the rhetoric about the relationship between principles and cases from the profession's practice of research. First, he noted that few questions of law can be answered "by direct reference to the abstract principles of the law, as taught in the school, or laid down by the commentators."[147] Constitutional and statutory provisions must be investigated and "the decisions of the courts bearing on the point must be found and compared, before the lawyer can say with any positiveness, 'thus the law is written.'" Lawyers also consult treatise writers, not to find "the opinions of a learned man, expert in legal lore," but to find "the *case law* on the subject, as determined not alone in the local jurisdiction, but as shown in the decisions of the courts throughout the whole United States." Before the West reporter system, the lawyer could never be certain that such a nationwide search was complete. Official reports were slow, and unofficial reporting was haphazard. In the end, the lawyer "had to go into court uncertain whether he might not be met on the threshold by his opponent, with controlling precedents to which he had not had access, and of the existence of which he had not been made aware." With the regional reporter system these fears were assuaged. Critics call his innovation the "blanket system" of reporting, he wrote, but he found that to be a compliment, not a criticism. "No policy of insurance is so satisfactory to the insured as the blanket policy; and that is the sort of policy we issue for the lawyer, seeking insurance against the loss of his case through ignorance of the law as set forth in the decisions of the highest courts."

West gauged his market well. The success of his enterprise demonstrated how highly the profession valued access to all possible precedents. In spite of the rhetoric of principle, the case seems to have been the basis of research and practice. Supporters of the case method, therefore, were certainly wise to portray their teaching technique as a means of giving students tools which would be useful in practice. At Harvard, the collapse of the required curriculum was part of the transition to an emphasis on teaching technique rather than legal truth. Recognition of the possibility for practical instruction was more widespread than the small world of Cambridge, Massachusetts. As early as 1870 an anonymous writer in the *Western Jurist* defended law schools against the charge of providing solely theoretical instruction by noting that "the most important result of a course of professional study . . . is not so much the amount actually learned, as the mental habit acquired."[148] In 1875 William G. Hammond, then teaching law at Iowa, read a paper on legal education to the American Social Science Association. He considered several different teaching methods and asserted that each had its place. The study of cases, however, was the only way directly to train students in habits of thought useful to the practitioner. That study enabled the student to learn "not only rules, but the sources from which rules proceed; and he insensibly acquires a habit of measuring the greater or less elasticity of each rule in connection with diverse states of facts, which is, perhaps, the best possible substitute for actual practice in ripening the legal judgment."[149] Devotees of the Harvard system were even more explicit in praising the advantages of the case method for teaching students how to deal with the problems of practice. In 1893 the circular of the Columbia Law School, a document surely acceptable to Dean Keener if not actually written by him, emphasized that what the student did in the classroom—discussing cases and analyzing the relevant and actual grounds of decision—was "practically . . . what he will be constantly doing as a lawyer."[150] The *Columbia Law Times* saw matters the same way. The advent of the case method was an improvement, the editors believed, because "the student now studies the law in the manner in which he will be called upon to investigate a case when he comes to active practice."[151] Emlin McClain, the Iowa proponent of tables of cases, understandably found teaching through cases an important part of legal education: "Plunge [the student] into the midst of a difficulty and then let him help himself out, as a lawyer or a judge would, by means of an adjudicated case, and he at once recognizes the utility and discipline of case study."[152] Even Joel P. Bishop, who became a vociferous critic of Harvard's methods, was adamant that every student must learn to criticize cases:

> The student should, therefore, read case after case; and make, as he goes on, his own abstracts of the points decided therein, cut down to the smallest possible dimensions, yet not so close as to pare off any thing which the case absolutely decides. There is no exercise more important than this; and it is especially one to be advantageously done by students in a class, under competent instruction; as, for example, in a law school.[153]

Comments like those just presented indicate a widespread belief that students should be taught to "think like lawyers," and thinking like a lawyer depended on the close analysis of cases. An anonymous respondent to a highly critical review of Langdell's contracts casebook published in the *Southern Law Review*[154] described the practice of the case method in just those terms. Class discussion was devoted to ascertaining "the precise point involved in each case, . . . what the court apprehended was the precise point," alternative grounds for decision, and the analogies that could be drawn from the courts' reasoning.[155] This careful parsing of the case is at the heart of research in a common law system; it is necessary before any argument about what law should apply to a given situation can be made. As a Harvard student put it in 1893, under the case method the student "reads hundreds upon hundreds of cases, becomes familiar with the appearance of decisions, and, to some extent, with the practice of courts, and learns how to digest a long case quickly and accurately."[156] So central to the entire enterprise was this analysis that Eugene Wambaugh, a member of the Harvard law class of 1880 who introduced the case method of instruction to the law faculty at the University of Iowa, wrote an entire treatise on *The Study of Cases*. Its subtitle fairly describes its scope: "A Course of Instruction in Reading and Stating Reported Cases, Composing Head-Notes and Briefs, Criticising and Comparing Authorities, and Compiling Digests."[157]

Austin Abbott used a modified version of the case method which preserved a prominent place for the lecture in his classes at the ancestor of New York University.[158] In his eyes, the great advantage of the case method was the colloquy between students and professor, which duplicated in the classroom what lawyers do in practice. When lawyers discuss a doubtful point of law they "get down four or five recent or leading cases and examine them together, and a colloquy ensues which brings out an analysis of each case," and in that way an agreement is reached "as to what the law is on the point." "This is," he continued, "substantially the natural course with the Case system."[159] In a paper read to the American Bar Association in 1894, Keener summed up the practical advantages of the case method in terms which probably appealed to every practicing lawyer in his audience:

> The student is required to analyze each case, to discriminate between the relevant and the irrelevant, between the actual and possible grounds of decision, and having thus considered the case, he is prepared and required to deal with it in its relation to other cases. In other words, the student is

> practically doing, under the guidance of the instructor, what he will be required to do, without guidance, as a lawyer.[160]

With such training a young lawyer could be a valuable addition to an established practice, whether or not he had a firm grasp of the somewhat amorphous principles that were so often asserted to be the heart of the common law. He would also be more sensitive to the facts of the cases he read, a valuable quality when dealing with the complications of code pleading, so heavily dependent on properly setting forth facts on which relief could be granted.

Dwight's advice to his students on preparing a case for argument, given in 1890, was quite different. "The first thing to be done," he advised, "is to master the leading principles applying to the case." Only then should the reports be consulted. Dwight's advice on what the lawyer should do with the reports was brief. He should first make sure that all the authorities that could be cited by his opponent were good law by determining whether they have been overruled or whether "they conflict with well established principles." The lawyer must decide whether a case has been restricted to its facts, or distinguished from a later case, or consists of dictum, but Dwight gives no hint that he is concerned with teaching those techniques.[161] For Dwight legal education avoided intensive instruction in the analysis of cases. Instruction by the case method did, and presumably for that reason was a better method of preparation for the actual practice of the law in a legal world swamped by reported cases. A pedagogical innovation based on theories about the structure and goals of learning had become an intensely practical tool for training members of the profession.

6

A New Legal Science

Langdell was not alone in thinking about legal science. Langdell's construct was only one current in a broad stream of change. Even as the new dean was settling into his work in Dane Hall, a small group of young men in the Boston area had been investigating legal science for some years, discussing their findings in a group that would later be known as the Metaphysical Club and publishing some of their work in the *American Law Review*. Of this group, the most important were Nicholas St. John Green and Oliver Wendell Holmes, Jr. They based their conception of law on the facts of the decided cases, yet they found Langdell's work unsatisfactory. Holmes's thought, of course, is often contrasted with Langdell's to the latter's detriment. Even so, the three men were closer intellectual companions than generally has been realized. The similarities highlight the importance of the belief in the case as the source of law for understanding nineteenth-century American jurisprudence. The founding generation of case method teachers at Harvard all shared that belief.

Fact Based Legal Science

The goal of the advocates of a new legal science was familiar: they sought to order the principles of the common law. They also recognized that the traditional ordering schemes based on the old science of procedure were no longer viable. "We cannot help saying that useful as books often are which gather under a remedy or class of remedies such as injunction or action, the rights which it protects," Holmes wrote in 1871, "the day for such an arrangement is passed." Such arrangements were useful "earlier in the history of jurisprudence," when procedure was more highly developed than were rules, "but now we want principles as they are related to each other, not according to the accidental difference in the way of enforcing them."[1] The science of ordered principles fared no better.

The goal of legal scientists like Joseph Story had been to create a proper understanding of the system of law through the intelligent application of inductive methods. Because the system that was to be revealed existed independently as part of the nature of things and the forms of action provided a practical ordering of legal knowledge, there had seldom been much explicit discussion of how the much talked-of legal principles were to be arranged. In a sense, the proper arrangement merely awaited revelation; legal scientists did not need to construct it. There were, however, some explicit attempts at ordering—Blackstone's arrangement of his lectures around the broad categories of law of persons and the law of things, itself a reflection of Roman legal ideas, could at least be presented as an example of science. The prevalent theme of American evocations of orderly science was the superiority of the classificatory scheme of the Roman law.[2] Appeals to antiquity meant little, however, to Holmes and Green.

In 1871 Holmes contributed an article to the *American Law Review* on "Misunderstandings of the Civil Law." He gave several examples of the misuse of civil law concepts in the common law, including Lord Holt's opinion in *Coggs v. Bernard*, famous for its attempt to explain common law rules of liability in bailment in terms of Roman law principles and often regarded as an archetype of legal science. Holmes's major point, however, was that studying civil law had no place in training American lawyers because "it tends to encourage a dangerous reliance on . . . glittering generalities" to the detriment of "the exhaustive analysis of a particular case, with which the common law begins and ends."[3] He made the same points several times during the next two years, denying "that fundamental principles are more clearly brought out in the Roman than in the English law" and emphasizing the importance of "the solution of a particular case" to the common law.[4] In fact, the much vaunted principles of the civil law are meaningless to the modern world, since they "are obscured by traditions which prevented their consistent application, by historical difficulties which have to be overcome before the law can be understood, by principles of classification that have lost their significance, and by a philosophy that is no longer vital."[5]

As vigorous as were Holmes's objections to the exultation of Roman law, no one in the early 1870s expended more energy in exposing the fallacy of relying on Roman law concepts and the supposed system they imposed on the common law than Nicholas St. John Green, Holmes's colleague in the Metaphysical Club and fellow contributor to the *American Law Review*. Green's role in formulating pragmatism has long been a standard theme in accounts of the origins of that peculiarly American philosophy.[6] Since his ultimate goal was to make ideas clear by really understanding what we mean when we use words, Green left little room for transcendent principles. Typical of his technique was his criticism of ordinary legal language used to define causation—that there is no recovery for "uncertain damage" or for the remote or consequential results of the defendant's actions, and that damage must arise naturally or be the fair, legal, and natural result of the defendant's actions if the plaintiff is to recover. Such expressions are "vague; they mean little." Merely "stereotyped forms for gliding over a difficulty without explaining it," they explain nothing of how a court arrives at a decision.[7]

Green's developing criticism is most clearly seen in the reviews and articles he wrote for the *American Law Review* between 1870 and 1874. His starting point was that study of the history of the common law proves the futility of searching for some plan or system underneath its various rules. "As the English law upon any subject was never constructed upon a plan," he wrote, "it cannot be resolved into one. It is a mass which has grown by aggregation, and special and peculiar circumstances have, from time to time, shaped its varying surfaces and angles."[8] He sustained this theme throughout his work. In his first major article, "Proximate and Remote Cause," published in 1870, he explained one of Bacon's most famous maxims—*In jure non remota causa, sed proxima, spectatur* ("In law the immediate, not the remote, cause of any event is regarded.")[9]—in terms of its grounding in scholastic logic that classified causes as formal, final, material and efficient. Because the schoolmen's logic was false, the maxim was useless.[10] In his review of Joel Bishop's treatise on the law of married women, he traced the status of married women under the common law to its foundation on the law of capture and purchase.[11] The peculiarities of the law of slander and libel arise from its relationship to civil and canon law and the struggle of the common law courts to wrest jurisdiction from the courts Christian.[12] Formulation of the classic three degrees of negligence on which Jones heavily relied in his systematic presentation of the law of bailment rests on a misinterpretation of a civil law text.[13] Similar use of history can be seen in his notes to the eighth edition of Story's agency treatise and in the notes he wrote to cases reported in the first two volumes of the *Criminal Law Reports*.[14]

The lessons of history, therefore, cast doubt on the methods and concepts used to systematize the common law. What was left, then, on which to build legal science? Certainly, no a priori system, like that proper to the civil law or that allegedly found in obscure maxims, would do. There is no "chain of causation" that, properly understood, will tell us who is liable for an injury. There are no categories of negligence into which we can portion out human behavior and assign liability for tortious acts. Nor can a philosophical system be built on the chaotic collection of precedents necessary in the world of code pleading. Holmes and other book reviewers writing anonymously in the *American Law Review* often complained about the lack of arrangement in the law caused by the tendency to group legal rules "around a fact of dramatic instead of one of legal significance."[15] As early as 1869, in a review of Judah Philip Benjamin's treatise on the law of sales, Holmes set forth his vision of a proper philosophical arrangement of the law. "A book of reference on any subdivision of the law," he wrote, "must set forth at length, not only the principles constituting the specific difference of the subject-matter, but also those common to it and to many other classes of the same genus." Fraud, for instance, should be treated as an aspect of contract "or possibly under some still wider head, rather than repeated in every text-book dealing with every one of the different sorts of contract known to modern commerce."[16]

An anonymous review of the revision of the United States statutes criticized the commissioners producing the revision for following the "manual" method of arrangement, which is neither philosophical nor practical. According to the reviewer, the New York digest is a perfect example of the manual method in its unhappy treatment of negligence cases. Although the digest does have a heading "Negligence," not all the relevant cases can be found there. Many such cases are placed under the title "Railroads" simply because the defendant was a railroad corporation: the rules laid down in the cases apply to all cases of negligence, "yet, from some assumed notion of 'convenience,' the cases are taken away from the natural title 'Negligence,' and placed under the title 'Railroads,' with which they have no connection, except the accidental one of the party litigant being a railway corporation."[17] This arrangement by patterns of dramatic facts is not useless. As the term used above implies, it makes for a useful manual for the practitioner who is seeking an exact precedent, but it is totally insufficient as the basis for what Holmes considered a philosophical classification. He made the same point in his review of the second edition of Thomas Shearman and Amasa Redfield's treatise on the law of negligence. While the authors "were philosophical in their first step, . . . when they planted themselves upon a legal conception instead of a branch of trade" the arrangement was still that "of a working manual."[18] It is not, however, a work of scientific jurisprudence.

A truly scientific system would have to be built from the bottom up, from the cases that give examples of the legally significant facts on which recovery is based. The system thus created may be based on "rights," or "obligations," or "duties," but the foundation must be factual. Holmes made this point quite clearly in a letter to John Chipman Gray written in July 1877. The two friends had spent an evening discussing an article Holmes had recently written.[19] A few days later Holmes described to Gray "my ultimate object":

> viz: to point out a distinction which is of the first importance to a philosophical classification—which has two distinct things to do (1) to enumerate the groups of facts which generate a right or obligation—(2) to enumerate the facts which do *not* generate either, and yet give a man the right or obligation *as if* the generative fact were true.[20]

The facts, of course, are to be sought in the cases. As Green wrote when dismissing John Townsend's theorizing about slander and libel in terms of malice, "the latest decided cases upon this subject *make the law*."[21]

The importance of relevant as opposed to merely dramatic facts colored all aspects of Green's and Holmes's writings in the early 1870s. Consider Green's treatment of causation. As a substitute for the scholastic chain of causation he offered a definition of the term "proximate cause" that varied according to the nature of the inquiry being made. "When a cause is to be investigated for any practical purpose," he wrote, "the antecedent which is within the scope of that purpose is singled out and called the cause, to the neglect of the antecedents which are of no importance to the matter at hand." When the practical purpose is to determine whether or not a person has caused harm through negligence, his misconduct is the proximate cause of "those results which a prudent foresight might have avoided."[22] In order to determine what those results are, the investigator must understand what actually happens in the world when men and women act:

> The law makes us responsible for those effects of our voluntary acts which might have reasonably been foreseen, or which are of a kind analogous to effects which might thus have been foreseen. There is generally no other way of determining whether certain events, or whether events analogous to them in kind, were or might have been anticipated or foreseen, than by an appeal to experience.[23]

Negligence was a question of fact. Elsewhere Green responded to the conclusion that the question of whether or not someone has been negligent involves ascertaining, first, whether or not the law imposes a duty and, second, what the duty was. When those questions of law are settled, it must be asked whether "the conduct under investigation" violated the duty. That is a question of fact, because the duty is to take such care for the rights of others "which under the particular circumstances of the case might be reasonably expected from a person of mature age who is not deficient in prudence" and "whether that forethought has been exercised is a question of fact."[24] Indeed, the duty is itself a question of fact since it is an obligation to refrain from harming others, harm which in turn is defined by analyzing circumstances in which compensation has been awarded for harm, circumstances which are illustrated by cases.

Green extended this sort of analysis beyond private law. One of the clearest examples of his reliance on facts and the cases that report them can be found in his criticism of the opinion of the Massachusetts Supreme Judicial Court in *Commonwealth v. White*, printed as a note to the report of the opinion in the *Criminal Law Reporter*.[25] White was convicted of criminal assault for menacingly pointing at another a gun which White knew was not loaded. Green maintained that the supreme court's upholding of the conviction was incorrect. White's action should make him liable for civil damages for assault and would justify a battery in self-defense, but the sustaining of the criminal conviction rests on a misunderstanding of the precedents.[26] The whole history of the common law of crimes shows us that criminal intent is a necessary component of legal guilt. The pointing of an unloaded gun shows the absence of an intent and of a means to inflict harm. To sustain a criminal conviction for such behavior requires authority. Since there are many cases of assaults with firearms, "it is singular that no well considered case be found which maintains such doctrine."[27] Without the facts of reported cases there is no ground for the asserted rule.[28]

Holmes took the same approach in many of his early book reviews and articles. In 1871 he reviewed a work on negligence that attempted to use the classifications of the Roman law to explain what was and was not negligent action. For Holmes, as for Green, the entire matter of negligence is a question of fact. If negligence is alleged in the pleadings, it is for the jury "to say whether the party has used such care as a reasonable and prudent man would have used under the circumstances of the particular case whatever they may be." But where there is no question for the jury, "then all that can be said is that there is a positive rule of law that when facts A., B., and C. concur, and no qualifying fact is shown or presumable, the defendant is liable."[29]

Holmes developed this theme fully for the first time in his second major article, "The Arrangement of the Law, Privity."[30] Here he explained his theory of the factual basis of legal duties by analyzing the concept of succession to show that people succeed to the rights and property of others when the law recognizes a fictional identity between the first and the second person, so that the operative facts are true for the successor. Five years after the appearance of this article Holmes summed up its basic thesis in yet another essay appearing in the *American Law Review*. First, he noted that "all special rights are legal consequences of a special group of facts." It is common in modern law, however, for a person to acquire a special right, "although the facts upon which it is primarily founded are not true of him, or are true only in part." Yet the right is possessed, and in the case of succession at least the difficulty is solved by a "fictitious identification of distinct persons for the purpose of transferring or completing the right." He then proceeded to use examples from the history of the law to illustrate the truth of the generalization he had "arrived at analytically" five years before.[31]

Behind the concern with facts, with behavior as an outward manifestation of the mind, was the psychology that Green introduced to the Metaphysical Club. Alexander Bain defined belief as something on which a person was prepared to act.[32] Applying this insight to his profession, Green linked thought and action into a full-blown theory of legal intent. Reviewing the fifth edition of Isaac Ray's *A Treatise on the Medical Jurisprudence of Insanity*, he directly related the notion of intent to Bain's psychology. Since intent is only an idea, "it cannot be perceived by the senses; it can only be inferred from acts." The prosecutor proves the defendant's acts and the jury "are generally justified in inferring an intent of the defendant that the consequence of those acts, that the *corpus delicti*, should follow."[33] Like negligence, then, criminal responsibility is a legal concept shaped by facts about the way the world works, facts recorded in the great body of decided cases.

Holmes's ideas about tortious liability clearly show the link between this particular theory of psychology and an empirical legal science based on the facts of cases. His theory of legal liability is usually said to be objective, because it does not require any culpability in the actor for the actor to be held liable. More specifically, both criminal and civil liability are based not on the actor's consciousness but on community judgments about the tendency of the acts, a theory quite similar to that Green discussed in the early 1870s. In "The Theory of Torts" published in 1873 Holmes elaborated the idea that the standard for determining negligence is whether or not an actor has lived up to what the average member of the community would do in similar circumstances.[34] Further development of this notion suggests that Holmes's objective theory of liability rests on a psychology which holds that the workings of the human mind can only be inferred from behavior. As Holmes put it in *The Common Law*:

> The philosophical analysis of every wrong begins by determining what the defendant has actually chosen, that is to say, what his voluntary act or conduct has been, and what consequences he has actually contemplated as flowing from them, and then goes on to determine what dangers attended either the conduct under the known circumstances, or its contemplated consequence under the contemplated circumstances.[35]

The contemplation of which Holmes speaks is a legal concept to be proved by showing facts rather than an inquiry into state of mind.

The psychological basis of Holmes's theory of liability reflects the factual basis of his theory of the law, a basis evident in his earliest writings. Psychology was not, however, the only source from which Holmes drew inspiration. Far more obviously than Langdell, he was influenced by John Austin. The exact nature and extent of Holmes's debt to Austin is a complex question to which different answers have been suggested.[36] A definitive answer to the question requires a careful analysis of the complexities of Austin's thought, as well as of the entire tradition of English utilitarianism.[37] Even without such an elaborate analysis, however, it is possible to show that Holmes derived his idea of the nature of law from the belief that law is ultimately the application of force, an insight which certainly is related to Austin's conception of law as command. Holmes, however, rejected Austin's ideas about the relationship of the sovereign to law.

Holmes seems to have formulated his views for the first time in a series of lectures on jurisprudence he gave at Harvard College in spring 1872. Their substance is preserved only in the form of a "Notice" in the *American Law Review* that nominally reviewed an article on Austin by Frederick Pollock.[38] According to Holmes, law, at least "in the more limited meaning which lawyers give the word," is the rules enforced by the courts, which rules are not necessarily the commands of the sovereign. Such a statement is, of course, a rejection of one of Austin's basic premises and is, in turn, the result of rejecting Austin's concept of sovereignty. Holmes pointed out that the identity of the sovereign is defined by the fact of power. "That is to say," Holmes wrote, "the will of the sovereign is law, because he has power to compel obedience or to punish disobedience, and for no other reason." There are, Holmes maintained, real limits on the power of the political sovereign, a statement he supported by showing in his lectures "that there might be law without sovereignty, and that where there is a sovereign, properly so called, other bodies not sovereign, and even opinion, might generate law in a philosophical sense against the will of the sovereign." He pointed out that in the end no command of the sovereign could prevail against the "physical power" of that "large number" which in some societies has even been a "numerical majority of males, who have had no share in the political power."[39]

Once the Austinian conception of sovereignty was disposed of, Holmes easily showed that judges decide cases from many motives "outside their own arbitrary will, beside the commands of their sovereign." All the lawyer is concerned with, he pointed out, is what the judges will decide in the future, because "in a civilized state" what "makes lawyers' law" is not the will of the sovereign "but what a body of subjects, namely, the judges, by whom it is enforced, *say* is his will." The true source of law and the true subject of jurisprudence is any motive for judicial decision which lawyers can reasonably rely on being used to decided future cases. This first appearance of Holmes's "prediction theory of law" grew out of a belief that what judges do is the law.[40] While Holmes modified the specifics of Austin's idea of sovereignity, the idea that law is what is enforced by power remained a link to his English predecessor.[41]

The belief that the cases are the law continued to shape Holmes's thought. He eventually abandoned his youthful attempts to classify the law around duties—a basically Austinian undertaking that substituted duties for rights—in favor of an empirical basis of law. "The primary duty," he wrote Frederick Pollock in 1883, "is little more than a convenient index to, or mode of predicting the point of incidence of the public force."[42] More than thirty years later Holmes wrote to John Chipman Gray, who had inquired about "an article of yours, I think in the Am. [*sic*] Law Review to the effect that the best classification of the Law was on duties."[43] Holmes replied:

> The duty basis was the theme of my first article in the law Rev. Oct. 1870—Vol. 5 p. 1. "A long time ago, gentlemen," as old Parsons used to say in a melancholy voice, "a very long time ago." Later I became convinced that the machinery of rights and duties and duties was a fifth wheel—and partially expressed it in an address to the Boston Law School Jan 8/97 ["The Path of the Law"] that was printed in the Harv. Law Rev. My theme and present view is expressed in American Banana Co. v. United Fruit Co. 213 U.S. 347, 356 [1908] "Law is a statement of the circumstance in which the public force will be brought to bear upon men through the Courts.[44]

Five years earlier Holmes had been even blunter on the topic in a letter to Gray: "Personally I don't care a damn for the rights and duties business preferring to regard only the prophecy as to the incidence of the public force."[45]

Finally, like Austin and Langdell, Holmes believed that for purposes of study, law and morals must be separated. Holmes had made the point in print as early as 1867. In that year he reviewed the ninth edition of Story's *Equity Jurisprudence* by Isaac Redfield, former chief justice of Vermont, who was praised as an ideal lawyer always concerned with sound principles and the morality of the law. The young Holmes saw matters differently. Although Redfield was "an eminent and able man," his editing of Story exhibited the same flaws of his other works. "One of them," Holmes wrote, "is a habit of moralizing, which is notably out of place among the rules and precedents of courts." He then quoted Redfield's criticism of an English judge for doing justice rather than adhering to principle, something always to be deprecated by those who believe in principle and trust " 'consequences to Him with whom are all the issues of life.' "[46] Holmes's comment on that statement clearly excluded morality from court: "When the learned editor calls in the authority of religion to make weight against the authority of the Master of the Rolls, by doing so he only renders the want of legal authority more conspicuous."[47] In 1878 he was more explicit, using terms reminiscent of Langdell's letter to Theodore Woolsey:

> We may leave on one side the question of their [legal rights'] relation to moral rights, and whether moral rights are not in like manner logically the offspring of moral duties; these are for the philosopher who approaches the law from without, as part of a larger series of human manifestations. The business of the jurist is to make known the content of the law.[48]

In short, Holmes's thought resembled that of Austin in important ways. His modifications of Austin's ideas are an extension of the empirical side of Austin's thought. If Austin's conception of law was based on the reality of power, his scheme for the classification and arrangement of legal ideas nevertheless partook of more abstraction than Holmes was willing to accept. An appreciation of history led Holmes to this position. Holmes's view of the sovereign was based on what history showed to be the limits of the political sovereign's power.[49] He saw too many instances in which sovereign power was powerless to make law in the face of power held by others, that "numerical majority of males" who in the extreme could undo the sovereign's law by taking to the streets. What should not be overlooked, however, is that for all his criticism of Austin, Holmes still found the source of law in power:[50] what the public power enforces is the law. He came close to saying that might makes, if not right, at least law of the kind lawyers rightly study. For Holmes, rejecting Austin's conception of the sovereign's absolute power does not entail rejecting the basic idea of the nature of law which Austin expressed.[51]

Since the ultimate basis of the sort of systematic legal science sought by Green and Holmes was the decided case, they might be assumed to be advocates and allies of the contemporary transformation of the Harvard Law School. Indeed, Green, Holmes, and Gray occupied lectureships in Cambridge during this period. Green, however, left Harvard in protest against the new methods and helped found the new law school at Boston

University. The intellectual relationship between Holmes and Langdell has become a controversial point. Holmes wrote critical reviews of Langdell's work in the years before publication of *The Common Law*. Saul Touster has portrayed Holmes moving from criticism of Langdell's reliance on cases to acceptance of the case method, a transformation which led Holmes in *The Common Law* to reject "moral ideas" and "philosophy" in favor of a narrow, formalistic approach to law.[52] That interpretation, however, is misleading. Cases were the basis of both men's legal science.

Holmes was the author of the hostile notice of the Harvard Law School which appeared in the *American Law Review* in 1870.[53] Apparently soured on law schools by his experience at the unreformed Harvard, he found that school inadequate in almost every particular. The next year, in reviewing Bryce's recommendation that common lawyers study the civil law, Holmes observed that the common law "begins and ends with the solution of the particular case," so that "the best training . . . is found in our moot courts and the offices of older lawyers."[54] The implication is that effective learning comes by doing, a belief perfectly compatible with the ideas about education that accompanied introduction of the case method to Harvard Law School. Green was even more explicit, observing in a review in the same issue of the *American Law Review* that "the only way to obtain thorough knowledge upon any point, either of science or of art, is to seek it from original sources."[55] Instruction by the case method did exactly that, but Green and Holmes certainly did not see the resemblance.

The stumbling block was Langdell himself. Green found legal education at Harvard too theoretical and left to teach at a law school founded to give useful instruction in law. Holmes's reviews of Langdell's work identify the same problem. Reviewing the first part of Langdell's contracts casebook, he praised its historical arrangement: "Tracing the growth of a doctrine in this way not only fixes it in the mind, but shows its meaning, extent, and limits as nothing else can."[56] Holmes went on, however, to criticize Langdell's treatment of the cases on forbearance as "collected with an over-scrupulous minuteness." Langdell, it seems, had paid too much attention "to the other side of what is now settled." This failing, did not detract from the usefulness of the work, however.[57] Publication of the complete work in the same year was greeted by another anonymous Holmes review, which praised the dean for using a philosophical rather than a manual method of arrangement and pointed out the importance of inculcating in students the principles deduced from cases. While Langdell's innovation was still new, Holmes had some reservations about Langdell's scholarship. Studying cases as the source of the law was the way to learn principles, but Langdell's way of studying cases was defective.[58]

Nine years later Holmes expressed the same attitudes more fully in his review of the second edition of the contracts casebook. Now, Holmes characterized the dean as "perhaps, the greatest living legal theologian," concerned only with the "the formal connection of things, or logic, as distinguished from the feelings which make the content of logic, and which have actually shaped the substance of the law.''[59] Those ''feelings'' were the sort of lessons of history that concerned Green. The core of Holmes's criticism, however, was the same as in his first review of Langdell's work. The tendency to ''over-scrupulous minuteness'' decried in 1871 had blossomed into dogmatism—''the effort to reduce the concrete details of an existing system to the merely logical consequence of simple postulates''—as seen in the extensive summary of the law of contracts which Langdell added to the second edition of the casebook. Having exposed in print his idea of a complete system for the first time, Langdell was clearly determined to prove his interpretation, even if that meant reconciling decisions ''which those who gave them meant to be opposed'' by drawing them together ''by subtle lines,'' never dreamed of before.[60]

A fuller explanation of these criticisms appears in Holmes's chapters on contract in *The Common Law*. In each instance where Holmes referred to Langdell's work he found Langdell to be too concerned with theory and insufficiently engaged with the practicalities of the situation. For instance, Holmes discussed Langdell's treatment of the mailbox rule, which held that acceptance of an offer was not complete until the offeror received the letter signifying acceptance. Holmes described Langdell as arguing that ''the consideration which makes the offer binding is itself a promise,'' which must be offered to the other party. Since the acceptance is itself an offer, it must be communicated to the other party before it can be effective. Holmes found this ''unsound.'' When a promise is made and the return promise is accepted in advance, he said, ''there is not an instant, either in time or logic, when the return promise is an offer.'' Putting aside logic, however, ''if convenience preponderates in favor of either view, that is a sufficient reason for its adoption.'' In the case of the acceptance by letter, ''the offeree, when he drops the letter containing the counter-promise into the letter-box, does an overt act, which by general understanding renounces control over the letter, and puts it into a third hand for the benefit of the offerer.''[61] Holmes in fact had little patience for any of Langdell's elaborate theory of consideration in bilateral contracts and the related theory of offer and acceptance involved in the mailbox rule. He answered Langdell's assertions about consideration and wagers on past events with the observation that ''contracts are dealings among men, by which they make arrangements for the future.'' Any present fact about which they are ignorant was just as uncertain as any future fact, and a willingness to pay ''if the event turns out not to have been as expected'' was sufficient consideration for a contract.[62]

A more striking disagreement with Langdell appears in Holmes's discussion of the notion of equivalency, another concept involved in understanding the role of consideration in bilateral contracts. Broadly put, Langdell's observation was that in the case of a contract made by giving a promise for a promise, the performance of one is payment for the performance of the other, and, therefore, as Holmes put it, neither party ''can call on the other to perform without being ready at the same time himself.''[63] This, in turn, became an important principle for understanding the role of conditions in contract law. Holmes, however, did not believe that the proper judicial treatment of conditions depended on working out a principle of equivalence:

> Suppose A promises B to do a day's work for two dollars, and B promises A to pay two dollars for a day's work. There the two promises cannot be performed at the same time. The work will take all day, the payment half a minute. How are you to decide which is to be done first, that is to say, which promise is dependent upon performance on the other side? It is only by reference to the habits of the community and to convenience.[64]

Theory, the idea that "on the principle of equivalency a man is not presumed to intend to pay for a thing until he has it," is not sufficient to answer the question. The work is payment for the money and the money for the work. There is no reason in logic to say one man "intends" to pay before he has what he has bought and the other intends to give before he has been paid. What explains the cases is the amalgam of practice and belief that is summed up in history and which is the law:

> The fact that employers, as a class, can be trusted for wages more safely than the employed for their labor, that the employers have had the power and have been the law-makers, or other considerations, it matters not what, have determined that the work is to be done first. But the grounds of decision are purely practical, and can never be elicited from grammar or from logic.[65]

Holmes used as the fourth sentence of *The Common Law* the same sentence he used in the review that described Langdell as a "legal theologian": "The life of the law has not been logic: it has been experience."[66] Langdell was working with the right sources; he knew how to do legal science, he simply did it badly. The system he extracted from the cases was too logical, too concerned to draw distinctions and reconcile cases on grounds that existed only in his own mind. Holmes, in contrast, felt himself to be firmly grounded in the reality of history, human nature, and ways of the world.

Other observers of Langdell's scholarship saw the same problems. At the time of the controversy over finding a replacement for Holmes, both Gray and Ephraim Gurney complained to Eliot about Langdell's remarkably stubborn adherence to his views. Holmes himself was still of the same mind thirty years later when, after reading Langdell's *A Brief Survey of Equity Jurisdiction*, a collection of articles printed posthumously, he wrote to Sir Frederick Pollock that the work "has his [Langdell's] acumen and patient discussion of detail, but I think it brings out the narrow side of his mind, his feebleness in philosophising, and hints at his rudimentary historical knowledge." All in all, "I think he was somewhat wanting in horse sense."[67] The heart of Holmes's criticism is an objection to Langdell's intellectual rigidity and a priori approach, to his creation of what Pollock called "the Langdellian ether of a super-terrestrial Common Law where authority does not count at all," not to the study of the law through the study of cases.[68]

Indeed, for Holmes the decided case would be the ultimate arbiter of Langdell's worth as a theorist: "Even if Mr. Langdell's results should hereafter be overruled in particular cases, they will have done very nearly as much to advance the law as if they had been adopted. For they must be either adopted or refuted, they cannot be passed by."[69] For both Holmes and Langdell the law was in the cases, and the legal scientist looked to the cases to test the results of his studies.[70]

Harvard Teachers and Positive Law

It may seem strange to assert that Holmes and the founding members of the reformed Harvard faculty were intellectual allies, so often have reputations of the academics been battered with the club of "formalism." They all had in common, however, an adamant belief that the cases were the law. They also were more or less content with the idea that law depended on power. In the first place, as Langdell's system of contract law and his approach to equity jurisprudence illustrate, the legal principles that he probably believed to be true in some absolute sense were not designed to order society. They were substantive principles of contract law, a true understanding of which revealed order in the chaos of the common law, and thus were the modern substitute for the obsolete forms of action that had once structured understanding. The principles behind a true understanding of equity were similarly narrow, based not on good morals but on the procedural limitations of common law actions. In addition, Langdell's notion of science included a place for the legal experiment, as his controversy with Samuel Williston showed. Langdell's belief that a decision by a court would validate his version of the controverted theory indicates at least a sort of acceptance of the idea that what courts do is the law, an acceptance of the very test to which Holmes believed Landgell's work would be put.[71]

There is also more direct evidence. Langdell wrote but one essay of a jurisprudential nature, published in its final form in 1900 in the *Harvard Law Review*.[72] It was a thoroughly Austinian enterprise, based on the familiar distinction between rights and duties. Both rights and duties are "created" by the state, he said—obligations through the courts and duties through the legislature. There are other sorts of duties; "domestic or family relations give rise to a numerous class of duties." Such duties, however, are moral rather than legal and are not enforced by the courts. Even more striking is Langdell's discussion of equitable rights. He found them to be merely fictions "invented by equity for the promotion of justice." Equity reasons upon them and grants relief based on them, but they are not "rights." "It seems," Langdell wrote, "to be impossible that there should be any other actual rights than such as are created by the State." The language of command permeates the essay, establishing that for Langdell the state was the ultimate source of law: the infringement of a right is a tort, he said, because "the infringement constitutes equally . . . an act of disobedience to a prohibitory command of the State." The same situation pertains with regard to duties: "The State also commands every person within its limits to do every act which the State makes it his duty to do." Finally, the Austinian nature of the enterprise is enforced by the close attention Langdell paid to the concepts and classifications of Roman law in his discussion of obligations.

Langdell had absorbed much of the language of Austinian positivism. He also absorbed its concepts. A striking instance of his use of both is his contribution to the scholarly debate over the constitutional status of the territories acquired by the United States as a result of the Spanish-American War. The pending peace treaty with Spain and the recent annexation of the Hawaiian islands occasioned much speculation about the extent of congressional power over the newly acquired lands and the applicability of constitutional guarantees to them.[73] In early 1899 Langdell published an essay in the *Harvard Law Review* in which he elaborately analyzed every use of the term "United States" in the Constitution and concluded that its provisions applied only to the states of the union. Langdell began his analysis by pointing out that the term "United States" refers both to the territory of the nation and to a sovereignty. After his examination of the text of the Constitution, Langdell noted that the limitations imposed by the Constitution on the sovereignty of the United States "have reference primarily to the States, and owe their existence primarily to the fact that the sovereignty over the territory of each State is divided between the State and the United States"; that fact leads to "a strong presumption that such limitations have no application to territory which is subject to no State sovereignty, and in which the United States can exercise all the power which can be exercised within a State either by the State or by the United States."[74] In short, the United States can govern these newly acquired lands in any way it pleases and need not respect the guarantees of the Constitution.[75] For Langdell the federal government was clearly the only sovereign of the United States outside the territory of the several states. His view is strongly related to the Austinian concept of the sovereign and accepts few controls on positive law making.

Perhaps even more startling is Langdell's position on the railroad question. In the wake of the circuit court decision in *The Northern Securities Case*, Langdell wrote an article in which he maintained that the Sherman Anti-Trust Act did not apply to railway combinations and that the decree of the court forbidding the Northern Securities Company from voting or receiving dividends on its shares of the railroad companies was not authorized by the statute and was thus illegal.[76] More noteworthy, however, was Langdell's assertion that there was no need to apply the Sherman Act to railroads to safeguard against the sort of evils the statute had been designed to prevent. Railways harm the public only by charging unreasonable rates, he said, and "for such an injury the state already had an incomparably better remedy than any which the Sherman Anti-Trust Act can furnish, in its unquestioned power to regulate and control railway rates." In addition, competition is ruinous to railways and does not result in keeping "prices within reasonable limits." The only competition possible is at "competing points," and the only competition engaged in is giving "lower rates than they are entitled to receive" to those who can ship at competing points at the expense of those who cannot and have no choice of carriers. The answer for Langdell was either governmental regulation or outright governmental ownership. He observed that should "the state itself . . . undertake the duty of rendering to the public the services which are rendered by railway companies, every one would agree that its monopoly of such service should be complete and absolute." Moreover, when the state "delegates to railway companies the right to render these services, and imposes upon them the corresponding duties," it must regulate the railway business just as if it ran the railways itself. The state must plan comprehensively and permit new construction only with its permission and only where new roads are needed. In fact, the "ideal railway system" would be a single system comprehending all the roads in a state, controlled "either by the direct authority of the state, or the direct authority of those by whom the system is owned, acting, however, under such rules and regulations as the state from time to time sees fit to make."[77]

When his comments on the regulation of railroads are seen in the light of his attitude toward the constitutional status of the conquered territories, it seems fair to say that Langdell had few qualms about legislative power and more than an incidental appreciation for Austinian ideas of sovereignty. Langdell's legal science was a science of legal principles narrowly conceived. The circuit court decree in *The Northern Securities Case* was illegal only because Congress had not authorized such a remedy in the statute. Without positive legislative authority, the decree would have to be sanctioned by the doctrines of equity determined by a thorough examination of decided cases. Langdell found no precedents; the decree was illegal.[78]

James Bradley Thayer began his teaching career assuming that lecturing was the best method of teaching, but he overcame his doubts about the case method as a way to study and, like Langdell, turned his scholarly efforts to the history of law as embodied in cases, specifically in the field of evidence. For Thayer, law was what the courts did: "We mean [by law], at all events, a rule or standard which it is the duty of a judicial tribunal to apply and enforce." He begged the question of where the rule or standard came from—"how far it is the command of a supreme political power, and how far the silently-followed habit of the community"—but his careful attention to the history of the relationship between judge and jury leaves little doubt that he found all that was useful for a lawyer in the study of cases.[79]

More important, he conceded great power to the legislature. Thayer's views on the annexation question were much like Langdell's. He too believed that the United States had the fullness of sovereign power. The Constitution, moreover, did not deprive the national legislature "of power to do anywhere the things which are forbidden within the United States" because its prohibitions, "although they do not say it, deal only with certain circumstances and persons and places."[80] Such sweeping trust in Congress was congenial to Thayer. Seven years before his article on the question of the constitutional status of the conquered lands, he published what is perhaps the single most influential piece of legal scholarship in American history. "The Origin and Scope of the American Doctrine of Constitutional Law" began as an address to the Congress on Jurisprudence and Law Reform at the 1893 Chicago world's fair. Thayer published it as a pamphlet and reprinted it in the *Harvard Law Review*.[81] The paper examined the origin of the American notion of judicial review. Thayer concluded that the judiciary had been given a political function through the exercise of "the power to revise the action of other departments and to pronounce it null." Having come to this conclusion, Thayer counseled judges to use "methods and principles" appropriate to a political task. Those methods and principles include restraint,—giving the legislature the benefit of the doubt, in fact using in constitutional adjudication the same standard of "beyond a reasonable doubt" familiar from criminal law. In the end, the ultimate safety of the Constitution had to be entrusted to the "prudence, moral sense, and honor" of the people.[82]

More than any other member of the early Harvard faculty, John Chipman Gray is probably associated with a rigid view of the law. His treatise on the Rule against Perpetuities organized a vast array of sometimes contradictory cases into a single comprehensible framework which gave, it is usually assumed, one rule to govern all cases.[83] He also left behind the only full-length treatment of jurisprudence to be written by the founders of modern American law teaching. *The Nature and Sources of the Law* was inspired by Gray's encounter with Austin. In the preface to the first edition, published in 1909, he wrote:

> Some fifty years ago I came across a copy of Austin's "Province of Jurisprudence Determined," then little read in England, and all but unknown in this country; and since then, although my work has been mainly on other lines, the subject has seldom been for long wholly out of my mind.[84]

In more than fifty years of legal thought Gray became a disciple of an Austinian positivism modified by the insights of historical jurisprudence.[85]

Gray summed up Austin's contribution to jurisprudence in terms that emphasized the rejection of the transcendent. Austin brought to the jurisprudence of the common law the idea that law is not an ideal—"is not that which ought to be, but that which is."[86] Austin's theory of law as command, however, was incorrect, as Henry Maine had demonstrated by showing the various ways law can exist without an organized sovereign.[87]

Austin's basic contribution still remains intact: "If Austin went too far in considering the Law as always proceeding from the State, he conferred a great benefit on Jurisprudence by bringing out clearly that the Law is at the mercy of the State."[88]

His description of Austin's contribution to jurisprudence indicates that Gray understandably had little use for theories that found the source of law in something other than court decisions. He doubted whether there were any universal principles valid in all places at all times.[89] He deprecated the theory that judges only discover the law.[90] Such theories Gray attributed to a misleading analogy to physical science, which was popular with supporters of the declaratory theory. The analogy was inapt, because though philosophers do not make the laws of nature, judges most emphatically do make the law of the land. "The laws of nature are independent of human opinion," Gray wrote, "while the Law of the land *is* human opinion."[91] That opinion is usually the opinion of the judges, who draw on many sources in formulating it, including custom and morality.[92]

Gray believed that judges determined the law of a state. They most emphatically *made* law, and the result was influenced by many factors, including their own personalities and political opinions. Gray even argued that, had Marshall been a Democrat and a supporter of the United States Bank, our law would be very different—an illustration that seems designed to outrage advocates of the other point of view.[93]

If Gray so wholeheartedly accepted the notion that law was a construct, dependent on many different factors, including the personal political beliefs of the judges, his scholarly work would seem to embody an overwhelming contradiction. After all, he wrote the leading work on an intensely technical area of the law of property, which still bedevils the profession. Gray's treatise on the Rule against Perpetuities is indeed full of rules that are supposed to decide cases even in the face of demonstrable intent of the person who is responsible for the writing being construed. "In no part of the law is the reasoning so mathematical in its character" Gray wrote; "none has so small a human element."[94] When the work on perpetuities is considered along with the companion work on restraints on alienation, however, a picture emerges of a consistent thinker.

Gray's treatise on the Rule against Perpetuities is the classical statement of the common law rule, a rule which some maintain Gray did more to invent than he admitted. It deals with the amount of control the dead may maintain over the disposition of property by the living.[95] Gray believed that the rule could be applied with total accuracy; unlike most topics of legal discussion there was a standard against which all reasoning could be measured. Because of this unusual nature of the Rule against Perpetuities, the discussion in the treatise is different from legal discussion in general: "A degree of dogmatism, therefore, may be permitted here which would be unbecoming in other branches of the law."[96] Presumably contracts was one of those areas. Gray had severely criticized Langdell for excessive dogmatism only three years before the appearance of the first edition of the treatise.[97] He was not inconsistent; he was being a teacher of Anglo-American property law. The common law of real property is a complex and highly artificial system that allows for ownership and the benefits of ownership to be divided not only in the here and now but in the future, along what is often called the "plane of time." The concepts involved in these "future interests" are carefully defined and fitted together in a logical way. Once the premises are accepted, the system of future interests works.[98]

Gray began his treatise with an elaborate discussion of future interests. Once that discussion was out of the way, the Rule against Perpetuities can be applied mechanically—"No interest is good unless it must vest, if at all, not later than twenty-one years after some life in being at the creation of the interest."[99] It is the clear line the "the law has laid down" to balance the desire to provide for future generations with the desire of the members of posterity to control property they have inherited.[100] There is nothing transcendent in the rule as it stands. Like all law, it comes from judges. Because it has been made in the course of litigation, "it has grown to fit the ordinary dealings of the community."[101] The rule can be changed at any moment by legislation and often had been, usually in the direction of greater stringency. Because "it is a dangerous thing to make such a radical change in a part of the law which is concatenated with almost mathematical precision,"[102] such efforts have led only to greater confusion.[103] The best rule, that which is easiest to understand and administer, has grown up with the cases. Gray's treatise was devoted to explicating those cases and stating as clearly as possible the rule that emerges, an enterprise perfectly consistent with his theory of the nature and sources of the law.

Gray's consistency is even more apparent in his other major work, the treatise on restraints on alienation. Gray was moved to write the book by the decision of the United States Supreme Court upholding the doctrine of spendthrift trusts.[104] Such trusts allow their creators to limit the extent to which the creditors of a trust beneficiary can reach the trust assets in order to satisfy the beneficiary's debts. Gray recoiled in horror from that doctrine. It is immoral not to pay one's debts, he said. The spread of the spendthrift trust is an example of America's "shortcomings in the matter of commercial honesty." It is contrary to the fundamental policy of the common law. By sanctioning "inalienable rights of property," the doctrine of spendthrift trusts keeps people in "pupilage," which is contrary to a law which has always held "that it is not the function of the law to join in the futile effort to save the foolish and the vicious from the consequences of their own vice and folly." The doctrine also subverts democracy. By enabling "the children of rich men to live in debt and in luxury at the same time," the spendthrift trust creates a privileged class, "an aristocracy, though certainly the most contemptible aristocracy with which a country was ever cursed."[105] In the preface to the second edition Gray denounced as "one of the worst results of spendthrift trusts . . . the encouragement it gives to a plutocracy."[106]

The doctrine of spendthrift trusts is judge-made law. On what sources did the judges draw in making these decisions? They did not, Gray was convinced, desire to promote dishonesty or encourage the creation of a plutocracy. They were influenced, rather, by several meretricious aspects of contemporary society. One was the unfortunate tendency of states and municipalities to repudiate their debts. He found another in state statutes that exempt large amounts of property from execution in satisfaction of a judgment. The major influence, however, was the reaction against laissez-faire. Paternalism, as Gray saw it, was "the fundamental essence alike of spendthrift trusts and of socialism."[107] Gray loathed socialism. He revealed in these comments more than a little sympathy for the idea that the progress from status to contract was both an accurate description of the history of the common law and a triumph of progress. His attack on the cases validating spendthrift trusts, however, was based not on a notion of the proper social order but on a critique of the formalistic reasoning of those cases.

Much of Gray's treatise was devoted to carefully tracing the cases dealing with restraints on alienation of property, classified along the lines of the various estates and future interests that are the core of property law. The cases showed that restraints were always opposed. There was no authority for the approval of spendthrift trusts. Gray applied his analysis to the leading Massachusetts case.[108] The court stated that while a limitation on alienation is "repugnant" to a legal estate (an interest in land), it is not repugnant to an equitable estate (an interest in a trust). Such an argument assumes a coherent system that provides automatic answers to real questions. Gray would not brook that reasoning. Repugnancy could not mean "logical inconsistency." The legislature could invalidate restraints on legal estates, and "the courts would have no trouble upholding them." The system of estates in land could be manipulated by the legislature. The result might not be wise, but it would be binding on society.[109]

Once logical inconsistency is put aside, repugnancy could only be either a "metaphysical refinement" or a conclusion dictated by public policy. The former in Gray's eyes was not worth refuting, and the latter was simply untrue. Gray had already shown to his satisfaction that all public policy favored alienation of property.[110] In upholding spendthrift trusts, therefore, judges had misread the sources of the law embodied in precedents and made a serious mistake. They had abandoned themselves to the tendencies of the age, tendencies that Gray abhorred and about which, he believed, the judges should certainly think twice. The betrayal of precedent should at least indicate that judges must honestly state their reasons for decisions rather than hide behind false reasoning. Gray was attempting to be a modern scientific jurist. It was his job to arrange and clarify the law found in the cases in order to illuminate its relationship to society and to aid lawyers and judges in working with and within it.

Of the five Harvard law teachers, James Barr Ames was least touched by positivism. Ames was one of Langdell's earliest students, the first to follow Langdell in teaching by cases and his successor as dean of Harvard Law School. Given Ames's intellectual lineage, it is not surprising that he was a historian of the law. He never produced a comprehensive work, however. Instead, he expended much of his intellectual effort in preparing casebooks and much of his time in administering Harvard Law School and counseling its students.[111] Several of his essays on legal history were published during his lifetime in the *Harvard Law Review*. Others that appeared in the posthumous *Lectures on Legal History* were constructed from both his notes and those of some of his auditors.[112]

Enough of Ames's work exists, however, to permit general conclusions to be drawn. First and foremost, he was a critic of cases and of judges. The sort of legal principles Langdell believed in were real to Ames, as was the process of legal reasoning whose results could be used to test and to judge cases. A positive rule of law could be judged "unwarranted" "as a matter of legal reasoning," but not objectionable because the proper result was reached nonetheless.[113] Also real in Ames's mind were the rights and duties Langdell discussed in his work. The problem of succession by one person to the legal situation of another, which Holmes treated as a matter of facts, Ames treated as a matter of rights and duties, which of their nature can or cannot be transferred.[114] Finally, he believed that while the common law was "unmoral," equity represented a higher morality and, unlike Holmes, he saw in it much more than simply a different method of procedure.[115] Ames even went so far as to maintain that "wrongful motive" could make an act a tort.[116]

Besides disagreeing with Holmes's view of law, Ames appealed to morality and principles, thereby distancing himself from Austinian positivism. He could, nevertheless, sound very much like Holmes:

> The law is utilitarian. It exists for the realization of the reasonable needs of the community. If the interest of an individual runs counter to this chief object of the law, it must be sacrificed. That is why, [in some cases] the innocent suffer and the wicked go unpunished.[117]

Ames, moreover, never turned his analysis of law into a denial of legislative power. His own allegiance to Austinian positivism was not in the end intellectual but rather institutional. Whatever he thought about the role of morals in law, Ames clearly believed that law schools should teach only law and that the teachers should be lawyers (although given his own career they apparently need not be practitioners). Like his mentor, he believed that teaching other subjects from other disciplines had no place in a law school. Along with Langdell, Thayer, and Gray, he actively promoted a version of legal education compatible with positivism.

In fact, it was Ames who made the most striking statement of limitation of the law school curriculum to what was law by an Austinian definition. When William Rainey Harper began to plan a law school for the new University of Chicago, he turned to Harvard for help. Harper, Ames, and Eliot agreed that Harvard would lend Joseph Beale, one of the second generation of Harvard teachers, to be the first dean of the new school.[118] All went well until the men in Cambridge discovered that Harper intended to put on the law school faculty Ernst Freund, a political scientist with European legal degrees and experience of practice in New York.[119] Freund traveled to Cambridge and met with Beale and Ames who, while impressed with Freund both as a thinker and a potential colleague, were adamant about excluding him from any school over which Beale would preside. Before Freund's trip to Cambridge, he had prepared a circular describing the curriculum of the new school. As Ames told it, under Freund's plan "2/9 of the work leading to the degree should consist of subjects belonging properly in the departments of Political Science or Sociology." In addition, Freund proposed that the teachers of these subjects, who were not lawyers, should be admitted to the law faculty. Finally, Ames was not at all convinced that Freund was a true believer in the case method. "I did not ask him his views on that point," Ames admitted, but "certainly his belief in the general methods of the German Universities, and his general views as to the function of a law-school would predispose him against a thoroughgoing belief in us or our methods."[120]

Ames was determined to exclude both nonlegal subjects and academics without law degrees from the law school. Freund's plan included international law in the first year, taught by a member of the political science department, and upper-class electives in criminology, "relation of the state to industry," finance, railroad transportation, accounting, banking, experimental psychology, history of political ethics, comparative politics, diplomatic history of the United States and Europe, government of colonies, European political theory, and administrative law.[121] "We have no such subjects in our Curriculum," Ames wrote Harper, "and are unanimously opposed to the teaching of anything but pure law in our department." Ames even refused to consider such courses as part of a postgraduate year.[122] Joseph Beale was in total accord with his dean, writing Harper that by limiting the school to the teaching of law "in the strict sense of the word" Harvard aimed to "turn out thoroughly trained men, fit at once to enter upon the practice of a learned and strenuous profession."[123]

A compromise was reached. Although the historian of the University of Chicago Law School could find no trace of any response by Harper to Beale and Ames, Harper apparently informed Freund that he would not hold the same position on the law faculty as the "pure" lawyers.[124] Freund then abandoned the idea of a permanent appointment to the law faculty and agreed to limit his teaching to elective subjects.[125] On the whole, the Harvard view, so clearly articulated by its dean, had prevailed.

Ames's attitude toward Freund's proposals illustrates how strongly Harvard Law School teachers believed in the superiority of their school. The teachers behaved as if the world had to acknowledge their leadership and had no qualms about pushing leadership toward dictatorship. The apparent submission of the University of Chicago authorities shows that agressiveness had its rewards. It may also have had wider impact. Once again, the teachers put forward the idea that law was a demanding study, worthy of single-minded pursuit. Those who were legal experts, therefore, were indeed important people who deserved the same sort of respect given masters of other sciences. The collective ego of the Harvard Law School fed the collective ego of the bar.

7

Opposition

Despite the victory in Chicago, the rise to dominance of the Harvard model of legal education was not a triumphal progress. Within the school, debate and dissension went on for decades. Elsewhere, in writings about the training of aspiring lawyers, criticism of Harvard's methods was constant. This criticism occurred in two phases. In the first phase, impracticality in Harvard's methods was asserted. The belief that "instruction at [Harvard Law School] was particularly technical and historical, and when completed, necessitated an apprenticeship in some good attorney's office," found expression in the founding of Boston University Law School.[1] There teachers familiar with the practice of law offered not only an introduction to the science of law but also training designed to enable students to enter active practice on graduation.[2] Similar concerns surfaced in the debate about the diploma privilege in New York. The *Albany Law Journal* printed several editorials in the early and mid-1870s advocating legal education that would "familiarize [the student] with the details of practice and the examination of witnesses."[3] The imposition of a clerkship requirement by the court of appeals and its acceptance by Eliot and Langdell went far to answering these objections.

In the second phase of criticism, which became evident after the turmoil at Columbia in the early 1890s, more far-reaching issues were involved. By the turn of the century the contest between the case method schools and those offering traditional forms of legal education had become to a great extent a contest between two opposing visions of the nature of law.

The Case Lawyer

Early discussions of the usefulness of the case method dealt mainly with its origin in and perpetuation of Langdell's supposedly excessive theorizing. The premises of discussions about methods in legal education changed about the time of the changes at Columbia. By then the principal complaint was that the case method was *too* practical. In the view of critics, the case method produced "case lawyers," a reprehensible subspecies of the profession who devoted themselves to the mindless collection of precedents in an attempt to win judgments for their clients based only on the assumed weight of the collected cases rather than by an appeal to the principles of the common law. Such fears seemed plausible because the glory of Theodore Dwight's method was its attempt to teach those very principles, in contrast to the almost exclusive reliance of the case method on reading cases. Those who feared and despised the case lawyer expressed concerns similar to those voiced by opponents of pettifoggers in an earlier era. Edward Phelps, who ended his long legal and political career by occupying the Kent Professorship at Yale from 1881 until his death in 1900, provided a neat sketch of the case lawyer in a address to the graduating class of the Boston University School of Law in 1879:

> Some lawyers fail in their studies for *want of depth*. They do not go down to the foundation principles which underlie all propositions of law. They are always hunting about after *cases*. . . . It is *principles* that the lawyer needs to deal with. *Cases* only illustrate principles; they are not to be neglected or overlooked, they are to be studied and understood; they *illustrate* principles, but they do not *supply* them; they do not *make* them, except sometimes false principles, which lead the world astray, until some other Court takes courage to repudiate and put an end to them. The real and enduring principle does not come out of the case, but underlies and controls the case. Depth of study, thorough mastery of the principles of the case, is the touchstone and criterion; that alone makes the lawyer, in the high sense of the term.[4]

Like the pettifogger of old, the case lawyer litigated out of ignorance. Just as the pettifogger might try to manipulate the old forms of action and play tricks with writs, the case lawyer tried to answer every question by piling up precedents and could, in Phelps's view, "be brought to almost any conclusion that seems to be sustained by what is called authority."[5] The result, as another observer saw it in 1882, was trying cases "upon precedent rather than upon principle, and it is a matter of common remark among the elder school of lawyers and judges that the younger men at the bar rely too much upon books and too little upon the elementary doctrines by which all cases should be decided."[6]

This lament about the younger generation hints at a concern with the direction of legal education. The link between case method and case lawyer was made clear in an exchange of views on the methods of legal education in the pages of the *Yale Law Journal* in 1892. The participants were Phelps, William A. Keener, Christopher G. Tiedeman, then teaching at the University of the City of New York, and John Chipman Gray. Phelps, in much the same terms as he used in his earlier comments, lamented the concentration on cases to the neglect of principles:

> The unhappy tendency of our time, not merely in schools but to a considerable degree in the profession and in the courts, is to encumber the law with much that is called learning, sought to be deduced from millions

> of heterogeneous, often irreconcilable, and sometimes incomprehensible cases, each of which, instead of being a decision upon the point involved, is a dissertation upon the general law of the subject.[7]

Tiedeman explained how the case method caused the situation Phelps lamented. It might be possible to use cases to teach a "few men of extraordinary mental powers"; "the average student," however, will learn only the importance of precedent and will become

> what is so generally deprecated, a case-lawyer, who thinks the whole business of advocacy consists of persuading the court that the cases he cites in support of his side of the controversy, are to be followed, not because they enunciate a profound scientific truth, but merely because they have given judgment for the plaintiff or defendant on a similar statement of facts.[8]

Keener and Gray defended their approach to legal education with arguments that would become standard. Keener first described what the case method was not:

1. It does not consist in the study of isolated propositions of law.
2. It does not proceed on the theory that the law consist of an aggregation of cases.
3. It does not proceed on the theory that to learn law one must *memorize cases*.
4. It does not proceed on the theory that law is to be taught or learned in a law school by the reading of cases merely.
5. It does not leave the student to deduce the principles of law from the cases *by himself*.[9]

In the hands of a skilled teacher, the case method was teaching through the use of original sources rather than secondhand: "Instead of reading about principles [the student] is studying and investigating the principles themselves." He is also reading and studying the only authoritative statement of those principles, the recorded opinions of appellate courts. In short, the case method is anything but the blind worship of precedent. It is true scientific study of the law, relying on the sort of analysis a practicing lawyer uses in dealing with clients' problems.[10] Gray made many of the same points, emphasizing particularly the rigorous nature of study by the case method.

The principals in this printed debate were not so very far apart in their views of what should be taught. Keener particularly insisted that most critics' objections were based on misconceptions about the case method. He appeared to have the better of the argument on this score. It is improbable that the case method as practiced by teachers such as Ames, Gray, Thayer, and Keener amounted to mechanical examination of isolated cases without any reference to the principles of the subject being studied. Langdell himself believed that the study of cases leads to understanding the principles. A recent graduate's description of instruction at Harvard published in 1888 depicted the professor leading the student "up and down among the pure fundamental principles, [making] him argue about them, turn them over, handle and dissect them, until they are burnt into his mind."[11] Keener was totally candid when he told the American Bar Association in 1894 that the case method did not make case lawyers. The cases studied showed how principles are applied to facts—"[i]n other words, the case is simply material from which a principle is to be extracted."[12] Keener was repeating almost verbatim Gray's defense of the case method written in 1888 in response to some of its earliest criticisms. That method, Gray wrote, "uses the cases merely as material from which the student may learn to extract the underlying principles."[13]

These arguments defended a case method that was not quite what Langdell envisioned, however. Keener's fourth point is especially telling. Langdell believed that most cases were useless for systematic study, and he worked hard to reduce all of the law of contracts to a system. However much he believed in teaching only from the actual sources of the law, he certainly believed that study of the sources he selected would give the student all he needed to know about the law of contracts. His examinations tested knowledge worth having—that is, systematic understanding of the law as conveyed by a true legal scientist—and therefore were superior to bar examinations set by the state.[14] Keener described a pedagogical technique that teaches students how to learn, as well as imparts substantive knowledge. This aspect of the case method of teaching was present from the beginning, and certainly was important to Eliot's support of Langdell. Ames, however, played the more important role in its development. In 1931, Samuel Williston wrote to Karl Llewellyn that "with reference to *teaching* law . . . the training in plotting general rules and deducing consequences in the manner developed by Ames (rather than by Langdell) is not likely to be improved."[15] This shift in emphasis to the technique taught by the case method corresponds to the increasing concern with the proliferation of precedent and the importance of the decided case to legal research. No matter how useful the case method could be in practice, however, some members of the bar saw it as a serious threat to the profession and to the rule of law itself.

These criticisms began to be made in earnest after the turmoil at Columbia in 1891. For discussion of legal education, the revival of the American Bar Association's interest in the subject was the most important result of the retirement of Dwight, the installation of Keener, and the founding of the New York Law School. The organized bar had been interested in legal education in the 1870s and 1880s. The Association of the Bar of the City of New York, for example, was deeply involved in attempts to end the diploma privilege in New York State and to strengthen the requirements for admission to practice. The American Bar Association, in contrast, paid no attention to the matter throughout the 1880s. Its Standing Committee on Legal Education issued a report in 1879 approving study in law schools where law could be taught as a science rather than a trade, but nothing more was forthcoming. The subject of legal education was perhaps too involved in local peculiarities to receive much attention from a nominally national association of lawyers. Consideration of legal education more-over, was, closely tied to the question of admission to practice, a matter of strictly local concern. In any event, the next report of the committee, issued in 1890, began with a reference to "the record of masterly inactivity formed by the unremitting efforts of their predecessors for at least ten successive years." There was nothing humorous about the rest of the report. Like much of the commentary on legal education up to that time, the report focused on the need to educate students broadly in legal principles rather than merely introduce them to the infinite variety of facts involved in legal controversies.[16]

The 1890 report marked the end of "masterly inactivity." The committee produced lengthy reports in both 1891 and 1892 that severely criticized the case method on familiar grounds. In its 1891 report the committee stated: "We deprecate the use of cases alone without reference to the fundamental principles of the law of which we believe them to be in all cases the application."[17] The 1892 report was even more emphatic, asserting that the case method emphasized "the doubtful part of the law" and ignored "the great but settled principles upon which so much of the lawyer's reasoning depends."[18]

The ABA was also concerned with the breadth of law school education. Throughout the 1890s the committee not only criticized the case method for its supposed slighting of principles but also asserted that law schools should teach a broad array of subjects that today might be considered cultural. The argument usually was based on the idea that lawyers were the natural leaders of American society and government. Law schools, therefore, should teach the "science of government" or "political and social science," and even moral and political philosophy.[19] In 1895 the committee declared that all schools gave instruction that was "too technical" and devoted to training attorneys rather than jurists. "Little effort," the committee wrote, "is made to train the student for the higher duties of his profession and citizenship."[20] In address to the ABA in 1894, John F. Dillon went further and named names. He analyzed Harvard's course of instruction and concluded that "the subjects taught and the books used show more clearly than any general description the intensely technical and practical character of the course of instruction." The entire enterprise in Cambridge was lacking "in historical and comparative jurisprudence, and in the literature, science and philosophy of the law—in what may, perhaps, be compendiously expressed as general jurisprudence."[21]

One can imagine the Harvard teachers' response: general jurisprudence, political science, moral philosophy had no place in law school. All the early teachers were positivists, at least in the sense that identifies law with the power of the state and separates morality from law for purposes of study. For them "cultural" subjects were outside the province of jursiprudence. The Harvard curriculum faithfully reflected these beliefs. From the mid-1870s until the early years of the twentieth century, the first-year curriculum did not vary—contracts, torts, property, civil procedure at common law, and criminal law and procedure filled the days of first-year students. Over the years the number of second- and third-year electives increased, but, excepting constitutional law and jurisprudence, these courses were all devoted to specific areas of private law such as sales, trusts, partnership, bankruptcy, admiralty, and carriers.[22]

The lecture and recitation method of teaching, which the case method had supplanted at Columbia and eventually elsewhere, resembled teaching at the old Harvard Law School before Langdell. The broad view of legal education with its emphasis on moral truth also harked back to the old regime which Harvard, at least, had so firmly resolved to put behind it. The advocates of a broadened curriculum may have sounded too much like that epitome of the old Harvard, Emory Washburn. In 1868 Washburn lectured a meeting of the American Social Science Association on the "Law as an Element of Social Science." Washburn declared that law was more than the command of the sovereign; it was a reflection of public thought: "Law becomes, in this way, a part of Social Science itself, because it enters into every thing which relates to the social well being of every individual of which a community is composed."[23] He also maintained that it could and should reform public sentiment:

> If I have not misconceived the importance of good laws, or the source from which all law emanates, there is a mighty work to be done here and everywhere, to educate the people, to give direction and tone to public thought, to check the waywardness of passion, and create in the public heart a sentiment of national honor as well as love of country.[24]

Here is law pouring over into morality and becoming a tool for the general uplift of society. Washburn's law, and by association the broad legal education promoted by those who criticized Harvard, was not science; it was amateur moralizing.[25] Their approach was far closer to that of the antebellum Baconian scientists, whose entire outlook was summed up by Eliot's predecessor as president of Harvard, Thomas Hill, in an address to the American Social Science Association in 1865:

> The ultimate ends of common sense, of philosophy and of science are the same. They may be summed up in one,—rational, intelligible. The conviction of this primal truth springs up upon occasion for its use in every human mind. No man capable of scientific labor ever doubts that all phenomena are subject to law, that is, all phenomena succeed each other in an order which can be understood and expressed in the formulae of human speech. To discover this order, to comprehend it, to express it in words and teach others to see it, this is the labor and the play, the work and the wages of the human intellect.[26]

The link between the older idea of legal science and the criticism found in the ABA's statement on legal education was not coincidental. Behind the attack on Harvard and its methods was a notion of law which resembled that of the antebellum legal scientists. The Austinian equation of law and power was not acceptable to those who thought of law as the expression of timeless principles.

The Evils of Positivism

This alternative view of the law was clearly evident in the views of the revitalized ABA Committee on Legal Education. In its report for 1891 the committee engaged in an elaborate attack on the theory that the common law is the judicial opinions recorded in the reports. "It is not correct," according to the committee, "to say that the judges make the law." On the contrary, the law is a preexisting system of principles, a proposition the committee proved by an appeal to the nature of the physical sciences whose truths are not made by those who investigate them but are rather discovered. In both the physical sciences and in the law "the announcement of a new truth, the recognition of a new principle, *must* be accepted as the revelation of that which already exists, not as the introduction of a change."[27] The case method, therefore, is erroneous in theory because "the cases are not the original sources of law, and are but the application of principles to the particular facts."[28]

The conviction that the principles of the common law exist above and apart from the actual decisions that apply them to controversies is venerable. It formed the basis of the antebellum notion of legal science. Sir William Blackstone himself wrote that judges only declared the law and did not make it. At first glance, then, the reiteration of this idea in the 1890s is an example of the conservatism of the legal profession and of the persistence of familiar ideas. By the time the Committee on Legal Education of the ABA repeated the formulae of the declaratory theory of law, however, the theory had taken on a new meaning.

The antebellum science of legal principles was based to a great degree on belief in the power of inductive reasoning to discover the Creator's laws. The aspiration to the superhuman led thinkers like case method teachers to denigrate their ancestors as unscientific. By the late nineteenth century, however, believers in a permanent law of universal truth were less wedded to the appeal to the divine. Many were convinced that they could prove the transcendent nature of law in ways compatible with modern scientific inquiry. They sought to use historical jurisprudence to refute Austin's analytical jurisprudence. This use of history to illuminate and to defend the common law was unoriginal. Glorifying the common law as the embodiment of English liberty had been a staple of the Whig history that justified opposition to Stuart tyranny.[29]

By 1861, however, the relationship of law and history entered a new era in the English-speaking world. In that year Henry Sumner Maine published his *Ancient Law*. Maine's work traced the origin of legal rules into the past, especially the Roman past, and tried to explain the mechanisms by which the law had changed in response to changes in society. Maine's explanation of his enterprise clearly emphasized its scientific character:

> If by any means we can determine the early forms of jural conceptions, they will be invaluable to us. These rudimentary ideas are to the jurist what the primary crusts of the earth are to the geologist. They contain, potentially, all the forms in which law has subsequently exhibited itself.[30]

Ignorance of these early forms is responsible for the "unsatisfactory condition in which we find the science of jurisprudence." By ignoring the facts of legal history jurists place assumption over observation, and their unverified theories hold sway over "sober research."[31]

This philosophical aspect of *Ancient Law* was overshadowed, however, by what was assumed to be the historical message of the work. For many readers only one phrase in the entire work was important: "We may say that the movement of the progressive societies has hitherto been a movement *from Status to Contract*" [italics in original].[32]

Although as Frederick Pollock noted "it is not clear how far Maine regarded the movement of which he spoke as a phase of the larger political individualism which prevailed in the eighteenth century and a great part of the nineteenth, or what he would have thought of the reaction against this doctrine which we are now [in 1906] witnessing," many of Maine's readers found in his dictum support for their faith in laissez-faire.[33] They also found in it a convenient weapon with which to fend off Austin's analytical jurisprudence. Especially in the United States, *Ancient Law* was read as an exemplary use of history to correct Austin's errors. William G. Hammond lamented that during his sojourn in Germany, Austin fell completely "under the influence of the so-called philosophical school of jurists" and therefore had ignored the historical school whose leader was Savigny. Had the situation been reversed, "the study of scientific jurisprudence in England might have reached, a generation earlier, the point to which it has later been brought under the guidance of jurists like Sir Henry Maine."[34]

Perhaps the most famous exponent of this approach to law was James Coolidge Carter. Nothwithstanding his loyalty to his legal alma mater, Carter did not fully accept its faculty's ideas of the nature of law. His interest in jurisprudence seems to have begun with opposition to codification in general and of the civil code proposed in New York in particular. He was a member of the committee of the Association of the Bar of the City of New York charged with opposing the proposed code. The need to refute the claims for the code so energetically made by its author, David Dudley Field, led Carter "into inquiries concerning the distinctions between written and unwritten law."[35] From these inquiries came several important speeches and, finally, at the end of his life, the lectures on the subject prepared for presentation at Harvard Law School but only published posthumously as *Law: Its Origin Growth and Function*.

The message of Carter's work is simple: all law is custom and courts declare and do not make it. Custom is gradually established through sanctions, he said: first, through informal ones that include self-help; later, with the growth of "organised government," through societal enforcement of the decisions of acknowledged experts in what the customs are. This organized force is applied only "in the case of those breaches or alleged breaches of custom which endanger the peace of society." Eventually, "as civilisation advances, and population, industry, and wealth increase, the social organisation expands and advances," the job of ascertaining custom is lodged in "regular judicial tribunals . . . armed with the whole power of the State to directly enforce their decisions." The proceedings of these courts are recorded in permanent form and regarded "as authoritative declarations of binding custom." In this way they become precedents, and when litigation arises if "an apt precedent is found it is followed without further inquiry, and the precedents themselves are by the private work of jurists arranged in scientific form and go to make up the fabric of substantive law." Carter summed up his research with the assertion that "law, with the narrow exception of legislation, *is* custom, and, like custom, self-existing and irrepealable."[36] In fact, this customary law "may justly be called Divine; for, being identical with custom which is the form in which human nature necessarily develops conduct, it can have no other author than that of human nature itself."[37]

Carter's basis for this conclusion was mainly historical, based on a "survey of human life in all ages and in all stages of social progress." These stages included "primitive man," a nomad; man in settlements; man in a "social state"; literate society; arbitrary governments; the development of law and courts; and finally "man in the present enlightened age."[38] He also had no doubt that all nations and peoples had passed or would pass through these stages. His actual examples were drawn primarily from the history of England, especially when he dealt with the development of judicial tribunals. That was the history he knew best, he claimed, and, besides, "social progress elsewhere has not, as I suppose, in substance been different from that exhibited in England."[39] Even the details of these various stages are uniform across societies, he said. Carter's examination of the characteristics of the last stage of development was based on an examination of the courts of the United States and England "for the reason that we are best acquainted with them, and because we may be sure that the condition of courts in other countries, however varying from that of these, is not fundamentally different."[40] The fault with theories of law that find their essence in command is ignorance of the truth "that society, like every other phenomenon in nature, was a condition resulting from the operation of causes reaching back into periods infinitely remote."[41] For Carter and many others, the message of history is uniform and inescapable. As a speaker before the ABA put it in 1891 with specific reference to Maine's work: "In a modern industrial state, this freedom of individual contract, representing a long and toilsome progressive social development, becomes essential in any rational conception of individual liberty."[42]

In part because Austin's ideas were assumed to justify unlimited legislative power, the advocates of the preservation of property rights seized on the historical jurisprudence (which they believed was first voiced by Maine) to create an explanation of the nature of law that emphasized continuity and stability and provided new grounds for the old idea that judges merely declare the law rather than make it.

Like the antebellum legal scientists, they spoke the language of induction. Carter declared that "the province of science," including the science of law, is "rigidly confined to the observation and orderly arrangement of facts."[43] William G. Hammond, himself a law teacher, also argued that we only know the law through induction based on cases. In that sense cases are the law because we could not understand it without them, but they do not make the law. "No one believes," he argued, "that the observation and experiments by which our knowledge of physical science is constantly increasing, are so many additions to nature and its laws."[44] Law must be learned, he wrote in 1880, "like the law of the physical world, inductively" from "the decided cases of the past," which "are so many observations upon the practical working of these laws, [and] from which the true theory is to be inferred."[45] Thomas McIntyre Cooley, judge, teacher, and treatise writer, also asserted that judges discover law and found the proof for that assertion in the inductive nature of the legal process: "The case is not the measure of the principle; it does not limit and confine it within the exact facts, but it furnishes an illustration of the principle."[46] Like the antebellum legal scientists before them, these thinkers induced true law from cases. For some of them this law expressed the mind of the Creator, but for all of them its real power came from its connection with history.

The ability to appeal to history to support the unchanging principles of law was useful partly because it appeared to link evolution to the science of the law. For all these thinkers, the expression of law in rules changes with changing times. Carter blamed the seductive appeal of Jeremy Bentham's foolishness to the ignorance of the pre-Darwinian world: "The law of Evolution so dominating in its influence upon recent thought, had not been stated." Once it was understood that society evolves, it became clear that legal rules were the product of causes reaching far back into time and they cannot be changed by arbitrary legislation.[47] One harried supporter of analytical jurisprudence humorously described his dilemma in a world dominated by ideas of slow change:

> But quite certainly, in spite of all that can be urged, the cultivators of analytical jurisprudence will still be reproached with wanting historical-mindedness, a graver charge in these days when evolution is in the very air,—it has been humorously said,—than heresy or even petty larceny.[48]

Ironically, the arguments of these legal thinkers were not truly evolutionary. All of them accepted a theory of historical change based on stages of development, much like the historical thought of antebellum legal scientists. They saw no place for slow change reflecting a changing environment, or for the gradual emergence of new rules better suited to different times. Not every acknowledgment of change is evolutionary.

A full discussion of this alternative science of law would involve much more than an investigation of legal education.[49] It is clear, however, that for the advocates of legal truth the case method law school was the enemy. They promoted a different sort of legal education, which found a home during this period at the law school of Yale College. Especially after the coup at Columbia in 1890–1891, Yale became the citadel of alternative legal science. Under the leadership of Simeon Baldwin, the school resisted the case method and tried to provide a broad legal education designed to train society's leaders.

Baldwin was a railroad lawyer and politician, eventually becoming both governor of Connecticut and chief justice of its highest court.[50] From 1869 he played an important role in the life of the Yale law school, carrying a heavy burden of teaching, as well as providing financial support. He was a devoted and articulate promoter of the science of permanent principles, which he applied to legal education at Yale. He was also a prominent figure in the organized bar, one of the founders of the ABA, its president in 1890, and a long-time director of its bureau of comparative law.

For Baldwin, "the study of elementary law" was "the proper beginning of a legal education," because of the nature of law itself.[51] This elementary law was unwritten, and it was "a higher law than any which . . . legislatures could make or unmake." The decisions of appellate courts were valuable to the extent they expressed this higher law. The appellate decision was not "a source of supply from which law can be dug out by pains and difficulty." Not surprisingly, Baldwin identified "the evolution of all things wrought by time" as an important part of "the thought of our day" and invoked Maine for the conclusion that courts are the "echoes" of the unwritten law. It was "principles, not cases," that were "the building stones of law, here and everywhere, now and always."

The casebook, then, was not the proper basic tool of legal education. It was only "a series of fragmentary discussions of particular topics, interspersed with fragmentary portions of opinions from reported cases." The treatise, on the other hand, was "an orderly and succinct statement of the existing law on some particular topic, illustrated by apt examples, and fortified by references to reported cases."[52] It was there that "judicial precedents are sifted and legal doctrines finally clothed in appropriate terms and arranged in scientific order."[53] The best method of studying law was to have students read such books a chapter or two at a time and then require them "to be ready to explain the principles of decision applicable to states of fact slightly variant from those given in the examples put by the author."[54]

Baldwin repeated the commonplace that instruction from cases would create only case lawyers "to whom the natural appeal to authority is to a volume of reports" and who would believe that judges "are oracles—or idols," thus adding to the followers of Austinian foolishness. Instruction by the case method "tends to put the student back into the ranks of those of former generations who thought of law only as a rule prescribed by a superior authority." On the contrary, every decision depends on preexisting rights or duties and those must be understood before the case can be understood.[55]

Edward Phelps also believed in the primacy of principles that were an integral part of Anglo-American history. According to Phelps, lawyers should concern themselves not with cases but with "the foundation principles which underlie all propositions of law."[56] These principles formed part of what Phelps called the law of the land, which was unalterable by the legislature. They were "inherent in the human conscience," and "they derive their authority from the spontaneous and universal recognition of intelligent humanity, as well as from divine revelation."[57] The rights based on these principles—rights to life, liberty, and property—were therefore "placed beyond the reach of any department of the government."[58]

History confirmed the primacy of these rights, continued Phelps. In spite of the universal nature of these principles and the rights resting on them, they were also in some way the exclusive heritage of "the Anglo-Saxon race" and were embodied in a unique way in "the common law of England, which is likewise the common law of the English-speaking race everywhere." In addition, the common law also included certain "legal rights" that ensured the enjoyment of the fundamental rights. These legal rights were the growing part of the law that changed as society changed, but they could not be made by any authority.[59] They were valid and enforceable only to the extent that they reflected the condition of society. Phelps believed that society in some sense made law. He also clearly set out the antipositivistic implications of that belief:

> And no man has ever yet obtained a clear idea of [the foundation of law] who attempted to deduce its sanction from the maze of metaphysical speculation, or who failed to comprehend that law among a free people must have something else to stand upon besides positive authority, and must be inspired by a controlling and animating spirit, that has sway over the reason and the conscience of men. The days of arbitrary power in state, in church, or in rules have passed away, so far as we are concerned, to be seen no more.[60]

In sum, transcendent law was justified by its conformity to absolute morality and even revelation, incorporated into history and the common law which is the expression of history, and one with the nature of society.[61]

Under Baldwin, the Yale Law School put these theories into practice. In 1887 the school formalized its approach in an "education covenant to which all of the faculty of that day devotedly subscribed." It described the method of instruction as "mainly that of recitations." Both the "conviction" of the faculty and "the tradition of the University" held that "definite and permanent impressions concerning the principles and rules of any abstract science are best acquired by the study of standard text-books in private, followed by the examinations and explanations of the recitations room." Although lectures were used where "proper manuals" are wanting or where the pressures of time or "the rapid advance of learning" require it, the subjects lectured upon were always "covered by recitation work." The recitations, however, were not designed solely to test the student's preparation. Time was always reserved "for a free colloquial discussion" and for student questions.[62]

This sort of instruction was precisely that of the antebellum law school. The emphasis on principles so evident in Baldwin's views of legal education was carried forward by the course in elementary law required of all beginning students. Until 1895 the course was taught by William C. Robinson, who read lectures to his students, required them to memorize definitions and rules, and sent them to do collateral reading in treatises.[63] Robinson, like Baldwin, was no friend of positivism. In his view, law was a science, but a deductive science whose base is "immutable and universal principles." The law that exists today is inherited, "not from the courts and legislatures of past generations" but from preceding "social conditions."[64]

The Yale school also tried to create a broad legal education, at least for the scholar. As early as 1876 the school inaugurated a graduate course leading to a master of law degree. The curriculum included Roman law, comparative jurisprudence, oratory, constitutional history, and political science.[65] This course was designed to train legal scholars and those "who hope to take an active and intelligent part in politics, (using that term in its best and proper sense)."[66] While the graduate course was never a success when measured by the number of students who took the advanced degree, much of its curriculum was incorporated into the third year of law study required in 1896.[67] As late as the opening years of the new century, the dean of the law school was still promoting law as a "cultural study," the pursuit of which should count toward the bachelor's degree.[68]

Unfortunately for the believers in unchanging legal truth, the school devoted to its inculcation did not prosper. Baldwin was distressed at the tendency of graduates of Yale College to attend Harvard Law School.[69] In the privacy of his diary he fulminated against Harvard's reputation, although he admitted that "their class of students is certainly better than ours: that is, there are more good men and fewer poor sticks."[70] In 1898 the school went so far as to appoint a committee "to control the increasing annual exodus of Yale graduates to Harvard Law School."[71] The solution hit upon was to allow Yale students to receive the bachelor's degree and the law degree in a six-year course of study.[72]

More thoroughgoing adjustments were needed if the Yale Law School was to seriously challenge Harvard. For years the president of the university, Arthur T. Hadley, blocked requiring a college degree for admission, and as late as 1902 he stated his opposition in comprehensive terms. He rested his views in part on social considerations: the "poor man" simply cannot delay earning a living for the time it would take to complete both college and law school courses. By demanding the degree as a prerequisite of legal study, "we enhance the artificial difficulties which are already great enough at best, and tend to make the professions of law and medicine places for the sons of rich men only"; the result would be a "caste system." His views would have ranked as heresy in Cambridge or at Columbia, where thorough preparation presumably represented by the undergraduate degree was the necessary precursor of demanding legal instruction. Even worse, at least for his law school, Hadley had the temerity to assert "that the work of the manufacturer and the financier, the engineer and the journalist, involves the same sort of ability and character, and carries with it the same sort of social privileges and responsibilities, that are involved in that of the lawyer, the physician, or the minister." All that was needed to prepare for successful professional study was solid grounding in English, the ability to read "ordinary" Latin prose, some reading knowledge of French and German, and concrete mathematics—algebra, geometry, and trigonometry—"which do not require an exceptional type of intellect to master." To the extent that Harvard's success was based on rigorous training successfully pursued only by the brightest students and thus guaranteeing the intellectual preeminence of the profession, Hadley's views would not contribute to similar success for Yale Law School.[73]

Apparently, Hadley came to a better understanding of the spirit of the age. A few years after the president had dismissed the college degree as required preparation, Dean Rogers pointed out in his annual report that the reputation of every degree-granting institution depended on the public perception that its standards of admission and graduation are rigorous.[74] Yale finally required a college degree for admission in 1912. President Hadley explained his about-face by identifying "the preliminaries required of a law student" as "a certain maturity of thought and judgment, a grasp of general ethics, a power of clear thinking and clear statement." These qualities were best guaranteed by requiring the degree.[75] Dean Rogers agreed, at least in part, because the 1912–1913 academic year marked Yale's final conversion to the case method.

The turn to the case method at Yale had been gradual. It was first introduced in all its Harvard-style rigor in 1903 when Arthur Corbin and John W. Edgerton joined the faculty.[76] The innovation was only grudgingly accepted, each adoption of a casebook needing the specific approval of the entire faculty. At last, on April 27, 1912, the faculty resolved that any professor could use "the case system of instruction" without special approval. As Rogers put it, adoption of this resolution "meant that in the opinion of the Faculty whatever objections were originally entertained against this method of instruction has ceased to influence the thought of the Faculty as a whole." Rogers went on to state that the case method's value was the training it gave students. It was an inductive method that accomplished the three major aims of education: cultivation of "the powers of discriminating observation,'' strengthening of ''the logical faculty,'' and improvement of ''the judgment.'' Although the case method was ''a difficult system,'' it was ''profitable.''[77]

The formal explanation of Yale's conversion fails to indicate that the view of the nature of law, which had sustained opposition to the case method, had finally been abandoned. There are some hints, however, that a larger change in thinking accompanied the change in teaching method. First, blanket approval of the case method came about only after Baldwin's withdrawal from daily involvement with the school, Robinson's departure, and Phelps's death.[78] Second, to give more time ''for subjects of more practical and immediate importance to students preparing for the practice of law, the adoption of the case method was accompanied by the elimination of both the course in elementary law, designed to inculcate the great principles in the old-fashioned way, and the course in American diplomatic history.'' The demands of training in technical principles had eclipsed the older vision of a broad legal education. Finally, after 1912 instruction was given almost exclusively by full-time teachers ''withdrawn from the active practice of law.''[79] As the school turned to full-time academics, it was staffed with men who equated the case method with proper legal education.

There is another indication of the thoroughgoing nature of the change. Arthur Corbin was among the very first Yale faculty members to use the case method. Shortly after the school's total conversion, he wrote a brief article for the *Yale Review* which clearly put him in the camp of those opposed to the idea of law as permanent principles. Entitled ''The Law and the Judges,'' the theme of the article was the power of judges to make law, which ''is an expressed rule or principle of human action.'' While anyone can make such a rule, ''judges have by far the greatest influence'' since the rules they proclaim must be obeyed by at the least the parties to the suits tried before them.[80]

Corbin's allegiance to the positivist impulses of the case method appeared in his discussion of the nature of rules. They were not preexisting truths from which judges deduced the correct resolution of a particular controversy. The rules lived only in their application to disputes. Any rule proclaimed by a judge ''is an inductive conclusion . . . from preceding individual instances.'' These conclusions must be reached by drawing on all the sources of the law: constitutions and statutes, precedent, treatises, prevailing ideas of morality, and actual societal practice. Echoing Holmes, Corbin declared that ''law is not logic, nor does reason play the chief part in its creation. It grows in the semi-darkness of ignorance and emotion, it is based upon racial experience, and it represents the custom and the interest and the desire of the average man.''[81]

How should a judge approach this daunting task? Not, it seems, by reading treatises or meditating on the ultimate good. Rather, judges must get understanding by studying the reports that are ''a mighty storehouse of *facts*." The cases are various and provide authority "for both sides of almost any question."

> But they are instructive: they permit of a vast amount of comparison; they present material for testing a proposed rule by applying it to a great variety of cases; they cover all the fields of human conduct and endeavor; they supply arguments of learned and experienced men on both sides of vast numbers of questions.[82]

Cases are manifestly the key to law, and hence they must provide the basis of instruction.

8

Reconciliation

As the twentieth century began, prospects for cooperation between the bar and law schools seemed dim. In 1900 thirty-five law schools organized the American Association of Law Schools (AALS) to give the academic world an organization separate from the American Bar Association's legal education section. While the two organizations continued to meet together from 1900 until 1913, their relationship was not a happy one. The separation of the annual meetings was occasioned, according to the law teachers, by the older organization's disregard for both legal educators and legal education. The last straw was the decision to move the date of the ABA's meeting from August to October, a time particularly unpropitious for academics.[1] The differences, however, encompassed more than a disagreement over a convenient time to meet. The nature of legal education still divided the bar and some professors. In fact, the professors themselves were divided, but the nature of those divisions shows that the Harvard model was on its way to triumph in academia, in part because it eventually helped bring the schools and the bar together.

The Spread of the Case Method

The early years of the AALS were marked by frequent debates over the content of legal education, even though in one form or another some variety of case method had arrived almost everywhere.[2] Even in those schools like Yale where lectures and recitations were preferred methods of instruction, cases were used at least in the upper-class years.[3] At Georgetown, a lecture and recitation system using textbooks was in place in the mid-1880s, but by 1912 textbooks were supplemented with "leading cases," and in the upper-class years some courses were taught using casebooks and class discussion in which students were required to state the facts and law of the case and then to answer questions "upon the particular case, and upon similar statements of fact, with a view to developing a full knowledge of the principle."[4] In several schools, the arrival of the case method was a piecemeal affair, cases gradually supplementing and then supplanting the use of textbooks and treatises and questioning on the cases replacing recitation on the texts. At Michigan, for example, in 1895 of one-third of the courses "employed case materials in connection with either lectures or a textbook," and casebooks were used in all courses by 1920.[5]

At some schools, active university presidents took the lead in modernizing their law schools much as Seth Low did at Columbia. Starting in 1911, President George Vincent of the University of Minnesota hired case method teachers to replace a dean, William Sullivan Pattee, whose teaching left his students (many of whom were football players seeking refuge from the "severe discipline" of other branches of the university) with the impression that the law was "a vast plain, sketchily settled, having as its most notable landmarks huge monuments to the Christian virtues."[6] Lucius Polk McGehee of the University of North Carolina's law school brought a "sharp transition from the textbook to the casebook as the basis of instruction" when he became dean in 1910.[7] The modernization of North Carolina, however, was not secure until the president of the university insisted in 1923 that McGehee's successor be "an administrative head who knows legal education, who has been trained in modern methods" and who was ready to build rather than perpetuate the current state of affairs. As part of the preparation of his recommendations, President Harry Woodburn Chase visited what he must have regarded as the leading law schools in the country—Chicago, Harvard, and Columbia.[8] At Wisconsin, President Charles Kendall Adams "brought [Charles N.] Gregory into the College of Law specifically to modernize the school along the lines of Harvard."[9]

Two schools that used distinctive teaching methods associated with influential members of the faculty were converted to the case method through the efforts of particularly influential faculty members trained at Harvard. At the University of Virginia, the method of teaching associated with John Minor persisted into the 1930s. Minor attempted to provide an overall map of the law in the style of Blackstone's *Commentaries*. He handed out printed outlines or wrote them on the classroom blackboard and then provided details and anecdotes in his lectures. One admirer declared that Minor's aim was "to imbue his pupils with those instincts of right doing and right thinking without which they might become bookworms, phrase-mongers, plea-jugglers, and money-getters, but never lawyers."[10] After earning the S.J.D. degree at Harvard in 1922, Professor Armistead Mason Dobie brought the case method home to Charlottesville. Then, after Dobie became dean in 1932, the last vestiges of the Minor method disappeared. The historian of the University of Virginia School of Law describes Dobie as "colorful, vital, dynamic, sarcastic on occasion, and never at a loss for words." He was a dramatic and effective teacher and public speaker, and some of the success of the case method may have been due to the strength of his personality, as well as his position as dean.[11]

Hastings College of the Law also had a distinguished founder of a method of law teaching among its faculty. John Norton Pomeroy was a well-known writer of treatises, as well as a teacher.[12] His teaching method used cases, lectures, and discussions, but its most distinctive feature was the detailed systematization of the law that shaped the entire curriculum. Seeing the law as a whole, Pomeroy tried to convey knowledge that went beyond cases to history and jurisprudence. The Pomeroy system began to fade with its creator's death in 1885 and went into eclipse with the appointment of Robert W. Harrison to the faculty in 1901, three years after his graduation from Harvard Law School. Harrison was "extremely personable and well-liked, even loved, by his students," and "had considerable influence with his colleagues." Once again, the force of personality may have helped promote the case method.[13]

Law teachers did not agree, however, about the place in the curriculum of courses designed to teach such skills as drafting pleadings and interviewing clients. The Harvard teachers and their disciples and allies maintained that the case method regime, coupled with a curriculum of private law, taught all the skills one needed to succeed. A professor at Michigan put it succinctly: "The student can no longer learn a large part of the law copying forms of pleading—but must, perforce, study the fundamental basis of liability in order to know whether 'the facts constitute a cause of action.'"[14] His explanation of the worth of academic training for practice harks back to the changes caused by the Field Code and the abolition of the forms of action. Careful analysis of facts will give the knowledge and skills necessary. The divisions among teachers on this subject seem to reflect more than anything else the prospective careers of their students. As William Vance of the University of Minnesota told the bar association of his state, Harvard could avoid teaching how to draft pleadings and other technicalities of practice because on graduation its students entered established offices where they could learn these skills. In the west, as Vance put it, new graduates often entered practice on their own. They had to know these practical details or they would be unable to earn a living.[15]

The lack of agreement on the merits of teaching the elements of practice indicates one of the reasons for reconciliation between the Harvard style of legal academics and the articulate elite of the American bar. Harvard had entered into a new form of apprenticeship arrangement with the bar. Training students in a way of thinking about the law which seemed to promise the possibility of making sense of the ever-growing number of reported cases, Harvard then sent them to the law offices of the emerging large firms to learn that firm's way of doing business. When this practical advantage of the Harvard system was joined with the exaltation of the profession practiced by the advocates of thorough legal education, the basis of a firm alliance had been created.

The planners of the 1886 law school celebration of the Harvard bicentennial tried to link the reformed school to securing the prestige of the bar. The case method itself increasingly contributed to the academic status of the profession. The case method had been portrayed more and more as a method of study. This rhetoric had reached its culmination in 1907 when James Barr Ames declared that Harvard's goal was training in legal reasoning "by putting before the students the best models that can be found in the history of English and American law." Students who have examined "the opinions of the greatest judges that the English common law system produced" know what legal reasoning is "and are more likely to possess the power of solving legal problems than they would be by taking up the study of the law of any particular state."[16]

Ames's justification for the study of cases was shared by many schools. At Brooklyn Law School, cases were used along with textbooks, and the study of cases encouraged the student to develop a "legal trend of thought in the examination of the opinions of the most able and learned judges, thus enabling him to see the practical application of legal principles to facts."[17] The Northwestern Law School catalogue for 1894–1895 declared the object of case study to be "not merely to secure familiarity with the rules of law as actually enforced, but also to build up a legal mind, to train in the art of legal reasoning, and to cultivate the faculty of sound legal common sense."[18] At George Washington University cases were studied along with textbooks in order "to afford [the student] scientific training in accurate methods of study and of reasoning along legal lines."[19]

The power of the case method to teach legal reasoning thus became its ultimate justification. The last great case method controversy was discussed in just those terms. In 1914 the Carnegie Foundation sponsored a study of the case method by Josef Redlich, an Austrian legal scholar.[20] On the whole Redlich approved of the case method, but he suggested that more attention be paid to giving the student a brief systematic introduction to law before beginning case study. The suggestion that this instruction be offered by lecture unleashed vigorous debate at the 1915 meeting of the AALS. Those who ventured to find some worth in Redlich's suggestion were strongly attacked by case method teachers. The defense of the case method, however, was really an attack on the lecture. Harlan Stone, dean at Columbia, called lectures "educational medievalism" and observed that because of "the demands of 'college life,' undergraduate study seldom exhibits that thoroughness and intensity which characterizes the work of the professional student." Stone's colleague R. W. Gifford agreed: "Lecturing is similar to a certain extent, and has the same vice, as learning merely by reading, and that is that in so doing you are not using your mind to think." Beale, however, made the strongest attack on undergraduate education: "It is true that they lecture in most of our American colleges, and that is why men in college never learn anything, or care to learn anything."[21] The alleged ignorance of American undergraduates strengthened the appeal of case method as a means of promoting rigorous education.

These attacks on the lecture system, however, are as difficult to accept uncritically as are early attacks on the case method as a rote drill in the holdings of cases. In private, some case method teachers could be more conciliatory, at least toward those in authority over them. Stone explained to Nicholas Murray Butler of Columbia University that "the instructor in each course taken by first year men devotes considerable attention to fundamental legal conceptions, [for example,] instruction as to the nature of common law as distinguished from written law, the way in which common law was developed in England and brought to the United States; and various other aspects of the nature and the history of law."[22] Eventually such informal instruction would be formalized, often in courses on "legal method" designed to give beginning students some perspective on the studies they were about to undertake.[23]

The public stance of case method teachers, however, exalted the intellectual prowess of those who taught and learned using the case method. Around the time of World War I, some of these teachers agitated for a change in the basic law degree from bachelor of laws (LL.B.) to doctor of law (J.D.). At Michigan, the faculty noted that with an entrance requirement of two to four years of collegiate work and the use of reported cases as the basis of instruction, "which in most instances is of the seminary or proseminary type, the second bachelor degree became a grotesque anomaly."[24] Dean Henry M. Bates stoutly maintained in a letter to the president of the university that "the holders of this [law] degree under the Michigan plan are at least fully equal in training, scholarship and intelligence to the Doctors of Philosophy."[25] The demanding nature of legal education had become an important aspect of an emerging alliance with the bar. Surviving the case method law school was proof of intellectual superiority.[26]

The Failure of Sociological Jurisprudence

Feeding the ego of the bar would not have been enough to reconcile the members of the ABA and other articulate lawyers to the model of legal education that started at Harvard. There were real differences between the theories of law that underlay the different approaches to the methods of legal education. By the first decades of the twentieth century, the implications of Austinian positivism had lost some of their terror for the bar. The social strains of the 1880s and 1890s diminished with the new century. While laissez-faire and its legal analogue, freedom of contract, did not disappear from the American scene, the forces of reform had become more respectable. The attempt consciously to adapt American society to the changing conditions of material life increasingly became a middle-class crusade for what was called social justice.

The early twentieth-century reform movement can scarcely be summarized in a phrase, but "Progressive era" and "Progressive movement" remain convenient terms. The goal of Progressivism, social justice, is also a complex idea. It is certain, however, that part of the quest for social justice in the Progressive era involved improving the lot of laboring men and women. Much of this melioristic desire found expression in state statutes limiting the hours of work, improving working conditions, and requiring payment of wages in currency rather than in scrip and in the creation of workmen's compensation schemes. Such laws often fell afoul of the bar's fear of socialism and were frequently struck down by appellate courts in the name of freedom of contract. As the reform impulses these statutes represented entered the mainstream of American politics, however, the statutes themselves seemed to be less and less the product of the sovereign Austinian legislature run amok. The organized bar remained convinced that lawyers were the natural leaders of American society. The increasing divergence between popular political reform programs and the bar's position must have proved embarrassing.

If these developments in American public life were not disquieting enough, changes in society as a whole exacerbated the problem. The Progressive era was a time in which the concept and role of the professional acquired new importance. As social structures changed and America became more and more a national society, mastery over a politically neutral body of scientific knowledge became an important way to make one's place in society respectable and secure. As practitioners of one of the oldest professions, lawyers should have fitted easily into the scheme, but the political atmosphere made their claims to scientific neutrality appear hypocritical.

For whatever reason, the ABA lawyers became less fearful of change. A striking illustration of this transformation was the reception given Roscoe Pound's speech at the 1906 ABA convention on "The Causes of Popular Dissatisfaction with the Administration of Justice." In 1906 Pound was dean of the law school at the University of Nebraska. The recipient of a Ph.D. in botany from Nebraska, he had studied law for only one year at Harvard before returning to Lincoln to practice law. He had achieved great prominence in his native state by 1906, having served on the commission appointed to hear cases backed up on the docket of the Nebraska Supreme Court. He was at St. Paul at the invitation of the president of the ABA, who had heard him speak at the annual meeting of the Nebraska State Bar Association in 1905.[27]

Pound's diagnosis of the problem included several causes of dissatisfaction: American political institutions, which deemphasized bureaucratic control in favor of local government; the inherent tendency of all law toward uniformity; and the circumstances of an age of transition from extreme individualism to a more collective outlook. These causes, however, "will take care of themselves." "But too much of the current dissatisfaction," Pound continued, "has a just origin in our judicial organization and procedure." The principal result of the failings of judicial organization and procedure is "a deep-seated desire to keep out of court, right or wrong, on the part of every sensible businessman in the community."[28]

Demonstrating that the old fears were not totally dead, some members of the ABA denounced Pound's speech as a radical attack on the very heart of American law. These men could not even acknowledge collectivist tendencies except to reprobate them. A resolution to reprint the speech and distribute it to the members of the association and to a joint committee of Congress then considering a judiciary bill was met by vigorous attacks on Pound's propositions. In the end, the subject of the speech was referred to the Committee on Judicial Administration and Remedial Procedure.[29] The following year that committee reported that Pound had not been "iconoclastic" or "antagonistic" and urged the creation of a special committee to "Suggest Remedies and Formulate Proposed Laws to Prevent Delay and Unnecessary Cost in Litigation." The committee's recommendation was adopted, and the ABA officially bent its efforts toward procedural reform.[30]

During the first three decades of the twentieth century the special committee formed in 1907 focused its attention solely on procedure in the federal courts, leaving the state field to state bar associations. The committee was able to secure the passage of several bills reforming aspects of federal procedure. One required showing probable cause before the United States Supreme Court would grant a writ of habeas corpus. Others worked a limited procedural unification of law and equity, simplified the process for amending pleadings, broadened the scope of review by the United States Supreme Court, and required that new trials be refused if the errors complained of in the court below did not affect the substantial rights of the parties. The committee members also provided advice to the committee of the Supreme Court that wrote the new equity rules of 1912.[31]

The special committee published long reports in 1909 and 1910 on comprehensive procedural reform. These reports, which were Pound's work, advocated the creation of a system of procedure by rules of court rather than through statutory enactment. Achieving implementation of this notion on the federal level was left to another committee, headed by Thomas Shelton, which worked for congressional passage of a bill allowing the U.S. Supreme Court to make procedural rules for the law side of the federal courts. Although Shelton met nothing but frustration—Sen. Thomas Walsh of Montana kept the bill bottled up in the Judiciary Committee seemingly forever—after Shelton's death the reform was finally adopted, resulting in the Federal Rules of Civil Procedure.[32]

As pursued by the ABA, procedural reform would fulfill important professional aims. Removing rule-making from the legislatures would reinforce lawyers' claims to professional status: to the experts belonged the making of rules for the practice of expertise.[33] Improving the mechanism for managing business in the courts would, as Pound had frankly said in 1906, help preserve the profession's near monopoly of the means of resolving commercial disputes. In spite of the allure of that goal, the ABA's efforts for procedural reform made only slow progress, principally because nothing could be done without the cooperation of Congress.[34] The entire episode, however, showed that the ABA was willing to consider legal change under the inspiration and for a time even the leadership of an academic lawyer.

Pound's contribution to an accommodation of the organized national bar went beyond introducing it to the idea of academic expertise in accomplishing professional reform. He also formulated a variation of legal science designed to help lawyers accept the idea that law did change and that it was not the reflection of eternal principles. Drawing on European scholarship, Pound put together a sociological jurisprudence opposed to the "mechanical jurisprudence" of the nineteenth century.[35] Law would now serve society rather than oppose it in the name of sterile logic.[36]

Pound recognized that with the new century had come a new conception of justice—social justice as opposed to the older legal justice. Society had decided to pit "the organized brains of the community against the aggressive individual brain" to prevent exploitation and oppression.[37] This desire was reflected in legislation that put social interests above individual interests. Unfortunately, not only was legislation itself scorned by the common law tradition, but the anti-individualist notion embodied in the legislation ran contrary to the intellectual outlook that dominated the courts.[38]

To counteract the obstacles to the new legislation, sociological jurists insisted on six main points:

1. Study of the actual social effects of legal institutions and legal doctrines.
2. Sociological study in connection with legal study in preparation for legislation.
3. Study of the means of making legal rules effective.
4. A "sociological legal history" designed to show us how the law of the past grew out of social, economic, and psychological conditions, how it accorded with or accommodated itself to them, and how far we can proceed upon that law as a basis, or in disregard of it, with well-grounded expectations of producing the results desired.
5. The importance of reasonable and just solutions of individual causes.
6. [All with the hope of making] effort more effective in achieving the purposes of law.[39]

In short, the sociological jurist criticizes legal systems, doctrines, and institutions "with respect to their relation to social conditions and social progress."[40]

Once the sociological view of jurisprudence came to dominate legal thinking, all would be well. Pound, like John Chipman Gray before him, believed that the causes of the current problem were to be found in the intellectual realm and had nothing to do with politics or economics. Judges made antisocial decisions because they had antiquated ideas about law and society, said Pound. They were still living in a world in which the sole purpose of law was to free the human will and abolish the invidious distinctions based on status. Their opinions were based not on "class bias" or "purely economic influences" but on now-obsolete notions about the "progress from status to contract."[41] Judges remained mired in obscure metaphysics because they misused Maine's historical jurisprudence and failed to heed scholarship like Holmes's, which taught that social forces made the law. The bench and the bar needed reeducation, and the business of legal education belonged to the law school and its faculty. Just as faulty legal scholarship was responsible for the antiquated ideas that controlled the courts, so reformed teaching would train "the rising generation of lawyers in a social, political and legal philosophy abreast of our times."[42] It was the mission of that new profession to raise up a new generation of practitioners trained in a law appropriate to the modern world. If the schools failed in this task, lawyers would have to surrender "their legitimate hegemony in legislation and politics to engineers and naturalists and economists."[43]

It is impossible to know whether or not Pound was making a calculated appeal to the bar's self-image with such words. They must, however, have eased the way into the minds of the profession. The anger his 1906 speech caused was one of the last gasps of instant reaction against any suggestion that the legal system should accommodate itself to anything even remotely resembling socialism. Still, the quest for social justice did not instantly vanquish laissez-faire and freedom of contract. Leaders of the bar still spoke the language of inevitable progression from status to contract. In 1916 Elihu Root, then serving as president of the ABA, advised the association to trust in the gradual development of the law to solve the current problems, and even praised the bête noire of the sociological jurist—freedom of contract as the instrument of the destruction of a society based on status. He further cautioned: "We should not forget that every increase of governmental power to control the conduct of life is to some extent a surrender of individual freedom and a step backwards towards that social condition in which men's lives are determined by status rather than by their own free will."[44] He was a believer in the theory of law that Pound had labeled an anachronism. Harlan Stone, then dean of the law school at Columbia, attacked the concept of social justice as a basis for judicial decision and labeled sociological jurisprudence more a theory of legislation than of the judicial process.[45]

In spite of opposition, the notion of sociological jurisprudence was increasingly accepted because it proved to have little content. In the first place, it proved virtually meaningless for legal education. Given the importance attached to legal education in Pound's work and his position as dean of Harvard Law School from 1916, Pound could be expected to welcome expansion of the curriculum in a sociological direction. Pound's practice of legal education at Harvard, however, was remarkably narrow. He found abhorrent the plan of the dean of Northwestern's law school, John Henry Wigmore, to add a fourth year of legal study in which courses emphasizing the practical working of the law would be taught. Pound summed up his view in a letter to Stone: "It has been the glory of the better law schools of the country that they have stood resolutely for thorough work—for doing a few of the things best [worth] doing as well as they could, rather than for paper programmes attempting to cover everything."[46] Nor did he have any sympathy for clinical training or legal aid work, although presumably it would have brought the students into contact with some of the social forces that made a sociological jurisprudence necessary.[47] Pound was even opposed to separate courses in jurisprudence.[48] Making such additions to the curriculum would have distracted students from professional training.

Pound's views on the content of legal education had not advanced one whit beyond those of James Barr Ames and Joseph Beale. In part, Pound's reluctance to tamper with the Harvard curriculum may have been due to simple inertia. Institutional factors also played an important role. The school was large and the faculty few. Pound frequently complained that preparing to teach, grading, and the administrative tasks of the deanship occupied almost all his time. There was little left for cultivating new projects.[49] The entire experience sometimes left him depressed. In the mid-1920s he wrote Henry Bates, the dean of the University of Michigan Law School, that "frequently, I feel that the job of trying to run a law school here is a thankless task and almost a futile one."[50] His original scholarship, as opposed to the retailing of continental works, never got beyond an attempt to create yet another classification of the law. Even that attempt, undertaken first for the American Law Institute, was incomplete. He produced only a history of theories of classification and the bald statement of his own idea:

> Classification is a shaping and developing of traditional systematic conceptions and traditional systematic categories in order to organize the body of legal precepts so that they may be: (1) Stated effectively with a minimum of repetition, overlapping, and potential conflict, (2) administered effectively, (3) taught effectively, and (4) developed for new situations.[51]

Pound was still living in an intellectual world of rights and duties, still trying to make the sort of map of the legal system John Austin had attempted. He never got anywhere in drawing it. His plan for avoiding the pitfalls of a priori thinking could have been written a generation earlier: trace historical development rather than depend on reasoning after the event.[52] Sociological jurisprudence was not much more effective outside of academia. Attempts to influence the highest courts with sociological argument, excepting Louis Brandeis's victory in *Muller v. Oregon* in 1908, never bore fruit.[53]

What sociological jurisprudence came to mean, then, was not a body of doctrine but an attitude or even a rhetoric that emphasized the well-known ability of the common law to accommodate itself to the times and which emphasized even more strongly the importance of thorough training for forming good lawyers. As befits such a blandly acceptable notion, the rhetoric of sociological jurisprudence appeared more and more frequently. It can be seen in the works of prominent New York practitioners like Henry W. Taft and Frederick Rene Coudert.[54] It even penetrated the discourse of Harlan Stone. "The entire history of our law," wrote Stone in 1919, only five years after he had rejected the concept of social justice, "has been one of change and adaptation to meet new conditions, social and economic, and to conform to a more enlightened ethical perception."[55] In the face of the unordered, unscientific chaos of the American common law, Stone doubted that sociological jurisprudence had "any methodology, any formulae, or any principles which can be taught or expounded so as to make it a guide whether to the student of law or to the judge."[56]

Stone's words are revealing. For all the talk of fifty years, no real progress had been made in the great goal of systematizing the common law. The case method had been put forward as a means of learning enough about the law to allow classification to go forward, but the great task had never even been begun. The teachers were too busy consolidating their position; the practitioners in the bar associations were busy with their clients. The division over the worth of the positivistic approach to law prevented cooperation among teachers in the new model schools, traditional teachers, and the bar associations. After the World War I the situation changed. Cooperation replaced hostility, and practitioners and teachers were able to come together on common intellectual and professional ground in the American Law Institute.

The American Law Institute

Efforts were made before World War I to create a new classification of American law. The American Bar Association first took up the problem of classification in 1888 in response to a letter on the subject from Henry T. Terry, who called for an arrangement of American law according to "ultimate principles."[57] The committee formed in response to this appeal made elaborate reports in 1891 and 1902 but was discontinued after 1907 just as procedural reform received the association's sanction and attention.[58] The classificatory ideal survived the demise of the ABA committee. In 1910 one issue of the *Green Bag* was devoted entirely to the question of the creation of an American corpus juris, a gigantic classification and statement of the principles of American law. The centerpiece of the presentation was a long "Memorandum in re Corpus Juris" prepared by two practitioners, Lucien Hugh Alexander and James DeWitt Andrews, and a distinguished teacher, George Kirchwey of Columbia Law School. The heart of the proposal was creation of a group of law teachers who would write a complete statement of American law according to a scientific scheme of classification and then submit their work to an advisory board of practitioners, judges, and other teachers. In this way all American law could be "*completely exhibited as the product of the best thought in the profession*"[59] [italics in original].

This desire to bring together law teachers, judges, and practitioners was one of the first signs of reconciliation among the branches of the profession. It would reappear in the discussions surrounding the founding of the American Law Institute (ALI) thirteen years later. In the meantime, however, the 1910 agitation seems to have come to nothing. In 1916 the idea was revived within the ABA once more, probably in response to Elihu Root's presidential address of that year, "Public Service by the Bar."

Root's speech urged the profession to take an active part in society to ensure that the people of the United States benefitted from the best possible administration of justice. The true spirit of the profession required such service. "Commercialization" of the bar, the attitude that lawyering is merely "a career which affords a living without manual labor," must be opposed through strict control over admission to the bar and the requirement that admission be governed by the standards of the best law schools. Yet preserving standards is only part of the solution. Even the most honorable members of the profession need help in understanding America's rapidly changing law. Judges and lawyers engaged in the administration of justice needed a new American Corpus Juris Civilis which would "carry to the great mass of them, present and future, a comprehensive and discriminating understanding of the legal principles which form the thread of Ariadne for guidance through the labyrinth of decisions." Root did praise liberty of contract and laissez-faire, but far more significant for the future of cooperation with legal academics was his linking of the case method with the great goal of classification. Because the case method requires the student "by a truly scientific method of induction to extract the principle from the decision and to continually state and restate for himself a system of law evolved from its history," it trains lawyers who will create "naturally" a "systematic restatement of our law."[60] From the highest position in the American bar had come at last approval of the case method and the legal science it could help create.

The creation the following year of the ABA's Special Committee on the Classification and Restatement of the Law can probably be laid to the influence of Root's speech. This committee set its collective mind to producing the corpus juris; one of its leaders was the same James DeWitt Andrews of the 1910 project. Not much was accomplished during the war, but the committee came to life again in 1919, and from then until 1922 Andrews tried to convince the association that a corpus juris could be created through the dormant American Academy of Jurisprudence. Founded in 1914 by a group of luminaries including William Howard Taft, Elihu Root, George Wickersham, Frederick Coudert, Roscoe Pound, and Samuel Williston, the academy had the familiar aim of inquiring

> into all important principles of law which at the present time are in a confused, conflicting, and uncertain stage by reason of conflicting judicial decisions, to the end that the sound principles of right and justice may be discovered and such logical reasons therefore given as will preclude as far as possible future uncertainty and discussion and in this manner unify and clarify the law.[61]

The coming of the war ended the group's activities, and Andrews's attempt to revive it was frustrated by the coming of the ALI.[62]

The mid-decade revival of the classification idea was not limited to the elite practitioners represented in the ABA. In 1914 the elite law teachers of the Association of American Law Schools heard two speeches, one by Joseph Beale, who had by then returned to Harvard, on "The Necessity for a Study of Legal System" and the other by Wesley N. Hohfeld of Yale on "A Vital School of Jurisprudence and Law: Have American Universities Awakened to the Enlarged Opportunities and Responsibilities of the Present Day?"[63] Beale made yet another contribution to the rhetoric of principles, system, and science, differentiating the "philosophical system . . . of scientific principle" from the misstatements and misconceptions of the courts. What the law teacher teaches and what requires restatement is pure science. Hohfeld's paper was a detailed outline of such a systematic study. These two speeches, together with the appointment the following year of a committee to investigate the establishment of a center for jurisprudence later were designated by the director of the ALI as the starting point for his brief official history of the institute.[64] This beginning was slowed by the war, but when activity resumed in 1920 the denouement came rapidly.

After the war the movement to establish a formal mechanism to classify the law reemerged with vigor. The ABA and the AALS pursued the elusive goal, but this time together.[65] In March 1922 a member of the relevant AALS committee, William Draper Lewis, dean of the law school at the University of Pennsylvania, approached Elihu Root, "the leader of the American Bar," for his support. It was forthcoming, and on May 10, 1922, the AALS committee and some distinguished practitioners met under Root's chairmanship in New York City and formed the Committee on the Establishment of a Permanent Organization for the Improvement of the Law. This group produced a lengthy diagnosis of the failings of American law and called a meeting of leading lawyers, teachers, and judges for February 23, 1923, which, although it failed to impress Mr. Justice Holmes—who wrote Harold Laski: "You can't evoke genius by announcing a *corpus juris*"—accepted the report and created the American Law Institute.[66]

The report of the Committee on the Establishment of a Permanent Organization focused on the uncertainty and complexity of American law. No one could be blamed for this situation. The bench and bar were prisoners of a system that demanded the resolution of individual cases and thus worked against any ordered development of the law. Nevertheless the defects constantly undermined respect for the law and "disrespect for law is the corner-stone of revolution." If, however, judges and lawyers sufficiently understand legal science they will see "the real issues presented by the facts of a case," apply the appropriate principles, and thus bring law to greater certainty as well as better "adaptation to the needs of life."[67]

This scientific work was tailored to the methods of the case method schools. As Root pointed out in 1916, the case method was an unequaled tool for analysis of cases and extraction of principles. Law teachers had been saying that for decades. Other teachers and many practitioners responded that the principles were the wrong sort, insufficiently tied to eternal truth; thus the case method led to legislative supremacy. A lessening concern with radicalism helped allay these fears. The support the new model schools gave the social position of the bar also helped reconcile many to their methods. In addition, the old guard was passing away. More and more prominent and prosperous practicing lawyers were alumni of case method institutions; they had not become wild-eyed anarchists.

Another factor promoting cooperation had entered the equation by the 1920s: concern with the professional status of the bar. Status is a continuing theme in the story of the relationship between practitioners and law schools. Columbia's law school was founded to help improve the image of the bar, and the school fell into disfavor when it became the easy route to practice. Eliot and Langdell maintained the importance of promoting the status of lawyering as a learned profession. Some of the disagreement between practitioners and teachers in the late nineteenth century in part reflected different visions of professionalism. The emphasis on professionalism that emerged in the early twentieth century brought the ideal of scientific expertise, which could already be seen influencing those making careers for themselves in legal academics, into a new prominence. Practitioners and teachers who were advocates of universal timeless principles upheld a definite political position, which their legal science was designed to serve. The twentieth-century professional, like the scholar of positive law, was a scientific expert removed from politics.[68] Professionals were the masters of a neutral body of scientific knowledge, not advocates of partisan political views. In the twentieth century, therefore, the postulates of positivistic legal science became assets in the bar's quest for status. The separation of law and morality and the emphasis on the factual basis of legal science drawn from cases was no longer a threat to the right ordering of society, but was the foundation of a politically neutral professionalism.

The vision of legal education supported by the anti-positivistic approach also opposed the newer model of professionalism. A broad law school curriculum would dilute lawyers' claims to mastery of a useful body of knowledge and would call into doubt their self-sufficiency and autonomy. Using part-time teachers and recruiting teachers from the realm of practice would also injure the professional status of the bar, since the career of full-time legal academics testified to the scientific worth of law as a scholarly discipline, the proper study of which required an academic class.

The importance of cooperation among practitioners, judges, and teachers in promoting the professional image of lawyers can be seen in the rhetoric surrounding the founding of the ALI, which was focused on professionalism and cooperation. The authors of the report "realized that an alliance between treatise-writing professors and front-line practitioners and judges was the only battle plan for long-term success."[69] In the first place, the Report of the Committee to Establish a Permanent Organization insisted that the proposed organization "should not promote or obstruct political, social or economic changes'' but should remain on the high plane of science, leaving for the legislatures such questions as tax and fiscal policy, government administrative policy, and ''novel social legislation'' like old-age pensions or methods for composing differences between capital and labor.[70] Another familiar note was sounded when the committee blamed ''not a little of the existing uncertainty in the law'' on low educational requirements for admission to the bar and on the politicization of judicial office. Finally, the report strongly emphasized the legal profession's ''obligation to the American people to promote the certainty and simplicity of the law, and its adaptation to the needs of life,'' analogizing it to the ''duty of the doctors of medicine to organize to increase medical knowledge.''[71]

The ultimate glorification of the legal profession was saved for the report's speculations on the future of the proposed restatement. An early draft expressed the hope that if the restatements were done well enough, state legislatures would adopt the principles they contained as a ''guide and aid to the Courts'' with authority equal to that of the decisions of the highest court of the state.[72] This hope was reduced to a speculation in the final draft. It had lost urgency. The important thing became ''so to plan the work that the restatement from its inception shall be recognized as a work of great public importance for the execution of which the American legal profession as represented by its leaders on the bench, in practice, and in the schools, is responsible.'' The goal had clearly become exaltation of the profession and preservation of that leadership which Pound praised in his 1906 speech. As Elihu Root told members at the founding meeting, their action ''points the pathway where we will be acknowledged the natural leaders of the democracy in its struggles towards better life, towards permanency of institutions.''[73]

Agreement between leaders of the practicing bar and academics was not limited to a common vision of a legal science that would support lawyers' claims to professional status. During the same period in which the ABA and the AALS cooperated in creating the ALI, they also reached an agreement on strengthening the formal requirements for admission to the bar by imposing uniform requirements for admission to law school. The goal of the committed advocates of the case method law school had always been to require the bachelor's degree for admission to law school. The practicalities of American life, however, prevented widespread enactment of this requirement. Given the realities of access to higher education, broad imposition of such a requirement would simply turn potential students away from law school to other means of preparing for the bar. At the time of its founding the AALS required only that students at its member schools have a high school diploma. Debate on this topic within the association, along with that the related matter of part-time and evening instruction, continued for twenty years, usually along the same lines as the debate on teaching the skills of practice.[74]

Many of the advocates of higher standards looked with envy on the medical profession and the wonders they believed had been wrought by the Flexner report.[75] In the wake of Flexner's work, medical schools closed, enrollment fell, and the profession seemed to gain control over entry into its ranks.[76] They no doubt believed that Redlich's report on the case method would perform a similar office for the legal profession. It did not, but the leaders of both school and bar were pleased when the Carnegie Foundation offered to try again after World War I. To the eyes of believers in higher standards the threat to professional status was greater than ever. They saw the bar flooded by undesirables trained at third-rate law schools, many of which did no better than cram students for the bar exams and did nothing to instill them with the spirit of the profession.[77] Lawyerly fears of undesirables, principally immigrants and Jews, seem to have been a staple of the American profession, but after World War I they became acute. For those who believed in the scholarly law school, the statistics relating to legal education must have been frightening. Of the six largest law schools during the 1919–1920 school year, only one, Harvard, enrolling 883 students, required any college work for admission. Of the other five (Georgetown, New York University, George Washington, Fordham, and Suffolk), enrolling 4,061 students (16.58% of all law students), only two had full-time programs and all five had part-time afternoon or night programs. In the same year, 42.9% of the law students in the United States were enrolled in full-time schools, and only 13.9% of the total were enrolled in schools requiring at least two years of college work for admission.[78] The ABA appointed a committee on legal education, chaired by Elihu Root, to investigate the problem, while Alfred Z. Reed undertook the study for the Carnegie Foundation. The results of these studies were very different.

Reed's report basically advocated legitimatizing the actual situation. He reported there were two American bars which practiced two very different kinds of law, and the divisions ran along economic and class lines. Reed was therefore willing to have the night or part-time schools train the lower bar, leaving the training of the upper bar and the improvement of the law to the full-time schools of high standards.[79]

The Root committee totally rejected the idea of a divided bar but accepted the part-time school, provided it offered a course of as many working hours as there were in the standard three-year full-time program. It demanded, however, two years of collegiate education before entering law school. That requirement was seen by opponents of the new guidelines as limiting access to the bar along economic lines.[80] The AALS followed the Root committee's lead, rejected the divided bar, and agreed to accept part-time schools as members, while raising its entrance requirements over a number of years to two years of college. The departure from settled policy regarding part-time schools as members so infuriated Pound that he wrote to Harlan Stone suggesting that "Columbia and Harvard, and a few other institutions which have consistently stood for what ought to be in legal education . . . pull out of this Association and let it run as an Association of second-rate institutions."[81] Pound's fulminations came to nothing.

The ABA and the AALS each gave a little and patched up their differences as they tried to close the door through which entered those who could never be properly professional lawyers.

The agreement between the ABA and the AALS on standards for legal education and admission to the bar did not alter state laws governing admission in the slightest, but the agreement itself is highly significant. For once, the upper levels of the profession—both practitioners and teachers—were speaking with a unified voice on the subject of what made a good professional. At the same time, they both testified to the scientific nature of the law and their own great sense of responsibility to the nation—and thus reaffirmed their right to lead—through the American Law Institute.

The treaty between practitioners and teachers did not achieve perfect reconciliation. The resulting alliance carried within itself the seeds of its own destruction. Some law teachers, like Pound, were unhappy with any compromise of what they saw as high and necessary standards, no matter how strongly required by the practicalities of the situation, but on the whole the exclusionary intent of the new rules for legal education seems to have been widely supported.[82]

The weakest link, however, was the legal science that inspired the advocates of the case method. To some degree this sort of legal science lay behind the American Law Institute's work on the Restatements, although some participants may have had hopes for making them tools of reform. For one observer, at least, the Institute was not what he had hoped. Edgar N. Durfee, a professor at Michigan, spent part of the winter of 1930–1931 "in Law Institute work." He discovered to his surprise "that some of the eminent gentlemen with whom I there worked have not moved as from ancient Langdellian moorings as I has assumed everybody had."[83] Behind that assumption lay the dissolution of positivistic legal science.

The Coming of Realism

The intellectual assumptions on which the legal scientific enterprise were based had been under attack for decades by the time the ALI was born. As early as 1899 Jabez Fox, a Massachusetts judge "and sometime lecturer at Boston University law school," published in the *Harvard Law Review* a brief essay taking James Bradley Thayer to task for attempting to separate questions of law from questions of fact by defining questions of law as those decided by reference to a rule.[84] Fox maintained that law came only from decided cases, only from the mouth of the judge, whether there was a rule involved or not.[85] The following year Fox published another brief essay in the same journal, again criticizing some of Thayer's work on evidence and again pointing out the critical factor in the outcome of a case was the mind of the judge deciding it. Judges decide in different ways because they "have given different weights to divers competing considerations which cannot be balanced on any measured scale." For example, judges assess credibility differently, depending on their beliefs about the honesty of witnesses. Thus decisions about the admissibility of hearsay depend not on some rule applied with mathematical precision but on the personalities of the judges.[86] Not surprisingly, perhaps, Fox was also critical of attempts to explain decisions that claimed to find a rule or reason which the judges themselves had not announced. On that ground he faulted the first edition of Gray's treatise on perpetuities and Holmes's lectures on agency.[87] Fox recognized the usefulness of criticizing a case "because it is opposed to another case, or to a principle which has been established and defined by a line of cases," but not criticism designed to establish a principle "which the writer would be glad to see recognized, as more rational or as offering a fairer ground for the decided cases to rest upon than any which the courts have seen fit to adopt." What sort of criticism is that, he asked, "but a beating of the air?"[88]

Fox was not alone in taking academic legal scientists to task for lack of practical understanding. James Barr Ames precipitated a controversy when he severely criticized some provisions of the Uniform Negotiable Instruments Act in an essay published in the *Harvard Law Review* in 1900.[89] Ames had taught the subject and produced a casebook but did not even see a copy of the act until shortly before he wrote his comment.[90] Not only is "the fact that the commissioners did not call Ames into consultation in the forming of this statute, and that he did not see a draft while the project was under way . . . an eloquent demonstration of the detachment of academic jurists from the practical science of legislation during the 1890's,"[91] it also illustrates how much the situation had changed by the 1920s. Ames's intervention resulted in a flurry of publications, although it apparently had little effect on the triumphant progress of the model act. It did lead to his appointment by Massachusetts as a commissioner on uniform state laws and thus indirectly to Samuel Williston's long and fruitful relationship with the same body.[92] It also led, however, to some sharp criticism of Ames's entire intellectual approach and, by extension, that of all the academic scientists. John Farrell, a New York practitioner, accused Ames of making criticisms based on "an isolated or imaginary case" or "hypothetical cases or conditions created by the negligent acts of individuals who may be parties to the instruments" and insisted that such commentary was useless in evaluating a statute meant to deal with real business problems.[93]

There was opposition from within the ranks of teachers, as well. H. L. Wilgus of the University of Michigan pointed out in 1908 that the case method could easily degenerate into the kind of exercise that encouraged "intellectual gymnastics, in which all become tangled up in their own ingenuity,—courts are censured, the law as a practical, useful, actual rule of action is forgotten," and students and teachers engage in "a discussion of only imaginary, unreal, unpractical suppositions about impossible situations, signifying nothing."[94] John Wurts of Cornell told an audience at Yale much the same thing. One problem with the case method, he said, is recognized by "all but those who propose to follow the theory as distinguished from the practice of the law." The case method, he maintained, overdevelops the analytical faculty. Students learn to "love to split hairs and to argue technicalities which have nothing to do with the merits of the case except that, being raised, they delay or prevent consideration of the merits."[95] One teacher, Albert Kales of Northwestern, proposed a radical remedy for the "flood of easy speculation." Each law school, he believed, should specialize in the law of its particular state, and law teachers should practice as advocates, specializing in the argument of truly significant and difficult cases.[96] In that way teachers would truly participate in development of the law. It is useless to devote oneself to understanding some sort of overarching legal science of the common law because, no matter what the situation was when Langdell wrote, in the early twentieth century there was no general common law of the United States.[97]

Such attitudes spelled the beginning of the end for the regime of legal science. Academic legal scientists worked to establish a true understanding of what the law should be. For all their positivistic inclinations, they believed in the possibility of understanding what made law work, an understanding that would enable lawyers to predict what courts would decide. Holmes, of course, made prediction the heart of his theory of law, but it was essential to the very idea of a case-oriented positivistic legal science. The goal of scientists was the discovery of principles that governed all law. Once they were understood, lawyers could approach the solution of legal problems in a rational way. Frederick Pollock had set the tone as early as 1874: "We now have seen case-law has a scientific aim, namely, the prediction of events by means of past experience, and that the possibility of such prediction rests, as in other sciences, on a fundamental assumption of uniformity."[98]

A generation later, James Brown Scott, a case method teacher, said much the same thing, maintaining that cases on a particular subject could be analyzed, classified, and made to yield underlying principles. In this way a general principle was established, and when once the general principle was established, it could be—indeed, must be—applied to analogous cases.[99] In essence, Scott stated the aim of the American Law Institute.

Kales, however, pointed out the unfortunate fact that a general common law did not exist. The various jurisdictions gathered into the United States came to different conclusions about what principles were and what sort of conclusions they dictated. Fox's criticism of the Harvard teachers' excessive analysis hinted at a view that would be more fully developed soon after the ALI was founded. Judges, Fox believed, made their decisions based on opinions, some of which simply were not amenable to logical analysis or to change by logical persuasion. He had aimed his criticism at the one great assumption of case method scientists. As Holmes wrote in the précis of his lectures on jurisprudence, that subject could consider as a source of law only those motives for judicial action which, like constitutions, statutes, customs, and precedents "can be relied on as likely in the generality of cases to prevail." "Singular motives," he wrote, "like the blandishments of the emperor's wife, are not a ground of prediction, and are therefore not considered.''[100] Gray said much the same thing in somewhat the same words:

> Of course, the motive of a judge's opinion may be almost anything,—a bribe, a woman's blandishments, the desire to favor the administration or his political party, or to gain popular favor or influence; but these are not sources which Jurisprudence can recognize as legitimate.[101]

Fox criticized just this selective approach to understanding judicial motives. To ignore the mundane but real led the legal ''scientist'' to fruitless speculation and to the creation of systems with only a tenuous relationship to the real world of lawsuits and lawyering. Not long after the founding of the ALI, similar criticisms, voiced with more volume and greater precision, would come from a new group of legal scholars who are loosely grouped as ''legal realists.'' They would begin to destroy the careful harmony between logic and experience the founders of the modern law school had labored so long to create.

Epilogue

By the time the American Law Institute was founded, the new model law school had become a rigorous training ground for professionals. Leaders of the legal profession had once regarded the case method school as an incubator of dangerous ideas about the nature of law. It trained not competent leaders of society but mindless case lawyers whose understanding of their profession was limited to piling up citations. After World War I, however, the narrow technical nature of education in the case method school was more widely accepted as the model of professional competence. Whatever the various hopes and goals of those who helped create the American Law Institute, it did provide a mechanism by which practitioners, teachers, and judges could all cooperate in the great professional project of putting the rules into proper order. At least on the surface apolitical and technocratic, the work of the institute was the simple acknowledgment of the proper role of the legal profession. In a sense, then, the changes Langdell began bore fruit not so much as new methods of learning and understanding but as part of the transformation of American life in the late nineteenth and early twentieth centuries.

Langdell was an educator, of course, and his legacy to legal education has been controversial. In the 1920s and 1930s legal realism called Langdell's contributions into question. Some criticism emphasized what Langdell and his colleagues left out of legal education. As the importance of common law faded and statutes became more important, the limitation of legal education to parsing cases and explicating common law rules seemed less useful and less interesting.[1] John Johnson identified this shift to statute law as part of a transformation in sources of information important to courts, a transformation Langdellian legal education was ill-equipped to handle.[2] William Chase maintained that the narrowness of case method education stunted the teaching and thus the practice of administrative law, depriving government agencies of real power to police the market.[3] In addition, narrow technical training may have become less becomeless challenging for the legal professoriate. In John Henry Schlegel's view, by World War I legal academics had accomplished the systematic statement of the law that was the object of Langdell's science.[4] Legal realism then becomes, in part, "something for the tired and trapped legal academics to talk about."[5]

Langdell left something out, however, because he never believed it should be included. Langdell and his fellow scientists separated the common law from other studies because that was the road to science free from a priori moralizing. A striking illustration is Langdell's approach to the *Northern Securities Case*. The narrow principles of equity jurisprudence dictate the kind of relief that can be given, he said, but the real question of the best way to regulate railroads is one of what the modern world recognizes as economics. The two simply did not belong together in law school. One message this volume hopes to communicate is that Langdell was neither intellectually perverse nor unimaginative, nor stupid, just as Holmes was not totally original. Rather, both men were deeply situated in the intellectual life of their age, and their ideas about law were far more alike than different. The creation of a modern science of law was their common goal, and the separation of that science from every other science was their common method.

The second strain of criticism of Langdell's approach to legal education involves the supposed failure of case method instruction to help students learn the skills needed to be working lawyers. Over the decades, this challenge to the classic Harvard model has involved promotion of live client clinics designed to offer legal assistance to the needy, often run in conjunction with legal aid organizations, and, more recently, classroom training in skills such as interviewing, negotiating and counselling, using simulations and other techniques often dramatically different from the dialogue of the case method classroom.[6] For some, these innovations simply redress the balance between apprenticeship and school training which Langdell's approach distorted.[7]

Again, this study has tried to show that Langdell was deeply immersed in practice and that at least one source of his focus on cases was his experience of the changes the Field Code brought to law practice.[8] In addition, Langdell meant to train counsellors, but it cannot be said that he believed the United States had room for only one kind of lawyer. The uproar Alfred Reed caused by suggesting that the bar need not be populated by uniformly trained lawyers shows how the law schools came to link case method training with the prestige of the bar.

The attack on the case method as the enemy of training for practice is overwhelmingly ironic. Langdell certainly believed he was training students in the skills they needed to practice law. The world of code pleading required the ability to parse cases and isolate facts. All systematization of the common law depended on understanding the cases, and, as they proliferated, the ability to discriminate among cases presumably became increasingly valuable. Finally, the pedagogical justification for the case method explicitly linked classroom experience to the experience of practicing law.[9]

It is true that case method teachers did not pay much attention to other skills, and some reasons can be suggested. First, they expected every student to spend some time as a clerk to an experienced practitioner. Langdell's and Eliot's calm acceptance of the New York clerkship requirement indicates that they did not expect their school to teach skills beyond those imparted by thorough training in the original sources of legal understanding. Working with knowledgeable lawyers would teach neophytes the more practical aspects of applying that knowledge to the always different facts that real problems presented.

Second, and much more speculative, is the possibility that case method teachers relied on the homogenous social background of their students to provide the skills necessary to deal with people—to counsel, negotiate, and interview. Not every student was born with that background, but it may be that law teachers expected all students to be gentlemen by the time they arrived at law school. Since they would spend their professional lives dealing with other gentlemen, there was no need to worry about teaching skills that were so closely linked to a code of behavior presumably shared by every member of the profession.[10]

Whatever the shortcomings of the legal education Langdell and his colleagues created, present-day legal education is still shaped by the actions and beliefs of those teachers and scholars of the preceding century, and there is something appealing in the clear role for legal education they envisioned. They knew what they had to do and they went on to do it. In the process, they were confident that they were training their students to fulfill the most demanding tasks of a most demanding profession. It is a spirit that modern legal education would do well to recover.

Notes

A Note on Citation

Legal materials are cited in this book according to the conventions of legal scholarship. Under that scheme, cases are cited by name, volume of the reporter in which they appear, followed by the standard abbreviation of the name of the reporter, and finally the page on which the report of the case begins. Parenthetical matter following the citation includes the date of the decision as well as the name of the court deciding it if that information is not clear from the name of the reporter. A reporter which bears the name of a state (for example, N.Y. or Mass.) is assumed to report the decisions of that state's highest court.

Many standard legal treatises, such as Blackstone's *Commentaries*, Kent's *Commentaries on American Law*, and Parsons's work on contracts have appeared in numerous editions. Editions appearing after the author's death usually are prepared by adding to the case citations in the work and by appending notes rather than by altering the text. In order to facilitate reference to the author's original work, these later edictions usually preserve the original pagination (or the pagination of the last edition prepared by the author) by inserting in the text the original page numbers enclosed in square brackets and preceded by an asterisk. These so-called "star pages" are the standard of legal reference to these works. In this book star pages are supplied in parentheses following the page reference to the actual edition cited.

Preface

1. Grant Gilmore, *The Ages of American Law* (New Haven, 1977), p. 56.

Chapter 1

1. Robert E. Stevens, "Two Cheers for 1870: The American Law School," *Perspectives in American History* 5 (1971), 434; Grant Gilmore, *The Ages of American Law* (New Haven, 1977), p. 42.

2. Stevens, "Two Cheers for 1870," 440–441; Joseph Redlich, *The Common Law and the Case Method in American University Law Schools* (New York, 1914), pp. 23–25, 39.

3. Alfred Z. Reed, *Training for the Public Profession of the Law* (New York, 1921), pp. 371–372.

4. The locus classicus is the work of Jerome Frank. See, for example, idem, "A Plea for Lawyer Schools," *Yale Law Journal* 56 (1947), 1303, where Frank calls Langdell "a brilliant neurotic" and asserts that "[h]is pedagogic theory reflected the man." For further examples, see Thomas C. Grey, "Langdell's Orthodoxy," *University of Pittsburgh Law Review* 45 (1983), 11–12, and Gilmore, *Ages of American Law*, 45. In a review of the second edition of Langdell's contracts casebook Oliver Wendell Holmes, Jr., stigmatized him as "perhaps, the greatest living legal theologian." [Oliver Wendell Holmes, Jr.,] "Book Notices," *American Law Review* 14 (1880), 234. Notable exceptions to this strain of commentary are the two excellent articles by Anthony Chase: "The Birth of the Modern Law School," *American Journal of Legal History* 23 (1979), 329–348, and "Origins of Modern Professional Education: The Harvard Case Method Conceived as Clinical Instruction in Law," *Nova Law Journal* 5 (1981), 323–363.

5. Langdell's experience in practice is often forgotten. In a 1927 report the Yale Law School faculty, for example, asserted that Langdell had never practiced law. Laura Kalman, *Legal Realism at Yale, 1927–1960* (Chapel Hill and London, 1986), p. 109.

Chapter 2

1. For an important exception see Anthony Chase, "The Birth of the Modern Law School," *American Journal of Legal History* 23 (1979), 329, and idem, "Origins of Modern Professional Education: The Harvard Case Method Conceived as Clinical Instruction in Law," *Nova Law Journal* 5 (1981), 323.

2. Charles William Eliot, "The New Education," *Atlantic Monthly* 23 (1869), 215–216.

3. Burton Bledstein, *The Culture of Professionalism: The Middle Class and the Development of Higher Education in America* (New York, 1976), p. 126.

4. Hugh Hawkins, *Between Harvard and America: The Educational Leadership of Charles W. Eliot* (New York, 1972), p. 204.

5. Charles W. Eliot, untitled, undated address with heading "Harvard Law School? 1882," Charles W. Eliot Papers, Box 349, Harvard University Archives, Pusey Library (hereafter cited as Eliot Papers). Note that Eliot clearly expected new graduates of Harvard Law School to spend some time as unpaid clerks to established lawyers. On Eliot and practicality, see Lawrence R. Veysey, *The Emergence of the American University* (pbk., Chicago, 1970), pp. 86–98.

6. On some aspects of this tension, see Jerold Auerbach, "Enmity and Amity: Law Teachers and Practitioners, 1900–1922," *Perspectives in American History* 5 (1971), 551–601, and William R. Johnson, *Schooled Lawyers: A Study in the Clash of Professional Cultures* (New York, 1978), pp. 120–153, 155–159.

7. Joel Parker, *The Law School of Harvard College* (New York, 1871), p. 31. See also Arthur Sutherland, *The Law at Harvard: A History of Ideas and Men, 1817–1967* (Cambridge, 1967), pp. 148–156.

8. Charles Warren, *History of the Harvard Law School and of Early Legal Conditions in America*, 2 vols. (New York, 1908; rep. ed., New York, 1970), II: 303–318; Sutherland, *Law at Harvard*, 140–148.

9. Warren, *History of Harvard Law School*, II:336–339; Parker, *Law School of Harvard College*, 40–47.

10. Parker, *Law School of Harvard College*, 45, 51–55; Warren, *History of Harvard Law School*, II:336–338.

11. The 1870 report is quoted in full in Parker, *Law School of Harvard College*, 33–34. Parker's pamphlet is a comprehensive and biting response to criticisms of the old regime.

12. The 1869 report is reprinted in Warren, *History of Harvard Law School*, II:358–359.

13. [Oliver Wendell Holmes, Jr.,] "Harvard University Law School," *American Law Review* 5 (1870), 177. On Holmes's relationship to the note, see Mark DeWolfe Howe, *Justice Oliver Wendell Holmes: I. The Shaping Years, 1841–1870* (Cambridge, 1957), p. 205.

14. Warren, *History of Harvard Law School*, II:358–359.

15. Henry James, *Charles W. Eliot: President of Harvard University, 1869–1909*, 2 vols. (Boston and New York, 1930), I:263.

16. For the statutes, see Sutherland, *Law at Harvard*, 166, and Warren, *History of Harvard Law School*, II:371 n. 1.

17. Parker, *Law School of Harvard College*, 40. On the resemblance of the law school to the office, see James, *Charles W. Eliot*, I:266–267, and, more generally, Gerard E. Gawalt, "Massachusetts Legal Education in Transition," *American Journal of Legal History* 17 (1973), 47.

18. Charles W. Eliot, "Langdell and the Law School," *Harvard Law Review* 33 (1920), 522, reprinted under the same title in idem, *A Late Harvest: Miscellaneous Papers Written between Eighty and Ninety* (Boston, 1924), pp. 45–56.

19. R. E. Haynes to C. C. Langdell, February 2, 1870, Langdell Mss., Box 1, Harvard Law School Library, Manuscript Division.

20. Samuel L. Batchelder, "Christopher C. Landgell," *Green Bag* 18 (1906), 437. Batchelder was Emory Washburn's grandson and may have had firsthand information. Warren, *History of Harvard Law School*, II:311.

21. Quoted in Warren, *History of Harvard Law School*, II:360.

22. Eliot, "Langdell and the Law School," 518.

23. J. Warren to C. Warren, June 2, 1908, in Letters of Reminiscence presented by Charles Warren, Harvard Law School Library, Treasure Room (hereafter cited as Letters of Reminiscence, HLS/TR).

24. Warren, *History of Harvard Law School*, II:358–359. Warren says that Parsons resigned on December 11; the letter of resignation is dated December 1, and Eliot's reply accepting it is dated December 15. T. Parsons to C. W. Eliot, Cambridge, December 1, 1869, and Eliot to Parsons, Cambridge, December 15, 1869, both in President's Papers, C. W. Eliot, Box 66, 1869–1870, Harvard University Archives, Pusey Library (hereafter cited as President's Papers, C. W. Eliot by box number and, if applicable, folder title).

25. J. B. Thayer to C. W. Eliot, Boston, November 13, 1869, President's Papers, C. W. Eliot, Box 66.

26. G. O. Shattuck to C. W. Eliot, Boston, December 17, 1869, ibid.

27. J. C. Carter to C. W. Eliot, New York, December 24, 1869, ibid.

28. J. C. Carter to C. W. Eliot, New York, December 20, 1869, ibid.

29. Eliot, "Langdell and the Law School," 518.

30. Langdell apparently trained the school's longtime librarian, John Hines Arnold, in the finer points of careful book buying. *The Centennial History of the Harvard Law School* (1918), [Cambridge ?,] pp. 189–190.

31. Eliot, "Langdell and the Law School," 521–522.

32. W. A. Everett to C. Warren, n.p., February 10, 1908, Letters of Reminiscence, HLS/TR. Warren prints a portion of the letter quoted here in *History of Harvard Law School*, II:486.

33. See, respectively, notes 8, 29, and 7.

34. Thayer's memorandum book indicates that his litigation practice at least involved the collection of merchants' accounts. Memorandum Book A, LMS 2148 vol. 1, Harvard Law School Library, Treasure Room.

35. Howe, Mark DeWolfe. "The First Law School Lecture of James Bradley Thayer, Preliminary Note," *Journal of Legal Education* 2 (1949), 2–6, and J. C. Gray to C. W. Eliot, June 9, 1870, President's Papers, C. W. Eliot, Box 66.

36. *Annual Reports of the President and Treasurer of Harvard College, 1873–1874*, pp. 26–27. (This volume includes the reports of the deans of the various faculties. Successive volumes are hereafter cited as *Annual Report* and date). Langdell's comments cited in this paragraph can be found in C. C. Langdell, "Teaching Law as a Science," *American Law Review* 21 (1887), 123–124.

37. See "Birth of the Case Method."

38. Thayer, for instance, clearly needed his law school salary to meet current expenses. The substance of his negotiations with Eliot through fall 1873 was financial. He accepted only on the condition that his salary should be $5,000 a year as soon as the condition of the law school permitted it. "I think I can say I will go, if this can be done. But I cannot bear to leave my present place if I must begin vexing myself about the details of money matters and expect to have it to do hereafter." J. B. Thayer to C. W. Eliot, December 5, 1873, President's Papers, C. W. Eliot, Box 67. See also Thayer to Eliot, October 11, 1873, ibid.

39. "Each of his lectures contained a statement of general doctrine,examples of the application of the doctrine, a statement of real or apparent exceptions, examples of those exceptions, and ample citations of decisions. Judge Bradley, though now and then asking questions, did not encourage interference with his orderly presentation of a subject." *Centennial History*, 198. During his stint as a lecturer at the beginning of Langdell's deanship those students devoted to the new ways supplemented Bradley's lectures "by private study of White and Tudor's Cases on Equity" (p. 199).

40. Ibid., 213.

41. E. W. Gurney to C. W. Eliot, President's Papers, C. W. Eliot, Box 71, 1882–1883, folder 1883 G-L.

42. *Centennial History*, 198.

43. Warren, *History of Harvard Law School*, II:404.

44. Ibid., 407.

45. J. C. Gray to J. B. Thayer, n.p., n.d. [July 1878], James Bradley Thayer Papers, folder 20–1, Harvard Law School Library, Manuscript Division (hereafter cited as Thayer Papers).

46. Warren, *History of Harvard Law School*, II:411, 414.

47. J. C. Gray to J. B. Thayer, July 3, 1877, and July 11, 1878, Thayer Papers, folder 20-1.

48. Mark DeWolfe Howe, *Justice Oliver Wendell Holmes: II. The Proving Years, 1870–1882* (Cambridge, 1963), pp. 263–265.

49. James Barr Ames, *Lectures on Legal History* (Cambridge, 1913), p. 233. See also Howe, *Proving Years*, 273–280.

50. Howe, *Proving Years*, 257.

51. Ibid., 260.

52. Holmes "kept up his connection with" his office. Ibid., 266 (quoting Thayer).

53. *Annual Report, 1882–1883*, 27.

54. E. Gurney to C. W. Eliot, President's Papers, C. W. Eliot, Box 71, folder 1883 G–L.

55. W. A. Keener to C. W. Eliot, ibid., Box 70, folder 1882 H–K.

56. F. E. Parker to J. Q. Adams, December 29, 1882, ibid., Box 71, folder 1882 P–W.

57. Following quotes in this paragraph from J. C. Gray to C. W. Eliot, January 3, 1883, ibid., Box 71, folder 1883 G–L.

58. *Annual Report 1882–1883*, 27.

59. W. A. Keener to C. W. Eliot, January 11, 1883, President's Papers, C. W. Eliot, Box 71, folder 1883 G–L. The offer was apparently withdrawn in a letter from Eliot to Keener dated January 9.

60. Warren, *History of Harvard Law School*, II:432. At least one other name was canvassed after the offer to Keener was withdrawn. Eliot made inquires about Jeremiah Smith. See J. G. Noble to C. W. Eliot, April 20, 1883, President's Papers, C. W. Eliot, Box 71, folder 1883 M–Y, and ibid., April 21, 1883, suggesting the names of others who knew Smith who might be willing to give Eliot their impressions.

61. The board apparently solicited recommendations of Keener. See Henry J. Scudder to E. Rockwood Hoar, June 9, 1883, President's Papers, C. W. Eliot, Box 71, folder 1883 M–Y. Keener had worked in Scudder's office in New York, and Scudder's comments emphasize Keener's accomplishments as a practicing lawyer. Scudder wrote in terms designed, it would seem, to placate someone opposed to the appointment of teachers without extensive experience in practice. Scudder wrote: "United with a well ripened store of knowledge, [Keener] has what many students fail to acquire, a vigor of conviction that equips him for forensic conflict. Since leaving me, he has been in various active litigations and evinced all the purpose and practical courage that we recognize as the leading elements in counsel at the bar."

62. Reports to the Overseers, President, and Fellows, Series II, Vol. III, 1881–1884, p. 244, Harvard University Archives, Pusey Library.

63. F. E. Parker to J. Q. Adams, December 29, 1882, President's Papers, C. W. Eliot, Box 71, folder 1882 P–W. Parker reported that according to Joseph H. Choate, the judge's brother, the judge preferred the life of an academic to that of a practitioner.

64. J. G. Noble to C. W. Eliot, April 20, 1883, ibid., Box 71, folder 1883 M–Y.

65. E. H. Abbott to C. W. Eliot, March 27, 1890, ibid., Box 78, folder 1890 A–Bo.

66. J. B. Ames to C. W. Eliot, March 16, 1890, ibid.

67. Ames to Eliot, September 28, 1890, ibid.

68. Samuel Williston, "Jeremiah Smith," *Harvard Graduates Magazine* 30 (1921), 157. See also Joseph Beale, "Jeremiah Smith," *Harvard Law Review* 35 (1921), 1–8, who is even more oblique.

69. Williston, "Jeremiah Smith," 156.

70. Jeremiah Smith, "Notes for a Talk on Law as a Profession, February 25, 1890." This unpaginated autograph is in the Harvard Law School Library, Treasure Room, catalogued as L/MS/5001.

71. Ibid.

72. See note 5.

73. In his 1890 address, Smith echoed with uncanny accuracy certain portions of a lecture by Washburn ("Professional Training as an Element of Success") given

before the entire school in January 1861. Washburn had belittled the role of eloquence and pointed out the decline in the sorts of business likely to come to a young lawyer. Even if Eliot knew nothing of the earlier address, the similarities emphasize Smith's position as a representative of the class of practitioner-teachers and the possible hope on the part of Eliot and the overseers that he would bring the same sort of prestige to the school as had Washburn.

74. *Centennial History*, 256.

75. See the bibliography in ibid., 321–323.

76. Beale, "Jeremiah Smith," 4.

77. Batchelder, "Langdell," 440.

78. Warren, *History of Harvard Law School*, II:372.

79. Franklin G. Fessenden, "The Rebirth of Harvard Law School," *Harvard Law Review* 33 (1920), 495–496, 500.

80. Parker, *Law School of Harvard College*, 34; Warren, *History of Harvard Law School*, II:358; James, *Charles W. Eliot*, I:219–220, 257–260; Bruce Kuklick, *The Rise of American Philosophy: Cambridge, Massachusetts, 1860–1930* (New Haven, 1977), p. 136. For an earlier attempt to replace recitations in the college with lectures in order to encourage scholarly effort on the part of the faculty, see Robert A. McCaughey, *Josiah Quincy, 1722–1864: The Last Federalist* (Cambridge, 1974), p. 139.

81. C. S. Bradley to C. W. Eliot, January 19, 1870, President's Papers, C. W. Eliot, Box 66; *Centennial History*, 198.

82. Warren, *History of Harvard Law School*, II:372.

83. Fessenden, "Rebirth of Harvard Law School," 495–496, 500.

84. Parker, *Law School of Harvard College*, 23.

85. Emory Washburn, *Lectures on the Study and Practice of the Law* (Boston, 1871; rep. ed., Littleton, Colo., 1982), p. 53.

86. It may have been, however, much like the recitations used by Ashael Stearns from 1817 to 1829. Under Stearns "the chief work of the students was private reading of books recommended to them, with quizzes by the professor upon the passages read." *Centennial History*, 5.

87. This and the following quotes next two paragraphs from *Annual Report 1879–1880*, 14.

88. See chapter 3 in this volume.

89. The description of Washburn's teaching comes from *Centennial History*, 19.

90. This and the following quotes from Washburn, *Lectures on Study and Practice*, 45, 51–52, 62–65.

91. J. C. Gray to C. W. Eliot, June 9, 1870, President's Papers, C.W. Eliot, Box 66.

92. J. B. Thayer, Memorandum Book B, p. 5, LMS 2148, vol. 2, Harvard Law School Library, Treasure Room. This excerpt from the Memorandum Book is printed in Howe, "Preliminary Note," 4.

93. Memorandum Book B, ibid., 9.

94. Ibid.

95. Warren, *History of Harvard Law School*, I:361. Sir Frederick Pollock also found this aspect of Langdell's thought important. Frederick Pollock, "The Vocation of the Common Law," in Harvard Law School Association, *Report of the Ninth Annual Meeting at Cambridge, June 25, 1895 in especial honor of Christopher Columbus Langdell* (Boston, 1895), 17.

96. For the European background of Eliot's ideas of pedagogy, see Chase, "Birth of the Modern Law School," 343–346. Samuel Williston, *Life and Law: An Autobiography* (Boston, 1941), p. 199, gives Langdell priority in developing the idea that students should be taught from original sources.

97. Chase, "Origins of Modern Professional Education," 324–330.

98. Deborah L. Haines, "Scientific History as a Teaching Method: The Formative Years," *Journal of American History* 53 (1977), 898–899.

99. Not everyone, of course, agreed with the idea that the case method was training in the skills of practicing law. See chapter 5 in this volume. For similar developments in medical education, see Kenneth M. Ludmerer, *Learning to Heal: The Development of American Medical Education* (New York, 1985), pp. 50–52, 64–65, 71, 153.

100. Batchelder, "Langdell," 440.

101. Theodore W. Dwight, "Columbia College Law School, New York," *Green Bag* 1 (1889), 146.

102. William Wetmore Story, *Life and Letters of Joseph Story*, 2 vols. (Boston, 1851), II:37.

103. Keener in class: Roscoe Pound quoted in Sutherland, *Law at Harvard*, 203. Keener at Columbia: Julius Goebel, Jr. et al., *A History of the School of Law Columbia University* (New York, 1955), 429 n. 22, 138–139, 154. See also *Centennial History*, 41 ("Ames aimed to persuade; Keener to convince even against the will"). And see Williston, *Life and Law*, 74 ("[Keener's] logic was remorseless, and any student who ventured upon a difference of opinion with him found himself in an argument not likely to prove to his advantage").

104. "Book Notices" [anonymous review of Langdell, *A Selection of Cases on Sales of Personal Property*] *American Law Review* 7 (1872), 145. See also Oliver Wendell Holmes, Jr., "Book Notices" [review of Langdell, *A Selection of Cases on the Law of Contracts*], *American Law Review* 5 (1871), 539; *American Law Review* 6 (1872), 353.

105. Harvard Law School Association, *Report of the Organization and of the First General Meeting at Cambridge, November 5, 1886* (Boston, 1887), pp. 27–28.

106. Bledstein, *Culture of Professionalism*, pp. 25, 248–259.

107. George M. Fredrickson, *The Inner Civil War: American Intellectuals and the Crisis of the Union* (New York, 1965), p. 175.

108. Fessenden, "Rebirth of Harvard Law School," 503, 505.

109. James Barr Ames, "The Vocation of the Law Professor," in idem, *Lectures on Legal History* (Cambridge, 1913), p. 362.

110. Charles W. Eliot, "The Aims of the Higher Education" (1891), in idem, *Educational Reform* (n.p., 1897), pp. 223, 247.

Chapter 3

1. Joseph Story, "Codification of the Common Law" [1837], in William W. Story, ed., *The Miscellaneous Writings of Joseph Story* (Boston, 1852), p. 702.

2. For examples of Story's praise of Bacon, see William P. LaPiana, "*Swift v. Tyson* and the Brooding Omnipresence in the Sky: An Investigation of the Idea of Law in Antebellum America," *Suffolk University Law Review* 20 (1986), 775–776.

3. George H. Daniels, *American Science in the Age of Jackson* (New York,

1968), p. 65. See also Theodore Dwight Bozeman, *Protestantism in an Age of Science: The Baconian Ideal and Antebellum Religious Thought* (Chapel Hill, 1977), pp. 23–30.

4. Daniels, *American Science*, 65. A youthful John Adams illustrated an eighteenth-century view of the importance of arrangement in his discussion of genius: "Thus Order, Method, System, Connection, Plan, or whatever you call it, is the greatest Proof of Genius, next to Invention of new Wheels, Characters, Experiments, Rules, Laws, which is perhaps the first and greatest. Q[uery]. Does not the Word Invention express both these faculties, of inventing Wheels &c. and putting them in order." L. H. Butterfield, ed., *The Earliest Diary of John Adams* (Cambridge, 1966), p. 73. For examples of Bacon's influence on Adams, see L. H. Butterfield, ed., *Diary and Autobiography of John Adams*, 4 vols. (Cambridge, 1962), I: 177, 186, 266, 286; II:375, 386; III:264; IV:212.

5. James Wilson, *The Works of the Honorable James Wilson, L.L.D.*, 3 vols. (Philadelphia, 1804), II:43–44. For the story of the creation of the lecture course, see Clarks Page Smith, *James Wilson, Founding Father 1742–1798* (Chapel Hill, 1956), pp. 308–309.

6. Daniel Mayes, *An Address Delivered before the Trustees and Faculty of Transylvania University at the Opening of the Session of the Law Department on the 7th Nov. 1831* (Lexington, 1831), p. 16; Idem, *An Introductory Lecture Delivered to the Law Class of Transylvania University on the 5 of November 1832* (Lexington, 1832), pp. 17, 7.

7. On the Litchfield school, see Marian C. McKenna, *Tapping Reeve and the Litchfield Law School* (New York, 1986).

8. James Gould, *A Treatise on the Principles of Pleading in Civil Actions*, 4th ed., Franklin Fiske Heard, ed., (Albany, 1887), p. xiii.

9. Joseph Willard, *Address to the Members of the Bar of Worcester County, Massachusetts, October 2, 1829* (Lancaster, 1830), p. 113.

10. William Kent, "The Rise and Progress of Commercial Law in English Jurisprudence," in *Inaugural Addresses, Delivered by the Professors of Law in the University of the City of New-York, At the Opening of the Law School of the Institution* (New York, 1838), p. 49.

11. "Notes of Professor Greenleaf's Introductory Lecture, At the Present Term," *Law Reporter* 1 (1838), 218. A reprint of the "Notes" in the Harvard Law School Library, Treasure Room bear the inscription, in Greenleaf's hand, "With the Respects of S. Greenleaf" and the notation in another hand, "Gift of Prest. Quincy." Greenleaf no doubt considered the "Notes" to be at least an accurate summary of his views.

12. Edward D. Ingrham, "An Address delivered before the Law Academy of Philadelphia, at the opening of the Session of 1828–1829," 12 Hazard's Register of Pennsylvania 326 (1833) (hereafter cited as Hazard).

13. Joseph Hopkinson, "An Address delivered before The Law Academy of Philadelphia at the opening of the session of 1826–1827," 12 Hazard 290 (1833).

14. Thomas Sergeant, "A Lecture delivered before the Law Academy of Philadelphia, on Tuesday Evening, November 28, 1843," 3 Pa. L.J. 97 (1844).

15. William Rawle, "A Discourse on the Nature and Study of Law," (1832) 14 Hazard 182 (1834).

16. George Van Santvoord, *The Study of Law as a Science* (Albany, 1856), pp. 6–7.

17. Henry Nicoll, *An Address Delivered before the Graduating Class of the Law School of Columbia College . . . May 19, 1869* (New York, 1869), p. 4.

18. Theodore W. Dwight, *An Introductory Lecture Delivered before the Law Class of Columbia College, New York, Monday, November 1, 1858* (New York, 1859), p. 47; Julius Goebel, Jr., et. al., *A History of the School of Law, Columbia University* (New York, 1955), pp. 35–39, 126–128.

19. Phillip S. Paludan, *A Covenant with Death: The Constitution, Law, and Equality in the Civil War Era* (Urbana, Ill., 1975), p. 111.

20. George S. Hale, *Joel Parker* (Cambridge, 1876), p. 29.

21. Joel Parker, *The Law School of Harvard College* (New York, 1871), p. 22.

22. Emory Washburn, *Lectures on the Study and Practice of the Law*, 4th ed. (Boston, 1874), pp. 29, 50. Washburn's lectures were given at the request of the law students at Harvard and were first published in 1871. The inclusion of the same errata slip in the second and succeeding "editions" indicated that they are actually reprints.

23. "Art. VI—Whether Law Is a Science?" *American Jurist* 9 (1833), 349–352. Michael Lobban describes the form this sort of legal science took in England in the 1820s and 1830s. He maintains that English common lawyers believed that the common law "could not be defined by first principles: it could only be described by systematization" and that there was "a belief pervasive among common lawyers that jurisprudence was useful for describing and clarifying the common law, but not for defining the law a priori." *The Common Law and English Jurisprudence, 1760–1850* (Oxford, 1991), p. 220.

24. Thomas S. Kuhn, *The Structure of Scientific Revolutions*, 2d ed. (Chicago, 1970), pp. 1–9.

25. Bozeman, *Protestantism in an Age of Science*, 64–70.

26. John Milton Goodenow, *Historical Sketches of the Principles and Maxims of American Jurisprudence* (1819; rep. ed., Buffalo, 1972), p. 36.

27. "Whether Law Is a Science?" 350.

28. Joseph Story, *Commentaries on the Conflict of Laws* (Boston, 1834), p. 1 (§ 1). The importance ascribed to the influence of climate can be seen in cases dealing with the common law presumption that no male under the age of fourteen years is capable of committing the crime of rape. The Ohio Supreme Court explained the origin of the presumption in terms of "the moist and cold climate of England," noted that "in our climate, the age of puberty is frequently earlier than in that of England or the more northern States of this Union," and held that an infant under fourteen is presumed incapable of committing rape. But the presumption is rebuttable by proof that he has arrived at puberty. Williams v. State, 14 Ohio 222, 226–227 (1846). In 1855 a New York court came to the same conclusion using identical reasoning: the fact that "in this state, having a population composed of almost every variety of races and a climate as various as its population," males frequently come to puberty before the age of fourteen requires a modification of the common law presumption. People v. Randolph, 2 Parker's Crim. Rpts. 174, 178–179 (1855).

29. Story, *Conflict of Laws*, 70 (§ 72).

30. Ibid., 107–108 (§ 116).

31. Ibid., 2 (§ 1).

32. Joseph Story, "Growth of the Commercial Law" [1825], in Story, *Miscellaneous Writings*, 279.

33. R. Kent Newmyer, *Supreme Court Justice Joseph Story: Statesman of the Old Republic* (Chapel Hill, 1985), pp. 387–389.

34. Peter Stein, *Legal Evolution: The Story of an Idea* (Cambridge, U.K.,

1980), p. 64; and Robert A. Ferguson, *Law and Letters in American Culture* (Cambridge, Mass., 1984), p. 47.

35. Baron de Montesquieu, *The Spirit of Laws*, David W. Carrithers, ed. (Berkeley, 1977), pp. 104–105.

36. Story's concern with the perpetuation of the proper understanding of the American Revolution and of the republic it created is the pervading theme in Newmyer, *Joseph Story*.

37. Perry Miller, *Life of the Mind in America from the Revolution to the Civil War* (New York, 1965), pp. 129, 258–259; Dorothy Ross, "Historical Consciousness in Nineteenth-Century America," *American Historical Review* 89 (1985), 909–928.

38. Preceding quotes and discussion from Ross, "Historical Consciousness," 911–920.

39. Swift v. Tyson, 41 U.S. (16 Pet.), 1, 18 (1842).

40. Sir William Blackstone wrote "it sometimes happens that the judge may *mistake* the law," and that the decisions of the courts are evidence of the common law. William Blackstone, *Commentaries on the Laws of England*, 4 vols. (Oxford, 1765–1769; facsimile ed., Chicago, 1979), I:71.

41. Mayes, *Introductory Lecture . . . 1832*, 6–7.

42. James Kent, *Commentaries on American Law*, 12th ed., O. W. Holmes, Jr., ed., 4 vols. (Boston, 1873), I:*444.

43. Nathan Dane, *A General Abridgment and Digest of American Law*, 8 vols. (Boston, 1823), I:vii.

44. Art. III–Codification, and Reform of the Law—No. 1," *American Jurist* 14 (1835), 283.

45. Morton J. Horwitz, *The Transformation of American Law, 1780–1860* (Cambridge, 1977), pp. 42–47.

46. [William Curtis Noyes,] "Art. III—The Legal Rules Governing the Enjoyment and Use of Light," *American Jurist* 23 (1840), 58–59.

47. Preceding quotes from "Whether Law Is a Science?" 352–353.

48. Joseph Story, "Report on Codification" [1837], in Story, *Miscellaneous Writings*, 719.

49. Joseph Story, "Importance of Legal Studies" [1829], in Story, *Miscellaneous Writings*, 506. See also, "A Law Academy Tract," *Olwine's Law Journal* 1 (1850), 1; Thomas Sergeant, "Law as a Science," 3 Pa. L.J. 100–101 (1844).

50. See generally, Miller, *Life of the Mind*, and Charles M. Cook, *The American Codification Movement: A Study of Antebellum Legal Reform* (Westport, Conn., 1981).

51. Murdock v. Hunter, 17 F. Cas. at 1015 (C.C.D.Va. 1808) (No. 9941).

52. Baring v. Reeder, 11 Va. (1 Hen. & M.) 154, 158 (1806).

53. Ibid. at 162–163.

54. Marks v. Morris, 14 Va. (4 Hen. & M.) 463 (1809).

55. Rensselaer Glass Factory v. Reid, 5 Cowen 587, 632 (1825).

56. Robert v. West, 15 Ga 122, 133–134 (1854).

57. Bozeman, *Protestantism in an Age of Science*, 64–70. Bozeman shows that the interpretation Richard Whatley put forward in his 1826 *Elements of Logic*—Bacon intended "merely to direct [deduction] to its proper use, that is, as an interpreter of principles established inductively"—became an important part of American scientific thought.

58. People v. Randolph, 2 Parker's Crim. Rpts. 174, 177 (1855).

59. Rensselaer Glass Factory v. Reid, 5 Cowen 587, 628 (1825).

60. "Whether Law Is a Science?" 356.

61. Ibid., 355.

62. Ibid., 356.

63. Miller, *Life of the Mind*, 96–265.

64. James McClellan, *Joseph Story and the American Constitution: A Study in Political and Legal Thought* (Norman, 1971), pp. 24–25.

65. Maxwell Bloomfield, *American Lawyers in a Changing Society, 1776–1876* (Cambridge, 1976), p. 151.

66. The quoted phrase is taken by Bloomfield from the law magazines of the 1830s and later used by him to identify the alternative model of professionalism. Ibid., 143, and, generally, 136–190.

67. For a treatment of similar aspects of English legal thought, see Lobban, *Common Law and English Jurisprudence*, 207–219, 256–289.

68. For some indication of the early practice, see David Thomas Konig, *Law and Society in Puritan Massachusetts: Essex County, 1629–1692* (Chapel Hill, 1979), pp. 58–62. Konig finds the simplicity of land litigation procedure in Essex county the result of "a sophisticated adaptation of the common law" (p. 62). See also his "Editor's Introduction," to D. T. Konig, ed., *Plymouth Court Records, 1686–1859*, 16 vols. (Wilmington, 1978), I:149–172. Bruce H. Mann, "Rationality, Legal Change, and Community in Connecticut, 1690–1760," *Law and Society Review* 14 (1980), 187–221, implies that the simplicity of the procedure used in debt cases in early eighteenth-century Connecticut was in part the product of the small scale of economic life and a resulting lack of interpersonal relations based solely or primarily on the debtor/creditor relationship (pp. 193, 201, 207–208).

69. Herbert A. Johnson, "Civil Procedure in John Jay's New York," in idem, *Essays in New York Colonial Legal History* (Westport, Conn., 1981), pp. 169–170.

70. Samuel Tyler, *Memoir of Roger Brooke Taney, L.L.D.* (Baltimore, 1872), pp. 60–61.

71. Willard, *Address to Members of the Bar*, 79.

72. Preceding quotes all from Emory Washburn, *Sketches of the Judicial History of Massachusetts from 1630 to the Revolution in 1775* (Boston, 1840; rep. ed., New York, 1974), pp. 190, 196.

73. William E. Nelson, *Americanization of the Common Law: The Impact of Legal Change on Massachusetts Society, 1760–1830* (Cambridge, 1975), p. 72.

74. John A. Conley, "Doing It by the Book: Justice of the Peace Manuals and English Law in Eighteenth Century America," *Journal of Legal History* 6 (1985), 267–268.

75. Mann, "Rationality, Legal Change and Community," 207–208.

76. John M. Murrin, "The Legal Transformation: The Bench and Bar of Eighteenth-Century Massachusetts," in S. N. Katz, ed., *Colonial America: Essays on Politics and Social Development* (Boston, 1971), pp. 415–449.

77. Gerard W. Gawalt, *The Promise of Power: The Legal Profession in Massachusetts, 1760–1840* (Westport, Conn., 1979), pp. 7–30. The young John Adams, who saw himself as a model of the well-trained professional, made one of his first projects upon setting up his practice in Braintree an attack on the pettifoggers of the vicinity. Butterfield, *Diary and Autobiography of John Adams*, I:44–45, 64–65. For an interesting discussion of Adams's view of the virtues of elitism, see Daniel R. Coquillette, "Justinian in Braintree: John Adams, Civilian Learning and

Legal Elitism, 1758–1775," in *Law in Colonial Massachusetts, 1630–1800* (Boston, 1984), pp. 376–381. One of these pretenders, however, did best Adams in his first case.

78. Joseph H. Smith, "New Light on the Doctrine of Judicial Precedent in Early America, 1607–1776," in J. N. Hazard and W. J. Wagner, eds., *Legal Thought in the United States under Contemporary Pressures* (Brussels, 1970), pp. 9–39. Smith finds a vigorous doctrine of precedent in colonial America and the widespread use of English cases to resolve colonial questions, at least where no colonial statutes could be found on point.

79. Butterfield, *Diary and Autobiography of John Adams*, I:44–45, 64–65. For discussion of the case, *Field v. Lambert*, and of the difficulties with the pleading, see ibid., I:48–50, and idem, *Earliest Diary of John Adams*, 82–89. Adams's civilian learning was not without practical use. Coquillette, "Justinian in Braintree," 382–395.

80. See this section, text at note 86.

81. David Hoffman, *A Course of Legal Study*, 2d ed. (Philadelphia, 1846; rep. ed., Buffalo, 1968), pp. 372–373.

82. Alfred S. Konefsky and Andrew J. King, eds., *The Papers of Daniel Webster, Legal Papers: Volume I. The New Hampshire Practice* (Hanover, N.H., 1982), p. 6. See also Taney's memories of the difficulties of being obliged "to look for the rule [of pleading] in Comyn's Digest, or Bacon's Abridgment, or Viner's Abridgment, and the cases to which they referred." Tyler, *Memoir of Taney*, 56, 60–61.

83. Konefsky and King, *Webster, Legal Papers I*:6–7.

84. Joseph Story, "Autobiography," in *Story, Miscellaneous Writings*, 19–20.

85. Ibid., 20. For a defense of the importance of studying Coke, see Hoffman, *Course of Legal Study*, 215–231.

86. Joseph Story, *A Selection of Pleadings in Civil Actions, Subsequent to the Declaration. With Occasional Annotations on the Law of Pleading* (Salem, 1805; rep. ed., Buffalo, 1980).

87. Ibid., iv.

88. William W. Story, ed., *Life and Letters of Joseph Story*, 2 vols. (Boston, 1851), I:112.

89. "Review of Story's Pleadings," *Monthly Anthology and Boston Review*, 2 (1805), 484, quoted in McClellan, *Joseph Story*, 23–26.

90. Jenni Parrish, "Law Books and Legal Publishing in America, 1760–1840," *Law Library Journal* 72 (1979), 386.

91. Ibid., 401, and James Gould, *A Treatise on the Principles of Pleading in Civil Actions*, 4th ed., Franklin Fiske Heard, ed. (Albany, 1887), p. xi.

92. Wilson, *Works*, I:52–53.

93. This and preceding quotes from Gould, *Treatise on the Principles of Pleading*, xii.

94. Hoffman, *Course of Legal Study*, 352. See also Mayes, *Introductory Lecture . . . 1832*, 17–29.

95. This and preceding quotes from Creed Taylor, *Journal of the Law-School, and of the Moot-Court attached to it; at Needham, in Virginia*, Vol. 1 (Richmond, 1822), p. vii. Although Taylor lived until 1836, no further volumes of the journal were published. For further information on the school and Taylor, see W. Hamilton Bryson, *Legal Education in Virginia 1779–1979, A Biographical Approach* (Charlottesville, 1982), pp. 29–33, 589–595.

96. J. P. Kennedy, *Memoirs of the Life of William Wirt*, 2 vols. (Philadelphia, 1849; rep. ed., Buffalo, n.d.), I:362.

97. McFaul v. Ramsey, 20 Howard 523, 525 [1857, per Grier, J.].

98. At the conclusion of his article on the changes in procedure in debt collection cases in Connecticut, Bruce Mann suggests a good reason for the attachment on the part of lawyers to the forms of law: "Lawyers function best when they have a scheme of conceptual pigeonholes to classify the situations they encounter. While not a return to the terrible rigor of form pleading, increased technicality of pleading represented, from a lawyer's perspective, an internal simplification that allowed them to categorize things more precisely." Mann, "Rationality, Legal Change and Community," 213.

Nelson argues that although the weaknesses of the system were evident early, it persisted because "it provided lawyers with a conceptual framework for analyzing an otherwise amorphous body of legal rules." Nelson, *Americanization of the Common Law*, 87. G. Edward White describes the writ system in the early nineteenth century as "a surrogate for doctrinal classification." G. Edward White, *Tort Law in America: An Intellectual History* (New York, 1980), p. 9. The importance of the causes of action to understanding substantive law can be seen through even a brief perusal of the organization of Dane's *Abridgement*.

For other United States Supreme Court cases evidencing impatience with attempts to reform common law procedure, see Randon v. Toby, 52 U.S. (11 Howard) 493 [1850, per Grier, J.]; Bennet v. Butterworth, 52 U.S. (11 Howard) 669 [1850, per Taney, C. J.]; Green v. Custard, 64 U.S. (23 Howard) 484 [1859, per Grier, J.]; Farni v. Tesson, 66 U.S. (1 Black) 309 [1861, per Grier, J.].

The Supreme Court dealt with these reformed state procedures because of the diversity jurisdiction of the federal courts. Cases that would otherwise be litigated in the state courts can be brought in federal court if the parties are citizens of different states (and if certain other requirements are met). Until the passage of the Conformity Act of June 1, 1872 (5, 17 Stat. 196), which required procedure in diversity cases brought on the law side of the federal courts to conform "as near as may be" to the state procedure that would have governed had the case been brought in state court, the choice of procedure was governed by the Process Acts of 1789 (1 Stat. 93), 1792 (1 Stat. 275), and 1828 (4 Stat. 278 1). Robert Wyness Millar, *Civil Procedure of the Trial Court in Historical Perspective*, ([New York,] 1952), pp. 57–60. Generally speaking, these acts required that the federal court apply the state procedure that obtained at the time the process act became applicable to the state. The effect was to "freeze" state procedure as of that date. See Charles E. Clark and James W. Moore, "A New Federal Civil Procedure: I. The Background," *Yale Law Journal* 44 (1937), 400–401.

99. M.H. Hoeflich, "The Americanization of British Legal Education in the Nineteenth Century," *Journal of Legal History* 8 (1987), 245.

100. Quincy, 35.

101. Gawalt, *Promise of Power*, 16.

102. L. Kinvin Wroth and Hiller B. Zobel, "Introduction," in *Legal Papers of John Adams*, 3 vols., L. K. Wroth and H. B. Zobel, eds. (Cambridge, 1965), I: lvii–lviii (hereafter cited as *Adams Legal Papers*). See also Butterfield, *Diary and Autobiography of John Adams*, I:135–138, 159, 205–206; and Stephen Botein, "The Legal Profession in Colonial North America," in *Lawyers in Early Modern Europe and America*, Wilfrid Prest, ed. (London, 1981), pp. 135–136.

103. "Review of Story's Pleadings," 483, quoted in McClellan, *Joseph Story*, 24.

104. Diary of Aaron Barlow Olmstead, p. 211. New-York Historical Society (Misc. Microfilms, reel 14).

105. Ibid., 207.

106. Ibid., 211–212.

107. Alfred Z. Reed, *Training for the Public Profession of the Law* (New York, 1921), pp. 67–84; Gawalt, *Promise of Power*, 7–30, 129–158.

108. Reed, *Training for the Law*, 79–90.

109. Art. VI, sec. 8, cited in Francis N. Thorpe, *The Federal and State Constitutions, Colonial Charters and other Organic Laws*, 7 vols. (Washington, D.C., 1909), V:2664.

110. N.Y. Laws 1847, vol. I, C. 280, §75 (p. 342–343). It should be noted that since the ratification of the Constitution of 1846 the title "Supreme Court" has been borne by the statewide court of general jurisdiction. The highest court of the state is designated the "Court of Appeals." Const. of 1846, Art. VI, §§ 2,3, cited in Thorpe, *Constitutions*, V:2663.

111. Reed, *Training for the Law*, 89–90. The New Hampshire Supreme Court's rules for the regulation of attorneys and counsellors allowed candidates with a "liberal education" and a college degree, as well as a three-year clerkship, and candidates without the formal educational credentials, who had served a five-year clerkship, to be admitted on the recommendation of the bar of the county of the candidate's residence. A person who insisted on admission in accord with the minimum legislative requirement of citizenship and good moral character was required to present the evidence of citizenship and character in "affidavits by persons known to the court." Rules of Court Nos. 37, 38, 41 in 38 N.H. 581, 589–590 (1859).

112. Gawalt, *Promise of Power*, 184–185.

113. Ibid., 6.

114. Ibid., 188–192, quotation at 191. William R. Johnson finds that similar informal mechanisms disciplined the Wisconsin bar at a slightly later date. William R. Johnson, *Schooled Lawyers: A Clash in Professional Cultures* (New York, 1978), pp. 24–41.

115. *Adams Legal Papers*, I:lv.

116. Paul S. Clarkson and R. Samuel Jett, *Luther Martin of Maryland* (Baltimore, 1970), pp. 55–56.

117. Henry Marie Brackenridge, *Recollections of Persons and Places in the West*, 2d ed., enlarged (Philadelphia, 1868), pp. 116–117. On his father, Hugh Henry Brackenridge, lawyer, politician, justice of the Supreme Court of Pennsylvania, and author of *Modern Chivalry*, see Maxwell Bloomfield, *American Lawyers in a Changing Society, 1776–1876* (Cambridge, 1976), pp. 165–169.

118. John Neal, *Recollections of a Somewhat Busy Life* (Boston, 1869), pp. 113, 164.

119. James W. Gerard, *Address* [to the New York Law Institute, April 4, 1863], quoted in Henry W. Taft, *A Century and a Half at the New York Bar* (New York, 1938), p. 29.

120. *Adams Legal Papers*, I:lxvii–lxix.

121. Daniel H. Calhoun, *Professional Lives in America: Structure and Aspiration, 1750–1850* (Cambridge, 1965), p. 71.

122. Ibid., 76–78.

123. Printed in Report of the Committee on a Code of Professional Ethics, *American Bar Association Reports*, 31 (1907), 717–735.

124. Edward S. Martin, *The Life of Joseph Hodges Choate*, 2 vols. (New York, 1920), I:84–85; Gawalt, *Promise of Power*, 184–185.

125. Martin, *Life of Choate*, I:103–104.

126. As late as 1870 a writer in the *Western Jurist* estimated that "full three-fourths of the annual additions made to the American Bar come from private offices, and have never gone through the course of instruction furnished by a law school." "Law Schools and Their Course of Study. Second Article," *Western Jurist* 4 (1870), 125–129 (quotation from p. 129).

127. This and preceding quotes all from Parker, *Law School of Harvard College*, 17–19.

128. Story, *Life and Letters of Joseph Story*, II:36, 487.

129. "Art. XI—Sketch of the Law School at Cambridge," *American Jurist* 13 (1835), 124.

130. McKenna, *Litchfield Law School*, 63, 147, 166–167.

131. "Law Schools and Their Course of Study," 5. In 1895 James Bradley Thayer, then teaching at Harvard Law School, asked Simeon Baldwin, then teaching at Yale Law School, for information on Litchfield: "The student copied down most of what was said *verbatim* and the lectures must have been, I think, mainly dictations. I have found bound volumes of notes taken by my father as a student, which apparently are a literal reproduction of complete sentences as they fell from the lecturers' lips; the authorities being noted in the margin. . . . The student was expected to read more or less from these authorities, as the course ran along." Draft of S. E. Baldwin to J. B. Thayer on letter of Thayer to Baldwin, July 16, 1895, Baldwin Family Papers, Series I Box 52, folder 653, Yale University Library, Manuscript Division.

132. Preceding quotes all from Benjamin F. Butler, *Plan for the Organization of a Law Faculty. . . in the University of the City of New York* (1835), reprinted in Ronald L. Brown, *The Law School Papers of Benjamin F. Butler* (New York, 1987), pp. 130–132.

133. Ibid., 136.

134. [John C. Spencer,] "Proposed Law School, at Hamilton College, New York," *American Jurist* 13 (1835), 487. According to Butler the proposal was first published in the *New-York Mirror* in October, 1834. Butler, *Plan for the Organization*, 136.

135. [Spencer,] "Proposed Law School," 488.

136. Charles Richard Williams, *The Life of Rutherford Birchard Hayes*, 2 vols. (Boston, 1914), I:31–32.

137. Parker, *Law School of Harvard College*, 19–20.

138. Respectively, Ezra M. Prince to Charles Warren, n.p., n.d.; John D. Long to Charles Warren, n.p., October 7, 1907—in Letters of Reminiscence presented by Charles Warren, Harvard Law School Library, Treasure Room (hereafter cited as, Letters of Reminiscence, HLS/TR). Warren prints portions of the letters quoted in this paragraph and of others in *History of Harvard Law School*, II:175–184, 303–318.

Parker's aridity was noted outside the law school, too. Referring to the professor's participation in the Massachusetts Constitutional Convention of 1853, Richard Dana wrote: "Judge *Parker* disappointed everybody. He showed himself an honest man & a good dry technical lawyer, but he discussed questions of statesmanship & public policy, on the narrowest precedents, & in the driest manner. . . . The Judge persevered in attention to business, & spoke often, yet his voice was so low, & his manner so dry that he often had but some ½ dos. listeners." Robert F. Lucis, ed., *The Journal of Richard Henry Dana, Jr.*, 3 vols. (Cambridge, 1968), II:567.

139. Edward Everett to Joel Parker, Cambridge, October 6, 1847, Joel Parker Papers, Box 1, Massachusetts Historical Society. Reprinted in Charles Warren, *History of Harvard Law School and of Early Legal Conditions in America*, 2 vols. (New York, 1908; rep. ed., New York, 1974), II:113 n. 1.

140. Everett's letter did make an impression on Parker: "Your letter leads me to believe that this duty [to give instruction] would be somewhat less onerous than I had supposed it to be." Draft of Parker to Everett, October 14, 1847, Joel Parker Papers, Box I, Massachusetts Historical Society.

141. Everett P. Wheeler, "The Harvard Law School in 1857," *City College Quarterly* 13 (1917), 156. Wheeler admitted that he learned more from listening to the leaders of the Boston bar argue in court than from the professors in the law school (p. 158).

142. Joseph H. Choate, "A Fragment of Autobiography," in Martin, *Life of Choate*, I:81.

143. "Harvard Lectures," notebook in Container 22, Joseph H. Choate Papers, Manuscript Division, Library of Congress, Washington, D.C.

144. Alexander Wilson to Charles Warren, October 3, 1907; Gregory W. C. Noble to Charles Warren, October 8, 1907. Wilson was at the law school from 1851 to 1853, Noble in 1860–1861. Similar comments were made about the period 1847–1848: Walter Mitchell to Charles Warren, October 16, 1907. All three letters are in Letters of Reminiscence, HLS/TR. Warren mentions the phenomenon briefly in *History of Harvard Law School*, II:317. Warren also reprints portions of these and other letters of reminiscence in ibid., 175–184, 303–318.

145. *The Centennial History of the Harvard Law School* ([Cambridge ?,] 1918), p. 24.

146. Respectively, Charles E. Phelps to Charles Warren, Baltimore [1908] (typed transcription); Thorton K. Lathrop to Charles Warren, n.p., October 1, 1907, in Letters of Reminiscence, HLS/TR.

147. Butler, *Plan for the Organization*, 120–121.

148. Ibid., 132.

149. Ibid., 123.

150. "Syllabus," reprinted in Brown, *Law School Papers of Butler*, 223–229.

151. Brown, *Law School Papers of Butler*, 51, 196.

152. William Curtis Noyes, "Handwritten Notes, December 1843," in ibid., 231–232. The anonymous author of an article in the *Western Jurist* observed in 1870 of legal education that "in almost every case of success enough to attract attention, we find that such success has been directly connected with the labors and reputation of single teachers." "Law Schools and Their Course of Study," 8.

153. Brown, *Law School Papers of Butler*, 56.

154. Ibid., 45–50.

155. W. Kent to J. Story, Sept. 13, 1839, Joseph Story Papers, University of Michigan, Clements Library, quoted in Brown, *Law School Papers of Butler*, 46–50. Butler's plan frankly stated that "[t]he organization of the school, and its whole system of instruction, would be specially adapted to students who design to pursue their professions within this State" (p. 117).

156. Ibid., 52.

157. R. Kent Newmyer, "Harvard Law School, New England Legal Culture, and the Antebellum Origins of American Jurisprudence," *Journal of American History* 74 (1987), 817–818.

158. Alfred S. Konefsky, "Law and Culture in Antebellum Boston," *Stanford Law Review* 40 (1988), 1134–1136.

159. Butler, *Plan for the Organization*, 123. Butler also denigrated any extensive study of Roman law, which was widely regarded as the model of scientific jurisprudence. M. H. Hoeflich, "Law and Geometry: Legal Science from Leibniz to Langdell," *American Journal of Legal History* 30 (1986), 112–119.

160. LaPiana, "Idea of Law in Antebellum America," 771–832.

161. Edward L. Pierce, *Memoir and Letters of Charles Sumner*, 2 vols. (Boston, 1877), I:109.

Chapter 4

1. M. H. Hoeflich, "Law and Geometry: Legal Science from Leibniz to Langdell," *American Journal of Legal History* 30 (1986), 119–121, and Robert Stevens, *Law School: Legal Education in America from the 1850s to the 1980s* (Chapel Hill, 1983), p. 52.

2. Preceding quotes all from Christopher C. Langdell, "Preface to the First Edition," *A Selection of Cases on the Law of Contracts*, 2nd ed. (Boston, 1879), pp. viii–ix.

3. Christopher C. Langdell, "Teaching Law as a Science," *American Law Review* 21 (1887), 123–124.

4. *Annual Reports of the President and Treasurer of Harvard College, 1876–1877*, pp. 96–97. (This volume includes the reports of the deans of the various faculties. Successive volumes are cited as *Annual Report* and date.)

5. Anthony Chase, "Origins of Modern Professional Education: The Harvard Case Method Conceived as Clinical Instruction in Law," *Nova Law Journal* 5 (1981), 359.

6. *Annual Report 1876–1877*, 95–96.

7. Ibid., 95.

8. Langdell, "Preface to the First Edition," viii–ix.

9. Hoeflich, "Law and Geometry," 96–119.

10. C. C. Langdell, "Mutual Promises as a Consideration for Each Other," *Harvard Law Review* 14 (1901), 496, 503. It is interesting to note that rules which used to be important to pleading are here being treated as part of the law of evidence.

11. Grant Gilmore, *The Death of Contract* (Columbus, 1974), pp. 5–6, 13–14, and Thomas C. Grey, "Langdell's Orthodoxy," *University of Pittsburgh Law Review* 45 (1983), 1–6. For a brief explanation of the most influential view of what this classic or orthodox thought is, see Duncan Kennedy, "Toward an Historical Understanding of Legal Consciousness: The Case of Classical Legal Thought in America, 1850–1940," *Research in Law and Sociology* 3 (1980), 3–24; also, Morton J. Horwitz, *The Transformation of American Law, 1870–1960: The Crisis of Legal Orthodoxy* (New York and Oxford, 1992), pp. 9–31. "Classical formalism" or "orthodoxy" has received many definitions, but it is fair to say that they all emphasize what Horwitz has called the "legal architecture" of the resulting system (p. 10), marked by a high degree of abstraction and systematization. Edward A. Purcell, Jr., *Litigation and Inequality: Federal Diversity Jurisdiction in Industrial America, 1870–1958* (New York and Oxford, 1992), p. 394 n. 13 has a thorough summary of the literature. As Purcell notes, there is little agreement on whether formalism led to judicial decisions which explicitly favored corporate enterprise (ibid.). He does suggest (ibid., 396 n. 15) that among judges, at least, formalism is best understood as "a distinctive historical phenomenon" resulting from the clash

between a world view rooted in the nineteenth century and one which reflected the emerging values that would characterize the new century. Controversies in legal education bear out Purcell's suggestion. Chapters 6 and 7 below show that the case method teachers espoused a theory of law based on the belief that law came from power and were opposed by thinkers who believed that law was discovered, not made, and that its substance consisted of timeless principles. This latter view was closely related to the antebellum idea of law sketched in Chapter 2. I believe the "formalist" label, at least in its most pejorative meaning, belongs not to Langdell and the other case method teachers, but to their opponents, developing a distinction perhaps first suggested by Grey, "Langdell's Orthodoxy," 34, 35 n. 134.

12. The *Summary* began as an appendix to the contracts casebook, first published in 1871. The second edition of the casebook appeared in 1879 with a much more complete summary, which, in turn, was published separately in 1880 and in a further edition in 1883. Charles Warren, *History of the Harvard Law School*, 2 vols. (New York, 1908; rep. ed., New York: 1970), II:460. All subsequent references in this chapter are to the numbered sections of C. C. Langdell, *A Summary of the Law of Contracts*, 2nd ed. (Boston, 1880).

13. In Part II of the treatise, Story included agency, partnership, bailments, sales, guaranty, and the law of landlord and tenant. William W. Story, *A Treatise on the Law of Contracts Not under Seal* (Boston, 1844; rep. ed., New York, 1972), pp. viii–x.

14. Grant Gilmore, *The Ages of American Law* (New Haven, 1977), p. 45.

15. Theophilus Parsons, *The Law of Contract*, 2nd ed., 2 vols. (Boston, 1855), I:xiii–xxviii.

16. Francis Hilliard, *The Law of Contracts*, 2 vols. (Philadelphia, 1872), and Joel Prentiss Bishop, *The Doctrines of the Law of Contracts in their Principal Outlines, Stated, Illustrated, and Condensed* (St. Louis, 1878).

17. Bishop, *Doctrines of the Law of Contracts*, iii–iv.

18. Hilliard, *Law of Contracts*, includes sections on bills and notes along with sections on masters and servants. The latter, of course, was in the 1870s becoming part of the relatively new subject of torts. See G. Edward White, *An Intellectual History of Tort Law in America* (New York, 1980), pp. 12–19.

19. Langdell may have been the first theoretician of contract law in the United States, but the impulse to theorize seems to have appeared almost simultaneously in at least one other part of the common law world. According to P. S. Atiyah, 1867 marks the appearance of the first English work on contract, written by Martin Leake, resembling Langdell's: "Leake was the first author to write purely on the general principles of contract law, excluding the law relating to particular contracts." P. S. Atiyah, *The Rise and Fall of Freedom of Contract* (Oxford, 1979), p. 682.

20. Ibid., 162–163; and C. H. S. Fifoot, *Lord Mansfield* (Oxford, 1936; rep. ed., Aalen, Denmark, 1977), pp. 135–141, 243–245.

21. A. W. B. Simpson, *A History of the Common Law of Contract : The Rise of the Action of Assumpsit* (Oxford, 1975), pp. 322–323, 337–341, 365, 445.

22. Fifoot, *Lord Mansfield*, 244. Fifoot's statement is based on *Lee v. Muggeridge*, 5 Taunt. 36, 128 E.R. 482. Atiyah also characterizes the decision in that case as indicating acceptance of Mansfield's ideas. Atiyah, *Freedom of Contract*, 490. While there were American precedents opposing Mansfield's views, at late as 1836 he received strong support from a anonymous writer in the *American Jurist*, "Art.

III—Codification and Reform of the Law—No. III," *American Jurist* 16 (1836), 79–83.

23. Wennall v. Adney, 3 Bos. and Pul. 249 note (a), 127 E.R. 138.

24. Ibid., 127 E.R. at 140. See the criticism of the note's discussion of cases in "Codification and Reform of the Law—No. III," 79–83.

25. Simpson, *History of the Common Law of Contract*, 491–493.

26. Wennell v. Adney, 3 Bos. and Pul. 249 note (a), 127 E.R. at 139.

27. The foregoing sentence is, of course, only the briefest statement of a most complex matter. For a clear discussion of the traditional learning, see John Edward Murray, Jr., *Murray on Contracts*, 2nd ed. (Indianapolis, 1974), pp. 124–220. For a full discussion of Mansfield's views on the matter, see Fifoot, *Lord Mansfield*, 118–157 and James Oldham, *The Mansfield Manuscripts and the Growth of English Law in the Eighteenth Century*, 2 vols. (Chapel Hill and London, 1992), I: 223–232.

28. Littlefield v. Shee, 2 B. & Ad. 811.

29. Eastwood v. Kenyon, 11 Ad. & E. 438, 113 E.R. 482 (1840).

30. Atiyah, *Freedom of Contract*, 491.

31. 11 Ad. & E. 438, 438–441, 113 E.R. 482, 482–483 (1840).

32. Ibid. at 445–452, 113 E.R. 482, 485–487 (1840).

33. Quotes from and following discussion based on Story, *Treatise on the Law of Contracts*, 90, 92.

34. Ibid., 91–92 n. 4. The cases are Greeves v. M'Allister, 2 Binney 591 (Phila. Common Pleas 1809)—"When the interest of a man is promoted, though not at his request, and he deliberately engages to pay for it, the law very properly says, he shall fulfill his promise" (at 592) and Doty v. Wilson, 14 Johns. 378 (N.Y. Supreme Ct. 1817)—the moral obligation to pay is sufficient to uphold promise to pay it; benefit in conjunction with promise implies request.

35. Parsons, *Law of Contract*, 360.

36. Ibid.

37. Ibid., 359–361.

38. Langdell, *Summary of the Law of Contracts*, 89 (§ 71).

39. Ibid.

40. Ibid., 58 (§ 45).

41. Ibid., 59 (§ 46).

42. Ibid., 87 (§ 69).

43. Ibid., 91–92 (§ 72).

44. Ibid., 92–93 (§ 73).

45. Ibid., 93–94 (§ 74). Lord Denman suggested as much: "If the ratification of the wife [Sarah] while sole were relied on, then a debt from her would have been shown, and the defendant could not have been charged in his own right without some further consideration." Eastwood v. Kenyon, 11 A & E 438, 451, 113 E.R. 482, 487.

46. Story, *Treatise on the Law of Contracts*, 81–82 (§§ 127–129).

47. Bishop, *Doctrines of the Law of Contracts*, 151–152 (§§ 428–431).

48. Hilliard, *Law of Contracts*, 256–259 (§ 14).

49. Parsons, *Law of Contract*, 373–376.

50. This discussion and preceding quote from Langdell, *Summary of the Law of Contracts*, 103 (§ 81–82).

51. Ibid., 248–249 (§ 183).

52. Atiyah, *Freedom of Contract*, 165–167.

53. Langdell, *Summary of the Law of Contracts*, 106–111 (§ 87–88). The English courts seem to have reached similar conclusions; see Atiyah, *Freedom of Contract*, 438–440.

54. Story, *Law of Contracts*, 73.

55. Parsons, *Law of Contract*, 357; William Blackstone, *Commentaries on the Laws of England*, 4 vols. (Oxford, 1766; rep. ed., London, 1966), II:444–445.

56. For an elaborate analysis of the theory of a coherent system of legal rules, see Grey, "Langdell's Orthodoxy," 6–32.

57. For a lucid and brief outline of these changes, see A. W. B. Simpson, "Innovation in Nineteenth-Century Contract Law," *Law Quarterly Review* 91 (1975), 247–278, and, for a more interpretive approach, Gilmore, *Death of Contract*, 5–53.

58. Compare Parsons, *Law of Contract*, 399–408, with Langdell, *Summary of the Law of Contracts*, 1–23 (§§ 1–18); 193–194 (§§ 148–149); 197–204 (§§ 151–156).

59. Parsons' discussion of past or executed consideration consists primarily of analysis of the extent of parental obligation to provide for children since many of the cases involving the question arise in that circumstance. Parsons, *Law of Contract*, 247–260, 371. Langdell, on the other hand, discusses many of the same cases not in terms of their subject matter but in terms of his theories. Langdell, *Summary of the Law of Contracts*, 112–122 (§§ 90–98).

60. Langdell, *Summary of the Law of Contracts*, 82 (§ 65).

61. C. C. Langdell, "A Brief Survey of Equity Jurisdiction," *Harvard Law Review* 1 (1887), 55–72; idem, "A Brief Survey of Equity Jurisdiction: II.," ibid. 1 (1887), 111–131; idem, "Specific Performance," ibid. 1 (1888), 355–387; idem, "Bills for an Account," ibid. 2 (1889), 241–267; idem, "Bills of Equitable Adjustment," ibid. 3 (1890), 237–262; idem, "Creditors' Bills," ibid. 4 (1890), 99–127, 5 (1891), 101–138; idem, "Real Obligations," ibid. 10 (1896), 71–97; idem, "Classification of Rights and Wrongs," ibid. 13 (1900), 537–556, 659–678; and idem, "Equitable Conversion," ibid. 18 (1904–1905), 1–22, 83–194, 245–270. Reprinted in C. C. Langdell, *A Brief Survey of Equity Jurisdiction*, 2nd ed. (Cambridge, 1908).

62. Joseph Story, *Commentaries on Equity Jurisprudence, as Administered in England and America*, 2 vols. (Boston, 1836; rep. ed., New York, 1972).

63. Ibid., I:508 (§ 535).

64. Ibid., 517 (§ 548).

65. Ibid., 518 (§ 549).

66. Ibid., 506–508 (§§ 532–534).

67. Langdell, "Creditors' Bills," 106; idem, *Brief Survey*, 132.

68. In conformity with Langdell's usage, the term "executor" will be used hereafter, although the comments apply equally to the administrator of an intestate estate.

69. Langdell, "Creditors' Bills," 106–107; idem, *Brief Survey*, 132–133.

70. Langdell, "Creditors' Bills," 109; idem, *Brief Survey*, 135.

71. Langdell, "Creditors' Bills," 109–111; idem, *Brief Survey*, 136–137.

72. Langdell, "Creditors' Bills," ibid.; idem, *Brief Survey*, 137.

73. Langdell, "Creditors' Bills," 113; idem, *Brief Survey*, 138–139.

74. Langdell, "Creditors' Bills," 114; idem, *Brief Survey*, 139–140.

75. Charles G. Grafton to Charles Warren, Fond du Lac, Wisc., October 28, 1907, Letters of Reminiscence, Harvard Law School Library, Treasure Room (here-

after cited as Letters of Reminiscence, HLS/TR). Charles Phelps gave two versions of a similar recollection, one in Phelps to Charles Warren, [1908], ibid.; the other is quoted in James Barr Ames, "Christopher C. Langdell," in William Draper Lewis, ed., *Great American Lawyers*, 8 vols. (Philadelphia, 1909), VIII:470. This essay, the most complete biographical source, is reprinted in James Barr Ames, *Lectures on Legal History* (Cambridge, 1913), pp. 467–482.

76. C. G. Grafton to C. Warren, Fond du Lac, Wisc., October 28, 1907, Letters of Reminiscence, HLS/TR; Charles Warren, *History of the Harvard Law School and of Early Legal Conditions in America*, 2 vols. (New York, 1908; rep. ed., New York, 1970), II:176–178; Parsons, *Law of Contract*, I:x.

So pleased was Parsons with Langdell's work that it seems he allowed his by then ex-student to ghostwrite most of his treatise on bills and notes. Daniel W. Webster to C. Warren, Hiawatha, Kan., October, 11 [1907,] Letters of Reminiscence, HLS/TR.

77. Parsons, *Law of Contract*, I:x.

78. Ames, "Langdell," 472–474. D. W. Wilder to C. Warren, October 11, [1907,] Letters of Reminiscence HLS/TR, indicates that Langdell was working on Parsons's treatise on bills and notes in 1857–1858. Such work may have tided him over his difficulties in establishing himself in practice. He also contributed to the 1867 edition of *Bouvier's Law Dictionary*. William Schofield, "Christopher Columbus Langdell," *American Law Register* 46 (N.S.) (1907), 292.

79. City Bank of New York v. Perkins, 4 Bosworth 420, 422–436 (1859) and 29 N.Y. 554 (1864) (argued by Langdell). Others: Gillespie v. Torrance, 25 N.Y. 306 (1862); Manning v. Monaghan, 28 N.Y. 585 (1864); McBride v. The Farmers' Bank of Salem, Ohio, 26 N.Y. 450 (1863); Platt v. Lott, 17 N.Y. 478 (1858); The Belmont Branch of the State Bank of Ohio v. Hoge, 35 N.Y. 65 (1866); Van Buskirk v. Roberts, 31 N.Y. 661 (1864); Willitts v. Waite, 25 N.Y. 577 (1862).

80. See the biographical sketches in the *Green Bag* 4 (1892), 188, and the *Dictionary of American Biography*.

81. Ames, "Langdell," 473.

82. Robert Ludlow Fowler, "Constitutional and Related Aspects from 1801 to the Constitution of 1894," in D. McAdam et al., eds., *History of the Bench and Bar of New York*, 2 vols. (New York, 1897), I:158.

83. Francis Bergan, *The History of the New York Court of Appeals, 1847–1932* (New York, 1985), pp. 19–35.

84. Alison Reppy, "The Field Codification Concept," in A. Reppy, ed., *David Dudley Field: Centenary Essays* (New York, 1949), pp. 32–35.

85. An Act to Simplify and Abridge the Practice, Pleadings, and Proceedings of the Courts of this State, 1848 N.Y. Laws c. 379 § 118 [hereafter called the Code of Procedure (1848)]. In the 1849 enactment this provision became § 140, reading in part: "All forms of pleading heretofor existing, inconsistent with the provisions of this act, are abolished." An act to amend the act, entitled "An Act to Simplify and Abridge the Practice, Pleadings and Proceedings of the Court of This State," passed April 12, 1841, 1849 N.Y. Laws c. 438 [hereafter called the Code of Procedure (1849)]. For a full discussion of the effects of the code on the law of New York, see William P. LaPiana, "Just the Facts: The Field Code and the Case Method," *New York Law School Law Review* 36 (1991), 287–336.

86. Charles E. Clark, *Handbook of the Law of Code Pleading*, 2nd ed. (St. Paul, 1947), pp. 23–31; Robert Wyness Millar, *Civil Procedure of the Trial Court in Historical Perspective* ([New York,] 1951), pp. 52–57.

87. Goulet v. Asseler, 22 N.Y. 225 (1860).

88. George van Santvoord, *A Treatise on the Principles of Pleading in Civil Actions under the New York Code of Procedure*, new ed., Nathaniel C. Moak, ed. (Albany, 1873), pp. 2–4. This edition preserves van Santvoord's original text, Moak's additions being entered in square brackets, p. iv.

89. Ibid. As originally enacted, section 120 of the code required the complaint, the pleading, which began the plaintiff's suit, to be "A statement of the facts constituting the cause of action, in ordinary and concise language, without repetition, and in such a manner as to enable a person of common understanding to know what is intended." In the 1851 amendment of the code the definition of the complaint is found in subdivision 2 of section 142: "A plain and concise statement of the facts constituting a cause of action without unnecessary repetition." 1851 N.Y. Laws c. 479. van Santvoord maintained that the consensus of authority held the two provisions to have the same substantive meaning. van Santvoord, *Treatise on the Principles of Pleading*, 161–162. The later formulation does seem to be more sparing of professional sensibilities. Some, however, would not be reconciled. Charles O'Conor was a prominent New York practitioner, the length of whose career revokes Field's. His opposition to the Code of Procedure may have begun in his opposition, suggesting "pride and pique," to judiciary provisions of the 1846 constitution. Bergan, *History of the N.Y. Court of Appeals*, 28.

In 1870 South Carolina adopted the New York Code of Procedure. Two attorneys in Columbia wrote to O'Conor asking him to suggest books they might acquire to help them understand pleading and practice under the code. His answer was an extended criticism of the code and of "its sole author," David Dudley Field. O'Conor singled out for special criticism the requirement that only facts be pleaded. It is clear from his description of the kind of pleading resulting from that requirement that all science had been destroyed:

> Now, according to my conception, it requires somebody much more wise or more subtle than myself, or any special pleader I have ever been acquainted with, to define or find out what it is that should be stated in a regular pleading drawn in compliance with this requisite of the code. I am not aware that anyone has ever attempted to do it. The common practice in this state is to tell your story precisely as your client tells it to you, just as any old woman in trouble for the first time would narrate her grievances, and to annex by way of schedules, respectively marked A, B, C, & c., copies of any papers or documents that you may imagine may help your case. This is most emphatically a fair description of all the pleadings which come from the office of the chief codifier himself [Field].

Charles O'Conor to Pope & Haskell, March 14, 1870, reprinted from the Columbia *Guardian* in *Albany Law Journal* 1 (1870), 302–303, quotation at 303. For a modern view of the matter which described O'Conor's view as a "legalistic" interpretation of the code, see Clark, *Handbook of Code Pleading*, 129–130. Clark here describes as "the view most nearly approaching the code ideal and affording the most practically convenient results" one which sees the statement of facts required by the code as limited to what "a lay onlooker" would see as "a single occurrence or affair, without particular reference to the resulting legal right or rights."

90. van Santvoord, *Treatise on the Principles of Pleading*, 197–199.

91. Ibid., 5.

92. Ibid., 376.

93. Langdell, *Summary of the Law of Contracts*, 58–62 (§§ 46–47); 123–130 (§§ 99–103).

94. Theophilus Parsons, *The Law of Contracts*, 9th ed., John M. Gould, ed. (Boston, 1904), p. *431.

95. Gulian C. Verplanck, *An Essay on the Doctrine of Contracts* (New York, [1825]; rep. ed., New York, 1972), p. 7. On Verplanck, see Robert W. July, *The Essential New Yorker: Gulian Crommelion Verplanck* (Durham, N.C., 1951).

96. Verplanck, *Doctrine of Contracts*, 15.

97. Ibid., 155.

98. Ibid., 137, 173; 156–174, 222.

99. Ibid., 127.

100. E.L.P., "The Consideration of a Contract at Law and in Equity," *American Law Register* 2 (1854), 259.

101. Verplanck, *Doctrine of Contracts*, 107–131.

102. Horwitz emphasizes this aspect of Verplanck's work: Morton W. Horwitz, *Transformation of American Law, 1780–1860* (Cambridge, 1977), pp. 181–183.

103. Verplanck, *Doctrine of Contracts*, 37. Verplanck saw the object of all "scientific inquiry" the attaining of truth. July, *Essential New Yorker*, 206–209.

104. The fullest description of this conflict is Robert M. Cover, *Justice Accused: Antislavery and the Judicial Process* (New Haven, 1975); see especially pp. 197–200, and on the particular dilemma the conflict posed for Joseph Story, pp. 238–243. See also William E. Nelson, "The Impact of the Antislavery Movement upon Styles of Judicial Reasoning in Nineteenth-Century America," *Harvard Law Review* 87 (1974), 513, 525–547; idem, *The Roots of American Bureaucracy, 1830–1900* (Cambridge, 1982), pp. 41–61; White, *Tort Law in America*, 21–22; and Horwitz, *Crisis of Legal Orthodoxy*, 113–116.

105. Marvin Meyers, *The Jacksonian Persuasion* (Stanford, 1957).

106. For a summary of these tendencies and their influence on an important legal thinker whose contribution is discussed at length below, see Alan R. Jones, *The Constitutional Conservatism of Thomas McIntyre Cooley: A Study in the History of Ideas* (New York, 1987), pp. 21–32, 59–68, 142–165, 220–222; and also Nelson, *Roots of American Bureaucracy*, 10–16.

107. The foregoing is a brutally abbreviated summary of a large, thoughtful, and complex work. For brief statements of Atiyah's general approach see, Atiyah, *Freedom of Contract*, 1–7, 224–237, 292–294 ("[I]t is impossible to doubt the influence of political economy on the law of contract during this period [1770–1870]."), pp. 716–717.

108. Ibid., 492–493.

109. Rensselaer Glass Factory v. Reid, 5 Cowen 587, 620 (1825). The same view profoundly influenced the law of negligence as applied to carriers in New York. Robert J. Kaczorowski, "The Common-Law Background of Nineteenth-Century Tort Law," *Ohio State Law Journal* 51 (1990), 1154.

110. The fullest treatment of Austin's thought is Wilfred E. Rumble, *The Thought of John Austin: Jurisprudence, Colonial Reform, and the British Constitution* (London, 1985).

111. Ibid., 71–87.

112. C. C. Langdell to T. D. Woolsey, February 6, 1871, Woolsey Family Papers, Series I, Box 23, folder 433, Yale University Library, Manuscript Division.

113. Ibid.

114. Langdell, *Summary of the Law of Contracts*, 100 (§ 79).

115. Rumble, *Thought of John Austin*, 86–87.

116. Ibid., 4–5.

117. Christopher C. Langdell, "Dominant Opinions in England during the Nineteenth Century in Relation to Legislation as Illustrated by English Legislation, or the Absence of it, during that Period," *Harvard Law Review* 19 (1906), 151.

Chapter 5

1. *Annual Reports of the President and Treasurer of Harvard College, 1876–1877*, p. 92. (This volume includes reports of the deans of the various faculties. Successive volumes are cited as *Annual Report* and date.)

2. Robert T. Swaine, *The Cravath Firm and Its Predecessors, 1819–1947*, 2 vols. (New York, 1946), I:143–162.

3. "Admission to the Bar," *Albany Law Journal* 4 (1871), 309.

4. "Current Topics," *Albany Law Journal* 2 (1870), 413–414.

5. Swaine, *Cravath Firm*, I:166–169.

6. Maury Klein, *The Life and Legend of Jay Gould* (Baltimore, 1986), p. 69.

7. Such was the view of the editors of the *Albany Law Journal* who maintained in 1876 that the bar was as upright as it had ever been. "To be sure, there are a good many more disreputable men in the profession than previous to 1840, but that is simply because there are a great many more lawyers." "Admission to the Bar," *Albany Law Journal* 13 (1876), 142.

8. "Admission to the Bar," *Albany Law Journal* 4 (1871), 309; "Concerning Examinations for Admission to the Bar," ibid. 1 (1870), 351.

9. For a suggestion of the complexity of kinship networks among the elite, including merchants and lawyers, in antebellum Boston, see Alfred S. Konefsky, "Law and Culture in Antebellum Boston," *Stanford Law Review* 40 (1988), 1151–1155.

10. A. Nevins and M. H. Thomas, eds., *The Diary of George Templeton Strong*, 4 vols. (New York, 1952), II:478 (hereafter cited as *Strong Diary*).

11. Ibid.

12. *Strong Diary*, II:135–138; Julius Goebel, Jr., et al., *A History of the School of Law, Columbia University* (New York, 1955), p. 25.

13. Goebel et al., *History of Columbia Law School*, 29.

14. Quoted in ibid., 28.

15. *Strong Diary*, II:388; III:18.

16. Goebel et al., *History of Columbia Law School*, 33–34.

17. Theodore W. Dwight, *An Introductory Lecture Delivered before the Law Class of Columbia College* (New York, 1859), pp. 49–51. See also idem, *Education in Law Schools in the City of New York Compared with That Obtained in Law Offices* (New York, 1876), p. 4: "[T]he attorney is occupied with matters of form; the counsellor with the law itself or legal principles."

18. It should be noted that what Dwight offered was understood to be practical training. As Strong wrote: "The school cannot be established and will not win students unless training in practically useful and profitable knowledge (such as knowledge of the Revised Statutes and Wendell and Cowen and Hill [reporters of the decisions of the New York courts] as it is Dwight's office to impart) be its prominent feature." *Strong Diary*, III:13.

19. At the time Strong was elected to the board, eleven of its twenty-four

members were lawyers. *Strong Diary*, II:137 n. 19 Strong worked hard at securing lecturers from among the leading members of the New York bar. Ibid, 420, 422, 452. The history of the school observes that, besides supplementing Dwight's instruction, these appointments "actually served the much more important function of winning support for the new School among the members of the Bar." Goebel et al., *History of Columbia Law School*, 45. The relationships established with the lecturers who began teaching in the 1859–1860 academic year were long ones. One of the five died soon after appointment, two ceased under the pressure of professional duties in 1867 and 1875, and three kept on until their deaths in 1865, 1867, and 1872. Ibid., 398 n. 13.

20. N.Y. Laws 1860 c. 202.

21. The diploma privilege is said to have first appeared in Virginia in 1842. Alfred Z. Reed, *Training for the Public Profession of the Law* (New York, 1921), p. 249.

22. N.Y. Laws 1855, c. 310; ibid. 1859, c. 267; ibid., cc. 187, 202.

23. Matter of the Graduates, 10 Abbott's Prac. 348 (1860).

24. Ibid. at 357.

25. Matter of the Graduates, 11 Abbott's Prac. 301 (1860); a less full report of the case is found in 22 N.Y. 67 (1860) styled Matter of Cooper.

26. *Strong Diary*, III:29.

27. Ibid., 28.

28. *Annual Report 1876–1877*, 88–92.

29. Francis N. Thorpe, *The Federal and State Constitutions Colonial Charters and Other Organic Laws*, 7 vols. (Washington, D.C., 1909), V:2681–2687. The vote was 247,240 for and 240,442 against the article (p. 2693). For the story of the convention that drafted the article and the new constitution of which it was a part, see Francis Bergan, *The History of the New York Court of Appeals, 1847–1932* (New York, 1985), pp. 89–119. The new judiciary article was the only part of the proposed constitution to be put separately to the voters. The proposed constitution as a whole was rejected.

30. "Current Topics," *Albany Law Journal* 3 (1871), 275–276.

31. 4 N.Y. Laws (1871), pp. 2194–2197.

32. Ibid., 2196.

33. *Strong Diary*, IV:356.

34. "Current Topics," *Albany Law Journal* 2 (1870), 110, 413–414; "Admission to the Bar," ibid. 4 (1871), 309–310.

35. "Admission to the Bar," Ibid., 4 (1871), 309.

36. Charles F. Adams, Jr., and Henry Adams, *Chapters of Erie and Other Essays* (Boston, 1871; rep. ed., New York, 1967), p. 95. For an interpretation of Gould that emphasizes his business acumen and desire to create ongoing businesses, thus debunking his portrayal as a "robber baron," see Klein, *Jay Gould*, which also contains a discussion of the literature.

37. *Strong Diary*, IV:245.

38. Henry Nicoll, *An Address Delivered before the Graduating Class of the Law School of Columbia College* (New York, 1869), pp. 19–20. After playing an important role in organizing the Association of the Bar of the City of New York, Henry Nicoll resigned in disgrace in January 1875, having been found to have misappropriated funds of which he was trustee. George Martin, *Causes and Conflicts: The Centennial History of the Association of the Bar of the City of New York, 1870–1970* (Boston, 1970), p. 128; *Strong Diary*, IV:549–551.

39. On the founding of the association, see Martin, *Causes and Conflicts*, 3–39.

40. Ibid., 51–119, gives a careful and relatively dispassionate account of the proceedings against the judges—John H. McCunn, George G. Barnard, and Albert Cardozo—and Tweed. For a spirited defense of William Tweed and an equally spirited attack on the "reformers," see Leo Hershkowitz, *Tweed's New York: Another Look* (Garden City, N.Y., 1978).

41. Martin, *Causes and Conflicts*, 69–71.

42. Ibid., 131.

43. *Strong Diary*, IV:356.

44. N.Y. Laws 1871 c. 486 § 3. N.Y. Laws 1872 c. 260 ensured that all four schools—Columbia, Albany, New York University, and Hamilton—would continue to enjoy the diploma privilege.

45. In 1875 the supreme court in New York City admitted 36 men to practice. The number admitted by virtue of holding diplomas from Columbia and New York University was 250. Martin, *Causes and Conflicts*, 387. In Wisconsin, the diploma privilege was uncontroversial so "long as the traditional means of policing the legal profession—notably the 'convivial life' of the bar—were effective." William R. Johnson, *Schooled Lawyers: A Study in the Clash of Professional Cultures* (New York, 1978), p. 57.

46. *Strong Diary*, IV:480.

47. Ibid., 355.

48. Ibid., 364.

49. John W. Burgess, *Reminiscences of an American Scholar* (New York, 1934), p. 162.

50. *Strong Diary*, IV:544.

51. Burgess linked the lack of entrance standards to the diversity of the law school student body. Since only a common school education was required, "the son of a Hebrew old clothes vender of the East Side would be found sitting next to an aristocratic A.B. of Harvard or Yale." Burgess, *Reminiscences*, 181.

52. N. Davis to L. L. Delafield, February 12, 1876, in Lewis L. Delafield, *The Conditions of Admission to the Bar*, (Philadelphia, 1876), p. 18.

53. 4 Hun 815 (1875).

54. *Report of the Committee on Admission to the Bar Made to the Association of the Bar of the City of New York* (New York, 1876), p. 13.

55. While the committee's report made a strong case against the diploma privilege, the resolutions did not call on the legislature to abolish it. Rather, it was suggested that if the schools required eighteen months of actual instruction instead of the simple passage of eighteen months from registration to graduation, a graduate who spent a year in a clerkship could be admitted without examination as an acknowledgment of the superior training offered by schools. The requirement of clerkship would protect the public from young lawyers "without any knowledge of practice." The other resolutions called for open, written examinations set by impartial examiners who would be part of a permanent board, devotion on the part of members of the bar of more time to the training of their clerks, and a seven-year clerkship for those who were not college graduates. *Report of the Committee on Admission* (1876), 27–30.

56. Martin, *Causes and Conflicts*, 137–138.

57. "Report of the Special Committee on Admission to the Bar," *New York State Bar Association Reports* 4 (1880), 53–58; "Notes," *Albany Law Journal* 15 (1877), 520.

58. Goebel et al., *History of Columbia Law School*, 106, 432 n.132; Reed, *Training for the Law*, 262, where he states that at least some graduates whose admission was successfully opposed were admitted by another court.

59. Goebel et al., *History of Columbia Law School*, 107; Reed, *Training for the Law*, 262–263.

60. The rules may be found in "New Rules Regulating Admission to the Bar," *Albany Law Journal* 16 (1877), 242–243.

61. Rule 3, ibid.

62. The report for the 1876–1877 year is dated December 1877 (*Annual Report 1876–1877*, 97). See G. F. Hoar to C. W. Eliot, November 26, 1877, President's Papers, C. W. Eliot, Box 69 folder 1877, Harvard University Archives, Pusey Library; C. W. Eliot to S. E. Church, March 9, 1878, College Letterbook 90, pp. 139–145, Harvard University Archives, Pusey Library; Eliot to Church, March 14, 1878, ibid., 146–150; Church to Eliot, March 19, 1878, President's Papers, C. W. Eliot, Box 69 (1876–1880), folder 1878 (the chief judge writes Eliot that the rules have been amended that day "almost literally as you suggested").

63. "Amendment to Rules Regulating the Admission of Attorneys, March 19, 1878," *Albany Law Journal* 17 (1878), 235. In no event could anyone be admitted, however, without serving at least one year's clerkship.

64. In 1880 the New York State Bar Association debated resolutions of the Special Committee on Admission to the Bar, one of which called on the court of appeals to accord to Yale, Harvard, and the University of Virginia the same treatment given local schools. Although Delafield favored the resolution, it proved to be controversial and he withdrew it. *New York State Bar Association Reports* 4 (1880), 60–67.

65. *Annual Report, 1876–1877*, 30.

66. Robert Stevens, *Law School: Legal Education in America from the 1850s to the 1980s* (Chapel Hill, 1983), pp. 36–37; Charles Warren, *History of the Harvard Law School and of Early Legal Conditions in America*, 2 vols. (New York, 1908; rep. ed., New York, 1970), II:376–400.

67. *Annual Report, 1874–1875*, 28.

68. As their predecessors had been. See salary information for members of the faculty from the time of the death of Joseph Story in Warren, *History of Harvard Law School*, II:351–352.

69. Ibid., II:399.

70. *Annual Report, 1874–1875*, 26.

71. Ibid., 24–25, reprinted in Warren, *History of Harvard Law School*, II: 396–397.

72. Harvard Law School Association, *Report of the Organization and of the First General Meeting at Cambridge, November 5, 1886* (Boston, 1887), pp. 29–42 (hereafter cited as HLSA, *Organization and First Meeting*), reprinted in Oliver Wendell Holmes Jr., *Collected Legal Papers* (New York, 1920; rep. ed., New York, 1952), pp. 35–48, from which the following quotations are taken.

73. Holmes, "Use of Law Schools," in *Collected Legal Papers*, 45–46.

74. Following quotations in this paragraph from ibid., 36–42.

75. Oliver Wendell Holmes, Jr., "The Path of the Law," *Harvard Law Review* 10 (1897), 457; reprinted in idem, *Collected Legal Papers*, 167–202, from which the following quotations in this paragraph are taken.

76. Holmes, "Use of Law Schools," in *Collected Legal Papers*, 36; Mark DeWolfe Howe, *Justice Oliver Wendell Holmes I: The Shaping Years, 1841–1870*

(Cambridge, 1957), pp. 19–21; G. Edward White, "Holmes's 'Life Plan': Confronting Ambition, Passions, and Powerlessness," *New York University Law Review* 65 (1990), 1430–1435.

77. Karl Wayne Hobson, "The American Legal Profession and the Organizational Society, 1890–1930," unpublished Ph.D. dissertation (Stanford, 1977), pp. 224–234.

78. John P. Kennedy, *Memoirs of the Life of William Wirt*, rev. ed., 2 vols. (Philadelphia, 1856), I:240. Many lawyers in the young republic aspired to literary fame; see Robert A. Ferguson, *Law and Letters in American Culture* (Cambridge, 1984), pp. 87–95

79. HLSA, *Organization and First Meeting*, 63–68.

80. One speaker, Thomas Cooley, observed "how Harvard, by its teachings and by the leadership of strong minds, has built itself into the political institutions of the land, making every commonwealth and every municipality the better for its sound law and wholesome consitutional doctrine." Ibid., 57.

81. Ibid., 74.

82. Lawrence M. Friedman, *A History of American Law*, 2d ed. (New York, 1985), p. 637.

83. Hobson, "American Legal Profession," 141–208, has much statistical information on the rise of law firms, as well as literary evidence of the anxiety they caused some lawyers. The 1886 celebrations at Harvard took place in the middle of a decade (1882–1892) in which the number of large firms (four or more members) increased from thirty-one to fifty-eight (p. 168, table 8). Growth of firms accelerated in the 1890s. Much of this material is summarized in Wayne K. Hobson, "Symbol of the New Profession: Emergence of the Large Law Firm, 1870–1915" in Gerard W. Gawalt, ed., *The New High Priests: Lawyers in Post-Civil War America* (Westport, Conn., 1984), pp. 3–28.

84. On Holmes's changing image: "Holmes is a strange, enigmatic figure. Put out of your mind the picture of the tolerant aristocrat, the great liberal, the eloquent defender of our liberties. The Yankee from Olympus. All that was a myth, concocted principally by Harold Laski and Felix Frankfurter, about the time of World War I." Grant Gilmore, *The Ages of American Law* (New Haven, 1977), pp. 48–49. On fears of anarchy, see Arnold M. Paul, *Conservative Crisis and the Rule of Law: Attitudes of Bar and Bench, 1887–1895* (pbk. ed., New York, 1969), pp. 19–38.

85. Of the 573 members of the Harvard Law School Association listed in the record of the 1886 meeting, all but seventy-three were from New York or Massachusetts. HLSA, *Organization and First Meeting*, contains a list of members. The New York and Massachusetts members were preponderantly from Boston and New York City, while the remaining seventy-three showed an equally urban pattern, with Cincinnati, St. Louis, and Detroit the most popular locales. Hobson notes that urban lawyers were most likely to resort to the bar associations of the 1870s and 1880s and that, not surprisingly, these associations concerned themselves with the changes in professional life caused by urbanization (Hobson, "American Legal Profession," 233–237, 238–239), especially the promotion of social cohesion. The place of an alumni association in promoting the later goal is clear. Whether the urban nature of the membership of the HLSA was the product of self-selection among alumni or of the residence patterns of Harvard graduates, Hobson's analysis suggests both a need for fraternal relations among members of the urban bar and the role of the modernized Harvard Law School in promoting those relationships.

86. Goebel et al., *History of Columbia Law School*, 108–113.
87. Quoted in ibid., 112
88. Ibid., 113–114.
89. Ibid., 119.
90. Reed, *Training for the Law,* 196–197.
91. Goebel et al., *History of Columbia Law School*, 118.
92. W. A. Keener to President and Fellows of Harvard College, March 30, 1880, C. W. Eliot Papers, Official Papers 1887–1892, Box 262, Harvard University Archives, Pusey Library.
93. Goebel et al., *History of Columbia Law School*, 120–132.
94. Ibid., 124–128, 152.
95. Ibid., 148–152. Keener had no sympathy for a broad curriculum. W. A. Keener to Seth Low, December 21, 1892, President's Papers, Low Library. I owe thanks to James Wooten for bringing this letter to my attention.
96. Goebel et al., *History of Columbia Law School*, 98.
97. Theodore W. Dwight, "Columbia College Law School, New York," *Green Bag* 1 (1889), 145.
98. This and preceding quotes from Theodore W. Dwight, "Courses of Instruction in Columbia College Law School" *Columbia Law Times* 4 (1890), 33–36.
99. George Chase, "The 'Dwight Method' of Legal Instruction," *Cornell Law Review* 1 (1894), 77. Note the use of history as an example, and compare Chase's view with the rise of a new method of teaching the methods of historical investigation through the seminar and the examination of original sources. Keener drew an explicit parallel between the case method in law and new methods of studying history in William A. Keener, "The Inductive Method in Legal Education," *American Bar Association Reports* 17 (1894), 475.
100. Dwight, "Columbia College Law School," 149–150.
101. George Chase, "The New York Law School and the Harvard Law Review," *American Law Review* 26 (1892), 156. Chase's comments are contained in a letter to the editors of the *Harvard Law Review* responding to the comments on the new school cited below at n. 107. The editors of the *Harvard Law Review* refused to publish the letter, and Chase submitted it to the *American Law Review*.
102. Dwight, "Columbia College Law School," 146.
103. George Chase, "Columbia Law School—A Sketch of its History," *Columbia Law Times* 4 (1891), 4–5.
104. "The Law School Crisis," *Columbia Law Times* 4 (1891), 184–189.
105. "Middle Class Petition," *Columbia Law Times* 4 (1891), 248.
106. "Editorial," *Columbia Law Times*, 4 (1891), 178.
107. "The Columbia and New York Law Schools," *Harvard Law Review* 5 (1891), 147. It was this brief commentary that called forth Chase's reply, quoted at note 101.
108. "Editorial Comment," *Columbia Law Times* 5 (1891), 21–22.
109. "The Law School Crisis," 185.
110. This and preceding quotes this paragraph from "Editorial Comment," *Columbia Law Times* 6 (1892), 16.
111. John S. Hill, "The Blackstone Bugbear," *Columbia Law Times* 6 (1892), 43.
112. Stanwood Menken, "Methods of Instruction at American Law Schools: II. Columbia College, in the City of New York. School of Law," *Columbia Law Times* 6 (1893), 168.

113. Goebel et al., *History of Columbia Law School*, 152; James Wooten, "Law School Rights: The Establishment of New York Law School," *New York Law School Law Review* 36 (1991), 337–395.

114. Goebel et al., *History of Columbia Law School*, 162–168.

115. In his autobiography Williston remembered that the *Review* grew out of a small club of second- and third-year students dedicated to writing and discussing legal essays: "One or two of the earlier essays seemed to them good enough to deserve publication, and from this thought the project took the shape of founding a law review." Samuel Williston, *Life and Law: An Autobiography* (Boston, 1941), p. 83.

116. *Harvard Law Review* 1 (1887), 35.

117. *The Centennial History of the Harvard Law School* ([Cambridge ?,] 1918), pp. 140–141.

118. James Schouler, "Cases without Treatises," *American Law Review* 23 (1889), 2–3.

119. Warren, *History of Harvard Law School*, Appendix IV, II:520–521.

120. Untitled circular, reprinted in HLSA, *Organization and First Meeting*, 14; Winthrop H. Wade, "The Harvard Law School Association," *Harvard Graduates Magazine* (1907), reprinted in Warren, *History of Harvard Law School*, II:544–551.

121. This and following quotes and discussion from HLSA, *Organization and First Meeting*, 25–28.

122. Ibid., 60–63.

123. Ibid., 74–75.

124. Ibid., 75.

125. This and following quotes from ibid., 36–40.

126. This and following quotes from John C. Gray, "Methods of Legal Education: IV," *Yale Law Journal* 1 (1892), 160.

127. J. B. Thayer to S. E. Baldwin, July 21, 1895, Baldwin Family Papers, Series I, Box 52, folder 653, Yale University Library, Manuscript Division. In the letter Thayer discussed "our Cambridge celebration" of Langdell's retirement after twenty-five years as dean which was "a good thing": "With all his merits, we have long suffered from his very serious defects in certain ways." He then lamented Eliot's failure "to say a wise word or two about methods of teaching." He referred to his views in the preface to the casebook as his attempt to say "the right thing" and then noted "Langdell and Ames both agree with what I said there."

128. James Bradley Thayer, *Cases on Constitutional Law*, 2 vols. (Cambridge, 1895), I:vi.

129. James Barr Ames, "The Vocation of the Law Professor" (1901), *Lectures on Legal History and Miscellaneous Legal Essays* (Cambridge, 1913), p. 363.

130. Williston, *Life and Law*, 199.

131. Charles D. Drake, *Address Delivered May 8, 1878, at the Annual Commencement of the Cincinnati Law School* (Washington, 1878), p. 13. For other expressions of this point of view, see J. L. High, "What Shall Be Done with the Reports?," *American Law Review* 16 (1882), 434, and Editorial Comment, "Case Law—Audi Alteram Partem," *Central Law Journal* 22 (1886), 578.

132. See William P. LaPiana, "Just the Facts: The Field Code and the Case Method," *New York Law School Law Review* 36 (1991), 327–335.

133. Charles P. Kirkland, *Address to the Graduating Class of the Law School of Columbia College* (New York, 1866), p. 10.

134. High, "What Shall Be Done with the Reports?," 434. This profusion of precedents may have contributed to what one commentator saw as a growing lack of reverence for the doctrine of stare decisis among New York lawyers. William Green, "'Stare Decisis'," *American Law Review* 14 (1880), 627.

135. "Recent Legal Literature," *Central Law Journal* 11 (1880), 340.

136. High, "What Shall be Done with the Reports?," 429.

137. John F. Dillon, "Annual Address," *American Bar Association Reports* 7 (1884), 223–224, and idem, *The Law and Jurisprudence of England and America* (Boston, 1895), pp. 264–292.

138. Charles Tracy, *An Address Delivered before the Graduating Class of the Law School of Columbia College* (New York, 1868), pp. 16–17.

139. "Case Law—Audi Alteram Partem," 578–579.

140. Harvey Henderson, "The Origin and Utility of Case-Law," *Pittsburgh Legal Journal* 33 (1886), 305.

141. "Book Notices" [review of Gerard, *Title to Real Estate in the State of New York*], *American Law Review* 3 (1869), 543.

142. The original was entitled "Hair on the End of a Man's Nose," *American Law Review* 18 (1884), 129. The quotation is taken from the first of two editorials presenting readers' replies, "More Hair on the End of a Man's Nose," (p. 314).

143. "More Hair on the End of the Nose," 489. The replies are found in ibid., 314–317, 488–489.

144. "Editorial," *Central Law Journal* 22 (1886), 530.

145. James E. Briggs, "A Symposium of Law Publishers," *American Law Review* 23 (1889), 409.

146. Ibid., 407.

147. This and following quotes this paragraph from John B. West, "A Symposium of Law Publishers," *American Law Review* 23 (1889), 400–407.

148. "Law Schools and Their Course of Study," *Western Jurist* 4 (1870), 131.

149. William G. Hammond, "Legal Education in the North-West," *Journal of Social Science* 8 (1876), 175–176.

150. Quoted in "Methods of Instruction at American Law Schools: II. Columbia College in the City of New York," *Columbia Law Times* 6 (1893), 165.

151. "Editorial," *Columbia Law Times* 6 (1893), 171.

152. Emlin McClain, "The Best Method of Using Cases in Teaching Law," *American Bar Association Reports* 16 (1893), 406.

153. Joel P. Bishop, *The First Book of the Law; Explaining the Nature, Sources, Books, and Practical Applications of Legal Science, and Methods of Study and Practice* (Boston, 1868), p. 252.

154. "Langdell's Selected Cases on Contracts," *Southern Law Review* 5 (N.S.) (1880), 872.

155. "Langdell's Selected Cases on Contracts," *Southern Law Review* 6 (N.S.) (1880), 449.

156. Lloyd McKim Garrison, "Methods of Instruction at American Law Schools: III. The Law School of Harvard University," *Columbia Law Times* 6 (1893), 194.

157. Eugene Wambaugh, *The Study of Cases* (Boston, 1892). A second expanded edition was published in 1894 after Wambaugh had joined the Harvard faculty. See Warren, *History of Harvard Law School*, II:448.

158. See the description of Abbott's teaching methods in Charles W. Thomp-

son, "Methods of Instruction at American Law Schools: I. The University of the City of New York," *Columbia Law Times* 6 (1893), 136.

159. Austin Abbott, "Existing Questions of Legal Education," *American Bar Association Reports* 16 (1893), 386–387.

160. Keener, "Inductive Method," 482.

161. Theodore W. Dwight, "Method of Preparing a Case for Argument," *Columbia Law Times* 4 (1890), 4.

Chapter 6

1. [Oliver Wendell Holmes, Jr.,] "Book Notices" [review of Dicey, *A Treatise on the Rules for the Selection of the Parties to an Action*], *American Law Review* 5 (1871), 534–535.

2. M. H. Hoeflich, "Law and Geometry: Legal Science from Leibniz to Langdell," *American Journal of Legal History* 30 (1986), 112–118.

3. [Oliver Wendell Holmes, Jr.,] "Misunderstandings of the Civil Law," *American Law Review* 6 (1871), 37–49.

4. [Oliver Wendell Holmes, Jr.,] "Book Notices" [review of T. W. Greene, *Outlines of Roman Law*], *American Law Review* 7 (1873), 320; idem, "Book Notices" [review of Bryce, *The Academical Study of the Civil Law*], ibid. 5 (1871), 716. See also idem, "Book Notices" [review of *The Law Magazine and Law Review*, vol. 30], ibid. 5 (1871), 541–542; idem, "Summary of Events" [comment on the announcement of the *American Civil Law Journal*], ibid. 7 (1873), 579.

5. [Holmes], "Book Notices" [review of Greene], 320.

6. Philip P. Wiener, *Evolution and the Founders of Pragmatism* (Cambridge, 1949), pp. 153–171, 231–234; Max H. Fisch, "Justice Holmes, The Prediction Theory of Law, and Pragmatism," *Journal of Philosophy* 39 (1942), 85–97; idem, "Was there a Metaphysical Club in Cambridge?" in E. C. Moore and R. S. Robin, eds., *Studies in the Philosophy of Charles Saunders Pierce* (Amherst, Mass., 1964), pp. 4–28; idem, "A Chronicle of Pragmatism, 1865–1879," *Monist* 48 (1964), 441–466; Bruce Kuklick, *The Rise of American Philosophy: Cambridge, Massachusetts, 1860–1930* (New Haven, 1977), pp. 47–54.

7. [Nicholas St. John Green,] "Torts under the French Law" [review of Sourdat, *Traité général de la responsibilitié ou de l'action en dommages-intérêts en dehors des contracts*], *American Law Review* 8 (1874), 519.

8. [Nicholas St. John Green,] "Slander and Libel" [review of John Townsend, *A Treatise on the Wrongs called Slander and Libel, and on the Remedy by Civil Action for those Wrongs*, 2d ed.], *American Law Review* 6 (1872), 597.

9. Herbert Bloom, *A Selection of Legal Maxims, Classified and Illustrated*, 6th American ed. (Philadelphia, 1868), p. 165 (*215).

10. [Nicholas St. John Green,] "Proximate and Remote Cause," *American Law Review* 4 (1870), 201–216.

11. [Nicholas St. John Green,] "Married Women" [review of Joel Bishop, *Commentaries on the Law of Married Women under the Statutes of the Several States and at Common Law and in Equity*], *American Law Review* 6 (1871), 62–67, 73.

12. [Green,] "Slander and Libel," 604–609.

13. [Nicholas St. John Green,] "The Three Degrees of Negligence," *American Law Review* 8 (1874), 649–668.

14. These notes are reprinted in Nicholas St. John Green, *Essays and Notes on*

the Law of Tort and Crime (Menasha, Wisc., 1933). See especially "The Powers and Duties of Attorneys at Law," pp. 115–126; "The Requisites of an Indictment for Murder," pp. 155–158 (in which he makes comments about the relationship between scholastic logic and the common law similar to those in "Proximate and Remote Cause); "The Punishability of Children," pp. 170–180; "Rape under the Statutes of Westminster," pp. 199–204 ("The meaning of a statute passed in the dark ages cannot be determined by the ordinary rules of verbal criticism as if it were a statute of the present day," but rather must be read in light of the social facts of its own day, p. 199); "The Right to Repel Attack on the Dwelling-House," pp. 206–211 (elucidating the meaning of the maxim that one's house is his castle by citing historians, not cases).

15. [Oliver Wendell Holmes, Jr.,] "Book Notices" [review of *The Code of Iowa; Report of the Commissioners to Revise the Statutes of Iowa*; and Fitzjames Stephen, *Codification in India and England*], *American Law Review* 7 (1873), 318.

16. [Oliver Wendell Holmes, Jr.,] "Book Notices" [review of Benjamin, *A Treatise on the Law of Sales of Personal Property*], *American Law Review* 3 (1869), 541–542. For similar expressions, see the following Book Notices by an anonymous Holmes: [review of Roscoe's *Digest of the Law of Evidence in Criminal Cases*, 6th ed., by D. Power, American Notes by George Sharswood,] ibid. 1 (1867), 375–376; [review of J. Schouler, *A Treatise on the Law of the Domestic Relations*], ibid. 5 (1870), 113–114; and his first major article, "Codes and the Arrangement of the Law," ibid., 1–13 ("A well-arranged body of the law would not only train the mind of the student to a sound habit of thought, but would remove obstacles from his path which he now only overcomes after years of experience and reflection," because every subject would be treated "once and in the right place," and "the leading analogy between groups" would be pointed out. This has practical importance because "the perfect lawyer is he who commands all the ties between a given case and all others. But few lawyers are perfect, and all have to learn their business" (p. 3).

17. "The Revision of the United States Statutes," *American Law Review* 6 (1872), 220.

18. [Oliver Wendell Holmes, Jr.,] "Book Notices" [Review of T. Shearman and A. Redfield, *A Treatise on the Law of Negligence*, 2d ed.], *American Law Review* 5 (1871), 343.

19. O. W. Holmes, Jr. to J. C. Gray, July 13, 1877, Oliver Wendell Holmes, Jr., Papers, Box 33 folder 26, Harvard Law School Library Manuscript Division. (Hereafter cited as Holmes Papers.) The letter can also be found in the microfilm edition of the Holmes Papers (Frederick, Md., 1985), Reel 53, frames 256–259 (original) and Reel 24 frames 544–545 (typed transcript). The article referred to is evidently Oliver Wendell Holmes, Jr., "Primitive Notions in Modern Law, No. II," *American Law Review* 11 (1877), 641–660.

20. O. W. Holmes to J. C. Gray, July 18, 1877, Holmes Papers, Box 33 folder 26. The letter can be found in the microfilm edition of the Holmes Papers on Reel 53 frames 260–261 (original) and Reel 24 frame 546 (typed transcript).

21. [Green,] "Slander and Libel," 612.

22. [Green,] "Proximate and Remote Cause," 211, 214–215.

23. Ibid., 216.

24. [Nicholas St. John Green,] "Book Notices" [Review of T. Shearman and A. Redfield, *A Treatise on the Law of Negligence*], *American Law Review* 4 (1870), 351. According to Mark DeWolfe Howe's notes for his Holmes biography, this

anonymous review was attributed to Green by John Chipman Gray in notations to his copy of this volume of the *American Law Review*. Holmes Papers, microfilm edition, Reel 40 frame 791.

25. Commonwealth v. White, 110 Mass. 407 (1872), 2 Crim. L. R. 269. The note, "Threat of Violence as Criminal Assault," is reprinted in Green, *Essays and Notes*, 138–147.

26. Green, *Essays and Notes*, 139–143.

27. Ibid., 147.

28. It must be noted that Green is here dealing with a common law offense. The legislature could make behavior like White's a crime, but a court is bound by the factual circumstances which are the common law.

29. [Oliver Wendell Holmes, Jr.,] "Book Notices" [review of Campbell, *The Law of Negligence*], *American Law Review* 5 (1871), 537.

30. [Oliver Wendell Holmes, Jr.,] "The Arrangement of the Law, Privity," *American Law Review* 7 (1872), 46–66.

31. This and preceding quotes from Holmes, "Primitive Notions, No. II," 641.

32. Kuklick, *Rise of American Philosophy*, 50.

33. This and preceding quotes from [Nicholas St. John Green,] "Book Notices" [review of J. Elwell, *A Medico-Legal Treatise on Malpractice and Medical Evidence*, and I. Ray, *A Treatise on the Medical Jurisprudence of Insanity*], *American Law Review* 5 (1871), 708.

34. [Oliver Wendell Holmes, Jr.,] "The Theory of Torts," *American Law Review* 7 (1873), 652–663.

35. Oliver Wendell Holmes, Jr., *The Common Law*, Mark DeWolfe Howe, ed. (pbk. ed., Boston, 1963), pp. 127–128.

36. For a brief discussion of the various views of this question, which rightly emphasizes the extent to which they have been shaped by questions larger than the understanding of Holmes's thought, see Richard A. Cosgrove, *Our Lady the Common Law: An Anglo-American Legal Community, 1870–1930* (New York, 1987), pp. 110–112, 129–130 n. 67.

37. The first attempt to make such a comprehensive analysis is H. L. Pohlman, *Justice Oliver Wendell Holmes and Utilitarian Jurisprudence* (Cambridge, 1984). Pohlman comes to the conclusion that the ideas at the "core of Holmes's legal philosophy . . . are best understood as refinements of utilitarian jurisprudence" (p. 9).

38. [Oliver Wendell Holmes, Jr.,] "Book Notices" [review of *The Law Magazine and Review*], *American Law Review* 6 (1872), 723–725 (hereafter cited as [Holmes,] "Book Notices" [review of Pollock]); Howe, *Holmes: Proving Years*, 71.

39. This and preceding quotes from [Holmes,] "Book Notices" [review of Pollock], 723.

40. This and preceding quotes this paragraph from ibid., 724.

41. Michael Lobban emphasizes the abstract nature of Austin's sovereign, a discussion that suggests Holmes may have taken Austin's statements about sovereignty too literally. Michael Lobban, *The Common Law and English Jurisprudence, 1760–1850* (Oxford, 1991), pp. 245–256.

42. O. W. Holmes to F. Pollock, in Mark DeWolfe Howe, ed., *Holmes-Pollock Letters: The Correspondence of Mr. Justice Holmes and Sir Frederick Pollock 1874–1932*, 2 vols. (Cambridge, 1941), I:20–21.

43. J. C. Gray to O. W. Holmes, undated, Holmes Papers, Box 33 folder 23.

44. O. W. Holmes to J. C. Gray, October 27, 1914, Holmes Papers, Box 33 folder 26.

45. Holmes to Gray, November 3, 1909, ibid.

46. This and preceding quotes from Edward J. Phelps, "Isaac F. Redfield" (1877), in J. G. McCullough, ed., *Orations and Essays of Edward John Phelps, Diplomat and Statesman* (New York, 1901), pp. 222–223.

47. [Oliver Wendell Holmes, Jr.,] "Book Notices" [review of Story, *Commentaries on Equity Jurisprudence*, 9th ed. by Redfield], *American Law Review* 1 (1867), 554.

48. Oliver Wendell Holmes, Jr., "Possession," *American Law Review* 12 (1878), 702.

49. For a discussion of the relationship between Austin's, Maine's, and Holmes's ideas of sovereignty, see Pohlman, *Holmes and Utilitarian Jurisprudence*, 54–66.

50. Cosgrove, *Our Lady the Common Law*, 113.

51. Pohlman, *Holmes and Utilitarian Jurisprudence*, 48–75. Holmes and Green may also have been influenced along these lines by Chauncey Wright. See Daniel J. Wilson, *Science, Community, and the Transformation of American Philosophy* (Chicago and London, 1990), pp. 25–30.

52. Saul Touster, "Holmes a Hundred Years Ago: *The Common Law* and Legal Theory," *Hofstra Law Review* 10 (1982), 694–704. The link between Holmes and Langdell was most clearly made by Grant Gilmore, *Ages of American Law* (New Haven, 1977), pp. 48–56. For a critical assessment of recent Holmes scholarship, including observations on the connection between Holmes and Langdell, see Pohlman, *Holmes and Utilitarian Jurisprudence*, 144–164.

53. [Oliver Wendell Holmes, Jr.,] *American Law Review* 5 (1870), 177.

54. [Holmes,] "Book Notices" [review of Bryce], 716.

55. [Green,] "Book Notices" [review of Elwell and of Ray], 705.

56. [Oliver Wendell Holmes, Jr.,] "Book Notices" [review of Langdell, *A Selection of Cases on the Law of Contracts, Part I*], *American Law Review* 5 (1871), 540, 539–540 (1871) (hereafter cited as [Holmes,] "Book Notices" [review of Langdell, 1871]).

57. Ibid.

58. [Oliver Wendell Holmes, Jr.,] "Book Notices" [review of Langdell, *A Selection of Cases on the Law of Contracts*], *American Law Review* 6 (1872), 354.

59. [Oliver Wendell Holmes, Jr.,] "Book Notices" [review of Langdell, *A Selection of Cases on the Law of Contracts, with a Summary of the Topics Covered by the Cases*, 2d ed., and Anson, *Principles of the English Law of Contracts*] *American Law Review* 14 (1880), 234 (hereafter cited as [Holmes,] "Book Notices" [review of Langdell, 1880]). The involved story of the attribution of the review to Holmes is told in Touster, "*The Common Law* and Legal Theory," 695 n. 91.

60. [Holmes,] "Book Notices" [review of Langdell, 1880], 235.

61. This and preceding quotes from ibid., 239–240.

62. This and preceding quotes from ibid., 238–239. Several of the cases discussed in connection with this topic involve the idea of forbearance, Langdell's treatment of which Holmes in 1871 criticized as being too dogmatic. [Holmes,] "Book Notices" [review of Langdell, 1871], 540.

63. Ibid., 262.

64. Ibid., 263.

65. Ibid., 264.

66. Holmes, *The Common Law*, 5, and [Holmes,] "Book Notices" [review of Langdell, 1880], 234.

67. Holmes to Pollock, July 6, 1908, in Howe, *Holmes-Pollock Letters*, I:140.

68. Pollock to Holmes, September 17, 1897, in ibid., I:80.

69. [Holmes,] "Book Notices" [review of Langdell, 1880], 235.

70. C. C. Langdell, "Mutual Promises as a Consideration for Each Other," *Harvard Law Review* 14 (1901), 496, 503.

71. Ibid.

72. The following quotes and discussion in this paragraph are all from this source. C. C. Langdell, "Classification of Rights and Wrongs," *Harvard Law Review* 13 (1900), 537–556, 659–678. This work was a revision of "A Brief Survey of Equity Jurisdiction," ibid. 1 (1887), 55–72, and "A Brief Survey of Equity Jurisdiction: II.," ibid. 111–131. All these articles are reprinted in C. C. Langdell, *A Brief Survey of Equity Jurisdiction*, 2nd ed. (Cambridge, 1908).

73. For a brief survey of this literature, see James Edward Kerr, *The Insular Cases: The Role of the Judiciary in American Expansionism* (Port Washington, N.Y., 1982), pp. 27–35.

74. C. C. Langdell, "The Status of Our New Territories," *Harvard Law Review* 12 (1899), 371, 388.

75. Ibid., 389–392.

76. C. C. Langdell, "The Northern Securities Case and the Sherman Anti-Trust Act," *Harvard Law Review* 16 (1903), 539–554. The opinion of the Eighth Circuit can be found at 120 Fed. 721 (1903). The U.S. Supreme Court affirmed the lower court by a five to four vote over dissents written by Holmes and Edward White in 193 U.S. 197 (1904). On the case and its place in the history of antitrust law, see William Letwin, *Law and Economic Policy in America: The Evolution of the Sherman Antitrust Act* (New York, 1965), pp. 184–237.

77. Preceding quotes all from Langdell, "Northern Securities Case," 553–554. Thomas Grey notes that Langdell and his fellow legal scientists were not "enthusiastic supporters of big business," and that their natural political orientation was "to the Mugwumps, and later to the right wing of the Progressive movement." Thomas C. Grey, "Langdell's Orthodoxy," *University of Pittsburgh Law Review* 45 (1983), 35.

78. Ibid., 547–553. At the end of his life Langdell clearly stated the distinction between law and legislation. In a review of Albert Venn Dicey, *The Relation between Law and Public Opinion in England during the Nineteenth Century*, he noted that the title of Dicey's book was misleading. "As commonly used by lawyers," he wrote, the word law "means law as administered by courts of justice in suits between litigating parties," but Dicey used it "in the sense of legislation." Dicey's book was not about law at all. Christopher C. Langdell, "Dominant Opinions in England during the Nineteenth Century in Relation to Legislation as Illustrated by English Legislation, or the Absence of It, during That Period," *Harvard Law Review* 19 (1906), 151.

79. Preceding quotes all from James Bradley Thayer, "'Law and Fact' in Jury Trials," *Harvard Law Review* 4 (1890), 153.

80. James Bradley Thayer, "Our New Possessions," *Harvard Law Review* 12 (1899), 469–471, 479.

81. James Bradley Thayer, "The Origin and Scope of the American Doctrine of Constitutional Law," *Harvard Law Review* 7 (1893), 129–156. The essay is reprinted with Thayer's own emendations in James Bradley Thayer, *Legal Essays* (Cambridge, 1927), pp. 1–41.

82. Thayer, "Origin and Scope," in *Legal Essays*, 31–33.

83. Stephen A. Siegel, "John Chipman Gray, Legal Formalism, and the Transformation of Perpetuities Law," *University of Miami Law Review* 36 (1982), 439–464. For an attempt to place Gray squarely among the classical formalists, see Gregory S. Alexander, "The Dead Hand and the Law of Trusts in the Nineteenth Century," *Stanford Law Review* 37 (1985), 1189–1266.

84. John Chipman Gray, *The Nature and Sources of the Law*, 2nd ed., Roland Gray, ed. (New York, 1921), p. vii.

85. Some scholars have emphasized the "pragmatic" or positivist aspects of Gray's jurisprudence without dealing with his ideas of property law. Robert Samuel Summers, *Instrumentalism and American Legal Theory* (Ithaca, 1982); Niel MacCormick, "A Political Frontier of Jurisprudence: John Chipman Gray on the State," *Cornell Law Review* 66 (1981), 973–985.

86. Gray, *Nature and Sources*, 94.

87. Ibid., 88–89, 297.

88. Ibid., 89.

89. Ibid., 136, 144–150.

90. Ibid., 222–240, 283–292.

91. Ibid., 225.

92. Ibid., 291, 303–307.

93. Ibid., 226.

94. John Chipman Gray, "Preface to the First Edition" (1886), *The Rule against Perpetuities*, 3rd. ed. (Boston, 1915), p. ix.

95. On the history of the common law dealings with perpetuities, see Siegal, "Gray, Legal Formalism, and Perpetuities Law," 440–446.

96. Gray, "Preface" to *Rule against Perpetuities*, ix.

97. J. C. Gray to C. W. Eliot, January 3, 1883, President's Papers, C. W. Eliot, Box 71, folder 1883 G–L, Harvard University Archives, Pusey Library.

98. The standard student's text in the area is Thomas S. Bergin and Paul G. Haskell, *Preface to Estates in Land and Future Interests*, 2nd ed. (Mineola, N.Y., 1984).

99. Gray, *Rule against Perpetuities*, 174 (§ 201).

100. Ibid., 253 (§ 268).

101. Ibid., 616 (§ 870).

102. Ibid., 616 (§§ 870–871).

103. Ibid., 557–570 (§§ 728–752).

104. John Chipman Gray, "Preface to the First Edition," *Restraints on the Alienation of Property*, 2nd. ed. (Boston, 1895), p. xiii. The case is Nichols v. Eaton, 91 U.S. 716 (1876).

105. Ibid., iii, 242–248 (§§ 258–264).

106. Ibid., vi.

107. Ibid., vi-ix.

108. Broadway Bank v. Adams, 133 Mass. 170 (1882).

109. Gray, "Preface" to *Restraints on Alienation of Property*, 239–241 (§§ 255–257).

110. Ibid.

111. "Memoir of James Barr Ames," in James Barr Ames, *Lectures on Legal History and Miscellaneous Legal Essays* (Cambridge, 1913), p. 14.

112. "Preface," in Ames, *Lectures on Legal History*, v–vi. He also taught partnership, and his notes were used by other teachers. See Roscoe Pound to Henry M. Bates, July 5, 1917, Paige Box 1, folder July–Sept., 1917, Michigan Historical

Collections, Bentley Historical Library, University of Michigan, informing Bates that Pound is sending him typewritten notes of Ames's remarks on the cases in Ames's partnership casebook which he can use in preparing to teach the course while a visiting professor at Harvard.

113. James Barr Ames, "The Doctrine of Price v. Neal," (1891) in *Lectures on Legal History*, 281–282. Samuel Williston wrote to Karl Llewellyn that Ames made a point of questioning courts' statements of the reasons for their decisions. Williston to Llewellyn, July 24, 1931, Karl N. Llewellyn Papers, A.II.65.b, University of Chicago Law School. Henry Bates found merit in Ames's analyzing the legal nature of a partnership by treating it as an entity. He was convinced by Ames's teaching notes in which Ames showed "in case after case that the decision is absolutely inconsistent with any other theory than that of entity, though the court does not evolve that theory." Bates to Joseph H. Drake, February 8, 1918, Paige Box 1, folder February, 1918, Bates Papers.

114. James Barr Ames, "The Inalienability of Choses in Action" (1909), in idem, *Lectures on Legal History*, 210–218.

115. James Barr Ames, "Specialty Contracts and Equitable Defenses," in idem, *Lectures on Legal History*, 105, 115; idem, "The Origin of Uses" (1885), in ibid., 233–235; idem, "Purchase for Value without Notice" (1887), in ibid., 255; idem, "Can a Murderer Acquire Title by His Crime and Keep It?" (1897), in ibid., 321–322; idem, "Law and Morals" (1908), in ibid., 436–452; Oliver Wendell Holmes, "Early English Equity" (1885), in idem, *Collected Legal Papers* (rep. ed.; New York, 1952), pp. 1–24.

116. James Barr Ames, "How Far an Act May Be a Tort because of the Wrongful Motive of the Actor" (1905), in idem, *Lectures on Legal History*, 399–411.

117. Ames, "Law and Morals," 448.

118. Robert Stevens, *Law School: Legal Education in America from the 1850s to the 1980s* (Chapel Hill, 1983), pp. 39–40; Frank L. Ellsworth, *Law on the Midway: The Founding of the University of Chicago Law School* (Chicago, 1977), p. 63.

119. Oscar Kraines, *The World and Ideas of Ernst Freund: The Search for General Principles of Legislation and Administrative Law* (University, Ala., 1974), p. 2.

120. J. B. Ames to W. R. Harper, March 31, 1902, President's Papers 1889–1925, Box 19, folder 5, University of Chicago Archives, Regenstein Library (hereafter cited as President's Papers [Harper]).

121. Enclosure of Freund to W. R. Harper, March 2, 1902, ibid., Box 34, folder 17, showing a tabular arrangement of studies in the proposed school.

122. Ames to Harper, March 31, 1902, ibid., Box 19, folder 5.

123. Joseph Beale to W. R. Harper, April 2, 1902, ibid.

124. Ellsworth, *Law on the Midway*, 74.

125. E. Freund to W. R. Harper, May 20, 1902, President's Papers [Harper], Box 34, folder 17; Kraines, *Ernst Freund*, 191–192 n. 276.

Chapter 7

1. George Swasey, "Boston University Law School," *Green Bag* 1 (1889), 55.

2. Charles Warren, *History of the Harvard Law School and of Early Legal Conditions in America*, 2 vols. (New York, 1908), II:502–503.

3. "Editorials," *Albany Law Journal* 4 (1871), 74; see also ibid. 5 (1872), 97; ibid. 14 (1876), 206.

4. Edward J. Phelps, "Law as a Profession" (1879), in J. G. McCullough, ed., *Orations and Essays of Edward John Phelps, Diplomat and Statesman* (New York, 1901), p. 85.

5. Edward J. Phelps, "Sketch of the Life of Isaac Redfield" (1877), in McCullough, *Orations and Essays*, 222.

6. J. L. High, "What Shall Be Done with the Reports?," *American Law Review* 16 (1882), 439. For another vivid description of the case lawyer, see Edmund Whetmore, "Some of the Limitations and Requirements of Legal Education in the United States," *American Bar Association Reports* 17 (1894), 470–471: "He best argues his cases who considers not how he can match his facts with precedents, as he might match his hand in a game of dominoes, but how he can best rest the judgment that he seeks upon the right and reason of the law." William Johnson found similar attacks on the case lawyer in the rhetoric of the Wisconsin bar and found their basis to be moral: "Case lawyers, . . . , elevated reason above the moral sense and pridefully asserted that reason alone could guide judicial decisions." William R. Johnson, *Schooled Lawyers: A Study in the Clash of Professional Cultures* (New York, 1978), p. 118.

7. Edward J. Phelps, "Methods of Legal Education: I," *Yale Law Journal* 1 (1892), 141.

8. Christopher G. Tiedeman, "Methods of Legal Education: III," *Yale Law Journal* 1 (1892), 155.

9. William A. Keener, "Methods of Legal Education: II," *Yale Law Journal* 1 (1892), 144.

10. Ibid., 144–145, 149.

11. Sydney G. Fisher, "The Teaching of Law by the Case System," *American Law Register* 27 (N.S.) (1888), 418.

12. William A. Keener, "The Inductive Method in Legal Education," *American Bar Association Reports* 17 (1894), 484.

13. John C. Gray, "Cases and Treatises," *American Law Review* 22 (1888), 762.

14. *Annual Reports of the President and Treasurer of Harvard College, 1878–1877*, pp. 95–96.

15. S. Williston to K. Llewellyn, July 24, 1931, Karl Llewellyn Papers, A.II.65.b. University of Chicago Law School. See also Dean Ezra R. Thayer's comments in his annual report as dean of Harvard Law School, *Official Register of Harvard University* 8 (1909–1911), 126: "[Ames's] own skill as a teacher had much to do with the success of the method of instruction known by Mr. Langdell's name." Also John Henry Wigmore, dean of the Northwestern University School of Law, stated that Langdell commented on the cases in lecture while "two at least of his contemporaries [Thayer and Gray, perhaps] never used [Socratic questioning] to any important extent." *Report of the Dean of the Faculty of Law on an Educational Survey, 1925* (mimeo; Chicago, 1927), p. 48 (§ 27). Wigmore was a graduate of Harvard Law School where he had been a student of the first generation of case method teachers.

16. This and preceding quote from "Report of the Committee on Legal Education," *American Bar Association Reports* 13 (1890), 327, 334.

17. "Report of the Committee on Legal Education," *American Bar Association Reports* 14 (1891), 341.

18. "Report of the Committee on Legal Education," *American Bar Association Reports* 15 (1892), 340.

19. Ibid., 327; "Report of the Committee on Legal Education," ibid. 20 (1897), 361, 365; "Report of the Committee on Legal Education," ibid. 2 (1879), 27–28.

20. "Report of the Committee on Legal Education," *American Bar Association Reports* 18 (1895), 317.

21. John F. Dillon, "The True Professional Ideal," *American Bar Association Reports* 17 (1894), 420.

22. See the various tables of courses in Warren, *History of Harvard Law School*, II:405–406, 411–412, 414–415, and the annual reports of the Dean of the Law School in the *Annual Reports of the President and Treasurer of Harvard College*.

23. Emory Washburn, *Law as an Element of Social Science* (Boston, 1868), p. 14.

24. Ibid., 15.

25. On the gradual dissolution of the American Social Science Association in the face of the rise of specialized scholarship and scholarly associations, see Thomas L. Haskell, *The Emergence of Professional Social Science: The American Social Science Association and the Nineteenth-Century Crisis of Authority* (Urbana, Ill., 1977), and Mary O. Furner, *Advocacy and Objectivity: A Crisis in the Professionalization of American Social Science* (Lexington, Ky., 1975).

26. Abstract of Speech by Thomas Hill in American Social Science Association, *Documents Published by the Association* (Boston, 1866), p. 36.

27. This and preceding quote from "Report of the Committee on Legal Education," *American Bar Association Reports* 14 (1891), 342.

28. "Report of the Committee on Legal Education," *American Bar Association Reports* 15 (1892), 324.

29. J. G. A. Pocock, *The Ancient Constitution and the Feudal Law: English Historical Thought in the Seventeenth Century* (reissue, New York, 1987); Gerald Postema, *Bentham and Common Law Tradition* (Oxford, 1986), pp. 3–80.

30. Henry Sumner Maine, *Ancient Law: Its Connection with the Early History of Society and Its Relation to Modern Ideas* (London, 1861; rep. ed., n.p., 1986), p. 2. See generally, George Feaver, *From Status to Contract: A Biography of Sir Henry Maine, 1822–1888* (London, 1969), and R. C. J. Cocks, *Sir Henry Maine: A Study in Victorian Jurisprudence*. (Cambridge, 1988).

31. Ibid., 3.

32. Maine, *Ancient Law*, 141. For a discussion of readers' reaction to this famous sentence, see Stephen A. Utz, "Maine's *Ancient Law* and Legal Theory," *Connecticut Law Review* 16 (1984), 823.

33. Frederick Pollock, *Introduction and Notes to Sir Henry Maine's "Ancient Law"* (London, 1906), p. 36. Maine's biographer emphasizes his "Whiggish flexibility and lack of dogmatism" on economic questions. Feaver, *From Status to Contract*, 293 n. 45.

34. William G. Hammond, "John Austin and His Wife," *Green Bag* 1 (1889), 49. Modern scholarship indicates that Austin was not ignorant of the historical school of jurisprudence during his stay at the University of Bonn in late 1827 and early 1828 and in fact studied with a *privatim docens* who was himself a disciple of the historical school. W. L. Morison, *John Austin* (Stanford, 1982), pp. 17–20.

35. The following quotations are all from this source. James Coolidge Carter, *Law: Its Origin Growth and Function* (New York, 1907), p. v.

36. Ibid., 169–171, 173.
37. Ibid., 231.
38. Ibid., 119.
39. Ibid., 55.
40. Ibid., 66–67.
41. Ibid., 268.
42. Frederick N. Judson, "Liberty of Contract under the Police Power," *American Bar Association Reports* 14 (1891), 233.
43. Carter, *Law: Its Origin Growth and Function*, 219.
44. William G. Hammond, "Note 30," in Sir William Blackstone, *Commentaries on the Laws of England*, W. G. Hammond, ed. (San Francisco, 1890), p. 216.
45. William G. Hammond, "Note N. On Precedent and the Doctrine of Authority in the Law," in Francis Lieber, *Legal and Political Hermeneutics*, 3rd. ed. (St. Louis, 1880), pp. 328–329. Hammond's notes follow Lieber's text and are numbered consecutively with it.
46. Thomas M. Cooley, *A Treatise on the Law of Torts or the Wrongs which Arise Independently of Contract*, 4th ed., D. A. Haggard, ed. (Chicago, 1932), p. 16 (§ 10).
47. This and preceding quote from Carter, *Law: Its Origin Growth and Function*, 268.
48. Charles Malcolm Platt, "The Character and Scope of Analytical Jurisprudence," *American Law Review* 24 (1890), 613.
49. For a fuller discussion, see William P. LaPiana, "Jurisprudence of History and Truth," *Rutgers Law Journal* 23 (1992), 519–559.
50. For biographical details, see the article on Baldwin in *The Dictionary of American Biography* (New York, 1935), I:544–547.
51. Simeon E. Baldwin, "The Study of Elementary Law, The Proper Beginning of a Legal Education," *Yale Law Journal* 13 (1903), 1–15. This article is based on Baldwin's presidential address to the Association of American Law Schools in 1903. The following quotations are all from this source.
52. Simeon E. Baldwin, "Teaching Law by Cases," *Harvard Law Review* 14 (1900), 258, 260.
53. Simeon E. Baldwin, *The American Judiciary* (New York, 1914), p. 60.
54. Baldwin, "Teaching Law by Cases," 260.
55. Preceding quotes all from Baldwin, "Study of Elementary Law," 10.
56. Edward J. Phelps, "Chief Justice Marshall and the Constitutional Law of His Time" (1879), in McCullough, *Orations and Essays*, 82.
57. Edward J. Phelps, "The Relation of Law to Justice," in McCullough, *Orations and Essays*, 95.
58. Edward J. Phelps, "Law of the Land," in McCullough, *Orations and Essays*, 120.
59. Ibid., 121–123.
60. Edward J. Phelps, "International Relations," in McCullough, *Orations and Essays*, 155.
61. The view of society as an organic reflection of divine order permeated the approach to scholarship at Yale in the nineteenth century, see Louise L. Stevenson, *Scholarly Means to Evangelical Ends: The New Haven Scholars and the Transformation of Higher Learning in America, 1830–1890* (Baltimore and London, 1986).
62. This and preceding quotes from Frederick C. Hicks, *Yale Law School: 1869–1894* (New Haven, 1937), p. 33.

63. Ibid., 44–45.

64. William C. Robinson, *A Study on Legal Education: Its Purposes and Methods* (Washington, D.C., 1895), pp. 4–6. See also idem, *Elements of American Jurisprudence* (Boston, 1900).

65. Hicks, *Yale Law School: 1869–1894*, 24–27.

66. Simeon E. Baldwin, "Graduate Courses at Law Schools," *Journal of Social Science* (1880), 132. Baldwin read the paper printed here at the 1877 meeting of the American Social Science Association.

67. Hicks, *Yale Law School: 1869–1894*, 26.

68. Report of Dean Henry Rogers in *Report of the President of Yale University and of the Deans and Directors of its Several Departments for the Academic Year 1903–1904* (New Haven, 1904), p. 155 (hereafter cited as *Report of the President of Yale* and date). See also Alfred Z. Reed, *Training for the Public Profession of the Law* (New York, 1921), p. 302.

69. Williston noted the same trend in a 1909 letter to Bates, July 12, 1909, Henry M. Bates Papers, Michigan Historical Collections, Bentley Historical Library, University of Michigan, Ann Arbor, Michigan. Paige Box 1, folder 1906–1909: "This I think is an indictment of the Yale School" which had "got badly behind the times."

70. Entry for February 26, 1900, quoted in Charles C. Goetsch, *Essays on Simeon Baldwin* (Storrs, Conn. (?), 1981), p. 41.

71. Frederick C. Hicks, *Yale Law School: 1895–1915* (New Haven, 1938), p. 40.

72. Ibid.

73. Preceding quotes all from *Report of the President of Yale, 1901–1902*, 18–19.

74. *Report of the President of Yale, 1903–1904*, 164.

75. *Report of the President of Yale, 1911–1912*, 18–19.

76. Hicks, *Yale Law School: 1895–1915*, 44, and Laura Kalman, *Legal Realism at Yale, 1927–1960* (Chapel Hill and London, 1986), pp. 98–101.

77. Preceding quotes all from *Report of the President of Yale, 1911–1912*, 227

78. Goetsch, *Essays on Simeon E. Baldwin*, 44.

79. This and preceding quotes from *Report of the President of Yale, 1911–1912*, 222, 230.

80. Arthur L. Corbin, "The Law and the Judges," *Yale Review* 3 (1914), 236.

81. Ibid., 239, 240, 250.

82. Ibid., 246.

Chapter 8

1. Jerold Auerbach, "Enmity and Amity: Law Teachers and Practitioners, 1900–1922, *Perspectives in American History* 5 (1971), 567.

2. Paul L. Martin, "The Trained Lawyer," *American Law School Review* 3 (1912), 100; Robert B. Stevens, *Law School: Legal Education in America from the 1850s to the 1980s* (Chapel Hill, 1983), p. 63.

3. *Catalogue of the Law Department of Yale University 1896–1897* (New Haven, 1896), p. 17.

4. *Catalogue of the Officers and Students of Georgetown College, District of Columbia for the Academic Year 1884–1885*, pp. 77–78. Quote from idem, *1912–1913*, pp. 167–168.

5. Elizabeth Gaspar Brown, *Legal Education at Michigan, 1859–1959* (Ann Arbor, 1959), pp. 201–209.

6. James Gray, *The University of Minnesota, 1851–1951* (Minneapolis, 1951), pp. 157–158. Vincent hired so well that after he left the presidency in 1917, William Vance, the dean, Ernest Lorenzen, and Edmund Morgan all went to Yale (p. 165).

7. Robert H. Wettach, ed., *A Century of Legal Education* (Chapel Hill, 1947), p. 47.

8. Ibid., 55, 57.

9. William R. Johnson, *Schooled Lawyers: A Study in the Clash of Professional Cultures* (New York, 1978), p. 107. Johnson makes it clear that Adams, a historian, was attracted to the case method as the analogue of the history seminar; both involved the study of original sources.

10. John Ritchie, *The First Hundred Years: A Short History of the School of Law of the University of Virginia for the Period 1826–1926* (Charlottesville, 1978), pp. 40–50; Stevens, *Law School*, 71 n. 86.

11. Ritchie, *First Hundred Years*, 74.

12. Thomas Garden Barnes, *Hastings College of the Law: The First Century* (San Francisco, 1978), pp. 88–89.

13. Ibid., 100–116.

14. H. L. Wilgus, "Legal Education in the United States," *Michigan Law Review* 6 (1908), 667.

15. William R. Vance, "The State-Supported Law School," *American Law School Review* 3 (1914), 411. See also George F. Wells (Dean of the University of North Dakota College of Law), "Discussion of Papers by Morgan and Oliphant," *American Law School Review* 4 (1917), 270. (It is important to train students in practice, especially in the schools of the west and middle west, "where the students must go out, and expect to go out, into practice at the very earliest opportunity, most of them upon leaving the law school.")

16. Preceding quotes all from James Barr Ames, "Comments on Kales's Paper," *American Law School Review* 2 (1907), 119.

17. *Catalogue of the Brooklyn Law School, 1902–1903*, p. 11.

18. *Catalogue of the Northwestern University, 1894–1895*, pp. 162–163.

19. *George Washington University Bulletin* 86 (1906–1907), 188–189.

20. Josef Redlich, *The Common Law and the Case Method in American University Law Schools* (New York, 1914). See also Stevens, *Law School*, 112–113, 128–129 n. 42.

21. Preceding quotes all from "Papers and Discussion Concerning the Redlich Report," *American Law School Review* 4 (1916), 93, 106, 107.

22. H. Stone to N. M. Butler, February 18, 1915, Harlan Stone Papers, Box 44, Subject File Columbia University Law School, folder 1915, Columbia University Archives.

23. Perhaps the most famous course of such lectures is Karl Llewellyn's *The Bramble Bush*, first given in 1929–1930 and published in 1951.

24. Report of Committee of the Law Faculty, Henry M. Bates Papers, Michigan Historical Collections, Bentley Historical Library, University of Michigan, Ann Arbor, Michigan. Paige Box 1, folder October–December, 1917.

25. H. M. Bates to H. B. Hutchins, February 2, 1918, Paige Box 1, folder February 1918, Bates Papers. Three years later Bates wrote to a friend of the "general demoralization" of higher education, but noted that "we have escaped

largely, in the better professional schools, because we have crowded on so much work that the necessary habits of study have steadied the situation." H. M. Bates to Frank L. Sage, February 15, 1921, Bates Papers, Paige Box 1, folder 1920–1921.

26. Chase's recommendations for the University of North Carolina Law School were well received by "the University alumni at the bar and on the bench." The letters quoted in the history of the school show that these practitioners considered the rigorous academic training offered by the leading schools the best possible training for the practice of law in the modern world. Wettach, *A Century of Legal Education*, 61–63.

27. David Wigdor, *Roscoe Pound: Philosopher of Law* (Westport, Conn., 1974), pp. 1–123.

28. Preceding quotes all from Roscoe Pound, "The Causes of Popular Dissatisfaction with the Administration of Justice," *American Bar Association Reports* 29 (1906), 395–417.

29. "Discussion of Pound's Paper," *American Bar Association Reports* 29 (1906), 11, 12, 55–65.

30. "Report of the Committee on Judicial Administration and Remedial Procedure," *American Bar Association Reports* 31 (1907), 505–512.

31. "Memorandum of Everett P. Wheeler," *American Bar Association Reports* 45 (1920), 62–63.

32. "Report of the Special Committee to Suggest Remedies and Formulate Proposed Laws to Prevent Delay and Unnecessary Cost in Litigation," *American Bar Association Reports* 34 (1909), 578–609; idem, ibid. 35 (1910), 614–650; "Report of the Committee on Uniform Judicial Procedure," ibid. 6 (1920), 509–526.

33. It is significant that under the most widely supported plan for procedural reform the judges would be making the rules. For a discussion of the image of the judge as the expression of the highest professional aspirations, see Stephen W. Botein, "'What We Shall Meet Afterwards in Heaven': Judgeship as a Symbol for Modern American Lawyers," in G. Geison, ed., *Professions and Professional Ideologies in America* (Chapel Hill, 1983), pp. 49–69.

34. In addition, Pound may also have hoped to accomplish something for law teachers. Uniform rules for the federal courts became the ideal foundation of the case method teaching of procedure and helped create a partial solution to the perennial problem of teaching practice in the classroom.

35. For sociological jurisprudence, see Roscoe Pound, "The Scope and Purpose of Sociological Jurisprudence," *Harvard Law Review* 24 (1911), 612, and idem, *Law and Morals* (Chapel Hill, 1924), pp. 150–153.

36. Wigdor, *Roscoe Pound*, 161.

37. Roscoe Pound, "Social Justice and Legal Justice," *Central Law Journal* 75 (1912), 459.

38. Ibid.; Roscoe Pound, "Courts and Legislation," *American Political Science Review* 7 (1913), 361–383; idem, "Common Law and Legislation," *Harvard Law Review* 21 (1908), 383–407. Much of what Pound wrote was repetitive. The notes to these paragraphs indicate only some of the sources that support the statement made. For a full list of Pound's writings on jurisprudence in this period, all of which have entered into the synthesis presented here, see the bibliography and Francis Setaro, *A Bibliography of the Writings of Roscoe Pound* (Cambridge, 1942).

39. Roscoe Pound, "The Scope and Purpose of Sociological Jurisprudence, Part III," *Harvard Law Review* 25 (1912), 513–515.

40. Ibid., 516.

41. Roscoe Pound, "Political and Economic Interpretations of Jurisprudence, *Proceedings of the American Political Science Association*, 9 (1912), 100. See also idem, "Liberty of Contract," *Yale Law Journal* 18 (1909), 454–487, and idem, "Taught Law," *American Bar Association Reports* 37 (1912), 977.

42. Roscoe Pound, "Do We Need a Philosophy of Law?," *Columbia Law Review* 5 (1905), 352. The phrase "faulty teaching" is from idem, "Social Problems and the Courts," *American Journal of Sociology* 18 (1912), 339.

43. Roscoe Pound, "The Need of a Sociological Jurisprudence," *Green Bag* 19 (1907), 612.

44. Elihu Root, "Public Service by the Bar," *American Bar Association Reports* 41 (1916), 372.

45. Harlan F. Stone, *Law and Its Administration* (New York, 1924), pp. 40–49, 212–214; idem, "The Lawyer and His Neighbors," *Cornell Law Quarterly* 4 (1919), 185.

46. R. Pound to H. F. Stone, July 13, 1917, Paige Box 8, Roscoe Pound Papers, Harvard Law School Library, Manuscript Division (hereafter referred to as Pound Papers).

47. R. Pound to H. F. Stone, February 26, 1916, Pound Papers, Ms Box 3, Early Period Addenda.

48. R. Pound to James Parker Hall, dean of the University of Chicago Law School, November 27, 1916, Pound Papers, Paige Box 8.

49. Wigdor, *Roscoe Pound*, 248–254.

50. R. Pound to H. M. Bates, March 30, 1925, Bates Papers, Paige Box 1, folder 25.

51. Roscoe Pound, "Classification of Law," *Harvard Law Review* 37 (1924), 944.

52. Roscoe Pound, "The Progress of the Law: Analytical Jurisprudence, 1914–1927," *Harvard Law Review* 41 (1927), 184.

53. Muller v. Oregon, 208 U.S. 412 (1908). See Alpheus T. Mason, *Brandeis: A Free Man's Life* (New York, 1946), pp. 248–251; Melvin I. Urofsky, *A Mind of One Piece: Brandeis and American Reform* (New York, 1971), pp. 39–42; and Philippa Strum, *Louis D. Brandeis: Justice for the People* (Cambridge, 1984), pp. 114–131.

"As one of Brandeis's law secretaries [James M. Landis] has suggested, Brandeis was 'living proof' of the kind of jurist Pound was seeking." Samuel Konefsky, *The Legacy of Holmes and Brandeis: A Study in the Influence of Ideas* (New York, 1956), p. 92. Brandeis's statement of his views is Brandeis, "The Living Law," *Illinois Law Review* 10 (1916), 461–471.

See generally, William P. LaPiana, "'A Task of No Common Magnitude': The Founding of the American Law Institute," *Nova Law Review* 11 (1987), 1114–1115.

54. Henry W. Taft, *Law Reform: Papers and Addresses by a Practicing Lawyer* (New York, 1926), p. 3; Frederick R. Coudert, *Certainty and Justice: Studies of Conflict between Precedent and Progress in the Development of Law* (New York, 1913), pp. 36–37.

55. Stone, "Lawyer and His Neighbors," 188. See also idem, "The Significance

of a Restatement of the Law," *Proceedings of the Academy of Political Science in the City of New York* 10 (1923), no. 3, *Law and Justice*, 6. On Stone's favorable attitude to sociological jurisprudence, see Stevens, *Law School*, 137, and Alpheus T. Mason, *Harlan Fiske Stone: Pillar of the Law* (New York, 1956), pp. 114–120. Mason asserts that Stone's, "Some Aspects of the Problem of Law Simplification," *Columbia Law Review* 23 (1923), 319–337, indicates his full conversion to sociological jurisprudence from the critical position evidenced in idem, *Law and Its Administration*.

56. Stone, "Some Aspects of Law Simplification," 327–328.

57. Letter from Henry T. Terry to the American Bar Association printed in "Report of the Committee on Arrangement of the Law," *American Bar Association Reports* 12 (1889), 327–338. Terry, a lawyer and scholar of sorts, spent most of the 1910s teaching at the Imperial University in Tokyo. As late as 1924 he was corresponding with Roscoe Pound on the problem of classification and proposed an elaborate system that Pound found much too dependent on Austin. R. Pound to William Draper Lewis, June 24, 1924, Pound Papers, Paige Box 32; see N. E. H. Hull, "Restatement and Reform: A New Perspective on the Origins of the American Law Institute," *Law and History Review* 8 (1990), 93 n. 85.

58. "Report of the Committee on Classification of the Law," *American Bar Association Reports* 14 (1891), 379–408; ibid. 25 (1902), 425–475; Hessel Yntema, "The American Law Institute," *Canadian Bar Review* 12 (1934), 327 n. 26.

59. "Memorandum in re Corpus Juris," *Green Bag* 22 (1910), 76–77.

60. Preceding quotes all from Root, "Public Service by the Bar," 365–366.

61. James DeWitt Andrews to William Howard Taft, n.d., Pound Papers, Paige Box 26. Members in the group from *American Bar Association Reports* 44 (1922) 92.

62. Andrews himself may have been a cause of the project's failure. After New York lawyer Frederick R. Coudert left the committee charged with creating the academy, Andrews asked Henry Bates to take his place. Bates asked Coudert's opinion, which was that Andrews "is a rather futile person and gets nowhere. Coudert to Bates, October 25, 1921, Paige Box 1, folder 1920–1921, Bates Papers. Bates replied that Coudert has simply confirmed his own impression, but that "the time has certainly come when something of this sort should be done." Bates to Coudert, October 27, 1920, ibid.

63. Joseph Beale, "The Necessity for a Study of Legal System," *Proceedings of the Association of American Law Schools*, 14th Annual Meeting (1914), 31–45, quote at page 38; Wesley N. Hohfeld, "A Vital School of Jurisprudence and Law: Have American Universities Awakened to the Enlarged Opportunities and Responsibilities of the Present Day?," ibid. 76–139.

64. William Draper Lewis, "History of the American Law Institute and the First Restatement of the Law: 'How We Did It,'" in *Restatement in the Courts* (St. Paul, 1945), I:1–2. On the events in the AALS see Hull, "Restatement and Reform," 60–65.

65. LaPiana, "Founding of the American Law Institute," 1118–1119; Hull, "Restatement and Reform," 74–76.

66. Lewis, "History of the American Law Institute," 2–3; Philip C. Jessup, *Elihu Root*, 2 vols. (New York, 1938), II:470–471. Mark DeWolfe Howe, ed., *Holmes-Laski Letters: The Correspondence of Mr. Justice Holmes and Harold Laski* (Cambridge, 1953), p. 482. For a detailed narrative of the meeting, see Hull, "Restatement and Reform," 76–80.

67. "Report of the Committee on the Establishment of a Permanent Organization for the Improvement of the Law," *American Law Institute Proceedings* 1 (1923), Part 1, 1, 6–7, 68, 35, 37, 74. (hereafter cited as "Report of the Committee, Part 1).

68. One of the leading legal realists, Herman Oliphant, illustrated these points in an address to the Academy of Political Science in 1923. He criticized the attempt to answer legal questions, to choose between two competing lines of case authority, by deciding "on principle." "The invalidity of the method is, of course, fundamental," he wrote. All "so-called general principles are but experimental rationalizations of our previous experiences," and therefore cannot dictate "the inevitable solution of *new* problems, which of necessity form no part of the experience rationalized." Even traditional ideas of public policy are not helpful since they are based "on an instinctive empiricism," the "common sense method." Modern society is so complex, he believed, that only experts can hope to understand it. Herman Oliphant, "The Relation of Current Economic and Social Problems to the Restatement of the Law: The Problems of Logical Methods, from the Lawyer's Point of View," *Proceedings of the Academy of Political Science* 19 (1923), 19, 21–22.

69. Hull, "Restatement and Reform," 82.

70. "Report of the Committee, Part 1," 4–5, 15–16.

71. Respectively, quotes from ibid., 74, 29, 64–65.

72. Committee on the Establishment of a Permanent Organization for the Improvement of the Law, *Draft Report*, November 1922, 24. The drafts of the committee's report are gathered in a volume entitled American Law Institute, *Preliminary Reports, Etc.*, in the Harvard Law School Library.

73. "Report of the Committee, Part 1," 24, and Remarks by Elihu Root, in ibid., Part 2, 55. Hull has emphasized the progressive impulses of at least some of the law professors involved in the founding of the ALI, especially those of Lewis. There is clearly a tension in the report of the Permanent Organization Committee exemplified by the contrast between the language quoted in the text and other portions of the report emphasized by Hull, "Restatement and Reform," 81–85. The tension is well illustrated by Oliphant, "Relation of Current Economic and Social Problems to the Restatement of the Law." On the one hand, he explained that the ALI would avoid those areas of law where "there are bitter struggles over broad social policy," such as the struggles between labor and capital and the scope of the due process clause in limiting social legislation, because they are political questions most often discussed on "the plane of prejudice and emotion" (p. 17). On the other hand, he believed that the ALI would have to choose between competing lines of case authority and advocated choice based on "the increasing body of expert knowledge" in such fields as business, criminology, and domestic relations. The appeal to experts supports Hull's characterization of some of the academics involved in founding the ALI as "progressive pragmatists." Hull, "Restatement and Reform," 83–85. Yet, at least by the time he helped organize the Johns Hopkins Institute of Law in 1929, Oliphant, along with Walter Cook and Hessel Yntema, the other "leading forces behind the institute," "proved contemptuous of the progressive belief that the reformer could be a scientist or neutral expert." Laura Kalman, *Legal Realism at Yale, 1927–1960* (Chapel Hill and London, 1986), p. 32.

Whatever the hopes of the participants for the ultimate form of the institute's work, however, it seems clear that all agreed on the importance of cooperation among all branches of the profession in the labor. As Frank E. Horack, Jr., wrote to

Llewellyn in 1940: "[W]e are getting greater acceptance and greater leeway from the bar. I think the American Law Institute has taken the curse off the word 'professor.'" F. E. Horack to K. Llewellyn, September 18, 1940, Karl Llewellyn Papers, Q.II.3., University of Chicago School of Law.

74. Auerbach, "Enmity and Amity," 575–580.

75. Abraham Flexner, *Medical Education in the United States and Canada* (New York, 1910).

76. Stevens, *Law School*, 102–103. For a thorough consideration and evaluation of the effect of the Flexner report on medical education, see Kenneth M. Ludmerer, *Learning to Heal: The Development of American Medical Education* (New York, 1985), pp. 166–190.

77. Auerbach, "Enmity and Amity," 586–601. Much of what follows is based on Auerbach's article, although the reader will note some differences in emphasis.

78. Alfred Z. Reed, *Training for the Public Profession of the Law* (New York, 1921), p. 452, and idem, *Present-Day Law Schools in the United States* (New York, 1928), pp. 531–535.

79. Reed, *Training for the Law*, 403–420; Auerbach, "Enmity and Amity," 588–591; Stevens, *Law School*, 116–117.

80. "Report of the Special Committee to the Section of Legal Education and Admissions to the Bar of the American Bar Association," *American Bar Association Reports* 46 (1921), 687–688; Discussion of the Report, ibid., 661–678.

81. R. Pound to H. F. Stone, January 2, 1923, Pound Papers, Ms Box 33, folder 15.

82. Auerbach, "Enmity and Amity," 591–600; Johnson, *Schooled Lawyers*, 155–159.

83. Edgar N. Durfee to K. Llewellyn, September 9, 1931, Llewellyn Papers, A.II.65.b.

84. James E. Herget, *American Jurisprudence, 1870–1970* (Houston, 1990), p. 151.

85. Jabez Fox, "Law and Fact," *Harvard Law Review* 12 (1899), 546.

86. Jabez Fox, "Law and Logic," *Harvard Law Review* 14 (1900), 42. Thayer responded to some of Fox's criticisms but did not address his comments on the nature of law and the judicial process. James Bradley Thayer, "Law and Logic," ibid., 139–142.

87. Jabez Fox, "The Criticism of Cases," *Harvard Law Review* 6 (1892), 195–200. Holmes's lectures, entitled "Agency. I." and "Agency. II." appear in ibid. 4 (1891), 345–364, and ibid. 5 (1891), 1–23.

88. Fox, "Criticism of Cases," 200. Gray did modify the specific position Fox criticized in subsequent editions of the treatise. John Chipman Gray, *The Rule against Perpetuities*, 3rd. ed. (Boston, 1915), p. 478 (§ 603a).

89. James Barr Ames, "The Negotiable Instruments Law," *Harvard Law Review* 14 (1900), 241–257.

90. Ibid., 242 n. 1.

91. Arthur E. Sutherland, *The Law at Harvard: A History of Men and Ideas* (Cambridge, 1967), p. 212.

92. Ibid., 213–214.

93. John Lawrence Farrell, *The Negotiable Instruments Law: An Answer to Dean Ames's Latest Criticisms* (n.p., 1904), pp. 17–18.

94. H. L. Wilgus, "Legal Education in the United States," *Michigan Law Review* 6 (1908), 662–663.

95. John Wurts, "Systems in Legal Education," *Yale Law Journal* 17 (1907), 93.

96. Albert M. Kales, "Should the Law Teacher Practice Law?," *Harvard Law Review* 35 (1912), 258–262.

97. Albert M. Kales, "An Unsolicited Report on Legal Education," *Columbia Law Review* 18 (1918), 25–26.

98. Frederick Pollock, "The Science of Case-Law" (1874), *Essays in Jurisprudence and Ethics* (London, 1882), p. 246.

99. James Brown Scott, "The Study of the Law," *American Law School Review* 2 (1906), 2.

100. [Oliver Wendell Holmes, Jr.,] "Book Notices" [review of Pollock], *American Law Review* 6 (1872), 723.

101. John Chipman Gray, *The Nature and Sources of the Law*, 2nd ed. (New York, 1921), p. 290. Because he believed that "the development of legal doctrine was affected by a large range of non-legal factors," Gray is often rightly identified as a precursor of legal realism. Morton J. Horwitz, *The Transformation of American Law, 1870–1960: The Crisis of Legal Orthodoxy* (New York and Oxford, 1992), pp. 182, 314 n. 88. The preceding quotation suggests, however, that Gray did not believe those factors were part of the subject matter of legal science, a belief which clearly differentiates his thought from that of many legal realists.

Epilogue

1. John W. Johnson, *American Legal Culture, 1908–1940* (Westport, Conn., 1981), pp. 52–72.

2. Ibid.

3. William C. Chase, *The American Law School and the Rise of Administrative Government* (Madison, 1982).

4. John Henry Schlegel, "Langdell's Legacy Or, The Case of the Empty Envelope," *Stanford Law Review* 36 (1984), 1529.

5. Ibid., 1530.

6. Robert Stevens, *Law School: Legal Education in America from the 1850s to the 1980s* (Chapel Hill, 1983), pp. 162–163, 214–216, 240–241.

7. William R. Johnson, *Schooled Lawyers. A Study in the Clash of Professional Cultures* (New York, 1978), pp. 102–115.

8. For a study of the interrelationship between English legal thought and the demands of practice, especially the procedural structure of the law, see Michael Lobban, *The Common Law and English Jurisprudence, 1760–1850* (Oxford, 1991), especially Chapter 9, "Rules and Remedies in Early Nineteenth-Century Law."

9. The pioneer in this aspect of the case method is Anthony Chase, "The Birth of the Modern Law School," *American Journal of Legal History* 23 (1979), 329–348, and idem, "Origins of Modern Professional Education: The Harvard Case Method Conceived as Clinical Instruction in Law," *Nova Law Journal* 5 (1981), 323–363.

10. Edward A. Purcell, Jr., *Litigation and Inequality: Federal Diversity Juris-*

diction in Industrial America, 1870–1958 (New York and Oxford, 1992), pp. 150–154, describes early twentieth-century hostility toward personal injury lawyers on the part of the elite bar, and William E. Nelson, "Contract Litigation and the Elite Bar in New York City, 1960–1980," *Emory Law Journal* 39 (1990), 413–462, suggests that a striking increase in litigation in New York City starting in the 1960s may be due in part to the increasing diversity of the business management elite and the resulting collapse of generally accepted standards of behavior.

Bibliography

Primary Sources

Manuscript and Archival Sources

Baldwin Family Papers, Yale University Library, Manuscript Division, New Haven, Connecticut.

Henry M. Bates Papers, Michigan Historical Collections, Bentley Historical Library, University of Michigan, Ann Arbor, Michigan.

Joseph H. Choate Papers, Library of Congress, Manuscript Division, Washington, D.C.

Charles W. Eliot Papers, Official Papers, 1869–1886, Harvard University Archives, Pusey Library, Cambridge, Massachusetts.

Learned Hand Papers, Harvard Law School Library, Manuscript Division, Cambridge, Massachusetts.

Oliver Wendell Holmes Papers, Harvard Law School Library, Manuscript Division, Cambridge, Massachusetts.

Christopher C. Langdell Manuscripts, Harvard Law School Library, Manuscript Division, Cambridge, Massachusetts.

Christopher C. Langdell Papers, Harvard University Archives, Pusey Library, Cambridge, Massachusetts.

Letters of Reminiscence presented by Charles Warren, Harvard Law School Library, Treasure Room, Cambridge, Massachusetts.

Karl Llewellyn Papers, University of Chicago Law School Library, Chicago, Illinois.

Diary of Aaron Barlow Olmstead, New-York Historical Society, New York, New York.

Joel Parker Papers, Massachusetts Historical Society, Boston, Massachusetts.

Edwards Pierrepont Collection, Yale University Library, Manuscript Division, New Haven, Connecticut.

Edwards Pierrepont Papers, Library of Congress, Manuscript Division, Washington, D.C.

Roscoe Pound Papers, Harvard Law School Library, Manuscript Division, Cambridge, Massachusetts.

President's Papers, 1889–1925, University of Chicago Archives, Regenstein Library, Chicago, Illinois.

President's Papers, Charles W. Eliot, Harvard University Archives, Pusey Library, Cambridge, Massachusetts.

Records of the Board of Overseers of Harvard College, Vol. IX, 1871–1882, Harvard University Archives, Pusey Library, Cambridge, Massachusetts.

Reports to the Overseers [of Harvard College], Academical Series II, Vol. II, 1874–1876, Harvard University Archives, Pusey Library, Cambridge, Massachusetts.

Jeremiah Smith, "Notes for a Talk on Law as a Profession, February 25, 1890," Harvard Law School Library, Treasure Room, Cambridge, Massachusetts.

James Bradley Thayer Memorandum Books A, B, C, and D, Harvard Law School Library, Treasure Room, Cambridge, Massachusetts.

James Bradley Thayer Papers, Harvard Law School Library, Manuscript Division, Cambridge, Massachusetts.

Woolsey Family Papers, Yale University Library, Manuscript Division, New Haven, Connecticut.

Books and Articles

Abbott, Austin. "Exisiting Questions of Legal Education." *American Bar Association Reports*, 16 (1893), 371–389.

Adams, Charles F., Jr. and Henry Adams. *Chapters of Erie and other Essays*. Boston, 1871; rep. ed. New York, 1967.

Aiken, William P. "Methods of Instruction at American Law Schools. IV. Yale University." *Columbia Law Times*, 6 (1893), 223–224.

Allen, Charles Claflin. "The St. Louis Law School." *Green Bag*, 1 (1889), 288–293.

Ames, James Barr. "Comments on Kales's Paper." *American Law School Review*, 2 (1907), 119.

______. *Lectures on Legal History*. Cambridge, 1913.

______. "The Negotiable Instruments Law." *Harvard Law Review*, 14 (1900), 241–257.

Anonymous. "Art. III-Codification, and Reform of the Law—No. 1." *American Jurist*, 14 (1835), 280–302.

______. "Art. VI—Opinions of Lord Mansfield on Commercial Law—His Judicial Character." *American Jurist*, 6 (1831), 65–86.

______. "Book Notices." [Review of Bigelow, *Leading Cases on the Law of Torts*]. *American Law Review*, 10 (1875), 154–156.

______. "Book Notices." [Review of Cooley, *A Treatise on the Law of Taxation*]. *American Law Review*, 10 (1876), 570–572.

______. "Book Notices." [Review of Gerard, Title to Real Estate in the State of New York]. *American Law Review*, 3 (1869), 543.

______. "Book Notices." [Review of Langdell, *A Selection of Cases on Sales of Personal Property*]. *American Law Review*, 7 (1872), 145.

______. "Book Notices." [Review of Pollock, *Essays in Jurisprudence and Ethics]*. *American Law Review*, 16 (1882), 767–770.

______. Book Review of Ames, *Selection of Cases on the Law of Bills and Notes*. *Southern Law Review*, 8 (n.s.) (1882), 259–262.

______. Book Review of Langdell, *Selected Cases on Contracts 2d*. *Southern Law Review*, 5 (n.s.) (1880), 872–873.

______. Book Review of Langdell, *A Summary of Equity Pleading*. *Southern Law Review* 3 (n.s.) (1877), 316–317.

______. "Langdell's Selected Cases on Contracts." *Southern Law Review*, 6 (n.s.) (1880), 448–450.

______. "Law Schools and Their Course of Study." *Western Jurist*, 4 (1870), 1–12, 125–137.

______. "A Law Academy Tract." *Olwine's Law Journal*, 1 (1850), 1–13.
______. "Notes of Professor Greenleaf's Introductory Lecture, At the Present Term." *The Law Reporter*, 1 (1838), 217–223.
______. "Recent Legal Literature." *Central Law Journal*, 11 (1880), 339–340. [A review of first bound volumes of the West Publishing Company's Northwestern and Federal Reporters.]
______. "Reform in Legal Education." *American Law Review*, 10 (1876), 626–641.
______. "The Revision of the United States Statutes." 6 *American Law Review*, (1872), 211–229.
Austin, John. *The Province of Jurisprudence Determined*. London, 1832; rep. ed., n.p., 1984.
Baldwin, Simeon E. *American Jurisprudence*. Akron, 1892.
______. *The American Judiciary*. New York, 1914.
______. "The Consitutional Questions Incident to the Acquisition and Government by the United States of Island Territory." *Harvard Law Review*, 12 (1899), 393–416.
______. "Graduate Courses at Law Schools." *Journal of Social Science*, 11 (1880), 23–29.
______. "The Study of Elementary Law as the Proper Beginning of a Legal Education." *Yale Law Journal*, 13 (1903), 1–15.
______. "Teaching Law by Cases." *Harvard Law Review*, 14 (1900), 258–261.
Batchelder, Samuel L. "Christopher C. Landgell." *Green Bag*, 18 (1906), 437–443.
Beale, Joseph H. "Jeremiah Smith." *Harvard Law Review*, 35 (1921), 1–8.
______. "Langdell, Gray, Thayer and Ames—Their Contribution to the Study and Teaching of Law." *New York University Law Quarterly Review*, 8 (1931), 385–395.
______. "The Necessity for a Study of Legal System." *Proceedings of the Association of American Law Schools, 14th Annual Meeting* (1914), 31–45.
Bishop, Joel Prentiss. *Common Law and Codification; or The Common Law as a System of Reasoning*. Chicago, 1888.
______. "The Common Law as a System of Reasoning,—How and Why Essential to Good Government; What Its Perils and How Averted." *American Law Review*, 22 (1888), 1–29.
______. *The Doctrines of the Law of Contracts in Their Principal Outlines, Stated, Illustrated, and Condensed*. St. Louis, 1878.
______. *The First Book of the Law; Explaining the Nature, Sources, Books, and Practical Applications of Legal Science, and Methods of Study and Practice*. Boston, 1868.
Blackstone, William. *Commentaries on the Laws of England*. Oxford, 1765; rep. ed., London, 1966.
______. *Commentaries on the Laws of England*. W. G. Hammond, ed. San Francisco, 1890. [This edition contains a full collation of the editions of the *Commentaries* which appeared during Blackstone's life as well as Hammond's own extensive notes to the text.]
______. *Commentaries on the Laws of England*. George Sharswood, ed. Philadelphia, 1893.
Bonney, Charles C. "Codification." *American Law Review*, 20 (1886), 22–29.
______. *Law Reform and the Future of the Legal Profession*. Chicago, 1883.
Brackenridge, Henry Marie. *Recollections of Persons and Places in the West*, 2d ed., enlarged, Philadelphia, 1868.

Briggs, James E. "A Symposium of Law Publishers." *American Law Review*, 23 (1889), 407–414.

Brown, Samuel Gilman. *The Works of Rufus Choate with a Memoir of His Life*. 2 vols. Boston, 1862.

Budd, Henry. "A Few Thoughts on the Relation of the Courts and the Law Schools to Legal Education." *American Law Register*, 27 (n.s.) (1888), 71–77.

______. "A Reply on the Subject of Legal Education." *American Law Register*, 27 (n.s.) (1888), 407–416.

Burgess, John W. *Reminiscences of an American Scholar*. New York, 1934.

Butler, Benjamin F. *Plan for the Organization of a Law Faculty and for a System of Instruction in Legal Science*. . . . [New York], 1835.

Butterfield, L.H., ed. *Diary and Autobiography of John Adams*. Volume I: *Diary 1755–1770*. Cambridge, 1962.

______, ed. *The Earliest Diary of John Adams*. Cambridge, 1966.

Campbell, Robert. "Introduction." In John Austin, *Lectures on Jurisprudence or the Philosophy of Positive Law*, pp. ii–lv. 2 vols. Jersey City, [1875].

Cardozo, Benjamin N. "A Ministry of Justice." *Harvard Law Review*, 35 (1921), 113–126.

Carter, James C. "The Ideal and the Actual in the Law." *American Bar Association Reports*, 13 (1890), 217–245.

______. *Law: Its Origin Growth and Function*. New York, 1907.

______. "The Provinces of the Written and the Unwritten Law." *American Law Review*, 24 (1890), 1–24.

Chase, George. "Correspondence. The New York Law School and the Harvard Law Review." *American Law Review*, 26 (1892), 155–158.

______. *The "Dwight Method" of Legal Education as Compared with Other Methods*. [New York?], n.d.

______. "The 'Dwight Method' of Legal Instruction." *Cornell Law Review*, 1 (1894).

______. *Lecture on Torts*. [New York?], 1887.

Chitty, J. *A Treatise on the Parties to Actions, the Forms of Actions, and on Pleading*, 4th Amer. ed. 3 vols. Philadelphia, 1825.

Clark, E.C. "Jurisprudence; Its Use and Its Place in Legal Education." *Law Quarterly Review*, 1 (1885), 201–206.

______. *Practical Jurisprudence: A Comment on Austin*. Cambridge, U.K., 1883.

Cooley, Thomas M. "Sovereignty in the United States." *Michigan Law Journal*, 1 (1892), 81–92.

______. *A Treatise on the Law of Torts or the Wrongs which arise Independently of Contract*, 4th ed. D.A. Haggard, ed. Chicago, 1932.

______. "The Uncertainty of the Law." *American Law Review*, 22 (1888), 347–370.

Corbin, Arthur L. "The Law and the Judges." *Yale Review*, 3 (1914), 234–240.

Coudert, Frederick Rene. *Certainty and Justice: Studies of the Conflict Between Precedent and Progress in the Development of the Law*. New York, 1913.

Cranch, William. "Appendix, Note (A)." In 5 U.S. (1 Cranch) 367–461.

Delafield, Lewis L. *The Conditions of Admission to the Bar*. Philadelphia, 1876.

______. Discussion of Report of Committee on Admission. *New York State Bar Association Reports*, 4 (1880), 49–67.

Dennis, William Henry. "Object-Teaching in Law Schools." *American Law Review*, 21 (1887), 228–237.

Dickson, Samuel. *The Methods of Legal Education*. Philadelphia, 1891.

Dillon, John F. "Bentham and His School of Jurisprudence." *American Law Review*, 24 (1890), 727–751.

______. "Codification." *American Law Review*, 20 (1886), 29–47.

______. *The Law and Jurisprudence of England and America*. Boston, 1895.

______. "Presidential Address." *American Bar Association Reports*, 15 (1892), 167–211.

______. "The True Professional Ideal." *American Bar Association Reports*, 17 (1894), 409–422.

Drake, Charles D. *Address Delivered May 8, 1878 at the Annual Commencement of the Cincinnati Law School*. Washington, D.C., 1878.

Du Ponceau, Peter S. *A Dissertation on the Nature and Extent of the Jurisdiction of the Courts of the United States*. Philadelphia, 1824; rep. ed., New York, 1972.

Dwight, Theodore W. *Address before the Graduating Class of Columbia College Law School*. New York, 1877.

______. "Columbia College Law School, New York." *Green Bag*, 1 (1889), 144–148.

______. "Courses of Instruction in Columbia College Law School." *Columbia Law Times*, 4 (1890), 33–36.

______. *Education in Law Schools in the City of New York Compared with That Obtained in Law Offices*. New York, 1876.

______. *An Introductory Lecture Delivered before the Law Class of Columbia College*. New York, 1859.

______. "Method of Preparing a Case for Argument." *Columbia Law Times*, 4 (1890), 1–8.

E.L.P. The Consideration of a Contract at Law and in Equity." *American Law Register*, 2 (1854), 257–279, 385–400, 449–459.

Eliot, Charles William. "The New Education." *Atlantic Monthly*, 23 (1869), 199–218.

______. *Educational Reform*. [Boston?], 1897.

______. "Langdell and the Law School." *Harvard Law Review*, 33 (1920), 518–525.

Farrell, John Lawrence. *The Negotiable Instruments Law: An Answer to Dean Ames's Latest Criticisms*. N.p., 1904.

Field, David Dudley. "Improvements in the Law." *American Law Review*, 22 (1888), 57–65.

Fisher, Sydney G. "The Teaching of Law by the Case System." *American Law Register*, 27 (n.s.) (1888), 416–421.

Fox, Jabez. "The Criticism of Cases." *Harvard Law Review*, 6 (1892), 195–200.

______. "Law and Fact." *Harvard Law Review*, 12 (1899), 545–552.

______. "Law and Logic." *Harvard Law Review*, 14 (1900), 39–43.

Frankfurter, Felix. *Brief for Appellant: District of Columbia Minimum Wage Case*. New York, 1923.

Frankfurter, Felix, and Harlan Phillips. *Felix Frankfurter Reminisces*. New York, 1960.

Garrison, Lloyd McKim. "Methods of Instruction at American Law Schools. III. The Law School of Harvard University." *Columbia Law Times*, 6 (1893), 193–194.

Gilmore, Eugene A. "Annual Address." *Handbook of the Association of American Law Schools, Proceedings of the Summer Meeting, and of the Eighteenth Annual Meeting* (1920), 140–156.

Gould, James. *A Treatise on the Principles of Pleading in Civil Actions*, 4th ed. Franklin Fiske Heard, ed. Albany, 1887.

Graham, David, Jr. "The Practice of the Law, as Illustrated in the Study of Pleading and Practice." In *Inaugural Addresses, Delivered by the Professors of Law in the University of the City of New-York*, pp. 44–64. New York, 1838.

Gray, John Chipman. "Cases and Treatises." *American Law Review*, 22 (1888), 756–764.

______. "Methods of Legal Education. IV." *Yale Law Journal*, 1 (1892), 159–161.

______. *The Nature and Sources of the Law*, 2d ed. New York, 1921.

______. *Restraints on the Alienation of Property*. 2d ed. Boston, 1895.

______. *The Rule Against Perpetuities*. 3d. ed. Boston, 1915.

[Green, Nicholas St. John]. "Book Notices" [Review of Shearman and Redfield, *A Treatise on the Law Of Negligence*]. *American Law Review*, 4 (1870), 350–353.

Green, Nicholas St. John. "Contributory Negligence on the Part of an Infant." *American Law Review*, 4 (1870), 405–416.

______. *Essays and Notes on the Law of Tort and Crime*. Menasha, Wisc., 1933.

______. "Married Women" *American Law Review*, 6 (1871), 57–73.
A review of Joel Bishop, *Commentaries on the Law of Married Women under the Statutes of the Several States and at Common law and in Equity*.

______. "Proximate and Remote Cause." *American Law Review*, 4 (1870), 201–216.

______. "Slander and Libel" *American Law Review*, 6 (1872), 593–613. [A review of John Townsend, *A Treatise on the Wrongs called Slander and Libel, and on the Remedy by Civil Action for those Wrongs*, 2d ed.]

______. "The Three Degrees of Negligence." *American Law Review*, 8 (1874), 649–668.

______. "Torts under the French Law." *American Law Review*, 8 (1874), 508–529. [A review of Sourdat, *Traité general de la responsabilitie ou de l'action en dommages-interets en dehors des contracts*.]

Green, William. "'Stare Decisis'." *American Law Review*, 14 (1880), 609–651.

Hammond, William G. "John Austin and His Wife." *Green Bag*, 1 (1889), 47–53.

______. "Legal Education in the North-West." *Journal of Social Science*, 8 (1876), 165–176.

Henderson, Harvey. "The Origin and Utility of Case-Law." *Pittsburgh Legal Journal*, 33 (1886), 301–305.

High, J.L. "What Shall Be Done with the Reports?" *American Law Review*, 16 (1882), 429–445.

Hill, John S. "The Blackstone Bugbear." *Columbia Law Times*, 6 (1892), 40–44.

Hilliard, Francis. *The Elements of Law*. Boston, 1835.

______. *The Law of Contracts*. 2 vols. Philadelphia, 1872.

Hoar, George Frederick. *The Function of the American Lawyer in the Founding of States*. New Haven, 1881.

Hoffman, David. *A Course of Legal Study*, 2d ed. Philadelphia, 1846; rep. ed., Buffalo, 1968.

Hohfeld, Wesley W. "A Vital School of Jurisprudence and Law: Have American Universities Awakened to the Enlarged Opportunities and Responsibilities of the Present Day?" *Proceedings of the Association of American Law Schools, 14th Annual Meeting* (1914), 76–139.

Holmes, Oliver Wendell, Jr. "The Arrangement of the Law, Privity." *American Law Review*, 7 (1872), 46–65.

______. "Book Notices" [Review of Addison, *The Law of Torts*, abridged ed.]. *American Law Review*, 5 (1871), 340–341.

______. "Book Notices" [Review of Benjamin, *A Treatise on the Law of Sales of Personal Property*]. *American Law Review*, 3 (1869), 541–542.

______. "Book Notices" [Review of Birghtly, *A Digest of Decisions of the Federal Courts*]. *American Law Review*, 5 (1871), 539.

______. "Book Notices" [Review of Bryce, *The Academical Study of the Civil Law*]. *American Law Review*, 5 (1871), 715–716.

______. "Book Notices" [Review of Byles, *A Treatise on the Law of Bills of Exchange, Promissory Notes, Bank-Notes, and Checks*]. *American Law Review*, 2 (1868), 328.

______. "Book Notices" [Review of Campbell, *The Law of Negligence*]. *American Law Review*, 5 (1871), 536–537.

______. "Book Notices" [Review of *The Code of Iowa; Report of the Commissioners to Revise the Statutes of Iowa*; Fitzjames Stephens, *Codification in India and England*]. *American Law Review*, 7 (1873), 318–320.

______. "Book Notices" [Review of Cooley, *Constitutional Limitations*]. *American Law Review*, 6 (1871), 140–142.

______. "Book Notices" [Review of Dicey, *A Treatise on the Rules for the Selection of the Parties to an Action*]. *American Law Review*, 5 (1871), 534–535.

______. "Book Notices" [Review of Greene, *Outlines of Roman Law*]. *American Law Review*, 7 (1873), 320.

______. "Book Notices" [Review of article by Hammond on criminal confessions in *The Journal of Psychological Medicine*]. *American Law Review*, 5 (1871), 742.

______. "Book Notices" [Review of Holland, *Essays Upon the Form of the Law*]. *American Law Review*, 5 (1870), 114–115.

______. "Book Notices" [Review of *Iowa Reports*, vol. 23]. *American Law Review*, 3 (1869), 357–358.

______. "Book Notices" [Review of Langdell, *A Selection of Cases on the Law of Contracts, Part I*]. *American Law Review*, 5 (1871), 539–540.

______. "Book Notices" [Review of Langdell, *A Selection of Cases on the Law of Contracts, with a Summary of the Topics covered by the Cases* and Anson, *Principles of the English Law of Contracts*]. *American Law Review*, 14 (1880), 234–235.

______. "Book Notices" [Review of *The Law Magazine and Law Review*, vol. 30]. *American Law Review*, 5 (1871), 541–542.

______. "Book Notices" [Review of *Massachusetts Reports*, vol. 103]. *American Law Review*, 6 (1872), 350–352.

______. "Book Notices" [Review of Pollock]. *American Law Review*, 6 (1872), 723–725.

______. "Book Notices" [Review of Ram, *The Science of Legal Judgment*]. *American Law Review*, 6 (1871), 134–135.

______. "Book Notices" [Review of Redfield and Bigelow, *Leading and Select American Cases in the Law of Bills of Exchange, Promissory Notes, and Checks*]. *American Law Review*, 5 (1871), 720.

______. "Book Notices" [Review of Roscoe, *Digest of the Law of Evidence in Criminal Cases*, 6th ed. by D. Power, American Notes by G. Sharswood]. *American Law Review*, 1 (1867), 375–376.

______. "Book Notices" [Review of Schouler, *A Treatise on the Law of the Domestic Relations*]. *American Law Review*, 5 (1870), 113–114.

______. "Book Notices" [Review of Shearman and Redfield, *A Treatise on the Law of Negligence*, 2d ed]. *American Law Review*, 5 (1871), 343.

______. "Book Notices" [Review of Story, *Commentaries on Equity Jurisprudence*, 9th ed. by Redfield]. *American Law Review*, 1 (1867), 554–555.

______. "Book Notices" [Review of Taylor, *A Manual of Medical Jurisprudence*, 6th Am. ed. from 8th English]. *American Law Review*, 1 (1867), 377–378.

______. "Book Notices" [Review of Thompson, *The American Reports*]. *American Law Review*, 5 (1871), 549–550.

______. "Book Notices" [Review of Townshend, *The Code of Procedure of the State of New York, as Amended to 1870* last paragraph only]. *American Law Review*, 5 (1871), 359.

______. "Codes and the Arrangement of the Law." *American Law Review*, 5 (1870), 1–13.

______. *Collected Legal Papers*. New York, 1920; rep. ed., New York, 1952.

______. *The Common Law*. Mark DeWolfe Howe, ed. Boston, 1963; pbk. ed., Boston, 1963.

______. "Primitive Notions in Modern Law." *American Law Review*, 10 (1876), 422–439.

______. "Primitive Notions in Modern Law. No. II." *American Law Review*, 11 (1877), 641–660.

______. "The Theory of Torts." *American Law Review*, 7 (1873), 652–663.

Hopkinson, Joseph. "An Address Delivered before The Law Academy of Philadelphia at the Opening of the Session of 1826–1827." *Hazard's Register of Pennsylvania*, 12 (1833), 289–292.

Howe, Mark DeWolfe, ed. *Holmes-Laski Letters: The Correspondence of Mr. Justice Holmes and Harold J. Laski*. 1 vol. ed. Cambridge, 1953.

______. *Holmes-Pollock Letters*. 2 vols. Cambridge, 1941.

Hoyne, Thomas. *Address to the Graduating Class of the Law School of the University of Chicago . . . June 30, 1869*. Chicago, 1869.

Hutchins, Harry Burns. "Legal Education: Its Relation to the People and the State." n.p., [1894].

Ingersoll, Charles. "An Address Delivered before the Law Academy of Philadelphia at the Opening of the Session of 1833–1834." *Hazard's Register of Pennsylvania*, 14 (1834), 278–283.

Ingrham, Edward D. "An Address Delivered before the Law Academy of Philadelphia, at the Opening of the Session of 1828–1829." *Hazard's Register of Pennsylvania*, 12 (1833), 324–327.

Ivins, William M. "Is the Common Law a Proper Subject for Codification?" *New York State Bar Association Reports*, 3 (1879), 187–204.

Judson, Frederick N. "Liberty of Contract under the Police Power." *American Bar Association Reports*, 14 (1891), 231–259.

Kales, Albert Martin. "Should the Law Teacher Practice Law?" *Harvard Law Review*, 25 (1912), 252–273.

______. "An Unsolicited Report on Legal Education." *Columbia Law Review*, 18 (1918), 21–42.

Keener, William A. "The Inductive Method In Legal Education." *American Bar Association Reports*, 17 (1894), 473–490.

______. "Methods of Legal Education. II." *Yale Law Journal*, 1 (1892), 143–149.

Kelly, Edmond. "Codification." *American Law Review*, 20 (1886), 7–13.

Kennedy, John P. *Memoirs of the Life of William Wirt*, rev. ed. 2 vols. Philadelphia, 1856.

Kent, James. *Commentaries on American Law*, 12th ed. O.W. Holmes Jr., ed. 4 vols. Boston, 1873.

Kent, William. "The Rise and Progress of Commercial Law in English Jurisprudence." In *Inaugural Addresses, Delivered by the Professors of Law in the University of the City of New-York, At the Opening of the Law School of the Institution*, pp. 44–56. New York, 1838.

Kirkland, Charles P. *Address to the Graduating Class of the Law School of Columbia College*. New York, 1866.

Konefsky, Alfred S. and Andrew J. King, eds. *The Papers of Daniel Webster, Legal Papers, Volume I: The New Hampshire Practice*. Hanover, N.H., 1982.

Krauthoff, L.C. "The Supreme Court of Missouri." *Green Bag*, 3 (1891), 157–190.

Langdell, Christopher Columbus. *A Brief Survey of Equity Jurisdiction*, 2d ed. Cambridge, 1908.

______. "Classification of Rights and Wrongs." *Harvard Law Review*, 13 (1900), 537–556, 659–678.

______. "Dominant Opinions in England during the Nineteenth Century in Relation to Legislation as Illustrated by English Legislation, or the Absence of it, during that Period." *Harvard Law Review*, 19 (1906), 151–167.

______. "Mutual Promises as a Consideration for Each Other." *Harvard Law Review*, 14 (1901), 496–508.

______. "The Northern Securities Case and the Sherman Anti-Trust Act." *Harvard Law Review*, 16 (1903), 539–554.

______. *A Selection of Cases on the Law of Contracts*. Boston, 1871.

______. "The Status of Our New Territories." *Harvard Law Review*, 12 (1899), 365–392.

______. "Teaching Law as a Science." *American Law Review*, 21 (1887), 123–125.

Latrobe, John H.B. *Address Delivered at the Commencement of the Law Department of the University of Georgetown, D.C.* Baltimore, 1874.

Laussat, Anthony. *An Essay on Equity in Pennsylvania*. Philadelphia, 1826.

Lawton, Alexander R. "Codification." *American Law Review*, 20 (1886), 17–22.

Lieber, Francis. *Legal and Political Hermeneutics*. Boston, 1839; rep. ed., Buffalo, 1970.

______. *Legal and Political Hermeneutics*. 3d ed. W.G. Hammond, ed. St. Louis, 1880. [This edition contains lengthy notes by Hammond appended to Lieber's text.]

Lucis, Robert F., ed. *The Journal of Richard Henry Dana, Jr.* 3 vols. Cambridge, 1968.

McClain, Emlin. "The Best Method of Using Cases in Teaching Law." *American Bar Association Reports*, 16 (1893), 401–409.

______. "The Law Curriculum: Subjects to be Included and Order of Presentation." *American Bar Association Reports*, 19 (1896), 467–492.

McCullough, J.G., ed. *Orations and Essays of Edward John Phelps, Diplomat and Statesman*. New York, 1901.

MacFarland, William W. "The Evolution of Jurisprudence." *American Bar Association Reports*, 16 (1893), 271–285.

______. *The Sources of Our Jurisprudence*. Ithaca, 1890.

Maine, Henry Sumner. *Ancient Law: Its Connection with the Early History of*

Society and Its Relation to Modern Ideas. London, 1861; rep. ed., n.p., 1986.

______. *Lectures on the Early History of Institutions*. London, 1875; rep. ed., London, 1966.

Martin, Alexander. "Codification." *American Law Review*, 20 (1886), 13–16.

Martin, Paul L. "The Trained Lawyer." *American Law School Review*, 3 (1912), 92–109.

Matthews, Albert. *Thoughts on the Codification of the Common Law*, 2d ed. New York, 1881.

______. *Thoughts on Codification of the Common Law*, 3d ed. New York, 1882.

Mayes, Daniel. *An Address Delivered Before the Trustees and Faculty of Transylvania University at the Opening of the Session of the Law Department on the 7th Nov. 1831*. Lexington, Ky., 1831.

______. *An Introductory Lecture Delivered to the Law Class of Transylvania University on the 5 of November 1832*. Lexington, Ky., 1832.

Menken, S. Stanwood. "Methods of Instruction at American Law Schools. II. Columbia College, in the City of New York. School of Law." *Columbia Law Times*, 6 (1893), 168–170.

Miles, W. Procher. *Address Delivered before the Law Class of the University of Maryland*. Baltimore, 1875.

Miller, Samuel F. "Codification." *American Law Review*, 20 (1886), 315–322.

Montesquieu, Baron de. *The Spirit of Laws*. David W. Carrithers, ed. Berkeley, 1977.

Nicoll, Henry. *An Address Delivered before the Graduating Class of the Law School of Columbia College*. New York, 1869.

Neal, John. *Recollections of a Somewhat Busy Life*. Boston, 1869.

Nevins, A. and M.H. Thomas, eds. *The Diary of George Templeton Strong*. 4 vols. New York, 1952.

[Noyes, William Curtis]. Art. III—The Legal Rules Governing the Enjoyment and Use of Light," *American Jurist*, 23 (1840), 46–64.

Oliphant, Herman. "The Relation of Current Economic and Social Problems to the Restatement of the Law: The Problems of Logical Methods, from the Lawyer's Point of View." *Proceedings of the Academy of Political Science*, 19 (1923), 17–24.

Parker, Joel. *The Law School of Harvard College*. New York, 1871.

Parsons, Theophilus. *The Law of Contract*, 2d ed. 2 vols. Boston, 1855.

Penfield, W.L. "Text-books vs. Leading Cases." *American Law Review*, 25 (1891), 234–248.

Phelps, Edward J. "Methods of Legal Education. I." *Yale Law Journal*, 1 (1892), 139–143.

Pierce, Edward L. *Memoir and Letters of Charles Sumner*. 2 vols. Boston, 1877.

Pierrepont, Edwards. *Oration on the Influence of Lawyers Upon Free Governments*. [New Haven], 1874.

Platt, Charles Malcom. "The Character and Scope of Analytical Jurisprudence." *American Law Review*, 24 (1890), 603–615.

Platt, Johnson T. *The Opportunity for the Development of Jurisprudence in the United States*. Philadelphia, 1886. [This pamphlet first appeared as an address to the American Bar Association under the same title, *American Bar Association Reports*, 9 (1886), 215–227.]

Pollock, Frederick. *Introduction and Notes to Sir Henry Maine's "Ancient Law"*. London, 1906.

Pound, Roscoe. "The Causes of Popular Dissatisfaction with the Administration of Justice." *American Bar Association Reports*, 29 (1906), 395–417.

______. "The Administration of Justice in the Modern City." *Harvard Law Review*, 26 (1913), 302–328.

______. "Anachronisms in Law." *Journal of the American Judicature Society*, 3 (1920), 142–148.

______. "Cardinal Principles to Be Observed in Reforming Procedure." *Central Law Journal*, 75 (1912), 150–153.

______. "Classification of Law." *Harvard Law Review*, 37 (1924), 933–969.

______. "Common Law and Legislation." *Harvard Law Review*, 21 (1908), 383–407.

______. "Courts and Legislation." *American Political Science Review*, 7 (1913), 361–383.

______. "The Decadence of Equity." *Columbia Law Review*, 5 (1905), 20–35.

______. "Democracy and the Common Law." *Case and Comment*, 18 (1912), 447–451.

______. "Do We Need a Philosophy of Law?" *Columbia Law Review*, 5 (1905), 339–353.

______. "The End of Law as Developed in Legal Rules and Doctrines." *Harvard Law Review*, 27 (1913), 195–234.

______. "Enforcement of Law." *Green Bag*, 20 (1908), 401–410.

______. "Justice According to Law." *Columbia Law Review*, 13 (1913), 696–713; 14 (1914), 1-26, 103–121.

______. *Law and Morals*. Chapel Hill, 1924.

______. "Law in Books and Law in Action." *American Law Review*, 44 (1910), 12–36.

______. "Liberty of Contract." *Yale Law Journal*, 18 (1909), 454–587.

______. "Making Law and Finding Law." *Central Law Journal*, 82 (1916), 351–359.

______. "The Need of a Sociological Jurisprudence." *Green Bag*, 19 (1907), 607–615.

______. "Organization of Courts." American Judicature Society, *Bulletin VI*. Chicago, [1914], 1–28.

______. "Political and Economic Interpretations of Jurisprudence." *Proceedings of the American Political Science Association*, 9 (1912), 94–105.

______. "A Practical Program of Procedural Reform." *Green Bag*, 22 (1910), 438–456.

______. "Preliminary Report on Classification of the Law." *Proceedings of the American Law Institute*, 2 (1924), 381–425.

______. "The Scope and Purpose of Sociological Jurisprudence." *Harvard Law Review*, 24 (1911), 591–619; 25 (1911–1912), 140–168, 489–516.

______. "Social Justice and Legal Justice." *Central Law Journal*, 75 (1912), 455–463.

______. "Social Problems and the Courts." *American Journal of Sociology*, 18 (1912), 331–341.

______. "Some Principles of Procedural Reform." *Ilinois Law Review*, 4 (1910), 388–407, 491–508.

______. "The Spirit of the Common Law." *Green Bag*, 18 (1906), 17–25.

______. "Taught Law." *Reports of the American Bar Association*, 37 (1912), 975–996.

Rawle, William. "Address to the Associated Members of the Bar of Philadelphia." *Hazard's Register of Pennsylvania*, 10 (1832), 273–283. [The address was delivered in 1824.]

______. "A Discourse on the Nature and Study of Law." *Hazard's Register of Pennsylvania*, 14 (1834), 180–186.

______. *Equity in Pennsylvania*. Philadelphia, 1868.

Reddie, James. *Inquires in the Science of Law*, 2d ed. London, 1847.

Redlich, Josef. *The Common Law and the Case Method in American University Law Schools*. New York, 1914.

Robinson, William C. *Elements of American Jurisprudence*. Boston, 1900.

______. *A Study on Legal Education: Its Purposes and Methods*. Washington, D.C., 1895.

Rodenbeck, Adolph J. *The Classification and Restatement of the Law*, [New York, 1919].

Rogers, Henry Wade. "Law Schools and Legal Education." *American Law Register*, 27 (n.s.) (1888), 341–355.

Root, Elihu. "Public Service by the Bar." *Reports of the American Bar Association*, 41 (1916), 355–374.

Schouler, James. "Cases without Treatises." *American Law Review*, 23 (1889), 1–10.

______. "Text and Citations." *American Law Review*, 22 (1888), 66–73.

Sergeant, Thomas. "Law as a Science." *Pennsylvania Law Journal*, 7 (1848), 100–101.

______. "A Lecture Delivered before the Law Academy of Philadelphia, on Tuesday Evening, November 28, 1843." *Pennsylvania Law Journal*, 3 (1844), 95–110.

Soule, Charles C. "A Symposium of Law Publishers." *American Law Review*, 23 (1889), 396–399.

[Spencer, John C.] "Proposed Law School, at Hamilton College, New York." *American Jurist*, 13 (1835), 486–490.

Stewart, John W. "Memoir of Honorable Edward J. Phelps." In J.G. McCollough, ed. *Orations and Essays of Edward John Phelps, Diplomat and Statesman*, vii–xv. New York and London, 1901.

Stone, Harlan Fiske. *Law and Its Administration*. New York, 1924 [1915].

______. "The Lawyer and His Neighbors." *Cornell Law Quarterly*, 4 (1919), 175–189.

______. "Progress in Law Improvement in the United States." *American Bar Association Journal*, 10 (1924), 633–637.

______. The Significance of a Restatement of the Law." *Proceedings of the Academy of Political Science in the City of New York*, 10 (1923), no. 3, *Law and Justice*, 3–6.

______. "Some Aspects of the Problem of Law Simplification." *Columbia Law Review*, 23 (1923), 319–337.

Storey, Charles W. "Three Kinds of Law Books." *American Law Review*, 16 (1882), 761–766.

Story, Joseph. *Commentaries on the Conflict of Laws*. Boston, 1834.

______. *Commentaries on Equity Jurisprudence, as Administered in England and America*. 2 vols. Boston, 1836; rep. ed., New York, 1972.

______. *A Selection of Pleadings in Civil Actions, Subsequent to the Declaration. With Occasional Annotations on the Law of Pleading*. Salem, 1805; rep. ed., Buffalo, 1980.

Story, William Wetmore, ed. *Life and Letters of Joseph Story*. 2 vols. Boston, 1851.

______, ed. *The Miscellaneous Writings of Joseph Story*. Boston, 1852.

______. *A Treatise on the Law of Contracts Not under Seal*. Boston, 1844; rep. ed., New York: 1972.

Sullivan, James. *The History of Land Titles in Massachusetts*. Boston, 1801; rep. ed., New York, 1972.

Swasey, George. "Boston University Law School." *Green Bag*, 1 (1889), 52–57.

Taft, Henry W. *A Century and a Half at the New York Bar*. New York, 1938.

______. *Law Reform: Papers and Addresses by a Practicing Lawyer*. New York, 1926.

Taylor, Creed. *Journal of the Law-School, and of the Moot-Court Attached to It; at Needham, in Virginia*. Richmond, 1822.

Thayer, James Bradley. *Cases on Constitutional Law*. 2 vols. Cambridge, 1895.

______. "'Law and Fact' in Jury Trials." *Harvard Law Review*, 4 (1890), 147–175.

______. *Legal Essays*. Cambridge, 1927.

______. "Our New Possessions." *Harvard Law Review*, 12 (1899), 464–485.

Thompson, Charles W. "Methods of Instruction at American Law Schools. I. The University of the City of New York." *Columbia Law Times*, 6 (1893), 135–136.

Thompson, John. "Appendix." 20 Barbour 668–675. [A memorial note of State Supreme Court Justice Seward Barculo.]

Thorpe, Francis N. *The Federal and State Constitutions Colonial Charters and other Organic Laws*. 7 vols. Washington, D.C., 1909.

Tiedeman, Christopher G. "Methods of Legal Education. III." *Yale Law Journal*, 1 (1892), 150–158.

Tracy, Charles. *An Address Delivered before the Graduating Class of the Law School of Columbia College*. New York, 1868.

Trumbull, Lyman. "Precedent versus Justice." Excerpts from Speech as President of Illinois State Bar Association, January 24, 1893. *Columbia Law Times*, 6 (1893), 146–149.

Tyler, Samuel. *Memoir of Roger Brooke Taney, L.L.D.* Baltimore, 1872.

van Santvoord, George. *The Study of Law as a Science*. Albany, 1856.

______. *A Treatise on the Principles of Pleading in Civil Actions under the New York Code of Procedure*, new ed. Nathaniel C. Moak, ed. Albany, N.Y., 1873.

Viele, Shelton T. "Is the Common Law a Proper Subject for Codification." *New York State Bar Association Reports*, 3 (1879), 171–186.

Urofsky, M.I. and D.W. Levy, eds. *Letters of Louis D. Brandeis: I (1870–1907): Urban Reformer*. Albany, N.Y., 1971.

Vance, William R. The State-Supported Law School." *American Law School Review*, 3 (1914), 409–416.

Verplanck, Gulian C. *An Essay on the Doctrine of Contracts*. New York, 1825; rep. ed., New York, 1972.

Wambaugh, Eugene. "Best Education for a Lawyer," quoted in *Columbia Law Times*, 6 (1892).

______. "The Present Scope of Government." *American Bar Association Reports*, 20 (1897), 307–324.

Washburn, Emory. *Law as an Element of Social Science*. Boston, 1868.

______. *Lectures on the Study and Practice of the Law*. Boston, 1871; rep. ed. Littleton, Colo., 1982.

______. "Testimony of Experts." *American Law Review*, 1 (1866), 45–64.

Weatherbe, Robert L. "Codification." *American Law Review*, 20 (1886), 322–331.

Wells, George F. "Discussion of Papers by Morgan and Oliphant." *American Law School Review*, 4 (1917), 270.

West, John B. "A Symposium of Law Publishers." *American Law Review*, 23 (1889), 400–407.

Wheeler, Everett P. "The Harvard Law School in 1857." *City College Quarterly*, 13 (1917), 154–157.

______. "Procedural Reform." *Case and Comment*, 18 (1912), 661–665.

______. "Procedural Reform in the Federal Courts." *University of Pennsylvania Law Review*, 52 (n.s.) (1917), 1–16.

______. "Reformed Legal Procedure, Federal and State." *American Law Review*, 47 (1913), 48–66.

Whetmore, Edmund. "Some of the Limitations and Requirements of Legal Education in the United States." *American Bar Association Reports*, 17 (1894), 461–472.

Wigmore, John Henry. "The Legal Clinic." *Case and Comment*, 23 (1917), 973–976.

______. "Nova Methodus Discendae Docendaeque Jurisprudentiae." *Harvard Law Review*, 30 (1917), 812–829.

______. *Report of the Dean of the Faculty of Law on an Educational Survey, 1925*. Chicago, 1927.

______. "Roscoe Pound's Address of 1906: The Spark That Kindled the White Flame of Progress." *Journal of the American Judicature Society*, 20 (1936), 176–178.

Wilgus, H.L. "Legal Education in the United States." *Michigan Law Review*, 6 (1908), 647–682.

Willard, Joseph. *Address to the Members of the Bar of Worcester County, Massachusetts, October 2, 1829*. Lancaster, 1830.

Williams, Charles Richard. *The Life of Rutherford Birchard Hayes*. 2 vols. Boston, 1914.

Williston, Samuel. "Jeremiah Smith." *Harvard Graduates Magazine*, 30 (1921), 155–159.

______. *Life and Law: An Autobiography*. Boston, 1941.

______. "Successive Promises of the Same Performance." *Harvard Law Review*, 8 (1894), 27–38.

Wilson, James. *The Works of the Honorable James Wilson, L.L.D.* 3 vols. Philadelphia, 1804.

Wroth, L. Kinvin and Hiller B. Zobel, eds. *Legal Papers of John Adams*. 3 vols. Cambridge, 1965.

Wurts, John. "Systems in Legal Education." *Yale Law Journal*, 17 (1907), 86–97.

Reports and Publications of Organizations, Institutions, and Governments

American Association of Law Schools, *Handbooks* and *Proceedings*, Volumes 14, 18–20 (1914, 1920–1922).

American Bar Association, *Reports*, Volumes 1–48 (1878–1923).

American Judicature Society, *Bulletins*, Numbers I–XIV (1914–1919).

American Law Institute, *Proceedings*, Volume 1 (1923).

American Social Science Association, *Documents Published by the Association*. Boston, 1866.

Association of the Bar of the City of New York. *Report of the Committee on the Amendment of the Law upon the Proposed Civil Code*. New York, 1881.

______. *Reports of the Special Committee To Urge Rejection of the Proposed Civil Code*. New York, 1882, 1883, 1884.

[Columbia University]. Circular of the [Columbia] Law School, "Methods of Instruction at American Law Schools. II. Columbia College in the City of New York." *Columbia Law Times*, 6 (1893), 164–167.

Harvard Law School Association, *Report of the Ninth Annual Meeting at Cambridge, June 25, 1895 in Especial Honor of Christopher Columbus Langdell*. Boston, 1895.

[Harvard University]. *Annual Reports of the President and Treasurer of Harvard College, 1870–1900.*

Report on Legal Education Prepared by a Committee of the American Bar Association and the United States Bureau of Education, pp. 17–18. Washington, D.C., 1893.

[Yale University]. *Report of the President of Yale University and of the Deans and Directors of its Several Departments, 1904–1912.*

Legal Periodicals

Albany Law Journal, vols. 1–52 (1870–1896).

American Law Review, vols. 1–34 (1866–1900).

Columbia Law Times, vols. 1–6 (1887–1893).

[Unsigned editorial commentary in the above periodicals is a valuable source of contemporary commentary on then current issues in legal education.]

Secondary Works

Alexander, Gregory S. "The Dead Hand and the Law of Trusts in the Nineteenth Century." *Stanford Law Review*, 37 (1985), 1189–1266.

Anonymous. "Edwards Pierrepont." *The Green Bag*, 4 (1892), 188.

Atiyah, P.S. *The Rise and Fall of Freedom of Contract*. Oxford, 1979.

Auerbach, Jerold S. "Enmity and Amity: Law Teachers and Practitioners, 1900–1922." *Perspectives in American History*, 5 (1971), 551–601.

Barnes, Thomas Garden. *Hastings College of the Law: The First Century*. San Francisco, 1978.

Bergan, Francis. *The History of the New York Court of Appeals, 1847–1932*. New York, 1985.

Birmingham, Robert L. "Holmes on 'Peerless': *Raffles v. Wichelhaus* and the Objective Theory of Contract." *University of Pittsburgh Law Review*, 47 (1985), 183–204.

Bledstein, Burton. *The Culture of Professionalism: The Middle Class and the Development of Higher Education in America*. New York, 1976.

Bloomfield, Maxwell. *American Lawyers in a Changing Society, 1776–1876*. Cambridge, 1976.

Botein, Stephen W. "'What We Shall Meet Afterwards in Heaven': Judgeship as a Symbol for Modern American Lawyers." In G. Geison, ed. *Professions and Professional Ideologies in America*, pp. 49–69. Chapel Hill, 1983.

Bozeman, Theodore Dwight. *Protestantism in an Age of Science: The Baconian Ideal and Antebellum Religious Thought*. Chapel Hill, 1977.

Bridwell, Randall and Ralph U. Whitten. *The Constitution and the Common Law: The Decline of the Doctrines of Separation of Powers and Federalism*. Lexington, Mass., 1977.

Brown, Elizabeth Gaspar. *Legal Education at Michigan, 1859–1959*. Ann Arbor, 1959.

Brown, Ronald L. *The Law School Papers of Benjamin F. Butler*. New York, 1987.

Bryson, W. Hamilton. *Legal Education in Virginia 1779–1979, A Biographical Approach*. Charlottesville, 1982.

Calhoun, Daniel H. *Professional Lives in America: Structure and Aspiration, 1750–1850*. Cambridge, 1965.

The Centennial History of the Harvard Law School. [Cambridge?], 1918.

Chase, Anthony. "The Birth of the Modern Law School." *American Journal of Legal History*, 23 (1979), 329–348.

———. "Origins of Modern Professional Education: The Harvard Case Method Conceived as Clinical Instruction in Law." *Nova Law Journal*, 5 (1981), 323–363.

Chase, William C. *The American Law School and the Rise of Administrative Government*. Madison, 1982.

Chester, Alden, ed. *Legal & Judicial History of New York*. 3 vols. New York, 1911; rep. ed., Buffalo, 1983.

Clark, Charles E. *Handbook of the Law of Code Pleading*, 2d ed. St. Paul, 1947.

Clarkson, Paul S. and R. Samuel Jett. *Luther Martin of Maryland*. Baltimore, 1970.

Cocks, R.C.J. *Sir Henry Maine: A Study in Victorian Jurisprudence*. Cambridge, 1988.

Conley, John A. "Doing It by the Book: Justice of the Peace Manuals and English Law in Eighteenth Century America." *Journal of Legal History*, 6 (1985), 257–298.

Cook, Charles M. *The American Codification Movement: A Study of Antebellum Legal Reform*. Westport, Conn., 1981.

Coquillette, Daniel R. "Justinian in Braintree: John Adams, Civilian Learning and Legal Elitism, 1758–1775." In *Law in Colonial Massachusetts, 1630–1800*, pp. 370–392. Boston, 1984.

Cosgrove, Richard A. *Our Lady the Common Law: An Anglo-American Legal Community, 1870–1930*. New York, 1987.

Cover, Robert M. *Justice Accused: Antislavery and the Judicial Process*. New Haven, 1975.

Daniels, George H. *American Science in the Age of Jackson* New York, 1968.

Ellsworth, Frank L. *Law on the Midway: The Founding of the University of Chicago Law School*. Chicago, 1977.

Feaver, George E. *From Status to Contract: A Biography of Sir Henry Maine*. London, 1969.

Ferguson, Robert A. *Law and Letters in American Culture*. Cambridge, 1984.

Fifoot, C.H.S. *Lord Mansfield*. Oxford, 1936; rep. ed. Aalen, Denmark, 1977.

Fisch, Max H. "A Chronicle of Pragmatism, 1865–1879." *The Monist*, 48 (1964), 441–466.

———. "Justice Holmes, The Prediction Theory of Law, and Pragmatism." *The Journal of Philosophy*, 39 (1942), 85–97.

———. "Was There a Metaphysical Club in Cambridge?" In E.C. Moore and R.S. Robin, eds. *Studies in the Philosophy of Charles Sanders Pierce*, pp. 4–26. Amherst, Mass., 1964.

Fisher, Sydney G. "The Administration of Equity through Common Law Forms." *Law Quarterly Review*, 1 (1885), 455–465.

Fletcher, William A. "The General Common Law and Section 34 of the Judiciary Act of 1789: The Example of Marine Insurance." *Harvard Law Review*, 97 (1984), 1513–1580.

Frank, Jerome. "A Plea for Lawyer Schools." *Yale Law Journal*, 56 (1947), 1303–1344.

Fredrickson, George M. *The Inner Civil War: American Intellectuals and the Crisis of the Union*. New York, 1965.

Freidel, Frank. *Francis Lieber: Nineteenth-Century Liberal*. Baton Rouge, 1947.

Freyer, Tony Allan. *Forums of Order: The Federal Courts and Business in American History*. Greenwich, Conn., 1979.

Friedman, Lawrence M. *A History of American Law*, 2d ed. New York, 1985.

______. "Law Reform in Historical Perspective." *St. Louis University Law Journal*, 13 (1969), 351–372.

Furner, Mary O. *Advocacy and Objectivity: A Crisis in the Professionalization of American Social Science*. Lexington, Ky., 1975.

Gawalt, Gerard E. "Massachusetts Legal Education in Transition, 1766–1840." *American Journal of Legal History*, 17 (1973), 27–50.

______. *The Promise of Power: The Emergence of the Legal Profession in Massachusetts, 1760–1840*. Westport, Conn., 1979.

Gillette, William. "Benjamin R. Curtis." In L. Friedman, and F.L. Israel, eds. *The Justices of the United States Supreme Court: Their Lives and Major Opinions*. 4 vols. II: 895–908. New York, 1980.

Gilmore, Grant. *The Ages of American Law*. New Haven, 1977.

______. *The Death of Contract*. Columbus, Ohio, 1974.

Goebel, Julius, Jr. et al. *A History of the School of Law Columbia University*. New York, 1955.

Goetsch, Charles C. *Essays on Simeon E. Baldwin*. N.p., 1981.

______. "The Future of Legal Formalism." *American Journal of Legal History*, 24 (1980), 221–256.

Goldman, Eric F. *Rendezvous with Destiny: A History of Modern American Reform*, rev ed. New York, 1955.

Gray, James. *The University of Minnesota, 1851–1951*. Minneapolis, 1951.

Grey, Thomas C. "Langdell's Orthodoxy." *University of Pittsburgh Law Review*, 45 (1983), 1–53.

Haines, Charles G. *The Revival of Natural Law Concepts: A Study of the Establishment and of the Interpretation of Limits on Legislatures with Special Reference to the Development of Certain Phases of American Constitutional Law*. Cambridge, 1930.

Haines, Deborah L. "Scientific History as a Teaching Method: The Formative Years." *Journal of American History*, 53 (1977), 896–912.

Haskell, Thomas L. *The Emergence of Professional Social Science: The American Social Science Association and the Nineteenth Century Crisis of Authority*. Urbana, Ill., 1977.

Hawkins, Hugh. *Between Harvard and America: The Educational Leadership of Charles W. Eliot*. New York, 1972.

Hepburn, Charles M. *The Historical Development of Code Pleading in America and England*. Cincinnati, 1897.

Herget, James E. *American Jurisprudence: 1870–1970*. Houston, 1990.

Hershkowitz, Leo. *Tweed's New York: Another Look*. Garden City, N.Y., 1978.

Hicks, Frederick C. *Yale Law School: 1869–1894*. New Haven, 1937.

______. *Yale Law School: 1895–1915*. New Haven, 1938.

Hobson, Karl Wayne. "The American Legal Profession and the Organizational Society, 1890–1930." Unpublished Ph.D. dissertation, Stanford University, 1977.

______. "Symbol of the New Profession: Emergence of the Large Law Firm, 1870–1915." In Gerard W. Gawalt, ed. *The New High Priests: Lawyers in Post-Civil War America*, pp. 3–28. Westport, Conn., 1984.

Hoeflich, M. H. "The Americanization of British Legal Education in the Nineteenth Century." *Journal of Legal History*, 8 (1987), 244–259.

______. "Law and Geometry: Legal Science from Leibniz to Langdell." *American Journal of Legal History*, 30 (1986), 95–121.

Hofstadter, Richard. *The Age of Reform, From Bryan to F.D.R.* New York, 1955.

Holdsworth, W.S. "The New Rules of Pleading of the Hilary Term, 1834." *Cambridge Law Journal*, 1 (1923), 261–278.

Horwitz, Morton J. *The Transformation of American Law, 1780–1860*. Cambridge, 1977.

______. *The Transformation of American Law, 1870–1960: The Crisis of Legal Orthodoxy*. New York and Oxford, 1992.

Howe, Mark DeWolfe. "The First Law School Lecture of James Bradley Thayer, Preliminary Note," *Journal of Legal Education* 2 (1949),

______. *Justice Oliver Wendell Holmes I.: The Shaping Years, 1841–1870*. Cambridge, 1957.

______. *Justice Oliver Wendell Holmes II: The Proving Years, 1870–1882*. Cambridge, 1963.

Hull, N.E.H. "Restatement and Reform: A New Perspective on the Origins of the American Law Institute." *Law and History Review*, 8 (1990), 55–96.

Jacobs, Clyde E. *Law Writers and the Courts*. Berkeley, 1954.

James, Henry. *Charles W. Eliot: President of Harvard University, 1869–1909*. 2 vols. Boston and New York, 1930.

Jessup, Philip C. *Elihu Root*. 2 vols. New York, 1938.

Johnson, Herbert A. *Essays in New York Colonial Legal History*. Westport, Conn., 1981.

Johnson, John W. *American Legal Culture, 1908–1940*. Westport, Conn., 1981.

Johnson, William R. *Schooled Lawyers: A Study in the Clash of Professional Cultures*. New York, 1978.

Jones, Alan R. *The Constitutional Conservatism of Thomas McIntyre Cooley*. New York, 1987.

July, Robert W. *The Essential New Yorker: Gulian Crommelion Verplanck*. Durham, N.C., 1951.

Kaczorowski, Robert J. "The Common-Law Background of Nineteenth-Century Tort Law." *Ohio State Law Journal*, 51 (1990), 1127–1199.

Kalman, Laura. *Legal Realism at Yale, 1927–1960*. Chapel Hill and London, 1986.

Kellogg, Frederic R. *The Formative Essays of Justice Holmes: The Making of an American Legal Philosophy*. Westport, Conn., 1984.

Kennedy, Duncan. "The Rise and Fall of Classical Legal Thought." Unpublished MS, Harvard Law School, 1974, 1975.

______. "Toward an Historical Understanding of Legal Consciousness: The Case of

Classical Legal Thought in America, 1850–1940." *Research in Law and Sociology*, 3 (1980), 3–24.

Kerr, James Edward. *The Insular Cases: The Role of the Judiciary in American Expansionism*. Port Washington, N.Y., 1982.

King, Peter J. *Utilitarian Jurisprudence in America: The Influence of Bentham and Austin on American Legal Thought in the Nineteenth Century*. New York, 1986.

Klein, Maury. *The Life and Legend of Jay Gould*. Baltimore, 1986.

Konefsky, Alfred S. "Law and Culture in Antebellum Boston." *Stanford Law Review*, 40 (1988), 1119–1159.

Konefsky, Samuel J. *The Legacy of Holmes and Brandeis: A Study in the Influence of Ideas*. New York, 1956.

Konig, David Thomas. *Law and Society in Puritan Massachusetts: Essex County, 1629–1692*. Chapel Hill, 1979.

______. "Editor's Introduction." In D.T. Konig, ed., *Plymouth Court Records, 1686–1859*. 16 vols. I: 149–183. Wilmington, 1978.

Kraines, Oscar. *The World and Ideas of Ernst Freund: The Search for General Principles of Legislation and Administrative Law*. University, Ala., 1974.

Kuhn, Thomas. *The Structure of Scientific Revolutions*, 2d ed. Chicago, 1970.

Kuklick, Bruce. *The Rise of American Philosophy: Cambridge, Massachusetts, 1860–1930*. New Haven, 1977.

LaPiana, William P. "A Jurisprudence of History and Truth: Conservative Legal Thought in the Gilded Age." *Rutgers-Camden Law Journal*, 23 (1992), 519–559.

______. "Just the Facts: The Field Code and the Case Method." *New York Law School Law Review*, 36 (1991), 287–336.

______. "Swift v. Tyson and 'The Brooding Omnipresence in the Sky': An Investigation of the Idea of Law in Antebellum America." *Suffolk University Law Review* 20 (1986), 771–832

______. "'A Task of No Common Magnitude': The Founding of the American Law Institute." *Nova Law Review*, 11 (1987), 1085–1126.

Letwin, William. *Law and Economic Policy in America: The Evolution of the Sherman Antitrust Act*. New York, 1965.

Lewis, William Draper. "History of the American Law Institute and the First Restatement of the Law: 'How We Did It.'" *Restatement in the Courts*, vol. I: 1–42.

Lobban, Michael. *The Common Law and English Jurisprudence, 1760–1850*. Oxford, 1991.

Loyd, Charles M. *The Early Courts of Pennsylvania*. Boston, 1910.

Ludmerer, Kenneth M. *Learning to Heal: The Development of American Medical Education*. New York, 1985.

McAdam, D., et al., eds. *History of the Bench and Bar of New York*. 2 vols. New York, 1897.

McClellan, James. *Joseph Story and the American Constitution*. Norman, Okla., 1971.

MacCormick, Niel. "A Political Frontier of Jurisprudence: John Chipman Gray on the State." *Cornell Law Review*, 66 (1981), 973–985.

McKenna, Marian C. *Tapping Reeve and the Litchfield Law School*. New York, 1986.

Mann, Bruce H. "Rationality, Legal Change, and Community in Connecticut, 1690–1760." *Law and Society Review*, 14 (1980), 187–221.

Martin, Edward S. *The Life of Joseph Hodges Choate*. 2 vols. New York, 1920.

Martin, George. *Causes and Conflicts: The Centennial History of the Association of the Bar of the City of New York, 1870–1970*. Boston, 1970.

Mason, Alpheus Thomas. *Brandeis: A Free Man's Life*. New York, 1946.

______. *Harlan Fiske Stone: Pillar of the Law*. New York, 1956; rep. ed., n.p., 1968.

Meyers, Marvin. *The Jacksonian Persuasion*. Stanford, 1957.

Millar, Robert Wyness. *Civil Procedure of the Trial Court in Historical Perspective*. [New York], 1952.

Miller, Perry. *The Life of the Mind in America from the Revolution to the Civil War*. New York, 1965.

Morison, S.E., ed. *The Development of Harvard University Since the Inauguration of President Eliot, 1869–1929*. Cambridge, 1930.

Morison, W.L. *John Austin*. Stanford, 1982.

Mowry, George E. *Theodore Roosevelt and the Progressive Movement*. Madison, 1947.

Murphy, Paul L. *The Constitution in Crisis Times, 1918–1969*. New York, 1972.

Murrin, John M. "The Legal Transformation: The Bench and Bar of Eighteenth-Century Massachusetts." In S.N. Katz, ed. *Colonial America: Essays on Politics and Social Development*, pp. 415–449. Boston, 1971.

Nelson, William E. *Americanization of the Common Law: The Impact of Legal Change on Massachusetts Society, 1760–1830*. Cambridge, 1975.

______. "Contract Litigation and the Elite Bar in New York City, 1960–1980." *Emory Law Journal*, 39 (1990), 413–462.

______. "The Impact of the Antislavery Movement upon Styles of Judicial Reasoning in Nineteenth Century America" *Harvard Law Review*, 87 (1974), 513–566.

______. *The Roots of American Bureaucracy, 1830–1900*. Cambridge, 1982.

Newmyer, R. Kent. "Harvard Law School, New England Culture, and the Antebellum Origins of American Jurisprudence," *Journal of American History*, 74 (1987), 814–835.

______. *Supreme Court Justice Joseph Story: Statesman of the Old Republic*. Chapel Hill, 1985.

Oldham, James. *The Mansfield Manuscripts and the Growth of English Law in the Eighteenth Century*. 2 vols. Chapel Hill and London, 1992.

Paludan, Phillip S. *A Covenant with Death: The Constitution, Law, and Equality in the Civil War Era*. Urbana, Ill., 1975.

Parrish, Jenni. "Law Books and Legal Publishing in America, 1760–1840." *Law Library Journal*, 72 (1979), 355–452.

Paul, Arnold M. *Conservative Crisis and the Rule of Law: Attitudes of Bar and Bench, 1887–1895*. 1960; pbk. ed. New York, 1969.

Plucknett, Theodore F.T. *A Concise History of the Common Law*, 5th ed. Boston, 1956.

Pocock, J.G.A. *The Ancient Constitution and the Feudal Law: English Historical Thought in the Seventeenth Century*. Reissue; New York, 1987.

Pohlman, H.L. *Justice Oliver Wendell Holmes and Utilitarian Jurisprudence*. Cambridge, 1984.

Postema, Gerald. *Bentham and Common Law Tradition*. Oxford, 1986.

Purcell, Edward A., Jr. *Litigation and Inequality: Federal Diversity Jurisdiction in Industrial America, 1870–1958*. New York and Oxford, 1992.

Reed, Alfred Z. *Present-Day Law Schools in the United States and Canada*. New York, 1928.

______. *Training for the Public Profession of the Law*. New York, 1921.

Reid, John Phillip. *Chief Justice: The Judicial World of Charles Doe*. Cambridge, 1967.

Reppy, Alison. "The Field Codification Concept." In A. Reppy, ed. *David Dudley Field: Centenary Essays*, pp. 17–54. New York, 1949.

______. "The Hilary Rules and Their Effect on Negative and Affirmative Pleas Under Modern Codes and Practice Acts." *New York University Law Review*, 6 (1929), 95–111.

Ritchie, John. *The First Hundred Years: A Short History of the School of Law of the University of Virginia for the Period 1826–1926*. Charlottesville, 1978.

Ross, Dorothy. "Historical Consciousness in Nineteenth-Century America." *American Historical Review*, 89 (1984), 909–928.

Rumble, Wilfred E. *The Thought of John Austin: Jurisprudence, Colonial Reform, and the British Constitution*. London, 1985.

Schlegel, John Henry. "Langdell's Legacy Or, The Case of the Empty Envelope." *Stanford Law Review*, 36 (1984), 1517–1533.

Schofield, William. "Christopher Columbus Langdell." *American Law Register*, 46 (n.s.) (1907), 273–296.

Siegel, Stephen A. "John Chipman Gray, Legal Formalism, and the Transformation of Perpetuities Law." *University of Miami Law Review*, 36 (1982), 439–464.

Simpson, A.W.B. *A History of the Common Law of Contract: The Rise of the Action of Assumpsit*. Oxford, 1975.

______. "Innovation in Nineteenth Century Contract Law." *Law Quarterly Review*, 91 (1975), 247–278.

Smith, Clarks Page. *James Wilson, Founding Father 1742–1798*. Chapel Hill, 1956.

Smith, Joseph H. "New Light on the Doctrine of Judicial Precedent in Early America, 1607–1776." In J.N. Hazard and W.J. Wagner, eds. *Legal Thought in the United States under Contemporary Pressures*, pp. 9–39. Brussels, 1970.

Spann, Edward K. *The New Metropolis: New York City, 1840–1857*. New York, 1981.

Stein, Peter. *Legal Evolution: The Story of an Idea*. Cambridge, U.K., 1980.

Stevens, Robert. *Law School: Legal Education in America from the 1850s to the 1980s*. Chapel Hill, 1983.

______. "Two Cheers for 1870: The American Law Schools." *Perspectives in American History*, 5 (1971), 405–548.

Stevenson, Louise L. *Scholarly Means to Evangelical Ends: The New Haven Scholars and the Transformation of Higher Learning in America, 1830–1890*. Baltimore and London, 1986.

Strum, Philippa. *Louis D. Brandeis: Justice for the People*. Cambridge, 1984.

Summers, Robert Samuel. *Instrumentalism and American Legal Theory*. Ithaca, 1982.

Sutherland, Arthur E. *The Law at Harvard: A History of Ideas and Men, 1817–1967*. Cambridge, 1967.

Swaine, Robert T. *The Cravath Firm and Its Predecessors, 1819–1947.* 2 vols. New York, 1946.

Touster, Saul. "Holmes a Hundred Years Ago: *The Common Law* and Legal Theory." *Hofstra Law Review*, 10 (1982), 694–704.

Twining, William. *Karl Llewellyn and the Realist Movement*. London, 1973.

Urofsky, Melvin I. "Louis D. Brandeis on Legal Education." *American Journal of Legal History*, 22 (1978), 189–201.

______. *A Mind of One Piece: Brandeis and American Reform*. New York, 1971.

Utz, Stephen G. "Maine's *Ancient Law* and Legal Theory." *Connecticut Law Review*, 16 (1984), 821–852.

van Ee, Daun. *David Dudley Field and the Reconstruction of the Law*. New York, 1986.

Veysey, Lawrence R. *The Emergence of the American University*. 1965; pbk. ed., Chicago, 1970.

Warren, Charles. *History of the Harvard Law School and of Early Legal Conditions in America*. 2 vols. New York, 1908; rep. ed., New York, 1970.

Washburn, Emory. *Sketches of the Judicial History of Massachusetts from 1630 to the Revolution in 1775*. Boston, 1840; rep. ed., New York, 1974.

Wettach, Robert H., ed. *A Century of Legal Education* Chapel Hill, 1947.

White, G. Edward. "Holmes's 'Life Plan': Confronting Ambition, Passions, and Powerlessness." *New York University Law Review*, 65 (1990), 1409–1479.

______. *Tort Law in America: An Intellectual History*. New York, 1980.

White, Morton G. *Social Thought in America: The Revolt Against Formalism*, new ed. Boston, 1957.

Wiebe, Robert H. *The Search for Order, 1877–1920*. New York, 1967.

Wiener, Philip. *Evolution and the Founders of Pragmatism*. Cambridge, 1949.

Wigdor, David. *Roscoe Pound: Philosopher of Law*. Westport, Conn., 1974.

Williams, Mitchell G. "Pleading Reform in Nineteenth Century America: The Joinder of Actions at Common Law and Under the Code." *The Journal of Legal History*, 6 (1985), 299–335.

Wilson, Daniel J. *Science, Community, and the Transformation of American Philosophy*. Chicago and London, 1990.

Wood, Stephen B. *Constitutional Politics in the Progressive Era: Child Labor and the Law*. Chicago, 1968.

Wooten, James. "Law School Rights: The Establishment of New York Law School." *New York Law School Law Review*, 36 (1991), 337–395.

Yeazell, Stephen. "The Ideology of Legal Method, 1880–1925." Unpublished seminar paper, Harvard Law School, 1974.

Yntema, Hessel E. "The American Law Institute." *The Canadian Bar Review*, 12 (1934), 319–350.

______ and George H. Jaffin. "Preliminary Analysis of Concurrent Jurisdiction." *University of Pennsylvania Law Review*, 79 (1931), 869–919.

Index